Engendering Slavic Literatures

EDITED BY

PAMELA CHESTER & SIBELAN FORRESTER

Indiana University Press

Bloomington & Indianapolis

1000832153

The paper used in this publication meets the minimum requirements of
American National Standard for Information Sciences—Permanence of
Paper for Printed Library Materials, ANSI Z39.48-1984.

Manufactured in the United States of America

Library of Congress Cataloging-in-Publication Data

Engendering Slavic literatures / edited by Pamela Chester and Sibelan
    Forrester.
        p.   cm.
    Includes index.
    ISBN 0-253-33016-5 (alk. paper). — ISBN 0-253-21042-9 (pbk. :
alk. paper)
        1. Slavic literature—Women authors—History and criticism.
    2. Women in literature.   3. Slavic literature—19th century—History
    and criticism.   4. Slavic literature—20th century—History and
    criticism.   I. Chester, Pamela, date.   II. Forrester, Sibelan
    E. S. (Sibelan Elizabeth S.)
    PG504.5.E54   1996
    891.8—dc20   95-25946

    1   2   3   4   5   01   00   99   98   97   96

CONTENTS

Introduction

PAMELA CHESTER AND SIBELAN FORRESTER

Women, Gender, and Slavic Studies

RECENT POLITICAL UPHEAVALS in Eastern Europe have brought about changes in the status of women and the advent of new constructions of gender. In some cases this means a reactionary return from Communist ideas to older and often nationalist ideals of womanhood and manhood. Scholars in and of these regions now face a whole new set of academic and existential problems. At the same time they enjoy greater access to Western and local theory and are free to apply a broader range of theoretical categories to the study of politics, history, and literature. In this collection we present the work of scholars who demonstrate the powerful results of including the category of gender in the study of Slavic literatures.

Integrating the category of gender into our approach to any literature enriches reading in many ways. Because the Slavic literatures are still so often read and taught from more traditional perspectives, the need to address issues of gender is particularly urgent. Questioning women's access to the literary process brings back texts that have been lost to readers for decades or even centuries, while examining how male and female authors construct gender casts fresh light on more familiar parts of a literary tradition. Above all, consideration of gender adds further excitement to our intellectual work. Perhaps more than scholars in other literary disciplines, Slavists have shown resistance to gender studies, and this too hints at the magnitude of the changes that a theoretical expansion can introduce. Yet, as the essays in this collection show, attention to issues of gender can build quite productively on the textual emphasis of the Formalist and Structuralist tradition, which has played such an important role in the development of Slavic studies in North America.

This enterprise is fueled by the confrontation between cultural and literary theories developed almost exclusively in the so-called "first world," and the social realities and cultural and theoretical artifacts of "second-world" nations. Challenges to the hegemony of Western theory have already been raised in "third-world" cultures and in postcolonial studies, and Slavists can learn much from scholars in these areas: they point up the similarities and variations among the writings and thought of the world's peoples, including, of course, our own. Feminist literary theory, instead of isolating the scholar in some "ivory tower," draws from many disciplines and integrates academic practice with the rest of human activity. This expansive influence should not seem unfamiliar to teachers of Slavic literatures, who have always been obliged to outline the historical, political, social, and other contexts of literary works for their Western students.

The essays in this volume do not represent any single theoretical orthodoxy. All are informed, to differing degrees, by a feminist stance and an awareness of Western literary theory—or, more correctly, awareness of a variety of theories—while each author uses the tools best suited to her task. The collection aims to build upon the excellent scholarship already published in Russian women's studies, by placing all the gender structures of works of literature in question and by interrogating the assumptions of Western theory when applied to non-Western or partially Western (dare we dilute the purity of binary categories?) literatures. When Western feminist theory, film theory, or psychoanalytic notions of the self are applied uncritically to Eastern European cultural scenes, the conclusions they produce face the danger of degenerating into absurdity. Sensitivity to local cultures, a Slavist's traditional asset, encourages selectivity from among the most profitable foreign theories and the most insightful local ideas. Each culture constructs gender and other categories of difference in particular ways; furthermore, each writer works idiosyncratically within and around these constructions in the products of her or his literary creativity.

Goals of this Volume

Our aim is to approach texts written by both women and men, setting their writings and careers in their temporal and social contexts. This task involves the recovery of works by women who were significant in their traditions and their own times, and the definition of "gynocritical" approaches to recognized women writers and to such traditional topics as the way male writers treat and depict women or the feminine in their works. All these aspects fit within the multidisciplinary field of women's studies, but we prefer to categorize this volume's combined theoretical tendency as gender studies: after all, masculinity, supposedly the unmarked category in the Structuralist diagram of gender polarization, is just as much a construction as femininity: in fact, it often depends on the contrast to femininity for its shape and the illusion of stability. Our contributors share the fundamental premise that attention to issues of gender should compel awareness of other crucial categories of human difference: in the Slavic nations, these are most often class, religion, ethnicity, and sexuality. Historical, economic, and other disciplinary data contribute to the authors' basically literary analysis. Most of the contributors to this volume practice feminist criticism, but the exact nature and extent of practice vary from essay to essay. We concentrate on how gender is constructed in a variety of literary texts from the nineteenth and twentieth centuries. Finally, the present volume includes contributions dealing with men's as well as women's writing, so as to give a fuller and more accurate picture of the contexts in which women and men write and are read.

As far as we know, this is the first collection of its kind in English to include a variety of non-Russian Slavic literary topics in addition to Russian material. In many ways the literatures mentioned here (Croatian, Polish, Russian, Serbian, and Ukrainian) have little in common, because of their different historical, religious, and cultural attributes. On the other hand, the basis of their definition as Slavic is a shared linguistic origin: words and the concepts they refer to preserve common cultural assumptions in their etymology and work by similar gender patterns. The Slavic nations also happen (along with several non-Slavic nations) to have shared the experience of imposed socialism for at least fifty years, with comparable influences on their literary life. Most Westerners, like most Russians, have been content to ignore or at best to translate the "other" Slavic literatures, assuming that Soviet political significance in Eastern Europe and Russian strategic and demographic dominance in the Soviet Union translated into absolute literary importance for Russia and Russian as well. Many scholars in the West who work on other Slavic literatures have justifiably felt that they should tend primarily to their own neglected piece of turf; academic and other institutional conventions have tended to encourage and reward such specialization. We have found that viewing writers, works, and genres from several different Slavic nations adds a welcome nuance to this volume: while literate Russian society has at times defined itself as a problematic margin of European history and culture, the non-Russian Slavic peoples have for decades been treated in the West as marginal to the Soviet Union. Women writers in Slavic countries, therefore, have been doubly marginalized, and for that reason a study of their literary positions and negotiations can be especially telling. In some cases, of course, the big discovery is that Russia and Russian literature have nothing to do with what other Slavic writers are doing, and thus that Western readers must correct their own mental map of the world as they approach these works. Nonetheless, study of the historical, geographical, and linguistic constellation of the Slavic nations is richer if we read without forgetting their interrelations. We would be very pleased if the Western familiarity with and interest in Russian literature could serve as a bridge to other Slavic writers, who have been neglected for reasons that have nothing to do with literary value.

For many writers in these "other" Slavic cultures, on the margin between Western Europe and Russia, Western European literary theory has offered a liberating alternative to the platitudes of Socialist Realism or of Russian-dominated Pan-Slavism. Still, the imported Russian literary culture and Soviet-style bureaucratic organization could at times be preferable to the worst market-oriented aspects of Western literary production. Sometimes familiarity with Russian texts offered the best material for reference to the West as well. For example, Russian history and literature provide formative subtexts as well as a tradition of manic word play in contemporary Croatian poets such as Dubravka Oraić, Josip Sever, and Ratko Venturin, themselves translators or scholars of Russian literature.[1] Many Slavic writers now worry that the traditional importance of the writer in Eastern Europe is eroding under the onslaught of Western and Western-style mass culture, as the moral role of literature shrinks or changes. Contemporary theories of identity and authorship can be of great value in understanding the changes now under way in Slavic literatures and writing—if only because Eastern European writers today are working with and amid them as well.

At the same time, having lived with one supposedly internationalist orthodoxy makes residents and writers of the Slavic nations understandably resistant to the

importation of other orthodoxies, be they economic or artistic. In this spirit, the
eleven essays in this collection challenge and adapt different strains of theory as
they examine particular writers or literary works. While taking advantage of the
work of Western theorists, the authors also locate points at which supposedly objective and culturally aware treatments of issues in literary representation in fact
universalize culturally specific, Western intellectual and artistic currencies. Theory
is liberating and useful when it broadens the reader's range of understanding and
allows reading at a higher level of sophistication, informed but not constrained by
personal or national background. Our hope is that these essays will further the
process of removing, or at least trimming, our cultural insensitivities to texts and
cultures we read, study, and teach. Western readers, working to remove the blinders of "outsiders" to Eastern Europe writings, must not come to worship the
blinders of the "insider," or replace one with the other.

The State of the Field

The past five or ten years have produced a number of stimulating contributions to Slavic gender studies, especially in the area of Russian literature and
culture. Scholars have continued to rediscover, chronicle, revalue, translate, and an-
thologize the work of Russian women writers, many of them long out of print and
thus lost to modern readers. Some scholars have concentrated on the accessibility
and analysis of individual authors and texts, while others have begun to build a
theoretical basis for the study of these texts. In the Soviet Union and now in Russia,
a number of contemporary and historical anthologies of women's writing have appeared.[2] The following roughly chronological list, though not exhaustive,
represents the new level of Western interest and scholarly practice in this area:
Pachmuss's anthology *Women Writers in Russian Modernism*,[3] Heldt's ground-
breaking *Terrible Perfection*,[4] Ledkovsky's *Russia through the Eyes of Women* (in
Russian and English translation),[5] Kelly's *History of Russian Women's Writing*, accompanied by a thick volume of translations,[6] Helena Goscilo's *Balancing Acts*,[7]
Russian and Polish Women's Fiction,[8] and *Fruits of Her Plume*,[9] Ledkovsky, Rosen-
thal, and Zirin's monumental *Dictionary of Russian Women Writers*,[10] Clyman and
Greene's *Women Writers in Russian Literature*,[11] Holmgren's *Women's Works in
Stalin's Time*,[12] Costlow, Sandler, and Vowles's *Sexuality and the Body in Russian
Culture*,[13] and Liljestrom, Mantyasaari, and Rosenholm's *Gender Restructuring in
Russian Studies*,[14] the last of which includes literature in the larger set of topics per-
taining to Russian society. The most recent explosion of publications shows that
Slavic literary studies are not merely catching up with other fields in the area of
women's studies: we witness a blossoming of interest in the topic among scholars,
teachers, and students.

One striking feature of this surge of activity among literary scholars in
women's and gender studies is that it began so late, relatively speaking. Not only
have Slavists lagged two or three decades behind Western scholars in bringing con-
siderations of gender and other categories into the common currency of discourse

in the field; in the disciplines of history and other social sciences, Slavists began the work of exploring women's and gender issues in the 1970s, at a time when such projects in literature were rare, or at least rarely published. Among the first of these contributions were *Women in Russia*,[15] edited by Atkinson, Dallin, and Lapidus, and Stites's *The Women's Liberation Movement in Russia*;[16] more recently Engel's *Mothers and Daughters*[17] and Holland's *Soviet Sisterhood*[18] appeared. The last few years have seen an upswell of interest in the field from a wide variety of standpoints: Hubbs's *Mother Russia*,[19] Attwood's *New Soviet Man and Woman*,[20] *Russia's Women*,[21] edited by Clements, Engel, and Worobec, and *Perestroika and Soviet Women*,[22] edited by Buckley, are just a few examples. An extended bibliography combining North American and Russian and Soviet writers and scholarly texts is provided in *Dialogues/Dialogi* by Aiken, Barker, Koreneva, and Stetsenko.[23] This wealth of material undoubtedly reflects the challenge and advantage for Slavists of working in environments which, unlike many departments of language and literature, include other disciplines and subdisciplines. Historians and social scientists continue exciting and innovative work which can serve as a model for literary studies of gender—a contact which gender studies invites and facilitates.

The Resistance:
Gender Studies vs. Academic Tradition in Slavics

Given that gender studies and women's issues have only recently entered Slavics as a discipline—as opposed to the practice of individuals—it is natural that most undergraduate and graduate training in theory and methods of scholarship either overlooks these topics altogether or offers a single introductory week, usually late in the semester, for a quick overview of the questions of gender. This practice, not, of course, confined to Slavic departments, perpetuates the problem in the next generation. Courses on feminist literary theory in particular are almost exclusively the domain of English and French departments. We believe that many factors contribute to the resistance to innovations which marks many Slavic departments; gender is still a problematic area for many Slavists, and there are particular reasons for this.

One source of the resistance is in the Slavic cultures themselves: women are so thoroughly coded as second-class citizens that in many circles ambitious people of either gender avoid association with anything labeled *zhenskie* (women's/female/feminine). To refer, for example, to a Russian woman writer or poet as *pisatel'nitsa* or *poetessa* conveys a negative judgment about her writing; serious women prefer to call themselves merely "writers" or "poets" and leave their gender out of the picture. Such an attitude, not surprisingly, characterizes not only natives of these cultures. Even the most American of North American Slavic departments can react with disapproval to a scholar's concern with women writers or gender studies rather than with more "serious" topics.

For many American Slavists the problem in accepting gender studies is not an absence of theory, but rather the hegemony of a single theoretical approach.

Formalism and Structuralism combine to form a standard method so dominant that it is hardly perceptible, especially to the undergraduate or beginning graduate student who has little basis for comparison. These approaches were elaborated by Slavs, and it makes perfect sense that their theoretical standpoints are most deeply entrenched, most likely to be taught and applied to Slavic literatures. They have a proven methodological and pedagogical value, especially for the beginning literary analyst: they offer a ready set of questions and concerns applied to a text in order to initiate analysis, easing anxiety about how to work in an unfamiliar literature and (often) language. When taught outside of historical context, however, these critical methods tend to neglect societal and biographical factors, and in them the polarized fixity of gender reveals a not-so-well-hidden bias toward the masculine.

Almost from its infancy, Russian Formalism faced the emerging Soviet orthodoxy's insistence on a Marxist analysis of literature. The deforming effect of Socialist realism, its emphasis on authors' class origins, and its ideologically motivated anti-aestheticism—all are obvious to critics in the West and even more so to critics educated in the Slavic countries. Formalism offered not only a way of focusing on the literary text, its forms, devices, and place within a shifting literary hierarchy, but also a subtle locus of resistance to the Communist menace on the literary front. This reinforced the method's dominance among Western Slavists and still tends to cast doubt on more socially sensitive critical approaches—especially in cases where their practitioners also happen to advocate Marxism.

Structuralism, developing as it did from Slavic roots on Western soil, continued the textual emphasis of Formalism. At its most extreme, however, Structuralism mutated into a set of statistical procedures, sometimes powered more by the psyche or the whim of the scholar than by responsible and flexible readings of a text. The method's attention to form, the ease with which it neglects possibly disruptive categories of identity, can have a particular appeal to readers from dominant racial, class, and ethnic groups. In the United States, these groups have been raised to view their own culture as the (inter)national culture of a new society, the "melting pot," in an ironic parallel to the Russian cultural hegemony in the Soviet Union and Soviet hegemony in Eastern Europe. Such readers, whatever their ages, have a vested if unconscious interest in avoiding critical approaches which might force them to question their own assumptions about writing and society. At the same time, Slavic scholars who lived under Soviet or Socialist regimes, knowing firsthand what rampant ideology can do to a society, may understandably recoil from what they see as narrowly political categories in literary study.

In poststructuralism, the set of critical practices that largely defines itself by its energetic movement away from extreme Structuralism, we value its attention to context and the opportunity to regain the political and sociological concerns that descendants of the Formalists marginalized or jettisoned. These include the factors added, or subtracted, by nationality and language as components of a text's and a human individual's identity: race, class, gender, sexuality, religion, and ethnicity. A poststructuralist reading assumes that theory and other concerns in different academic disciplines are and should be interconnected; further, it challenges the premise of a unitary supranational culture, whether Soviet or North American, and helps to reveal how much "international" cultures advance the culture of their dominant nationality.

We would distinguish this summarized vision of poststructuralist theory from deconstruction proper, which in some of its forms tends, like extreme degenerated Structuralism, to concentrate on the text to the exclusion of related issues; some deconstructionists approach texts as utterly mutable quantities, where no one reading can be definitely privileged over another. This insistence on relativity can be useful, but it does not address the reader's qualifications and the minimum level of knowledge about the text's national and biographical components that helps to prevent "bad" or unilluminating readings. Poststructuralism and deconstruction can both provoke the same kinds of anxiety, however: they cut us loose from what we have come to accept as the "facts" of literary analysis and of our society's and psyche's organization, raising issues we may find it more comfortable to ignore.

————

FEMINIST THEORY INSISTS that a text can be severed neither from its linguistic and social origins, nor from the biographical experiences of its writer(s) and readers. In many ways feminism works to fulfill the promise of Structuralism, to analyze with reference to all relevant factors, neither neglecting nor enshrining gender and other categories of difference, and exploring how and why the binary polarizations of a culture, literature, or literary text are *constructed*. It not only grounds our readings in lived experience; it also provides a solid anchor for theoretical superstructures, points where the web of scholarly analysis will hold firm rather than giving way at the first puff of hot air. If a scholar's theoretical assumptions are stated honestly, we believe, even the reader who does not share them is able to account for them and to move on in the discussion that interests us all.

East, West, and Feminist Theory: Tensions and Complexities

In practice, incarnations of feminist theory and feminisms can be as various and mutually contradictory as those of Formalism and Structuralism. Some general tendencies of feminism in the West are comparable to widespread ways of understanding gender in Eastern Europe today. Our societies work from the conflicting assumptions that women are just like men—and that men and women are diametrically opposed and ideally complementary. The Western "liberal feminist" view that women will be able to achieve great things if only they are granted "an even playing field" with men oddly resembles the Socialist argument that gender inequity rises from economic oppression, and that there is no "natural" difference between the sexes beyond anatomy. In Eastern Europe this dogma has "allowed" women to sweep streets or perform heavy manual labor, and then go home to a full roster of domestic duties. Such historical background adds weight to the more traditional and grammar-based assumption of many Slavs that women are essentially *unlike* men and should be specially protected, even that a return to

traditional gender roles is morally preferable. This point of view figures prominently in Francine du Plessix Gray's 1990 book, *Soviet Women: Walking the
Tightrope.*[24] Paradoxically, it also tellingly resembles the assertions of so-called
"radical" or "cultural" feminists in the West, who often argue that women are not
only different from men but superior and better qualified to run society. Unquestioning acceptance of these oversimplified positions is not uncommon in either
East or West.

   Still, even before the collapse of the Soviet Bloc, serious attention to women's
issues and gender (*gendernye*) studies had taken root in parts of Eastern Europe. A
small number of Russian scholars have studied in Western Women's Studies
programs, and since 1990 scholars have founded the Moscow Center for Gender
Studies and a program of "Women's Courses" (named in honor of the first public
higher education for women in late-nineteenth-century Russia, and structured
quite differently from Western programs in Women's Studies). The group of feminists expelled from the USSR in 1979, including Tat'iana Mamonova and Iuliia
Voznesenskaia, has continued writing and publishing in the West. In the capitals of
the former Yugoslavia, both writers and scholars acquired a high degree of theoretical sophistication, including feminist theories. In other Slavic countries the
picture varies: some female scholars became well informed, or at least interested,
in Western feminisms despite the distorted image presented by the mass media,
while for the majority feminism was tainted after its self-interested cooptation by
socialist regimes; most women wanted nothing to do with it. (In the same way,
many young women in the United States will state thoroughly feminist demands
or opinions, but then hasten to add, "But of course I'm not a feminist. . . . ") Rendered suspicious and angry by life under Communism, women in Eastern Europe
today may trust the ideals of their traditional cultures, patriarchal or not, before
the prescriptions of outside "experts." In nations which now perceive themselves as
under siege by decadent Western culture, internal economic collapse, or military
aggression, women are pressured to perform their patriotic duty, to identify along
ethnic or national lines rather than by gender, or to accept a construction of femininity that is profoundly limited and limiting but nonetheless appealing in its
resonance with local tradition. Indeed, national literary canons provide powerful
formulations of such traditional constructions of gender. In this kind of atmosphere women writers and theorists may, as we have mentioned, deny the
importance of their gender in order to be taken seriously; the opposite strategy, insistence on the importance of a writer's gender as a way to attract and hold an
audience, is still rare in most Slavic literary milieux.

   The Western feminist can be seduced by hope that some of the wrongheaded-
ness we see on every side would be demystified and even corrected if only women
in other countries adopted *our* ideals of women's liberation. It is a shock to learn
that a majority of teenage Russians consider prostitution a highly desirable career,
or that female graduate students at prestigious universities believe that methods of
contraception other than abortion cause grotesque birth defects. Contact with
women in Eastern Europe, the problems they face and their strength and adapta-

tions in the face of difficult changes, can fire up a Western scholar's interest and sympathy in a way that is laudable indeed—as long as she or he does not respond with a further dose of cultural imperialism. Our goal is scholarly research and, ideally, eventual real-life contact of greater depth and subtlety. The contributions to this volume represent a wide and stimulating range of approaches to these issues in literature.

Gender in Slavic Literatures

The essays in this volume interrelate and overlap in their themes and theoretical grounding. Sandler, Pratt, and Kolchevska deal with women's autobiography, while Chester turns to men's autobiography; Forrester examines the links between women's texts and male-written contexts. Filipowicz and Zaborowska explore how women are mythologized in Polish historical and religious frameworks; Pratt shows that Russian women memoirists shape their truest identity through focus on the Other, a practice determined in part by Russian Orthodox tradition. Both Burgin and Forrester ground their work in lesbian theory. Lukić and Pavlychko introduce the connections between women writers' lives, theories, and practice in male-dominated, often conservative climates. The figure of the mother and relevant psychological theories are central to Kolchevska and Chester's work, and also underlie Sandler's reading of recent lyric poetry. Both Costlow and Sandler illuminate the Russian text through film theory. Brief quotations from languages that do not use the Latin alphabet as well as Russian and Ukrainian names are given in Library of Congress transliteration, unless they are already better known by other spellings (such as Tolstoy), for convenience of cross-reference in most libraries of North America.

———

WE HOPE THAT this book will convey something of the excitement of feminist and gender theory to scholars as well as undergraduate and graduate students, and that conversations initiated here will carry on in new directions.

———

THE EDITORS WISH to acknowledge the financial, scholarly, and moral support which has made this volume possible. Pamela Chester has worked with a fellowship from the National Endowment for the Humanities; Sibelan Forrester held a postdoctoral fellowship from the Social Science Research Council and received research support from Oberlin College and Swarthmore College.

Among the many colleagues who generously shared ideas and helpful suggestions, we would particularly like to thank Marina Balina, Charles Byrd, Charlene Castellano, Michael Finke, Jehanne Gheith, Antonina Gove, Celia Hawkesworth, Marina Ledkovsky, Judith Robey, Timothy Scholl, Anthony Vanchu, Laura Weeks, Mary Zirin, and the participants in the discussion group on women in Slavic and East European studies at the University of Illinois Summer Research Laboratory, which in 1993 and 1994 was run by Diana Greene. Our contributors themselves brought a matchless fund of comments, knowledge, and energy to this project. Rob de Lossa's translation from Ukrainian and Alexander Pivovarsky's gracious willingness to serve as a courier enabled us to include Solomea Pavlychko's essay in the collection. We enjoyed the superb administrative assistance of Retha Ball at Oberlin College, Eleonore Baginski at Swarthmore College, and Barbara Rotger at Harvard University's Ukrainian Research Institute.

Finally, we thank our families for their love and support; we wish to dedicate our work to our daughters, Lucy Chester and Yelena Forrester.

Notes

1. See Oraić, *Urlik Amerika* (Zagreb: SNL, 1981), Sever's translation of Mayakovsky's verse, *Trinaesti apostol* (Zagreb: Mladost, 1982), or Venturin's *Vječna riječ na straži* (Zagreb: Mladost, 1981). The fine poems written by Oraić (e.g., "Pjesma u boci. Iz pjesničke ostavštine Osipa Mandeljštama") and Venturin in response to the war in Croatia in 1991–92 have yet to attract critical attention in the West, perhaps because their condemnation of American and European (in)action, though still at times mediated through references to Russian culture, cuts too close to home.

2. Some of these titles include *Dacha na Petergofskoi doroge: Proza russkikh pisatel'nits pervoi poloviny XIX veka*, comp. V. V. Uchenova (Moscow: Sovremennik, 1986); *Tol'ko chas: Proza russkikh pisatel'nits kontsa XIX–nachala XX veka*, comp. V. V. Uchenova (Moscow: Sovremennik, 1988); *Tsaritsy muz: Russkie poétessy XIX-nachala XX vv.*, comp. V. V. Uchenova (Moscow: Sovremennik, 1989): *Vechernii al'bom: Stikhi russkikh poétess*, comp. L. Baranova-Gonchenko (Moscow: Sovremennik, 1990); *Zhenskaia logika: Sbornik zhenskoi prozy*, comp. L. V. Stepanenko and A. V. Fomenko (Moscow: Sovremennik, 1989); *Ne pomniashchaia zla: Novaia zhenskaia proza*, comp. L. L. Vaneeva, ed. N. A. Ryl'nilova (Moscow: Moskovskii rabochii, 1990); *Novye amazonki: Sbornik*, comp. S. V. Vasilenko (Moscow: Moskovskii rabochii, 1991).

3. Temira Pachmuss, trans. and ed., *Women Writers in Russian Modernism: An Anthology* (Urbana: University of Illinois Press, 1978).

4. Barbara Heldt, *Terrible Perfection: Women and Russian Literature* (Bloomington: Indiana University Press, 1987).

5. Marina Ledkovsky, ed., *Rossiia glazami zhenschchin* (Tenafly, N.J.: Hermitage, 1989) and *Russia through the Eyes of Women* (Tenafly, N.J.: Hermitage, 1990).

6. Catriona Kelly, *A History of Russian Women's Writing, 1820–1992* (Oxford: Clarendon Press, 1994), and ed., *An Anthology of Russian Women's Writing, 1777–1992* (Oxford: Clarendon Press, 1994).

7. Helena Goscilo, *Balancing Acts* (Bloomington: Indiana University Press, 1989).

8. Helena Goscilo, ed. and trans., *Russian and Polish Women's Fiction* (Knoxville: University of Tennessee Press, 1985).

9. Helena Goscilo, ed., *Fruits of Her Plume: Essays on Contemporary Russian Women's Culture* (Armonk, N.Y.: M. E. Sharpe, 1993).

10. Marina Ledkovsky, Charlotte Rosenthal, and Mary Zirin, eds., *Dictionary of Russian Women Writers* (Westport, Conn.: Greenwood Press, 1994).

11. Toby Clyman and Diana Greene, eds., *Women Writers in Russian Literature* (Westport, Conn.: Praeger, 1994).

12. Beth Holmgren, *Women's Works in Stalin's Time: On Lidiaa Chukovskaia and Nadezhda Mandelstam* (Bloomington: Indiana University Press, 1993).

13. Jane Costlow, Stephanie Sandler, and Judith Vowles, eds., *Sexuality and the Body in Russian Culture* (Stanford: Stanford University Press, 1993).

14. Marinna Liljestrom, Eila Mantyasaari, and Arja Rosenholm, eds., *Gender Restructuring in Russian Studies: Conference Papers—Helsinki, August 1992*, Slavica Tamperensia 2 (Tampere, 1993).

15. *Women in Russia*, ed. Dorothy Atkinson, Alexander Dallin, and Gail Warshofsky Lapidus (Stanford: Stanford University Press, 1977).

16. Richard Stites, *The Women's Liberation Movement in Russia: Feminism, Nihilism and Bolshevism, 1860–1930* (Princeton: Princeton University Press, 1978).

17. Barbara Alpern Engel, *Mothers and Daughters: Women of the Intelligentsia in Nineteenth-Century Russia* (Cambridge: Cambridge University Press, 1985).

18. *Soviet Sisterhood*, ed. Barbara Holland (Bloomington: Indiana University Press, 1985).

19. Joanna Hubbs, *Mother Russia: The Feminine Myth in Russian Culture* (Bloomington: Indiana University Press, 1988). Though it advances some debatable ideas, this book has interested and inspired readers in many disciplines.

20. Lynne Attwood, *The New Soviet Man and Woman: Sex-Role Socialization in the USSR* (Bloomington: Indiana University Press, 1990).

21. *Russia's Women: Accommodation, Resistance, Transformation*, ed. Barbara E. Clements, Barbara A. Engel, and Christine D. Worobec (Berkeley: University of California Press, 1991).

22. *Perestroika and Soviet Women*, ed. Mary Buckley (Cambridge: Cambridge University Press, 1992).

23. Susan Aiken, Adele Barker, Maya Koreneva, and Ekaterina Stetsenko, *Dialogues/Dialogi: Literary and Cultural Exchanges between (Ex)Soviet and American Women* (Durham and London: Duke University Press, 1994).

24. Francine du Plessix Gray, *Soviet Women: Walking the Tightrope* (New York: Doubleday, 1989). We find this book very problematic, but it gives an excellent presentation of the opinion that equality in the Soviet Union went "too far."

ENGENDERING SLAVIC LITERATURES

PART I

THE NINETEENTH CENTURY

Abusing the Erotic

Women in Turgenev's "First Love"

JANE COSTLOW

AT THE MIDPOINT of his novella of doomed infatuation—a work acclaimed as its author's most "enchanting and brilliant story"[1]—Turgenev dramatizes the initiation into sexual knowledge that is the story's central concern. Vladimir, the story's hero, clambers onto a garden wall only to leap down at the command of his beloved Zinaida. "You keep insisting that you love me," she says. "Jump down to me on the road, if you truly love me."[2] Zinaida's word is Vladimir's command, and in the next instant the boy lies stunned and briefly unconscious on the ground. Vladimir's leap enacts the identification of sexual coming-to-knowledge with a "fall," an identification central to Judeo-Christian culture. But Vladimir's "fall" is immediately followed by a loss of consciousness, however brief. It is in this moment of lost consciousness—at first real, and then feigned—that Turgenev's story shifts for a moment into a kind of blessedness, evoking everything that is lost in the larger world of the novella. Zinaida leans over the boy, addressing him for the only time in the story with the intimate "thou" (*ty*) and covering him with tender kisses. "'My dear little boy,' she said, leaning over me, and anxious tenderness sounded in her voice, 'how could you do that, how could you heed me . . . I love you . . . stand up'" (45). To address Vladimir as a little boy and cover him with gentle kisses is to bestow on him a kind of maternal concern in which tenderness and eroticism are conjoined. To speak words of love and an injunction to stand is to bring the boy back to life in a gesture not unlike a mother's toward her vulnerable child. Zinaida is hardly "maternal" in the larger story, nor does it seem that Vladimir wants from her a mother's affection. Nonetheless, "First Love" is in large part a story of a boy's education in what it means to desire. "Know how to desire," his father tells him, "and you will be free; you will command" (31). What happens in Vladimir's "fortunate fall" is a blissful escape from the violent desires of the rest of this story, an evocation of attention and connection that is gentle, tactile, loving. It is an intimation of the obverse of the world Vladimir comes to *see*—and finally to *know*: a world in which Eros is the child less of Aphrodite than of Ares, a world marked by sadistic ritual, imposing will, and a voyeuristic eye.

"The touch," Madeleine Grumet reminds us, "is older than the look."[3] We enter the world with imperfect sight and unfocused vision; we are bound to others and to life itself by touch, taste, and sound. Our eyes mature as organs of sensation only gradually, and as vehicles of knowledge and love they are at first inseparable from the patterns of touch that encircle our vulnerable bodies. To say this is perhaps to imagine origin in a way that flirts with nostalgia and romance: we are reminded of

Freud's "oceanic bliss" and Kristeva's "semiotic," idealized imaginings that feminist critics have cautioned us from accepting too easily.[4] I evoke an initial state marked not by vision but by touch—and a childhood marked by vision intertwined with the other senses—not for nostalgic purposes, however, but to suggest adult alternatives to a world of spectacle and violence. "First Love" narrates the passage to knowledge as a journey of sight: what the boy sees is a woman's body—alluring, statuesque, abused. The tale Turgenev tells is a narrative of eros and the eye; of a boy's accession to the world of his father, in which desire—and "love"—will be structured as a spectacle of objectified violence. After the final revelation of desire and bodily harm—when Vladimir sees his father strike Zinaida, and Zinaida kisses the wound—the boy will profess his love for his father, his willingness, presumably, to endorse what he has overseen. But we can, I think, interrogate Vladimir's journey to knowledge and "maturity," the way his story positions woman as both fetish and mime, the inevitability of *this* vision of love. When Vladimir falls into unconsciousness and the bliss of Zinaida's tenderness, he falls into sightlessness—his eyes are closed. Does Turgenev intimate, in this moment, a place of relationship *outside* the voyeuristic contract of objectification and will? Can we see something other than bodies abused in this tale of first "love"? Can we find a kind of attention that does not reinscribe paternal law, the myth of violent will as the only path to pleasure and connection? Finally, can a woman close her eyes and remember a kind of touch that precedes, and precludes, violence?

Turgenev's story of love is obsessed with seeing. Vladimir's sentimental education is staged (quite literally) as a series of moments in which he *watches*, is transfixed, and does not understand. The story's tension is to a great extent predicated on this disjunction of knowledge and sight; "maturity" comes when understanding catches up with vision, and Vladimir finds language for what he sees: "That's what love is . . . that is passion." These are the boy's simple predicates of fact, once he has seen his father strike Zinaida. Before Vladimir can name what he sees, though, he watches with a precarious innocence. He watches a cluster of men being struck by a woman with "explosive" flowers (11); he watches as Zinaida uses one of her admirers as a pedestal to her statue-like body (26); he watches as she sticks a pin into another's finger (33–34); he watches unperceived as Zinaida reads a book (21); again unperceived, he spies on his father's nocturnal visits to the wing of the house that Zinaida and her mother rent (60–61). One of Zinaida's admirers is named Belovzorov[5]—but if there is any innocent eye in this tale, it can only be Vladimir's, for even when he himself enters the stage of debauch, it is as one who does not understand what he does. Lushin, the doctor, and the one of Zinaida's admirers who figures as a kind of moral mentor for Vladimir, is alone in urging him to an awakening of sight: "Now then, young man . . . how can you, as bright as you are, not see what's going on around you?" (39).

The novella positions Vladimir as an equivocal observer—not wholly removed, because he comes to participate in (and to enjoy) Zinaida's erotic games; and neither innocent nor damned—because, as Zinaida suggests, there is as yet "no law written for him," since "Monsieur Voldemar is with us for the first time" (24).

The position Vladimir occupies vis-à-vis the world of "mature" passion and games is made quite explicit in the story's first scene of watching.[6] The boy sets out on his customary garden walk, but is suddenly stunned (the Russian, *okamenel*, reverberates with petrification, turning to stone) by what the narrator calls a "strange sight" (*strannoe zrelishche*). Several steps from where he stands, Vladimir sees a "tall, shapely girl" surrounded by four men; "she hit each of them in turn on the forehead with those small gray flowers whose name I don't know, but which are well known to children: these flowers form small baglets and break with a crack when you strike them against something hard" (11). The sight of this odd ritual sparks in Vladimir the desire to be included in its apparently gentle violence: "[I] would have given everything on earth just to have those charming fingers hit me on the forehead, too" (11). He is "unmanned" as the gun he carries falls to the ground, and he surrenders to the synesthesia of desire as he consumes with his gaze (*pozhiral vzorom*) the neck, arms, hair, eyes, lashes, and cheek of this striking woman. Vladimir's voyeuristic pleasure is interrupted, however, by "someone's voice," whose abrupt scolding shifts the boy from the position of the one watching to the one watched. "'Young man, oh young man'—someone's voice suddenly said near me—'surely it's not permitted to stare like that at other people's young ladies?'" (11) The desirous gaze is checked by the voice of prohibition and propriety; Vladimir's trance ends as he is caught in the play of two glances—for at the sound of the reprimanding voice, Zinaida turns her eyes on the boy who had been watching her.[7] Vladimir is poised between the "ironic" gaze of the doctor who had scolded him, and the "huge gray eyes" of the girl, positioned both literally and symbolically between shame and pleasure—between *styd* (as the narrator puts it) and *veselost'*. "I was very ashamed and very happy" (11).

This brief passage captures—as spectacle, *zrelishche*—the complex gestures, relationships, and allegiances that drive Turgenev's story. The boy watches Zinaida engaged in erotic play, but he is in turn watched by Lushin, a kind of good father in a story that more explicitly casts paternity as distance, unconcern, and will (*volia*). The flowers that serve as weapons are marked, curiously, as "unnamed"— the first emblems of anominalism in a text that flirts with what can be said and what can't. The scene is lushly erotic, as is the whole text, but it is an eroticism of violence, spectacle, control.[8] And finally, the woman's body stands as a monument of power, but it transpires that she is already possessed—she is, as Lushin says, *chuzhaia*, someone else's goods. To call her this is to insist not merely on propriety but on property: Lushin functions in this scene as a voice of shame, but one grounded in ownership more than morality. Someone *owns* Zinaida, and the desire she seems to represent is not in truth her own.

What Turgenev tells us here is a version of what Hélène Cixous has called "the first story in the world,"[9] the story of desire, transgression, and knowledge we find in Genesis. The biblical tale, we remember, hinges on eating, sight, and the voice of an angry God; as in Genesis, Vladimir is wrenched from a delicious knowledge by an as yet disembodied voice that calls him to shame and renunciation. Turgenev's garden story is not yet ready, however, to resolve in death and exile from pleasure—

that will come later. Its initial impulse is to remain poised between shame and pleasure, *before* the fall, holding onto a kind of knowledge not predicated on refusal. Vladimir wants Zinaida, and has not yet submitted to the words of prohibition that will be his father's law. The father's law—the law of will and power, of supreme egotism, but also a law that insists on its prior rights to the object of the son's affections—will be irrevocably instated only at the story's end, when Vladimir once more watches a "game" of violence and submission. But in that "game" the perpetrator will be his father, and Zinaida will kiss the wound left on her flesh by her lover's whip. "That's what love is . . . that is passion," the story insists—and we are meant, I think, to agree.

I want at this point to pose quite explicitly the issues raised by "First Love," for if the story is Turgenev's "most enchanting," then we need to be quite clear about how this tale attempts to charm. The story is constructed of sexuality, violence, and voyeuristic pleasures—and returns to moments of erotic "play" that involve games of dominance and pain. Stated thus, Turgenev's enchanting story seems perilously to partake of the pornographic imagination—the line between eroticism and pornography being fluid at best, and deeply contextual. Turgenev is not someone we normally associate with pornography; his own inclination was to link the French master of the pornographic—the Marquis de Sade—with Dostoevsky.[10] In his more muted way, however, Turgenev equals Dostoevsky in this narrative's givenness to cruelty, and in its construction of the beloved woman's body as itself a kind of fetishized implement of pain.

The moment of cruelly inflicted pain that is revelatory for Vladimir comes at the story's end, when his father strikes Zinaida with his whip—but prior to that, the instruments of torture are mostly Zinaida's: we see her first, as I've noted, hitting her admirers on the forehead; she strikes Vladimir on his fingers when they're bound with wool she's winding (17); as Vladimir kisses her fingers he's scratched by her nails (26); Zinaida sticks a pin in the doctor's hand (33–34); Zinaida speaks of her amusements as "striking people against each other" (33); her surname, Zasekina, alludes to the verb *zasech'*, to flog to death. What such repetitions accomplish is an association of Zinaida and eroticized violence, an association in which Zinaida plays the active role—plays, if you will, the role of sadist to the cluster of masochistic males in her entourage. The role she plays is the one that *seems* to embody power and will; it is Zinaida, we remember, who calls the shots and directs the action in the raucous evening of play that introduces Vladimir to the fallen house of the Zasekin family—the fallen world of eros and flogging. In this sense, Vladimir's first vision of Zinaida is exemplary, for it frames her as powerful and controlling, and creates of her body an icon of will and strength. The older narrator twice returns to the woman's "slender body" that causes his own weapon to fall: "my weapon slipped down onto the grass" (11). If Zinaida sometimes uses implements—flowers, a pin—to inflict pain, what strikes Vladimir and brings him to submission in this first encounter is the body itself, represented as a slender tower of erotic force.

I want to turn for a moment to the work of feminist film critics—in particular, to an essay by E. Ann Kaplan—in order to understand just what it is we're looking at in this "enchanting" story. Grounding her work in psychoanalytic understandings of the film process, which assume that film mimics the processes of the unconscious, Kaplan looks carefully at the formal ways in which the camera structures what we see on the screen. Women on screen are the objects of several gazes—the gaze of the camera/director, of other men within the filmic space, of an imaginary viewer in a potential audience. Central to Kaplan's argument is the notion that these gazes are predominantly, perhaps inevitably, male, and that the effect of the male gaze is to objectify the woman's body, more precisely to fetishize that body—that is, to render it phallus-like, long and slender, thus mitigating male dread of a wholly different women's sexuality.[11] Women on camera, Kaplan argues, are objects seen by men, viewed as available for male desire, as potentially submissive to male will: "Men," Kaplan reminds us, "do not simply look; their gaze carries with it the power of action and of possession that is lacking in the female gaze" (311). Sight, even the look of love, is linked to a world of power that frames even seemingly idyllic romance; in Zinaida's world, even the carnivalesque world of her erotic evenings is framed by a powerful (male) presence beyond those walls.

To return to Turgenev: One does not have to accept the global validity of Kaplan's argument to acknowledge that a story such as "First Love" constructs moments of seeing that conform to those the film critic analyzes. The male gazes upon the slender body of a woman, a dynamic that Turgenev calls attention to when he "lays bare" the frames that contain this voyeuristic moment: Vladimir watches Zinaida, but then Lushin watches Vladimir, and of course the fireside compatriots of the older Vladimir "watch" it all, via the mechanism of his carefully crafted text.[12] What is left open in this discussion, though, is the issue of power and gender—for Vladimir, at least at first, seems *not* to have the power which Kaplan insists is crucial to the male gaze; that power (the power to impose will and derive pleasure) circulates in the story between a gendered, older pair. It seems to shift from Zinaida (powerful in the story's first half, submissive at its ending) to Vladimir's father (elusive at first, revealed finally as the instrument of will and arbiter of fate). What I want to suggest, however, is that that circulation of power is in fact illusory—that power in this story is never Zinaida's—and that the only moment in the story that is truly hers (the moment of sightlessness I opened with) returns us to the complexity of sexuality, power, and pain for Turgenev. It may also return us to the world of politics beyond love.

It is too banal to say it, but it needs to be said: There is no "real" woman here, just a figure that represents projected male desire, Zinaida as the wish fulfillment of Vladimir/Turgenev.[13] When Vladimir's father strikes Zinaida at story's end, his gesture is conclusive in a way that none of Zinaida's ever are, because he holds power in the world, because he's a man, older, richer. The structure of Turgenev's story builds toward this crucial, climactic moment, giving to this final vision an epistemological and linguistic power ("That's what love is . . . that is passion") that

Zinaida's gestures do not have. The law of this father is control: the whip is an in-strument of will, just as his carefully meted gestures toward his son act both to distance and to bind filial affection.[14] Lushin, I've suggested, is the story's other father—kinder, seemingly more concerned for Vladimir's moral and emotional education. It is no accident, then, that this father is present at Vladimir's first vision of Zinaida, for he reminds us that this whole transaction takes place within the world of the fathers: Zinaida's games merely mime the gestures of the truly power-ful. If, as Luce Irigaray has suggested, mimesis can become for women a form of parodic and liberating repetition, Zinaida's acting out of power knows no libera-tory moment.[15] Both Zinaida and Vladimir will ultimately have to submit to a patriarchy grounded in will, cruelty, and shame. Indeed, Lushin's ethos of shame seems inextricably linked to the ethics of will that Vladimir's father expounds. Vladimir stands briefly poised between Lushin's "shame" and Zinaida's apparent offer of pleasure: what intervenes is Vladimir's father, who reveals possession of Zi-naida by striking her. What links shame and will is the woman: Zinaida elicits shame as she evokes vulnerable sexuality; the father's will emerges as an impulse of denial and control.[16]

To grow older, this story suggests, is to have one's eyes opened; to find a lan-guage for spectacles of cruelty; to acquiesce in the dynamic of will that is desire. "Know how to desire," says Vladimir's father, "and you will be free, you will com-mand" (31). Even if Vladimir will never become his father, the story accepts the father's definition of love and of the world. Eros is imprisoned by spectacle and vi-olence, and there seems no way to imagine anything else.[17]

Except for that moment of sightlessness, the moment of Vladimir's "fall" and Zinaida's tender kisses, a moment that seems to escape the objectification and vi-olence of the rest of the story precisely *because* the boy closes his eyes, as though only the elision of this adolescent gaze enables the woman to initiate a different kind of relationship—one that aborts the provocative gaming of so much of the story. I suggested in opening that Zinaida functions in this moment as a kind of maternal presence, and Vladimir as a not-yet-seeing, not-yet-upright child. In a larger, more literal sense, mothers seem quite absent from this story: both Vladimir's and Zinaida's mothers lurk as mildly grotesque figures, the first obsessed with propriety and her husband's infidelities, the second an illiterate impoverished princess incapable of regulating her daughter's wild ways. The only other mother in the story—we realize with some surprise—is Zinaida herself, who dies only days after childbirth (74).[18] This explicit association of mothers with the grotesque—and with death—is not unimportant; but I want to suggest that there is a larger sense in which the mother is present in this patriarchal story. The mother who is present is Turgenev's own—Varvara Petrovna Lutovinova; Zinaida is, in a sense, her progeny—if not Varvara herself.

Turgenev readily acknowledged a powerful autobiographical element in "First Love," but he emphasized in this regard the portrait of his father: "In 'First Love' . . . I depicted my father. Many have reproached me for that, and in particular re-proached me for not hiding it. But I think there's nothing harmful in it. There's nothing for me to hide."[19] Turgenev's mother is absent from this account; what Turgenev "hides," though, is the genesis of his knowledge of love and pain. As April Fitzlyon reminds us, "From childhood [Turgenev] was accustomed to the idea that women could hold power and exercise it. . . . he was also accustomed to the idea that women could be cruel."[20] Varvara Lutovinova, by all accounts, was a woman of enormous capacity for cruelty, a landowner who was capricious and unsparing in her willingness to inflict pain, both emotional and physical.[21] She stands, in fact, as a kind of mythic, archetypal monster of serfdom, as the vehicle of the horrors her son was to work to abolish with his writing. Can we not imagine Turgenev's artistic work as a kind of slaying of this dragon, a battle not only with Bloomian male precursors, but with the specter of his mother, the embodiment of a cruel order and manipulative love? Are Zinaida's erotic games—her willingness to inflict physical pain and emotional anguish—not modeled on the tortures his mother inflicted? If voyeurism, for Freud, was a revisitation of a primal scene, framed in later life by the voyeur's more controlling vision, perhaps Vladimir/Turgenev's voyeuristic visitations of Zinaida's cruelties aim at controlling and expunging the terrible recognition of maternal violence. For if the textual Zinaida is implicated in a patriarchal dynamic of eros as hostility, the historical Varvara played out her role as the cruel weapon of an unjust regime. There is no place in Turgenev's biography for the nostalgic imagination of the mother, as there is, say, in Tolstoy's: Turgenev's mother is cruel and distant, as enamored of violence as the fictional father who ultimately strikes his beloved. The deaths that close "First Love"—Zinaida's own, and the death of the unknown pauper—function perhaps as a kind of narrative retribution, punishing the mothers for not escaping the cruelty and shame of the world. The child (in all of us) would like to imagine something better.

The moment of sightlessness, of Vladimir's fall, still functions, to my mind, as a utopian figure in Turgenev's story, but as an allusion to gentleness and love that have no correlates, in either Turgenev's life or text. To be utopian is to be nowhere, but such a moment is important in its potential to pull us beyond the voyeuristic logic that seems so inevitable in this story and in the world. The father's equation of desire with command, his insistence that will (*volia*) is the greatest good, articulates a truth of our world as of Turgenev's. "What is sexually exciting in Western culture," one recent analyst suggests, "is hostility, violence and domination, especially but not necessarily directed against women."[22] One of the projects of feminist thought—a project with which I identify in my reading of "First Love"—has been to name the reality and persistence of hostility as sexuality, but to move beyond that articulation toward an imagination and enunciation that might bespeak a different kind of eros.[23] To imagine such eros is to desire a different kind of relationship to the body and to physicality itself; to hope for knowledge that doesn't objectify; to imagine gazes that are mutual and attentive, rather than charged with hostility and the desire for power.[24] "First Love" imagines such eros only briefly, elliptically; its greatest energies and strengths lie in its articulation of a story about acquiescing to power. "First Love" is anchored in the world of men, a world which exchanges and objectifies women for its pleasure. Vladimir offers up visions of Zinaida for his companions' appreciation—just as Turgenev offers the story itself to his friend Annenkov.

To suggest some link between these two of Turgenev's women—between Zinaida and Varvara Lutovinova—is to suggest a link not only between biography and text, but between the erotic aggressions of intimate life and the violence of class and economic relations. The story of Zinaida and Vladimir and his father articulates the cruelties of eros; the story of Varvara Lutovinova and her serfs bespeaks the violence of unchecked economic power. There is, however, a more specific, textual, way in which that link is effected.

In *Spring Torrents*, another of Turgenev's narratives of love, the narrator proclaims that "First love is exactly like a revolution: the regular and established order of life is in an instant smashed to fragments; youth stands at the barricade, its bright banner raised high in the air, and sends its ecstatic greetings to the future, whatever it may hold—death or a new life, no matter." This rhetoric constructs an analogic relationship between love and politics that is more specifically embodied in "First Love": the analogy in that story emerges more visually than rhetorically, and locates the connection between sexual and economic violence in the abuse of the body. At the very beginning of his memoir, the older Vladimir recalls how he stood and watched in the wallpaper factory that occupied one of the wings of his mother's estate. There were *two* wings on that estate: the other was rented by the Zasekin family. The scene Vladimir watches in the factory is, like the scene of Zinaida's games and like his father's striking of Zinaida, a scene of physical assault: "More than once I went there to watch as ten thin, disheveled boys in greasy coats, with haggard faces, jumped incessantly on wooden levers that clamped down on the press's square blocks, thus imprinting the bright wallpaper patterns with the weight of their frail bodies" (10). This moment of sociological *realia* might strike one as anomalous in this story that is so unconcerned with the political world, that seems to reach back to childhood in nostalgic flight from Russia "on the eve" of reform. "First Love" has in fact most frequently been read as standing apart from the more historically concerned novels of the period. But this vision of young boys' bodies jumping on levers and imprinting wallpaper is not anomalous, I would suggest. These boys "jump," as Vladimir will for Zinaida, but they jump for masters' economic gain, rather than to fulfill a romantic ritual. Just as Zinaida's body becomes a kind of tool of erotic devastation, so these boys' bodies are appendages of a machine; the final emblem of erotic violence in "First Love"—the welt that Zinaida kisses—is prefigured here in the imprint of body on paper.

There are several ways we might read this scene, a scene clearly linked to the voyeuristic revelations of the rest of the story. We could read it as a sublimated erotic gaze, directed at an object—young boys—too forbidden for more explicit incorporation in the narrative. We can read it as a reminder of the vast distance that separates Vladimir from these other boys—not much younger than he—who will never know the freedom of erotic and emotional adventure he knows that summer. Or we can read it as emblematically linked to Zinaida's story, reminding us that like these boys, Zinaida is materially vulnerable to exploitation. Most compelling to me, however, is the power of this scene to make connections between the intimate world of eros and a larger political world: the hierarchy, hostility, and exploitation that flourish in "love" don't exist in a vacuum. "To the extent that either sexual relations or other power relations are structured by a dynamic of domination/submission ... the community as a whole will be structured as domination."[25] Despite its movement toward an imagined past, "First Love" stands squarely in the world of pre-reform Russia, rent by relations of domination and abuse, in both erotic and political realms. First Love is a Revolution not because the spirit soars, but because in both the body is hideously used, and the order of master and slave that seemed to be destroyed is only turned upside down. The moment of touching tenderness is lost forever, something imaginable only in a never-never land beyond (or before) imposing will and the voyeuristic eye.

Notes

1. Richard Freeborn, *Turgenev: The Novelist's Novelist* (London: Oxford University Press, 1960).

2. I. S. Turgenev, *Polnoe sobranie sochinenii i pisem v dvadtsati vos'mi tomakh* (Moscow: Izd-vo Akademii nauk SSSR, 1960–68), vol. 9, pp. 4–5. All subsequent references are to this edition and will be made in the body of my essay.

3. Madeleine Grumet, *Bitter Milk: Women and Teaching* (Amherst: University of Massachusetts Press, 1988), p. 99.

4. See, for example, Domna Stanton, "Difference on Trial: A Critique of the Maternal Metaphor in Cixous, Irigaray, and Kristeva," in Nancy Miller, ed., *The Poetics of Gender* (New York: Columbia University Press, 1986), pp. 157–82.

5. The name derives from two roots: *belyi* (white) and *vzor* (gaze or look).

6. As I will note later, this is not truly the story's first scene of watching—but it is the first to involve Zinaida.

7. Turgenev's prose seems uncannily to describe the boy's trance as aborted masturbatory pleasure, implying a physical involvement in the scene that implicates him in its violence. Vladimir is described as "turning to stone" (*okamenel*) when he sees Zinaida, only to melt (*obomlel*) when the voice intervenes.

8. There has been little, if any, serious attention to the eroticism of the story. Frank Seeley, in his recent study of Turgenev, uses the terms "masochist" and "sadism" (of Vladimir and Zinaida, respectively) without taking them seriously, and insists that the story's final blow (when Vladimir's father strikes Zinaida) "was assuredly not struck by way of asserting or establishing the man's mastery over the woman." *Turgenev: A Reading of His Fiction* (Cambridge: Cambridge University Press, 1991), p. 157.

9. Hélène Cixous, "Reaching the Point of Wheat, or A Portrait of the Artist as a Maturing Woman," *New Literary History* 19, no. 1 (Autumn 1987): 1.

10. Inspired in part by Mikhailovskii's essay on the "cruel talent" of Dostoevsky, Turgenev referred to the latter as the Russian de Sade in two letters, one to Saltykov-Shchedrin and one to Annenkov. In both letters he expressed disgust at the wild adulation expressed for Dostoevsky at his funeral: "I also read Mikhailovskii's article on Dostoevsky. He's truly noted the fundamental aspect of his work. He could have recalled that there's a similar phenomenon in French literature—i.e., the infamous Marquis de Sade. That one even wrote a book: 'Tourments et supplices,' in which with great delight he dwells on the transgressive pleasure derived from inflicting elaborate torments and suffering. In one of his novels Dostoevsky also carefully describes the pleasures of a certain lover. . . . And just think, all the Russian bishops sang funeral services [*panikhidy*] to this, our own de Sade, and even read sermons about the universal love of this universal man!" *Polnoe sobranie sochinenii i pisem, Pis'ma*, vol. 13, p. 49.

11. E. Ann Kaplan, "Is the Gaze Male?" In Ann Snitow et al., eds., *Desire: The Politics of Sexuality* (New York: Monthly Review Press, 1983), pp. 311–12. Cited hereafter within the text.

12. Elizabeth Cheresh, in her new study of Turgenev, notes the way in which Vladimir's insistence on writing his account—rather than merely telling it—is linked to a desire to control response to the story. *Beyond Realism: Turgenev's Poetics of Secular Salvation* (Stanford: Stanford University Press, 1992), p. 163.

13. Compare Kaplan: "Women in film, thus, do not function as signifiers for a signified (a real woman) as sociological critics have assumed, but signifier and signified have been elided into a sign that represents something in the male unconscious." "Is the Gaze Male?" p. 310.

14. "I loved him, I admired him, he seemed to me the model of what a man should be—and dear God, how passionately I would have been attached to him if I hadn't constantly felt his distancing [*otkloniaiushchei*] hand" (30). "Sometimes gaiety came over him, and then he was ready to play and tease with me like a boy (he loved any strong physical movement); once—only once— he caressed me with such tenderness that I almost burst into tears" (30).

15. For a critical discussion of Irigaray's notion of mimicry and its potential to "disrupt" patriarchal discourse, see Toril Moi, *Sexual/Textual Politics: Feminist Literary Theory* (London, New York: Methuen, 1985), pp. 139–43.

16. If we remember the single moment ("vsego tol'ko raz!") of tenderness expressed toward his son, then the father's is also a will determined to control his own more tender impulses.

17. The editors of the Academy edition of Turgenev's works note the consistency of Turgenev's definition of love in "First Love" with such stories as "Zatish'e" and "Perepiska": "love in the story is understood as a tragic feeling, inevitably entailing the slave-like submission of one of the parties" (462).

18. The text is inexplicit, but it is possible that Zinaida had borne an earlier child, Vladimir's illegitimate half-brother: Turgenev is careful to mark the time that elapses between Vladimir's witnessing of the meeting between his father and Zinaida, and the sudden stroke (*udar*) that leads to his father's death. The stroke is caused by a letter that upsets him enormously, received eight months after that momentous, overseen meeting (72). Maidanov, one of Zinaida's acquaintances, later recalls to Vladimir that there had been "consequences" (*posledstviia*) of the "istoriia" of that summer (74).

19. From the memoirs of N. A. Ostrovskaia, quoted in Turgenev, *Polnoe sobranie sochinenii i pisem . . .* , *Pis'ma*, vol. 11, pp. 459–60.

20. April Fitzlyon, "I. S. Turgenev and the Woman Question," *New Zealand Slavonic Journal* (1983), p. 164.

21. For an account of Lutovinova based largely on the memoirs of Varvara Zhitova, see Tamara Zviguilsky, "Varvara Petrovna Loutovinova (1788–1850), mère d'Ivan Tourguéniev," in *Cahiers, Ivan Tourguéniev, Pauline Viardot, Maria Malibran*, vol. 4 (Paris, 1980), pp. 42–70.

22. Nancy Hartsock, *Money, Sex and Power: Toward a Feminist Historical Materialism* (Boston: Northeastern University Press, 1985), p. 166.

23. This impulse is apparent in the work of Nancy Hartsock, Ann Ferguson, and Audre Lorde, among others. See Hartsock, *Money, Sex and Power* (New York: Longman, 1983), chapter 7; Ann Ferguson, *Blood at the Root: Motherhood, Sexuality and Male Dominance* (London: Pandora, 1989), chapter 4; and Audre Lorde, "Uses of the Erotic: The Erotic as Power," in Laura Lederer, ed., *Take Back the Night: Women on Pornography* (New York: Morrow, 1980), pp. 295–300.

24. The imagination of a gaze that is mutual rather than objectifying forms something of a leitmotif in the work of some feminist thinkers. See, for example, E. Ann Kaplan, who ends her discussion of the "male gaze" with an allusion to the "*mutual* gazing" that was part of the "mutual, pleasurable bonding that we all, male and female, enjoyed with our mothers." "Is the Gaze Male?" p. 324. Similarly, Hélène Cixous ends the essay cited above with the following ruminations: "What is the *'point of wheat'*? [It] could be defined as a kind of economy of attention." "Reaching the Point of Wheat," p. 19; and Sara Ruddick, who has elaborated a morality grounded in the practice of parenting, centers her discussion on the act of loving attention. Ruddick, "Maternal Thinking," *Feminist Studies* 6, no. 2 (1980): 342–67.

25. Hartsock, *Money, Sex, and Power*, p. 155.

The Deconstruction of Sappho Stolz

Some Russian Abuses and Uses of the Tenth Muse

DIANA L. BURGIN

PLATO IS CREDITED with naming a Tenth Muse, though without specifying her sphere of influence: "Some say there are nine Muses: how careless! Look—Sappho of Lesbos is the tenth."[1] This is one of the earliest and most authoritative of the efforts of wise men and poets in Western civilization to name, define, or employ Sappho, an Aeolian Greek poet about whose life little is known for sure beyond the approximate date and place of her birth (c. 612 B.C.E., on the isle of Lesbos). To compensate for Sappho's biographical elusiveness, a great deal has been invented about her, including, from classical times, a double: not *that* Sappho, the poet, but the other Sappho, a courtesan.

The most popular and long-lived legend connected with Sappho, the story of the poet's unrequited love for a handsome youth, Phaon, which led her to commit suicide by leaping into the sea from the Leucadian promontory, gained widespread credence in the version written by Ovid (but attributed to Sappho herself) in the fifteenth epistle, "Sappho's Letter to Phaon," of *Heroides*. In the eighteenth century the Phaon episode was still believed to be the central fact of Sappho's putative biography, and virtually all Sapphic fictions in prose and verse grew out of it.[2]

It has recently been argued by Joan De Jean in her exhaustive study *Fictions of Sappho, 1546–1937* that the Sappho we know and remember today is in large part "a figment of the modern imagination."[3] Central to the workings of that imagination are the two remaining unarguable facts about Sappho—she was a woman and a poet. Because of this startling (to many) combination of her sex and her vocation, Sappho "has . . . served as a kind of touchstone for attitudes toward creative and independent women and women-identified women."[4]

This essay seeks to give a brief history of Sappho in Russian poetic culture. It will focus in particular on uses and abuses of Sappho by Russian poets and philologists that are culturally revealing and shed new light on the importance and manipulation of gender in Russian poetry. If one can argue that all uses of Sappho are alike, then it is also true that each nation-state uses and abuses her in its own way. To wit, Sappho Stolz, a minor character included in part three, chapter eighteen of *Anna Karenina*, a very Tolstoyan and therefore most Russian use.

Sappho Stolz is a Petersburg *haute monde* celebrity and courtesan of distinctively ambiguous gender and sexuality. Parodically hyperfeminine in the style of a female impersonator, she nevertheless smokes cigarettes, a marker in Russia of the 1870s of a liberated woman and a feminist: Sappho Stolz entered the drawing-room "on high-heeled shoes" with "brisk, little steps, and shook hands with the ladies vigorously *like a man*."[5] From his male, heterosexist perspective, Tolstoy proceeds to contrast Sappho Stolz to Lisa Merkalova, another society belle, clearly and invidiously implying that Sappho plays dominant butch to Lisa's passive femme: Lisa was as "soft" and undisciplined as Sappho was severe and stately.

Sappho Stolz is markedly un-Russian. By giving her a German surname, Tolstoy might have been indicating his awareness that in his time, German Hellenists were considered the most authoritative interpreters and philological "husbands" of Sappho. As a mannish woman, Tolstoy's Sappho Stolz plays upon the ancient tradition of *mascula Sappho*, an epithet coined by Horace in his First Epistle, and she embodies Tolstoy's fear and hatred of liberated, sexually aggressive ("masculine") women as well as his cherished belief that such women were not native to Russia.[6]

The "real" Sappho of Lesbos is mentioned only once in the ninety volumes of Tolstoy's *Complete Collected Works*, and interestingly, the sole reference occurs in one of the variants to a later scene in *Anna Karenina*.[7] Describing a general dinner discussion of the question whether women are "capable" or not, Tolstoy writes in this variant: "Some people said no, pointing to the fact that there had been no great people [who were women]; others said yes, naming Sappho, George Sand, Joan of Arc, and Catherine."[8] It is noteworthy that Sappho is placed in a company of four "great" women, all of whom were associated with transgressive gender and sexual behavior, cross-dressing in the case of Sand and Joan of Arc, female same-sex relationships in the case of Sand, Catherine (the Great, one assumes), and Sappho. Tolstoy obviously conflated genius with masculinity and mannish women with lesbians.

The Sappho (Stolz) of *Anna Karenina* represents masculinized female sexuality. She is worshipped by foppish, effeminate, too richly fed men such as her current swain Vaska, who "had come into the drawing room behind Sappho, and followed her about as though he were chained to her, keeping his sparkling eyes fastened on her as if he would like to eat her." Ten out of the twelve times Sappho Stolz's name is mentioned (in two and a half pages of the Russian text), she is called simply Sappho, which makes it seem as if she is not merely named after Sappho of Lesbos, but *is* she—both the courtesan and the poet. This minor character thus represents Tolstoy's reading of the Original Woman Poet.

Tolstoy's Sappho has beauty, bold manners, a large head, and a "big, much-exposed bust," attributes that lend her image the anima-like aura of a phallic mother. "The impulsive abruptness of her movements was such that at every step the lines of her knees and thighs were clearly visible"—she is frankly and dynamically sexual. Her most remarkable attribute, however, is "the extravagant extreme of her dress" ("ee tualet byl doveden do krainosti"), the way she is constructed. The narrator wonders lasciviously as he concludes his description of Sappho: "One involuntarily wondered where in the undulating, bolstered up mountain of material at the back" the real, graceful little body, "so naked in front and so hidden behind and below, really came to an end."

For all its misogyny and quintessential irreverence, this travesty of Sappho contains a serious and true perception of the Original Woman Poet in modern dress. To grasp this perception one must think of Sappho Stolz's "real, graceful, little body" as Sappho of Lesbos's real, fragmentary, and undressed corpus, which many male admirers over the centuries have described as "severe," "simple," and "stately." In the Russian text of the description cited above, the word "body" (*telo*) occurs at the very end of a long sentence. It is separated from the last adjective that modifies it, "graceful" (*stroinoe*), by two participial phrases in a classic example of Russo-Germanic syntax: *stroinoe, stol' obnazhennoe sverkhu i stol' spriatannoe szadi i vnizu telo*. The syntactical dress of the word "body" puts it and the woman's body (corpus) it signifies "under a mountain of material at its back."

The history of Sappho in Russian literary fashion began in the mid-eighteenth century with the first translations of her corpus, at that time consisting of essentially two poems: a hymn or ode to Aphrodite, and three stanzas of a lyric that begins, *fainetai moi kenos isos theoisin* ("It seems to me that one is equal to the gods"). Both poems were first translated into Russian prose from the original Greek by Grigorii Kozlitskii in 1759 and appeared in the November issue of Sumarokov's journal *The Busy Bee*. Sumarokov, himself a major eighteenth-century dramatist, did poetic translations of both poems from Kozlitskii's prose versions, but the majority of Russian translators of Sappho until the early twentieth century depended on French translations of her work, in the case of "fainetai moi," which shall concern us here, Boileau's.

During the first third of the nineteenth century there was a vogue for Sappho in St. Petersburg literary journals, where a spate of poetic translations and the first Russian Sapphic imitations and fictions appeared. The majority of these Sapphic works were translations from French.[9] Sappho's popularity in Russia at this time reflected the classical and graecophile tastes of Napoleonic Europe in general and Tsar Alexander I in particular and may also have been connected with the emergence of Russian women poets, a couple of whom were dubbed "the Russian Sappho" by their male contemporaries. As in western Europe at that time, the epithet had no connotations of the poet's sexual orientation because Sappho was considered a heterosexual poet.

After quoting a now-forgotten Russian poet who noted, "There is a Sappho in Russia and Sappho is not alone," a contemporary Russian literary scholar, E. G. Sviiasov, names three Russian Sapphos—Kheraskova, Bunina, and Lokhvitskaia—and opines (in the case of the first two) that "these very flattering comparisons were made most likely . . . because the authors in question belonged to the female sex."[10] Sviiasov mentions Batiushkov in connection with Bunina's naming, but does not cite the "Madrigal to a New Sappho" (1809) in which Batiushkov named her: "You are Sappho, I am Phaon, / —that I do not dispute. / But to my misfortune you / to the sea know not the route."[11]

Batiushkov's quatrain reveals his familiarity with the French Sapphic tradition in which Phaon is a poet and Sappho's poetic rival. He uses this tradition to allude to the role Bunina played in early nineteenth-century Russian literary politics—she was an active and respected supporter of the archaist-Shishkovite party. The madrigal also speaks to the gender politics of Russian poetry (in nearly any time) by expressing a young male poet's opinion of an older female contemporary. Simultaneously, Batiushkov alludes to Bunina's personal relationship with Ivan Dmitriev, a well-known Sentimentalist poet, with whom she enjoyed a "close literary friendship . . . and was rumored by her contemporaries even to have been in love."[12] Batiushkov gives an ironic twist to the traditional Sappho-Phaon love fiction, however, by implying that rejection is not enough to rid a man of the new Sappho. The Russian Phaon's misfortune testifies to the Russian Sappho's resiliency and shows a misogynistic, begrudging respect for Bunina's character, if not her talent or seductiveness. Unfortunately, I have not been able to find out what Bunina's own attitudes to Sappho were, or how she felt about being called a new one. Her own poetic association with Sappho appears to have been restricted to her translation of "fainetai moi," which she probably made from Boileau, whose works she translated into Russian.

In the West, "fainetai moi" proved to be the most problematic poem fragment in Sappho's corpus because of its homoerotic content:

> It seems to me *that one* is equal to the gods,
> *the man who[soever]* sits opposite you
> and listens nearby to you *speaking* sweetly
> and *laughing* charmingly, which, truly,
> terrifies the heart in my breast.
> For as I look briefly at you, so nothing
> comes to me to say,
> but my tongue has snapped, a subtle
> fire suddenly has run beneath my skin,
> with my eyes I see nothing, my hearing hums,
> sweat pours over me, trembling
> seizes all of me, I am *pale-greener*
> than grass, I seem to myself to be little
> short of death.[13] (Emphasis added)

The female speaker in the poem expresses desire for another woman, and the female gender of both the object of desire and the desiring subject is subtly but clearly marked. At the beginning of the poem the feminine participles "speaking" (*foneisas*) and "laughing" (*gelaisas*) define the addressee as a woman. The poetic speaker reveals her gender only once, near the end of the poem as we have it, in the feminine form of the comparative adjective *chlorotera* ("greener," "pale-greener," "paler"), itself the subject of centuries of heated debate as to what, precisely, Sappho meant by it.[14]

According to a recent survey, "fainetai moi" has yielded more translations and imitations in Russian than any other classical or western European poem. Seventeen versions of it were published between 1804 and 1828 alone.[15] In the remainder of this essay I examine several Russian translations of this poem with the aim of deconstructing their specific and changing cultural contexts.

From the sixteenth century to the early twentieth, all translators of "fainetai moi" read the poem heterosexually, or as an expression of the Sapphic speaker's internally mediated desire and jealousy. Such a reading depended on interpreting the relative pronoun phrase in lines one and two, *kenos . . . oner ottis* ("that one . . . the man who[soever]"), to denote a specific man who is present in the narrative of the poem and who ostensibly *creates a story* from the female speakers' feelings. The word *ottis*, however, is an indefinitive relative pronoun, "whosoever he may be," which means that Sappho did not specify either a concrete individual, or a man actually present in the poem, or a heterosexual love story dependent on his presence. At the same time she did not exclude these possibilities.[16]

By defining the "man whosoever" that Sappho intentionally left ambiguous, translators of the poem made him the focus of the female speaker's attention, desexualized her desire for her addressee and "female friend," and circumvented the problem of the poem's female homoeroticism. Sappho's lyric was widely understood to express her violent jealousy for a female rival rather than her violent desire for another woman. In the Russian translating tradition, several poet-translators interpreted "fainetai moi" as primarily an outpouring of female jealousy.

The great eighteenth-century poet Gavrila Derzhavin enjoyed a nearly lifelong poetic relationship with Sappho, central to which were the nine different translations he made of "fainetai moi." The complexity and intensity of Derzhavin's poetic interaction with Sappho deserves an essay in itself. Here I must limit myself to one interesting aspect of his involvement with "fainetai moi." His first translation of the poem dated from 1770 and was made from Boileau's French translation. As a Russian, however, Derzhavin apparently wanted to get closer to Sappho than the French intermediary allowed. His nationalist feelings were indicated in his explanation of why he included two translations of "fainetai moi" in the 1808 edition of his collected works, one from Boileau and another from a Russian trot he had made of the Aeolian Greek original. "The French language," Derzhavin explained, "is incapable of the same power [*sila*] of laconic expression as the Greek; but the opposite is proved by Russian."[17] Embedded in the tortured phrasing of this statement is the nationalist poet's desire to assert his fledgling poetic culture's separateness from (and superiority to) the French *arbiter dictum* and European literary model by establishing the native bonds that Russian enjoyed with classical Greek and the Original Woman (Mother) Poet, Sappho.

After Derzhavin, the Russian poet who experienced the most intimate bonding with Sappho appears to have been Pavel Katenin. In composing his complex and original 1838 Sapphic fiction, "Sappho: A Cantata," Katenin was vexed by his literal and figurative distance from Sappho's corpus. He turned to Pushkin for help in coming closer to Sappho, asking, in a letter from Stavropol' of June 1, 1835, if Pushkin did not know some Hellenist "who could make a slavish translation *en vile prose* of Sappho's two tiny poems: 'To Venus' and 'Heureux qui,' etc.?"[18] He repeated his request the following month in a letter of July 7: "Sappho is enchantingly sketched out in my imagination, and continues to entice; but firewood cannot be chopped without an ax, and I most humbly repeat my request to send the latter, that is, a few Greek verses jacketed in the most modern prose, as *vile et servile* as possible."[19]

This passage conveys Katenin's view of Sappho as an alluring foreign poet/seductress and potential fuel for his Russian poet's hearth (she is firewood). Sappho is all the more enticing for Katenin's not being able to have her. He lacks the tool (an ax) to make her serviceable, and that tool turns out to be Sappho's own "tiny" Greek corpus, which he constantly refers to in Boileau's French translation, yet wants encased in a slavishly useful Russian body bag.

Katenin's cantata amply demonstrates his reverence for Sappho, but his respect for the Original Woman Poet lies uncomfortably with his treatment of "fainetai moi," which he translated and interpolated into his Sapphic fiction as if Sappho were singing it herself through him:

The Song of Sappho to Phaon

How blessed he is, equal to the gods,
The one who sits opposite you, [Phaon],
Hears nearby the sounds of your speech,
Sees your smile!
Oh, what then, gods, happens to me!
The heart in my breast is torn asunder;
I have only to see [him], my tongue sticks in my throat,
My voice cannot speak.
Suddenly a subtle flame inside me,
Running in a circle, burns my body;
[As for] my hearing and my gaze—only darkness in my eyes,
Only noise in my ears.
My face will break out in a cold sweat,
Trembling will overcome the whole of me [*fem.*];
I will pale like grass; death is near,
My spirit freezes.[20]

Katenin's translation, ironically one of the better ones, nevertheless badly abuses Sappho's text. By entitling his fictional Sappho's poem "Sappho's Song to Phaon," Katenin changes the gender of the Original Woman Poet's addressee and gives him an identity.

Many translators of "fainetai moi" have assumed that the most prominent man in Sappho's life must have been the object of her desire in her most passionate poem. Consequently, Phaon has frequently been conflated with the only male in the text of "fainetai moi," namely, the initial "that one . . . the man who." Katenin, therefore, followed standard procedure in locating Phaon in the text of "fainetai moi." He departed from convention, however, in identifying Phaon as the addressee of the poem rather than as the man admiring the addressee. His changes of gender in Sappho's text ended up, moreover, suggesting a male homoerotic interaction between Phaon and his male admirer that makes Sappho, the involuntary female onlooker, distraught with jealousy.

Katenin was actually the second Russian translator of "fainetai moi" whose translation obliterated the poem's female homosexual content while introducing a (perhaps unconscious) male homosexual scenario into it. The eminent poet and translator Zhukovskii did likewise in his 1807 version, entitled "Sappho's Ode." The inflected pronoun form *odnim* ("alone," instrumental case) at the end of the first line immediately marks the Sapphic speaker's addressee as a man who is the object of another man's desire:

> That man is blessed who near you burns with you alone [*masc.*],
> Who is enchanted by the charm of your speech,
> Whom your eyes seek, your smile enraptures:
> He is equal to the gods![21]

In an addendum to his discursive notes on Derzhavin's Sappho translations (1869), the Russian classical philologist Iakov Grot quotes Zhukovskii's translation of "fainetai moi" as a curiosity precisely because Zhukovskii, Grot writes, "made Sappho address a man rather than her female friend." Although Grot has argued earlier in his notes that Sappho felt "ideal" (*ideal'naia*) rather than "base" physical passion for her female friend in "fainetai moi," he implies that Zhukovskii must have thought otherwise because he "clearly intended to remove [from Sappho's text] an attitude alien to the morals of the modern world."[22] Grot appears oblivious to the irony that Zhukovskii's purified Sapphic text could be considered sexually marked in the same way as Sappho's morally suspect poem. Alternatively, Grot, like the majority of nineteenth-century philologists in Europe and Russia, may have privileged Greek male homosexuality as by definition an "ideal" form of love that required no moral defense as female same-sex love did.

Grot's treatment of Sappho and her morally suspect lyric "fainetai moi" illustrates a culturally significant aspect of the Russian perception of Sappho in general: its desire to achieve an innocent look. However disingenuous that innocent look may be, it has kept Sappho's great-poet robes from becoming as soiled in Russian poetic use as they have at times become in Western literatures. On the other hand, because Russian Sapphic innocence can and often does hide a multitude of misogynistic and homophobic sins, Sappho has never been—with one exception, which I discuss at the end of this essay—the empowering presence for major Russian women poets that she has been in the West.

Russian philological and critical views of Sappho have drawn and continue to draw heavily on the work and theories of two nineteenth-century German Hellenists, Johann Gottlieb Welcker and Ulrich von Wilamowitz-Moellendorff, whose authority on Sappho remained unquestioned well into the twentieth century. Welcker's influential work on Sappho, written in the early nineteenth century, was focused less on Sappho than on Greek male homosexuality in its Platonic manifestation. It was Welcker who advanced the latter as a moral ideal crucial to the building of nation-states. He asserted that Sappho was the spokesman for the companion ideal of female Platonic eros and chastity. At the turn of the twentieth century, Wilamowitz rearticulated the theory of Sapphic chastity and developed the hypothesis that Sappho was the leader of a religious community and school for girls, and that her relations with the young women mentioned in her fragments reflected her special pedagogical and spiritual role in their lives.

Following Welcker and Wilamowitz, Russian philologists from the mid-nineteenth century until today typically affirm the presence of female same-sex love in Sappho's poems while denying its physicality—they uniformly argue that it is a manifestation of ideal love; that is, it exists only as an idea. From the 1890s, Russian commentaries on Sappho have vociferously denied this ideal love the name it had by then given rise to in common parlance.

Vikentii Veresaev, an open admirer of Welcker, exemplified the Russian philological denial of the word for Sappho's love in the name of love for Sappho's word. In the "Introduction" to his 1915 translation of Sappho's complete fragments, he dismisses the idea that uppercase Sapphic love, what he later describes as "Sappho's passionate love for women and lack of erotic feeling for men," is the same sort of "perverted, unnatural" love which his contemporaries call "sapphic" (lowercase) or "lesbian love." The notion that Sappho was homosexual, or even sexual, Veresaev argues, is one of the many myths that have grown up around her, along with her fatal, unrequited love for Phaon and "the gossip that she sold her love to men for money."[23]

Today, when the locus of Sapphic philological authority has moved from Germany to England, and the weight of Western scholarly opinion has shifted in support of a homosexual Sappho, one senses the difference between Russian and Western perceptions of Sappho more acutely. That difference becomes clear through a comparison of the views of Joan De Jean, writing in the late 1980s, and Ol'ga Freidenberg, writing in the elate 1940s, but enthusiastically seconded by Sviiasov in his 1991 study on Sappho in Russian poetry of the Silver Age.

At first glance, De Jean's statement "Sappho is, quite simply, a problem, certainly among the most sensitive issues in the history of literature" (p. 2) seems to echo a remark by Freidenberg in a 1946 letter to Pasternak: "I am now working on Sappho, one of the most difficult problems in classical literature."[24] But while De Jean sees the essence of the Sappho problem in "standards imposed on female sexuality" and "received ideas about female same-sex love," Freidenberg, in the 1949 published "Theses" for her still-unpublished monograph on Sappho, rejects the Western ("bourgeois") "lesbian theory," which she had earlier called "the height of vulgarity" in her politically uncensored diary.[25]

It is important to emphasize that Freidenberg never argues against the presence of female same-sex love in Sappho's lyrics. On the contrary, she takes that for granted as a textual fact, noting that in Sappho's songs "women sing of their love for women, not for men."[26] Freidenberg's quarrel is with modern terminology and its inapplicability to ancient, hermetic texts. She rejects the term "lesbian" because for her and the Russian intellectual culture she represents, it denotes something perverse and vulgar that characterizes a time and place far removed from what she calls the "historical specificity" of Sappho's Lesbos and her classical genre.

Freidenberg's proposed solution of the "Sappho problem" has a nationalistic dimension which is also reminiscent of nineteenth-century German philological thinking and aspirations. "The task of Soviet classical philology," she wrote, "is to liberate Sappho's songs from vulgar treatment, to return to them the lofty origi-

nality which will make it possible to assess correctly their historico-literary significance" (*Theses*, 190–91). Freidenberg's 1949 Soviet philological "liberation" of
Sappho from the clutches of the decadent West tellingly echoes the goals of
Welcker's 1816 essay as articulated in its title: "Sappho Liberated from a Prevailing
Prejudice" ("Sappho von einem herrschenden Vorurtheil befreyt"). Reviving the
theory of Sapphic chastity, Freidenberg asserts a "lesbian-free" Sappho in the interests of her supranational philology. By freeing Sappho from vulgar Western
treatment and abuse, Soviet philology will control the revelation of the real, pure
Sappho just as Welcker and his newly emergent German national philology of the
previous century claimed to have rescued the Tenth Muse from French abuse.

Russian poets' and philologists' discourse of Sapphic chastity managed to preserve the loftiness of the Original Woman Poet, but by placing her in the category
of a de-gendered ideal, they severed her connection with real women poets and
failed to foster respect in the culture for the latter. The latent hostility to Sappho,
which one finds in the West in the long tradition of Sapphic fiction making that
began in the Renaissance, can be discerned in Russia in the attitudes of male poets
and critics to their female counterparts. The Russian tradition of Sapphic name
calling, initiated, as we have shown, in the early nineteenth century by poets such
as Batiushkov, reached its peak intensity during the Silver Age. It is exemplified by
the poet Vladislav Khodasevich, who, in a 1916 book review, referred to a whole
group of his female contemporaries disparagingly as "ladies' poets" and "youthful
offspring of Sappho."[27] The epithet "Sappho" had come to denote merely the biological link of a Russian female poet to the great Sappho. Only male poets, and
female poets willing to eschew their gender in favor of the putatively ungendered
(but grammatically masculine) name of "poet," could enjoy a spiritual and genuine poetic kinship with the Original Woman Poet.

In *Fictions of Sappho* De Jean summarizes two ways in which Western male
writers have traditionally used Sappho: "young male writers strive for literary manhood by enacting their simultaneous attraction to a male and to a female literary
origin, . . . displaying only admiration for the male predecessor while displacing
their hostility onto Sappho in her role as the original woman writer"; "those male
authors somehow able to identify with the original woman writer, to succeed in a
special variant of . . . 'playing the other,' in this case, revoicing a most problematic
other, a woman who wrote of woman's desire for woman" (p. 8).

It seems to me that Sappho is not quite so problematic an other for male poets
as De Jean argues, in view of the prevalence of the *mascula Sappho* stereotype and
the widespread, cross-cultural tendency to perceive not only lesbian desire but any
desire expressed by a female subject as essentially "masculine." This suggests that
many male poets perceived Sappho, despite her sex, as sharing their gender, that is,
as being familiarly rather than strangely "other."

Around 1890, at the beginning of the Silver Age, Russian poetic interest
in Sappho intensified again. This second vogue did have demonstrable ties with
the vastly increased presence of women writers in Russia at this time and with the

women's liberation movement. One humorous and misogynistic indication of this was reflected in an epigram by the poet and philosopher Vladimir Solov'ev: "The solution of the woman question / will, truly, come to us from Lesbos."[28]

The decadent culture of the nineties hailed a new Russian Sappho, Mirra Lokhvitskaia. Like the old Russian Sappho, she lacked the authority or desire to name herself, as the original Sappho of Lesbos had, or to empower herself in Sappho's name the way Western lesbian poets of the time were doing. She acquired her Sapphic status not because her creativity had any intimate connection with Sappho's, but for the old reason that she was a female poet, and for a new Silver Age reason—she wrote, by the male-determined standards of the period, unabashedly erotic lyrics. For that reason, no doubt, Lokhvitskaia's typical female poet speaker, a woman burning with desire, was thought by some of her contemporaries to be "masculine" because her desire was more "physiological than spiritual."[29]

It is worth noting, however, that in one of Lokhvitskaia's three Sapphic fictions, "Sappho Visits Eros" (1891), appropriately subtitled "A Fantasy," the poet freshened the hopelessly stale plot of Sappho's unrequited love for Phaon by giving it a happy ending. The "Fantasy" narrates a visit Sappho makes to Aphrodite's house only to find that her beloved goddess is not home; she is away at a wedding. In Aphrodite's absence, Sappho frees the goddess's son (Eros) from the gilded cage in which his mother is punishing him (unjustly, he protests). In return, Eros makes the traitor Phaon return to Sappho's embraces, a happy surprise which greets the Tenth Muse when she arrives home in Mytilene.[30] In fantasizing this new Sapphic fiction, similar in mood to the late-eighteenth-century French bourgeois comedies created from Sappho's alleged life story, Lokhvitskaia in effect "rescues" Sappho from the power of the *female* goddess (with whom Sappho of Lesbos enjoyed a privileged and *creatively enabling* alliance) while empowering the *boy-god* Eros to usurp his mother's power and position in Sappho's life.

In the wake of Lokhvitskaia's premature death, the pages of Russian provincial journals exploded with Sapphic fictions, hysterical outpourings by male and female hacks on the subject of a desperate Sappho's suicide from unrequited love for Phaon.[31] By contrast, *fin de siècle* Sapphic fictions in the West were asserting a homosexual Sappho, both as a cultural model of decadent modernism and as the original woman-identified poet. Because of their almost total silence on female same-sex love, Russian Silver Age Sapphic fictions resemble those written in France in the late eighteenth century. If the latter, as De Jean suggests, can be linked with Foucault's thesis that "sexuality began to be morally problematic in the early eighteenth century" (De Jean, p. 117), might not Russian Silver Age Sapphic fictions provide literary cultural evidence that in Russia, sexuality acquired a similar moral complexity only in the years preceding World War I?

After the new discoveries of Sappho's fragments, which began in the 1890s and culminated in the Egyptian papyri finds at Oxyrynchus, translating activity in Russia increased.[32] Two poetic, metrically correct translations of Sappho's complete, extant oeuvre appeared: Viacheslav Ivanov's in 1914 and Vikentii Veresaev's the following year. Veresaev's translations are generally faithful to the originals and plain, while Ivanov's are often flamboyantly unfaithful. But such infidelity in a Russian male admirer of Sappho, one, moreover, who knew her original texts, suggests the kind of interesting and ambivalent poetic involvement with the Tenth Muse that I have discussed in other examples. In several ways, Ivanov's interaction with Sappho and his version of "fainetai moi" summarize the ambiguities of Russian male poets' attitudes to the Original Woman Poet.

Love

It seems to me: like the gods blessed and free
He who sits with you, *speaks with you,*
Looks a dear woman in the eyes and hears nearby
The affectionate babble
Of [her] tender lips! . . . Of smiling lips he catches
The breath . . . While I,—should I from afar merely glimpse
Your face—I sense not the heart in my breast,
I cannot open my lips!
My poor tongue is mute, and through my veins a subtle
Flame runs like a hot chill;
A din is in my ears; my eyes grow dark, are dimmed;
My legs falter . . .
All over [*fem.*] I tremble, grow numb; dampened with sweat
Is the pale ice of my brow: just as if death is coming . . .
One step—and I, with lifeless body,
Shall sink to the ground.[33]

First of all, the title Ivanov gave "fainetai moi," "Love" (*Liubov'*), is ambiguous and misleading. It could describe the feelings of the female speaker, but if that was Ivanov's intention, then he attached a modern misinterpretation to those feelings. As Freidenberg, among others, has noted, "the eros which the Greek lyricists describe does not at all correspond to the feeling of love."[34] Ivanov's title could also refer to the relationship he creates in the poem, following traditional translating practice, between the "blessed he who[soever]" and "a dear woman" he is talking to. In Sappho, one recalls, the young woman is talking, and an any man is admiring her in silence. If Ivanov meant his title to characterize the young heterosexual couple in his translation, then he wished to imply, again following standard practice, that the female Sapphic speaker is an onlooker, viewing a happy couple composed of one of her favorites, perhaps, and the lucky man who has her attention. The speaker's own response to the young woman is described not as something immediate and in motion as the poem proceeds, but as the general response that is triggered in her whenever she should glimpse the young woman, even from afar. Ivanov's Sappho is strangely disconnected from her emotions and from her erotic experience. In his poem only the interaction between the young woman and her male admirer has actuality, while the relationship between the female speaker and her female object of desire remains wholly in the realm of hypothetical (idea) reality. This is exactly the reverse of Sappho's lyric in which the speaker's attack of eros seems to take place in actuality while the "any man's" attraction to the speaker's addressee is at best potential, and maybe even hypothetical.

Ivanov gave actuality to the male admirer in "fainetai moi" in part no doubt because of his view of Sappho's life and poetic status, a view he expounds in the "Introduction" to his translations of Sappho and Alcaeus. Ivanov revoiced the now discredited, but in his time widely accepted, theory of Wilamowitz (with whom he had studied in Germany) that Sappho was the head of a religious community and school for aristocratic young women. Following Wilamowitz again, Ivanov explains Sappho's strong but chaste "erotic feelings" for her supposed female pupils as a central component of her idiosyncratic, "purely Hellenic understanding of her educational task, a task at once moral-religious, artistic and erotic" (Ivanov, 25).

Ivanov's translations of Sappho evoked controversy in classical philological journals. One of the poet's friendly critics delicately alluded in his review to Ivanov's practice of augmenting the originals, "in some cases beyond the limits of philological accuracy," and said this practice could be justified only by the translator's "poetic task." In Ivanov's own words, that task was "'to make a collection of lyrical fragments as complete as possible so that neither a single meaningful image nor a single definite thought is sacrificed.'"[35]

The last two stanzas of "Love" reveal the Russian poet-translator of Sappho at his augmenting best and suggest why Ivanov found a philologically accurate Sappho out of sympathy with his poetic Sappho, and the Sappho preferred by Russian poetic culture. Nobody would know from Ivanov's "fainetai moi" that metaphor is alien to Sappho, or that the assault from Eros that the female speaker suffers constitutes a real, physical attack, as Freidenberg has noted, "a seizure by the god, . . . deathbearing theophany in a pitiable, weak mortal." Ivanov weakens namely the physicality of Eros's assault and the physiology of the original Sappho's description of sexual desire that must have seemed to his Russian Victorian taste to exceed even a "masculine" attitude to erotic experience. He circumscribes and metaphorizes the physical symptoms of the female speaker's "seizure by the god." When nearing the fatal moment she says, "sweat pours over me, trembling seizes all of me" (*kad de m'idros kakheetai, tromos de paisan agrei*), Ivanov's Sappho notes almost fastidiously, "All over I tremble, grow numb; dampened with sweat the pale ice of my brow" (*Vsia drozhu, mertveiu; uvlazhnen potom / blednyi led chela*). The original Sapphic speaker is all sensation, while Ivanov's is numbed; her sweat-streaming body is translated into one part of it, the brow, suggestively symbolic of mind. Having superimposed his mind on the Sapphic speaker's whole female body, Ivanov then causes his own metaphor to melt into a sweating block of ice.

Sappho concludes the third stanza of her lyric with a single, "definite thought" expressed once in six words (in the original Greek): "I seem to myself to be little short of death" (*tethnaken d'oligo 'pideues fainom' em' aut[a]*). Ivanov's translation replaces this with a twelve-word circumlocution (in Russian) that conveys Sappho's thought of seeming near death in three approximate ways: "just as if death is coming . . . / One step—and I, with lifeless body, / Shall sink to the ground" (*slovno smert' prikhodit . . . / Shag odin—i ia, bezdykhannym telom, / Sniknu na zemliu*). More disturbing, Ivanov's translation of the last stanza of "fainetai moi" excises and replaces with part of its augmented self the most lexically mysterious of the Sapphic speaker's unpleasant physical symptoms, *chlorotera de poias emmi* ("greener than grass am I").

Robbed of its immediacy, terrifying theophanic religiosity, and physical reality of female same-sex desire, Sappho's distant, mysterious text becomes familiar to a Russian Silver Age reader, and open to Ivanov's aggressive male Symbolist poetic desire. He designs his own "extravagant get-up" for Sappho's corpus. Since he works from the inside out rather than the outside in, his procedures seem on the surface to be the reverse of Tolstoy's. Ironically, they yield a similar result.

Let us recall, for a moment, Tolstoy's Sappho Stolz (the parody Sappho) and his implied perception of Sappho of Lesbos (the original Sappho). Sappho Stolz's extravagantly extreme dress overwhelmed her real, graceful, little body with contrived and artificial bustles and corsetry, clumsy, unharmonious, unwieldy clothes that were in every sense, even in opposite senses, too much. The late-nineteenth-century construction of Sappho, as Tolstoy reveals through his travesty of it, was too revealing and overexposed of her upper torso and too titillatingly secretive and unrevealing of her lower half. Both excesses, in Tolstoy's view, had the same effect: they drew disproportionate attention to Sappho's sexuality and therefore gave an untrue and ungraceful appearance to her body (corpus). Finally, Tolstoy's parody of Sappho belied the emotional depth of the original Sappho. Sappho Stolz arouses the lust of men and women while feeling nothing herself. Her body moves without expressing inner, moral movement (emotion) as if she is an overendowed, empty doll.

In translating the new, expanded, but ever-fragmentary Sappho of the *fin de siècle* into "authentic" Russian poetry, Ivanov tried manfully to fill the emptiness in the corpus of the Tenth Muse. Rather than overwhelm Sappho's real, graceful, little body with extravagant, provocative clothes as his nineteenth-century fathers had done, Ivanov attempted to get inside the "bodies" of Sappho's fragmentary poems and perform a kind of reconstructive surgery by inserting artificial (dead) implants. Such surgery required that the patient's body be put to sleep, however. Ivanov succeeded in filling Sappho's poems out, but in the process of reconstruction, the original lines often lost their reality and their grace. In Ivanov's authoritative Russian reconstructions, Sappho became more perfect, and, consequently, almost permanently anesthetized, as cold, immobile, and lifeless as the benumbed and lifeless body of the Sapphic speaker in "Love." If there is any eros in that speaker's suffering of desire, then it is a pale, cerebral, necrophiliac eros, death-loving, rather than the death-dealing eros of the original Sapphic poem.

Ivanov's augmentations and reconstructions of Sappho suggest that his desire for the original woman poet trapped him with a lure impossible to avoid. He wanted "to make Sappho as complete as possible" when he knew that Sappho is nothing if she is not incomplete. The Egyptian discoveries made this clearer to Ivanov's generation than to any before it as they revealed a corpus exhumed from the dead, literally, in strips—the papyri were used as mummy wrappings—and proved that Sappho was not available to anyone whole. Neither Ivanov (and here I suggest a third possible reading of his "Love") nor "any *man* who sits near

[Sappho] and listens to [her] speaking sweetly" can put her back together again and return her *parthenia*, a word that occurs frequently in Sappho's fragments, a word redolent of beauty and loss that for the ancient Greeks meant "virginity" in the sense of being an unmarried woman, whole unto herself.[36] Denying his incapacity to make Sappho whole, Ivanov, the Russian Silver Age seeker of a pure, dead poet-muse, makes her over (and over) by filling her up with bits of himself.

If Derzhavin, in his self-designated role as Russian poet-hero and husband to Sappho, wished to assert his intimacy with Sappho and his superiority to her legendary poet-consort (Phaon) and her numerous French poet-lovers in posterity; if Katenin wanted Sappho, with the help of Russia's national poet, Pushkin, to fire his Russian creative hearth; and if Tolstoy desired to expose and debunk all other male authors' and authorities' fashionable sexual vulgarizations of Sappho in order to assert, by implication, his unique possession of the real Tenth Muse—then Ivanov, coming at the end of the Petersburg period in Russian "Sapphistry," can be seen to have aspired to the final Russian male authorship, through reconstruction, of Sappho.

One of the most avid readers of Ivanov's Sappho when she first appeared in 1914 was Sofiia Parnok (1885–1933), Russia's only openly lesbian poet.[37] Parnok immediately began writing Sapphic stanzas, examples of which she included in her first book, *Poems* (1916). Her passion for Sappho spanned two important love affairs (with the young poet Marina Tsvetaeva, 1914–16, and with the Moscow actress Liudmila Erarskaia, 1916–22), aspects of which Parnok wrote out in some of her Sapphic poems, and her desire for Sappho reached its peak intensity in 1918–19, when Parnok was living in the eastern Crimean town of Sudak.[38] Ironically, Parnok had already parted emotionally and creatively from Sappho by 1922, when her anthological collection of Sapphic poems, *Roses of Pieria*, was published. The appearance of *Roses* even annoyed her because, as she wrote to Maksimilian Voloshin, "After a six-year hiatus (and such a stormy one!) this small anthological collection looks somehow 'too esthetic' and that upsets me very much."[39]

From the standpoint of Russian literary history, however, Parnok was too dismissive of her Sapphic poems. Although it was, predictably, the "too esthetic" metrical and formal aspects of Parnok's Sapphic stanzas that excited the most comment and appreciation from her prerevolutionary contemporaries (and did prove anachronistic after the 1917 Revolution), the original perspective on Sappho and the unique creative interaction with her which Parnok's Sapphic poems express constitute a radical contribution to the Sappho tradition in Russian poetry. Parnok in fact developed Ivanov's "authoritative" Sappho in a new direction and reinterpreted the idea of what it means to attain to the "real" Sappho and translate the Original Woman Poet into Russian.

According to Parnok's first "Sapphic Stanzas," which were probably written in 1914, Sappho's "Aeolian lyre" stimulated Parnok's creativity and caused "music to flow in [her] veins."[40] She was inspired "to release into freedom, pour from [her] heart / stringed sounds" (#38). In the poem's last stanza, Parnok's speaker realizes that Sappho has stirred her Lesbian imagination and her racial memory of "the unforgettable pleasures of unforgettable songs / that my hetaeras[41] sang of old / in Sappho's school." This poem makes it clear that Parnok desired Sappho as strongly as Ivanov or any of the other Russian male poets I have discussed in this essay. Unlike them, however, Parnok desired not so much to possess as to merge with Sappho in order to be Sappho again, to re/member her both as a poet and as a lover of women.

As I have shown in the foregoing pages, for several Russian male poets, becoming intimate with Sappho depended largely on knowing Greek, or even "a slavish" prose version of her Greek. Parnok did not know Greek, and she made no attempt to learn it in order to get closer to Sappho. She accepted Ivanov's translations as linguistically accurate—mistakenly as it turned out, but even if she had known that some of Ivanov's translations were not faithful to the original, she most likely would not have been concerned. The intimacy with Sappho that Parnok desired did not depend on knowledge of Sappho's dialect. Parnok's Sapphic poems reveal that she believed herself to have a priori, extralinguistic knowledge of Sappho. Parnok knew (recognized) Sappho "across the centuries" as her kin, a "sister of a single faith" (#61). Therefore, what knowing Greek was to Russian male poets' sense of intimacy with Sappho, knowing her own was to Parnok's intimacy with the Original Woman Poet.

Parnok lets Sappho's fragments stand, for better or for worse, in Ivanov's translations, and uses them, rather than Sappho herself, as the epigraphs and points of origin for her own Sapphic songs. Instead of translating Sappho's fragmentary *texts* literally, from their ancient, dead language into her modern, living, yet nonetheless foreign tongue, Parnok, I would argue, strove to translate Sappho's missing *contexts* metaphorically, from their ancient, dead lyricism into her modern, living, and spiritually kindred lyricism. In one of her Sapphic poems, Parnok visualizes herself as a latter-day poet-maiden of "Sappho's school" and comments on the contextualizing impulse behind her creative "translations" and continuations of Sappho's fragmentary opus: "It seems to the maiden—she is dreaming out your dreams, Sappho, / singing out your songs that have not sounded down to us" (#68).

In other Sapphic poems Parnok maintains the integrity of her poetic speaker while simultaneously merging her with her "sister," Sappho. The first love lyric that Parnok wrote to Marina Tsvetaeva, in February 1915, takes off from one of Sappho's single-line fragments, allegedly written to her beloved girl, Atthis: "Like a small girl you appeared in my presence ungracefully" (#59). In her poem Parnok re-originates the context of Sappho's ancient line, using it as the epigraph (the beginning) and the refrain (the eternal message) of her modern lesbian song. That song's speaker (Parnok) and her beloved small girl (Tsvetaeva) play out their love affair according to the ancient model established by Sappho and Atthis. The ancient model is, of course, missing except for one line, but the modern Lesbian poet (Parnok) knows its whole presence surely and intuitively because the one extant line of Sappho's has struck her with knowledge of its entire context in the same way as one of Eros's arrows strikes a person with realization of her whole love: "'Like a small girl you appeared in my presence ungracefully'— / Ah, Sappho's single-line shaft pierced to my very core!" (#59). Parnok suggests here that in order to know the "real" Sappho, one has to be smitten by her. Where the Russian male poets I have discussed all, to varying degrees, aggressed upon the body of Sappho's texts in order to have her, or at least to dress her, Parnok opens herself to Sappho's essence. Where the Russian male poets who desired Sappho sought possession of Sappho's originating female lyrical power, Parnok seeks merger, identity, and parity with it.[42]

Parnok wants to realize Sappho's spiritual presence in all her extant body's gaping absence by "releasing into freedom" her own, inviolable inner Sappho. In this her Sapphic poems resemble the lyrical contextualizations of Sappho's fragments written out by the American-French lesbian poet Renée Vivien in her 1903 volume *Sappho* as well as the re-origination of Sappho by Vivien's lover, Natalie Clifford Barney, in her 1910 poetic drama "Equivoque."[43] Barney and Vivien created their lesbian-identified Sapphic fictions to rescue Sappho from the male decadent poets (Baudelaire, Verlaine, and Louÿs) and to reclaim her not only as the Original Woman Poet, but as the Original Lesbian Poet, an enterprise that required "de-heterosexualizing" Sappho's legendary biography. Parnok's treatment of Sappho bespeaks a similar agenda, and "too esthetic" or not, her Sapphic poems remain the only serious use of Sappho in Russian poetry that affirms the Original Woman Poet as a great poet and an active (sexual) lover of women. The lesbian politics of Parnok's re-originating "translations" of Sappho become clear in one of the poems of the cycle "Dreams of Sappho" (#66). After uttering her lyrical admonition to her hetaeras, "Believe me, someone in the future will remember us," Parnok's Sappho sinks on her female lover's breast, falls asleep, and dreams of the fulfillment of her own words. Aphrodite appears to Sappho in her dream (as Parnok dreams it out) and says with gentle irony: "'Here is fame, Sappho: people arguing who you addressed your eternal love songs to . . . , youths or maidens?'" (#66).

One of the many not-so-gentle ironies of Parnok's creative life lies in the fact that the poem in which she comes closest to being Sappho (and spontaneously so, without the mediation of Ivanov's translation) is a lyric that contains no reference to Sappho, no hint of Sappho's stanza, no apparent external connection with Sappho whatsoever—a lyric, moreover, that was written in 1929, almost a decade after Parnok herself said she had "become cold" to Sappho. I have in mind Parnok's last love lyric to Marina Tsvetaeva, "You are young, long-limbed!" which was inspired by the poet's attraction to a young reader and namesake of Tsvetaeva's, Marina Baranovich. Not only do the inner movement and structure of "You are young" reveal how potently Sappho was immanent within Parnok, they bear a striking resemblance to the rhythm and structuring of Sappho's "fainetai moi." Therefore, I would like to conclude this essay, which began with Sappho Stolz, with a brief deconstruction of Sappho-Parnok in the hope of teasing out the "real, graceful, little body" of the Original Lesbian Poet who is embedded and alive in Parnok's modern poetic text:

You are young, long-limbed! With such
a marvelously molded, winged body!
How awkwardly and with such difficulty
you drag around your spirit, anguish-stunned![44]
Oh, I know that spirit's way of moving
through whirlwinds of the night and ice-floe gaps,
and that voice that rises indistinctly,
God alone knows from what living depths.
I recall the darkness of bright eyes like those.
As when you read, all voices would grow quiet,
whenever she, a madman raving verses,
with her frenzy would ignite our souls.
How strange that you remind me so of her!
The same rosiness, goldenness,
and pearliness of face, and silkiness,
the same pulsating warmth.
And the coldness of serpentine wiles
and slipperiness. . . . But I've forgiven her,
and I love you, and through you, Marina,
the vision of the woman who shares your name. (#220)

First of all, like its unconscious model, "fainetai moi," Parnok's poem (and re/membering of her Atthis) narrates the speaker's two visions of her desired addressee. Sappho's speaker in "fainetai moi," we recall, imagines or sees her addressee at a public function as she mesmerizes some/any man. Parnok's speaker similarly sees (in her mind's eye) her addressee at a public reading as she mesmerizes her audience. Sappho's speaker then focuses on how sight of the addressee affects different parts of her own body—her voice, tongue, skin, eyes, ears, and whole body—moving her to orgasm. Complementarily, Parnok's speaker focuses on how re-sight of the different parts and sensations of her addressee's body—her long legs, voice, eyes, face, pulsing warmth, and serpentine cold—affect her and move her, in re/membering them, to a climax of forgiveness and a confession of love. Parnok's oxymoronic play on heat and cold also recalls "fainetai moi" and Sappho in general, for the Lesbian poet was the originator of the now hackneyed fire-and-ice metaphor of physical passion.

In expressing her desire and love, the speaker of Parnok's poem inscribes the feminine gender of her desiring subject and of her desired object in a manner that also re-originates Sappho's procedure in "fainetai moi." As Sappho does with the feminine participles *foneisas* ("speaking") and *gelaisas* ("laughing"), Parnok, with the adjectives *molodaia* ("young") and *dlinnonogaia* ("long-limbed"), asserts the feminine gender of her desired addressee(s) immediately, at the beginning of her poem, but withholds the climactic revelation of her speaker's feminine gender (and the lesbian contents of the poem) until the end of the poem, where, like Sappho, she inscribes her gender in a single word. Sappho affirmed the feminine gender of her speaker with the comparative adjective *khlorotera* ("pale-greener") and Parnok reveals her speaker's femaleness with the past tense verb *prostila* ("have forgiven").[45]

Parnok's idea of love as forgiveness represents the spiritual antithesis of the violent sexual attack suffered by Sappho's speaker, but at the same time such intense (com)passion suggests a kind of recovering of (and from) the passion sickness that afflicted/afflicts the Sapphic speakers of both poems. In "You are young" Sappho-Parnok employs the power of recovery or re/membering, which defined her interaction with the Original Lesbian Poet from its inception, and goes her ancient "sister" one better—an interesting instance of creative sororal sibling rivalry. The end of Parnok's re-originating "transcontextualization" of Sappho's "fainetai moi" contains not one surprise, as its ancient model does, but two: not only is the desiring subject of "You are young" female, she desires two women, one from her past and one in her present.[46]

I would argue, moreover, that on the metapoetic level of interpretation, the poet speaker of "You are young," through her desire for her past and present hetaeras, is celebrating her desire for a third, very distant, but eternally present woman, the woman who has enabled, does enable, and will continue to enable her creative desire as that anomaly of anomalies, a Russian lesbian poet. The third and essential desired addressee of Parnok's "You are young," and perhaps of all her personally addressed love lyrics, is, of course, Sappho of Lesbos—the same and yet essentially different Sappho who, "with such a marvelously molded, winged body" (corpus), has been made, in Russian male poetic use and abuse, to "drag her spirit awkwardly and with such difficulty" across the centuries, "anguish-stunned."

Notes

Unless otherwise noted, all English translations of Russian originals cited in this essay are mine (D.L.B.).

1. From the *Palatine Anthology*. Quoted by David A. Campbell, ed. and trans., *Greek Lyric I: Sappho and Alcaeus* (Cambridge, Mass.: Harvard University Press, 1982), p. 49.

2. In one of the most influential of these fictions, Claude de Sacy's *Les Amours de Sapho et de Phaon* (1775), Phaon is a poet like Sappho and competes with her in what the eighteenth century considered Sappho's special genre, pastoral poetry. De Sacy's novel was translated into Russian in 1780. See Joan De Jean, *Fictions of Sappho, 1546–1937* (Chicago: University of Chicago Press, 1989), pp. 168–69.

3. Ibid., p. 1.

4. Christine Downing, *Myths and Mysteries of Same-Sex Love* (New York: Continuum, 1991), pp. 217–28.

5. Leo Tolstoy, *Anna Karenina*, trans. Rosemary Edmonds (Baltimore: Penguin Books, 1954), p. 321. In subsequent quotations from the novel I have occasionally amended Edmonds's translation. Quotations of the Russian text come from Lev Tolstoi, *Anna Karenina* (Moscow, 1963), part III, chapter XVIII, pp. 267–70.

6. Most cultures reveal a desire to isolate female same-sex love as an exotic phenomenon that is quite foreign to themselves.

7. L. N. Tolstoi, *Polnoe sobranie sochinenii* (Moscow: "Khudozhestvennaia literatura," 1939), vol. 20, p. 346, no. 101 (ruk. no. 42).

8. In this variant Tolstoy's mouthpiece, Levin, participates in the discussion and opines that there are "duties especially native to women" (to bear, nurse, and bring up young children) and "duties especially native to men" (to fight, work, plow, go to sea, etc.). In Tolstoy's view, writing

poetry presumably falls under the employments "native to men," among the etceteras. Thus, Sappho, like the other great women, was guilty of transgressing "natural" gender roles.

9. Examples of Russian translations of eighteenth-century French Sapphic fictions include the enormously popular *Poems of Sappho* published by Golenishchev-Kutuzov in 1805 and *Poems of Sappho with Explanatory Annotations* published by Anastasevich in 1808.

10. E. V. Sviiasov, "Safo v vospriiatii russkikh poetov (1880–1919e gg.)," in *Na rubezhe XIX i XX vekov. Iz istorii mezhdunarodnykh sviazei russkoi literatury* (Leningrad: Nauka, 1991), p. 258.

11. Translation of the Russian text in Konstantin Batiushkov, *Polnoe sobranie stikhotvorenii* (Moscow-Leningrad, 1964), p. 242. As she was for most poets in posterity, so for Batiushkov the original Sappho was almost synonymous with love. See *Liubov' eshche gorit vo Safinykh mechtakh* ("Love still burns in Sappho's daydreams") from the poem "Daydream" ("Mechta"), p. 56. Batiushkov also marked Bunina's death with the words *Ischezla Safo nashikh dnei* ("The Sappho of our days has vanished"), which is quoted (but misdated) by Sviiasov in "Safo v vospriiatii," p. 258.

12. N. V. Bannikov, *Russkie poetessy XIX-go veka* (Moscow, 1979), p. 21. Grot alludes to this interpretation of Batiushkov's "Madrigal" in an addendum to his fascinating notes on Derzhavin's Sappho translations in Gavrila Derzhavin, *Sochineniia, s ob"iasnitel'nymi primechaniiami Ia. Grota*, 2e akademicheskoe izdanie (St. Petersburg: Imperial Academy of Sciences, 1869), vol. 2, p. 31.

13. This English translation of Sappho's "fainetai moi" (usually referred to as Fragment 31) is based heavily on John Windler's in his essay "Double Consciousness in Sappho's Lyrics," in *The Constraints of Desire: The Anthropology of Sex and Gender in Ancient Greece* (New York: Routledge, 1990), p. 178. The original Greek texts of this and other of Sappho's fragments that I have consulted are those in David Campbell's edition, *Greek Lyric I* (Cambridge, Mass.: Harvard University Press, 1982). The text of fragment 31 appears on pp. 78, 80.

14. Russian native speakers who heard the first version of this essay when I read it as a paper at Harvard University's Russian Research Center commented that in Russian, the quality of being "greener than grass" in the context of the poem carries strong connotations of illness, weakness, and nausea in the passion-stricken female speaker. For that reason, interestingly, some of the Russians in the audience rejected the notion that what the speaker of "fainetai moi" describes in the poem could be called "love," or even sexual passion.

15. E. V. Sviiasov, "Antichnaia liricheskaia poeziia v russkikh perevodakh i podrazhaniiakh XVIII–XX vekov. O bibliografii," *Russkaia literatura* (1988): 206–15.

16. See De Jean's thought-provoking discussion of fragment 31 in *Fictions of Sappho*, p. 324.

17. Quoted in the commentary to Derzhavin's 1797 translation of "fainetai moi" (which he entitled "Sappho") in *Sobranie stikhotvorenii Derzhavina* (Leningrad: Biblioteka poeta, 1957), p. 427. By calling Sappho's poem "Sappho," Derzhavin follows the practice of countless translators and identifies the female speaker of the lyric with the poet who created her, thus making the lyric appear autobiographical. Derzhavin's 1797 translation marks neither the speaker nor the addressee as feminine. His lyric and Sapphic fiction, "To Sappho" (*Safe*), of three years before (1794) suggests that Derzhavin believed Phaon to be the "blessed man" who admires and loves Sappho's "female friend," the addressee and object of the female speaker's jealousy in "fainetai moi." In "To Sappho" Derzhavin asserts himself as the creative rival of Phaon and expresses the wish that he might have been Phaon. Beneath this wish lies Derzhavin's more potent desire to be one with Sappho and to vie with her lyrically. If his wish came true, Derzhavin concludes in "To Sappho," "then zephyr and thunder [earlier described as Sappho's two characteristic tonalities] might fly from my all-powerful lyre, and I would depict the life and death of Plenira [Derzhavin's lyrical name for his wife whose death he is mourning in "To Sappho"] as you your own [life and death]" (*Togda s moei vsesil'noi liry / Zefir i grom by mog letet'; / Kak ty svoiu, tak ia Pleniry / Izobrazil by zhizn' i smert'*). Sappho (you) is to Derzhavin (I) as Sappho's own life and death are to Derzhavin's wife's life and death. By implication, Sappho is both the poem's second desiring male subject (the lyrical alter ego of Derzhavin, the poet in mourning) and its doubly absent female object of desire (Phaon's dead mistress—Phaon is the speaker of the first two stanzas of Derzhavin's poem—and

Derzhavin's dead wife). This is a clear case (and the first) in the history of Russian poetry of what De Jean has termed male "poetic doubling" of the original woman poet (*Fictions of Sappho*, p. 7).

18. Aleksandr Pushkin, *Polnoe sobranie sochinenii* (Moscow: Academy of Sciences, 1948), vol. 16 (letters), p. 32. In a previous letter of May 16, 1835, Katenin first mentioned his cantata-to-be, writing that he would like to read Pushkin two poems, one of which, "The Song of the Oarsman," he intends for a cantata that he cannot compose because he wants "to include poems of Sappho herself, and in Stavropol' there is not an original, a dictionary, or an exact translation to be had" (p. 27).

19. Pushkin, *Polnoe sobranie sochinenii* (1948), vol. 16, p. 39.

20. Translation from the Russian text in Pavel Katenin, *Izbrannye proizvedeniia* (Moscow-Leningrad: Biblioteka poeta, 1964), pp. 241–42. It is noteworthy that Katenin's Sappho, as depicted in the Cantata as a whole, is perceived as a sacrifice demanded by fate whose death represents the apotheosis of a national poet and incarnation of the beautiful: "Death was the singer's preordained fate; / her body was lost to the waves' abyss forever, / and her lyre, gift of Castalian nymphs, female companion of songs: / such has been the lot of beauty from the beginning of the world" (Katenin, *Izbrannye* [1965], p. 250). In view of Pushkin's direct involvement in facilitating Katenin's relationship with Sappho's "Greek verses," one wonders whether in the portrayal of Sappho's sacrificial death Katenin was not making an encoded statement about his feelings about Pushkin's death in January 1837, that is, about a year before his Sapphic cantata was published. Katenin's possible conflation of Sappho and Pushkin implies the androgynous character of both national poets.

21. Translation from the Russian original in previously cited Gavrila Derzhavin, *Sochineniia* (St. Petersburg, 1869), vol. 2, p. 31.

22. Ibid.

23. Vikentii Veresaev, *Sochineniia* (Moscow, 1948), vol. 3, p. 369.

24. "Boris Pasternak—Ol'ga Freidenberg," *Druzhba narodov* 9 (1988): 242.

25. Elliott Mossman, comp., ed., and trans. (with Margaret Wettlin), *The Correspondence of Boris Pasternak and Olga Freidenberg, 1910–1954* (New York: Harcourt, Brace, Jovanovich, 1982), p. 294.

26. O. M. Freidenberg, "Safo," in *Doklady i soobshcheniia filologicheskogo instituta LGU*, vyp. 1 (Leningrad, 1949), p. 190. My thanks to Professor Kevin Moss of Middlebury College for providing me a copy of this article.

27. Vladislav Khodasevich, "Sof'ia Parnok. *Stikhotvoreniia*," *Utro Rossii* 274 (1916). Ironically, Khodasevich, a good friend and admirer of Parnok, distinguished the Russian "offspring of Sappho" from Parnok, who, in attempting to reclaim Sappho as the original *lesbian* poet, was probably the only true "daughter of Lesbos" that Russian poetry has produced.

28. Translation of the Russian text in Vladimir Solov'ev, *Stikhotvoreniia. Proza. Pis'ma. Vospominaniia sovremennikov* (Moscow: Moskovskii rabochii, 1990), p. 107.

29. Quoted by Sviiasov in "Safo v vospriiatii russkikh poetov," p. 259.

30. Mirra Lokhvitskaia, *Stikhotvoreniia* (Moscow, 1896), vol. 1, pp. 182–84.

31. See Sviiasov, "Safo v vospriiatii russkikh poetov."

32. In the years 1914–16, the journal of classical philology *Germes* (*Hermes*), for example, published several Russian translations and reworkings of Sappho's newly discovered and previously known fragments.

33. Translations of the Russian text in Viacheslav Ivanov, *Alkei i Safo. Sobranie pesen i liricheskikh otryvkov* (Moscow, 1914), p. 85.

34. O. M. Freidenberg, "Proiskhozhdenie grecheskoi liriki," *Voprosy literatury* 11 (1973): 113.

35. E. Diehl, "Eoliiskie liriki v perevode Viacheslava Ivanova," *Germes*, December 1914, p. 462. Diehl quotes from Ivanov. Diehl is writing in defense of Ivanov's translations, which had been criticized (for the poet-translator's decision to retain the original meters) by K. Grinevich in an article ("Versus Sapphicus") published in a previous issue of *Germes* (October 1914, pp. 420–28). From the eighteenth century on, the most vociferous polemics about Sappho in Russian

poetry focused not on her gender or sexual orientation (as was the case in the West) but on her metrics and the structure of her verse.

36. For a fascinating discussion of what virginity meant in ancient Greek culture, see Giulia Sissa, "Maidenhood without Maidenhead: The Female Body in Ancient Greece," in *Before Sexuality: The Construction of Erotic Experience in the Ancient Greek World*, ed. Halperin, Winkler, and Zeitlin (Princeton: Princeton University Press, 1990), pp. 339–65.

37. For a discussion of Parnok's life and work in English, see Diana Lewis Burgin, *Sophia Parnok: The Life and Work of Russia's Sappho* (New York: New York University Press, 1994).

38. Being by the "melodious" Black Sea, in the putative homeland of the Amazons, stimulated Parnok to remember her ancient creative roots on Lesbos, the Isle of Women, another legendary Amazon settlement, and the geographical point where the putatively mythical Amazons and the allegedly real Sappho intersect and become conflated in Western literary tradition after *Ovid*.

39. Quoted in Burgin, *Sophia Parnok*, pp. 172–73.

40. Parnok's poems are quoted in my English translations of the original Russian texts in S. Parnok, *Sobranie stikhotvorenii* (Ann Arbor: Ardis, 1979), and will be referenced henceforth by their number in that edition, given in parentheses after the quotation, as in this case (#38).

41. In the archaic context of Parnok's Sapphic lyricism, I use the word "hetaera" to translate her *podruga*, which itself is a close translation of Sappho's *etaira*, meaning "female companion" and "friend," with whom a romantic/sexual relationship is not specified but is not excluded. *Podruga* has a similarly broad range of contextual meanings in contemporary Russian, from girlfriend/woman friend to sexual/romantic partner of the female sex, to life partner of the female sex (*podruga zhizni*), or "wife."

42. Parnok's full identification with Sappho comes across in the poem "You sleep, my hetaera" (#67). In writing out Sappho's fragment: "Sleep on your hetaera's breast, sleep on her tender breast," Parnok's speaker puts herself in the position of Sappho's poet addressee in posterity who simultaneously executes Sappho's command (to sleep on her hetaera's breast) and re-originates the Lesbian poet's postorgasmic creative mood.

43. The metapoetic significance of Sappho to all lesbian poets in posterity seems implied in lines spoken by Barney's Sappho to her hetaera Timas: "Tu me désireras à travers son désir / Et tu redonneras mon nom à ton plaisir" (Natalie Clifford Barney, *Actes et Entr'actes*, 1910, p. 67).

44. These lines bear striking but apparently chance resemblance to the following sentence in Radclyffe Hall's *The Well of Loneliness*: "All her life she must drag this body of hers like a monstrous fetter imposed on her spirit" (London: Corgi Books, 1968, p. 217).

45. The central idea of love as forgiveness that *prostila* expresses suggests, moreover, the "day of forgiveness" (*den' proshchenyi*) to which Tsvetaeva had referred in her "good-bye poem" to Parnok, "In days of yore, you were like a mother to me" (*V ony dni ty mne byla, kak mat'*), written at the end of April 1916. Tsvetaeva had predicted in her poem that on "the day of forgiveness" her and Parnok's "unreturnable time of yore" would be returned to them.

46. The idea of love "from premonition" and/or "from recollection" recurs throughout Parnok's love lyrics and characterizes the free (amarital), feminine erotic life of Parnok's Artemisian, quintessentially lesbian poetic speaker.

THREE

The Daughters of Emilia Plater

HALINA FILIPOWICZ

THE STORY OF Emilia Plater (1806–1831), Poland's national heroine, has the right feminist content. She put herself in a position of *double* revolt: against foreign oppression of the Polish-Lithuanian Commonwealth and against patriarchal assumptions about gender identities.[1] She rejected the submissive roles which male power as well as Russian supremacy had reserved for her. The story, in its most familiar form, tells of the glory of a young woman who cared little about public opinion and fought with great distinction in the national cause.[2] What Plater reportedly said of her contemporary, a Greek heroine who caught her imagination, may be said about her as well: "Men, in the course of their duty, can but challenge death. Bouboulina goes beyond—she braves public opinion besides."[3]

When the Polish insurrection against Russia broke out in 1830, Plater was determined to drive the Russians out of Lithuania. She invented a bold plan to seize the fortress of Dynaburg, but a patriotic committee in Vilnius rebuffed her. Undaunted by "the ignorant presumption of the men," she acted on her own initiative.[4] She raised a regiment of volunteers and joined the insurrection, although her male commanders and companions-at-arms repeatedly urged her to abandon the military way of life. Plater thus belies the traditional association of only the male gender with action, valor, leadership. She refuses to conform to the patriarchal standards of femininity and masculinity, whereby women are "passive," while men "lead challenging or even risk-taking lives."[5] In short, she possesses the necessary experience to qualify as a feminist heroine and to fulfill a demand for images of "self-reliant, independent, strong, courageous" women with whom female readers or spectators can identify.[6]

The feminist emphasis on the representation of strong women in literature is not, of course, unproblematic. To create such characters is not necessarily a feminist act. If their activities are shown as exceptional only because they are women, it is evident that the textual practice reverts to sexism. On the other hand, it would be naive to assume that the experience of a female character who meets the degrading and oppressive demands of patriarchy always incites female readers or spectators to imitation. Regardless of the author's intention, her role may be to expose, not to perpetuate, patriarchal practices. She may enable other women to become conscious of their own oppression by male power. She may even provoke them to dare to be different from her. Thus, despite her own powerlessness, she may empower them to question, perhaps even oppose, the social and political strategies of patriarchal oppression.[7]

But there is more at issue. As Toril Moi has cautioned in her incisive study of feminist critical practice, the insistence on the need for strong women in literature is "reminiscent of the Soviet Writers' Congress's demand for socialist realism in 1934. Instead of strong, happy tractor drivers and factory workers, we are now, presumably, to demand strong, happy *women* tractor drivers."[8] Such demands rest on the assumption that literature should be judged by "standards of authenticity."[9] After all, so the argument goes, there have always been women who managed to resist the relentless sexism of patriarchal society. It is time, then, "to begin rectifying psychological oppression by seeking out and publicizing positive role-models, time to uncover those strong female writers and characters who have been overlooked by literary criticism."[10] Seen in this perspective, literature becomes "a more or less faithful *reproduction* of an external reality to which we all have equal and unbiased access, and which therefore enables us to criticize the author on the grounds that he or she has created an *incorrect* model of the reality we somehow all know."[11]

To put it differently, the call for images of strong women involves not only "the highly questionable notion that art can and should reflect life accurately and inclusively in every detail,"[12] but also the controversial contention that art can and should engineer human behavior—that it can and should create a *correct* model of reality. My task, then, is not to determine whether representations of Plater in Polish literature are truthful to life or whether they have been effective in raising the consciousness of Polish women and mobilizing them to action.[13] Rather, I want to examine new questions: What has Polish culture made of Plater's *double* transgression? How is the patriarchal concept of immutably fixed gender identities reconciled with the model of female patriotism which Plater represents—or is it reconciled at all?

Predictably, an investigation into the cultural reception of Plater shows that her patriotic self-sacrifice has been readily accepted, but that the feminist content of her story has disappeared under the edifying image of a national heroine. Adam Mickiewicz's immensely popular poem "The Death of the Colonel" ("Śmierć pułkownika"), written in 1832, pays tribute to Plater's heroic virtue by promoting her from captain to colonel. It even ushers her into the timeless dimension of myth by declaring her a leader in the insurrection. Mickiewicz has wrought this metamorphosis through his ability to embody an urgent set of symbols.[14] At the same time, he has removed Plater from a realm of action. We see "the virgin hero" (*dziewicabohater*) on her deathbed, not on a battlefield. She is cleansed of carnality and glorified by death.[15]

It is possible, of course, to counter my critique by arguing that "The Death of the Colonel" is indebted to Julian Ursyn Niemcewicz's "Stefan Czarniecki" (1816) and that both poems draw on a literary convention whereby death sets the seal on a hero's perfection. However, to choose this convention for Plater is not an ideologically neutral gesture since it confirms the prevailing image of women as passive recipients of authoritarian/male discourse. In Mickiewicz's poem, Plater stages her deathbed scene in imitation of Czarniecki's and thus becomes a reflection of a masculine self. The assumption that women depend on men for their identities and actions underlies also Wacław Gąsiorowski's *Emilia Plater* (1910). The novel draws on the historical fact of the separation of Plater's parents when she was ten years old. After her mother's death in 1830, Plater sought her father out, but he refused to have anything to do with her. In the novel, the rejection has the effect of pushing her into imitative maleness: she finds out about the outbreak of the insurrection in Warsaw and resolves to take action precisely at the moment when she has had the final, unsuccessful conference with her father.

The case of numerous biographies of Plater is more complex—and interesting. Accounts of her life are approximate and rely on a body of tradition established by Józef Straszewicz's *Émilie Plater. Sa vie et sa mort* (1835), whose evidence is adulatory and filled with literary flourishes. His ideological project was to promote the Polish cause in the West, and Plater was useful to the political purpose of exposing the inhumanity of the archenemy of Western civilization, the devil-ridden Russia. The subsequent biographers never question Straszewicz's authority, and they hardly alter his schema of the "essential" scenes in her life. Yet their treatment of the inherited material reveals their own ideological agenda.

My discussion is neither a survey of Plater's biographies nor an attempt to show a *real* woman behind the façade of Straszewicz's glorification of Plater. I take three examples—the biographical accounts by Bolesław Limanowski, Felicja Boberska, and Kazimierz Żurawski[16]—to identify the ideological uses to which the Plater figure has been put under different political circumstances: in 1861 (on the eve of the anti-Russian insurrection of 1863–64), in 1880 (at the height of the Positivist ideology of peaceful reforms), and in 1911 (during the turbulent period after the revolution of 1905).

When Limanowski and Żurawski bring Plater's fainting spells and riding mishaps into the foreground, the reader may conclude that Plater's Amazonian likeness had to be softened and obscured to be countenanced at all. The emphasis on the fatigue and physical stress that Plater underwent may be seen as a strategy of upholding what she has threatened—the essentialism of gender identities set up by patriarchy in order to control women. She is not to be a figure who would lead to a weakening of gender divisions; hence the biographers hasten to reinforce the traditional notion of femininity. Of course, a different interpretation is possible as well. The frailty Plater had to overcome may be regarded as a commonplace of heroes' lives—a commonplace which makes them more human while adding to their heroism.

Limanowski and Żurawski cite Plater's comment about Bouboulina. They admit that men urged Plater to go home. But the reader's suspicion returns that both authors after all are upholding presuppositions about male supremacy and female passivity. When Limanowski and Żurawski attribute the plan to attack Dynaburg solely to Plater's cousins, it is evident that they cannot accommodate the full notion of her self-confidence.[17] And when they are silent about why she came back empty-handed from her trip to Vilnius, they are unwilling to acknowledge the extent of patriarchal resistance which she confronted even before she joined the insurrection.

Is a biography by a woman more sensitive to the feminist content of Plater's story? Felicja Boberska repeats after Straszewicz that Plater was the sole author of the plan to stage a siege of Dynaburg, but because she was a woman she was excluded from the deliberations of the citizens' committee in Vilnius. In Limanowski's account, Plater has mainly an auxiliary function, and little is made of her participation in battle. Boberska, on the other hand, consistently shows Plater taking charge, although she also sweetens her Amazonian image.[18] Lest we misconstrue Boberska's ideological intentions, however, she declares that "the ideal female laborers in the national vineyard" are philanthropists and educators.[19] She upholds Klaudyna Potocka, Emilia Sczaniecka, and Klementyna Hoffman as the models of female patriotism and thus becomes a solid defender of the patriarchal status quo. Plater and the other women who fought in the insurrection went against "the womanly nature."[20] "We do not at all consider them models worthy of imitation," Boberska smugly concludes, "but their sincere and boundless sacrifice merits recognition."[21]

The readiness to belittle Plater on the grounds that she was not like Potocka, Sczaniecka, or Hoffman, to rewrite or to suppress certain aspects of her story, indicates that its feminist implications have not gone unnoticed. The fissures, contradictions, and silences in texts about Plater suggest that Polish culture is ill at ease with her model of female patriotism but, given the vicissitudes of Polish history, it cannot afford to leave her out. She has been elevated to the national pantheon of heroes, where she can legitimize a claim that Polish women are superior to "German, English, and French women" because they have been "formed from a different grade of clay."[22] While her contemporary Nadezhda Durova (known as the Cavalry Maiden) has been "an embarrassment to the Russian straitjacket of 'femininity,'"[23] Plater has been venerated as a charismatic leader of the Polish struggle against invaders. At the same time, she constitutes a discomfiting presence in Poland's male-constructed cultural history. Plater's story, then, prompts much close questioning of the widely held view that the great and holy cause of Poland's independence integrated men and women because they shared the responsibility to free their country from the shackles of foreign oppression.[24] Her story offers a speculum for the penetration and illumination of the tangle of national mythology and gender mythology.

2

Emilia Plater features prominently in Margaret Fuller's *Woman in the Nineteenth Century* (1845), a book that marked an era in American protofeminist thought. She is the only Polish woman to inhabit the pages of Fuller's study. She is introduced as a revolutionary who was "an embarrassment and a puzzle" in the eyes of men.[25] Moreover, it is in "Countess Colonel Plater" that Fuller finds "the figure I want for my frontispiece."[26] While Polish authors have dwelled on the "unwomanly" nature of the countess's activities, Fuller discovers in Plater a helper in her campaign against patriarchal practices. She cites Plater's gender transgression as evidence to support her eloquent demand for equal opportunity:

> But if you ask me what offices they [women] may fill; I reply—any. I do not care what case you put; let them be sea-captains, if you will. I do not doubt there are women well fitted for such an office, and, if so, I should be glad to see them in it, as to welcome the maid of Saragossa, or the maid of Missolonghi, or the Suliote heroine, or Emily Plater.
>
> I think women need, especially at this juncture, a much greater range of occupation than they have, to rouse their latent powers.[27]

However, American society was not ready to accept Fuller's Polish helper. Of all the women discussed in the book, it was Plater who made many American readers ill at ease. In a letter to Caroline Sturgis, Fuller wrote: "The newspaper editors . . . are more indignant at my praise of Emily than at any of my other sins."[28]

Following an established convention, Fuller compared Plater's career to that of Joan of Arc. Unlike her French spiritual mentor, however, Plater is not among the well-documented figures of history. The prime source of knowledge about her life is the arresting tribute by Straszewicz, her relative and companion-in-arms. In *The Life of the Countess Emily Plater*, he follows an accepted patterning of a perfect heroic life and constructs a model biography for patriotic edification and mobilization. Consequently, it is easy to question his account and to suspect that Plater did not fire a single shot at the enemy.[29]

There is an inevitable tendency in the search for national heroes to exaggerate their actions. Plater's exact importance in the insurrection is hard to measure. Her real influence came later, after her death. Whether or not she played a leading role in the military campaign becomes insignificant beside the historical fact that the Poles have thought that she did. She is a figure of history, but she also occupies an eminent position in national mythology. Through Mickiewicz's "The Death of the Colonel," her story is part of the common stock of knowledge that Polish children learn in school. She has become an emblem of anti-Russian resistance and a model of female heroism held up for admiration.

The story of Plater has been told in detail many times—so many times, in fact, that it invites a reaction against the idealization with which she has been glorified. Józef Bachórz has tried his hand at subjecting the Plater story to scrutiny in two different publications: one is an essay in a weekly magazine, the other a scholarly article.[30] The fact that he has aimed to reach the general reader as well as the specialist suggests the urgency of his revisionist project.

Caustic about his compatriots' reverence for Plater, Bachórz insists on setting the record straight. He compares accounts of participants in the insurrection of 1830–31 and concludes that the cherished image of Plater is not true to life. Yet he fails to consider the proposition that no one has unbiased access to "truth." He thus falls prey to the fiction that it is possible for anyone to speak from a position unmarked by cultural, social, political, and personal factors. Wojciech Goczałkowski, whose memoirs are an important source for Bachórz's demystification of the Plater myth, vigorously upheld patriarchy's belief in immutably fixed gender identities. He was willing to acknowledge Plater's patriotic fervor, but he did not approve of her public activity. He regarded soldiership as a masculine prerogative which women wielded only through usurpation.[31] Ignacy Domeyko, whose support Bachórz enlists as well, granted women the right to fight for Poland's liberation but hastened to add that he did so "perhaps out of courtesy" to Plater, who was present during the conversation.[32]

In an authoritarian and manipulative gesture, Bachórz pretends that there is neutral, value-free criticism. Yet his demythologizing efforts reveal his own biases. He argues from a position that supports the traditional prohibition on "the military emancipation of women."[33] Moreover, he diminishes Plater's patriotic motivation by attributing her public activity partly to her low self-esteem. She was poor, unattractive, and unmarried, and the wish of her father, who had been separated from his wife and was about to marry another woman, was to have nothing to do with her. Consequently, Bachórz continues, she had to find a way of compensating for her physical defects and private frustrations.[34]

Bachórz's refusal to take Plater for granted has mobilized others to take a stand.[35] But her story is still presented as a stable monolith not subject to the law of time and change, while in fact Plater is one of the fascinating, even disturbing examples of how culture works on history to re-create its protagonists. She is a figure who always takes her identity, chameleon-like, from the ideological environment in which she appears.

In 1880, Boberska did not write about Plater merely to pay tribute to the national heroine on the fiftieth anniversary of the insurrection of 1830–31. Although she did not invite women to identify with Plater the warrior, she assimilated her with ease to a different political climate and to demands of a different ideology. She invoked the example of Plater not as an inspiration for armed struggle, which seemed a suicidal gesture after the unsuccessful uprising of 1863–64, but as an affirmation of certain moral and national values. Implicit in Boberska's account is the assumption that Plater's refusal of marriage with an enemy of Poland makes her a heroine in the sphere of moral action.

The Plater who rejected a Russian suitor by saying, "I am a Polish woman,"[36] fits the ideology of moral resistance against invaders and satisfies the demands of patriotic education for women. Boberska was an advocate of both. Her program for the national survival under foreign occupation was firmly planted on moral and educational ground. "God helps those who help themselves," argues Boberska, thus appropriating the central idea of the post-1864 Positivist ideology.[37] She wants Polish women to see in the history of their female predecessors a source of cultural and psychological self-confidence so that they could assume the role of custodians of patriotic virtue, and thus of the collective identity. The future of Poland, she tells her female readers, is in their hands because it is their obligation to instill patriotism and national pride in the young generation.[38]

Three decades later, Żurawski also placed his hopes in the patriotic edification in which the story of Plater would occupy a prominent place. Unlike Boberska, however, he did not intend his presentation primarily for a female audience. According to Żurawski, "all Polish men and women" can be imbued—via Plater—with the same light of patriotism.[39] But there is more at issue. His insistent appeal to a sense of national unity of all social classes suggests that he adopted Plater as a palladium of the conservative ideology of social solidarity.[40] She was for him a symbol of patriotic sacrifice which joins the classes. To mobilize his audience for a concerted effort toward the common good—Poland's prosperity, strength, and, eventually, independence—he was willing to overlook social conflicts and the material conditions of the working class.

Żurawski's fervent and rousing plea for national unity capitalized on the precedent established by Mickiewicz's "The Death of the Colonel." Never mind that the historical Plater died on the estate of a Polish nobleman. The image that "The Death of the Colonel" has implanted in cultural memory is that of a virgin warrior who dies in a humble cottage, surrounded by grief-stricken peasants. While Straszewicz's biography emphasized the splendor of the ancient aristocratic house of the Platers, Mickiewicz's poem has transformed Countess Plater into a heroine of the people and for the people, in the tradition of Joan of Arc.

Limanowski's account presents another kind of problem. To emphasize the identification of Plater with the people, he published the 1861 version of her biography under the assumed identity of a peasant, Janko Płakań. But the issue for Limanowski is not the conservative postulate of social solidarity. His preface to the 1911 edition makes it clear that he speaks from the ideological position of a Polish socialist who believes that the struggle for Poland's independence must be bound with a social revolution.[41] In his hands, the Plater story serves to awaken peasants to a patriotic duty of driving the invaders out of their homeland. As I have argued, Limanowski's reconstruction of her story does not advance the idea of gender equity, which stands behind Plater's transgression. In fact, his perspective is often hostile to the feminist implications of her flight from the patriarchal conventions of gender. In his account, as in Boberska's and Żurawski's, Plater's uncrushable yearning is to be free—as a Pole, not as a woman.

If Plater is not a cultural monolith but rather a suitably versatile cipher for a host of causes, it is inevitable to ask: What are the ideological assumptions encoded in the representations of Plater in works other than popular biographies? This question must, at least for the moment, be left hanging. First, it is necessary to ask: How was Plater possible? What accounts for the Poles' readiness to accept her as the national heroine even though she inverted the God-given order and defied what seemed the natural destiny of the female sex?

The axis of Plater's story is one of the most tantalizing puzzles of European history: the dismembering of Poland by Russia, Prussia, and Austria (1795–1918). The Polish history, so to speak, was organized with a dramatic sense: first the glory of Renaissance Poland, then reversal, the destruction of hopes, and the tragic fall, just as the country embarked on an ambitious program of reforms. By the end of the eighteenth century, Poland lost its territory and political autonomy to Russia, Prussia, and Austria. In the decades following the annexation, almost every generation of Poles went further than the moral demands of resistance to aggression allow, and in the name of "our freedom and yours" refused to lay down their arms.

In the Polish struggle for liberation, women were present in the ranks of conspirators, and occasionally in the ranks of insurgents as well. The extent of their patriotic involvement has led to one of the fundamental assumptions in the history of Polish culture—a claim that Polish women have had a unique standing in modern European history. While women in the West were conventionally feminine spectators of the drama of history, the fall of Poland necessitated the rise of the Polish women. Mickiewicz drew on such claims when, on June 17, 1842, he proudly told his audience at the College de France in Paris:

> The Polish woman does not excite her nerves by reading romances. She is not a delicate nymph, a passionate Italian or a witty queen of salons; she is a daughter devoted to her father, a wife ready to follow her husband to the ends of the earth. . . .
>
> Such is the inevitable path of humanity: first, it is necessary to make a sacrifice in order to acquire a certain right. In this way, the Polish woman secures her emancipation; she has greater freedom than women anywhere else. . . . Women will attain importance in society not by debating about their rights or announcing deluded theories, but by acts of sacrifice.
>
> In Poland, the woman takes part in conspiracies along with her husband and her brothers; she gives help to prisoners, putting her life in jeopardy; she is tried as a traitor of the state and exiled to Siberia. . . . Small wonder that she does not lack the courage to mount a horse and to lead troops to battle. . . .
>
> I repeat: the great issue of the emancipation of women is much more advanced in Poland than in any other country.[42]

To a feminist reader, the most striking aspect of Mickiewicz's exalted speech is not necessarily the traditional concept of woman as an adjunct to man (father, husband, brother), but rather the insistence on women's sacrifice offered at the altar of progress. Unlike men, they must carry a double burden. They must barter for their emancipation as Poles as well as women.

Despite Mickiewicz's uplifting claims, patriarchal ideology imposed restrictions on women's potential in Poland just as elsewhere in Europe. The struggle for independence offered Polish women a real if limited possibility of participating in the national—public—cause. At the basis of Mickiewicz's argument lies a thoroughly democratic idea: the story of Plater, which he briefly summarizes, proves that the path of heroism is open to everyone, regardless of gender. But the emphasis on Polish women's patriotic mobilization at the time of national need obscures their actual social, economic, and legal condition and thus, perhaps unwittingly, justifies the ruling patriarchy. Every emancipatory act Mickiewicz mentions is directed against foreign oppression of Poland, not against the patriarchal system. It is a program for unusual times—for the times of national calamity when the traditional order has been disrupted. What will be the status of the Polish women when the invaders are driven out? Mickiewicz's lecture offers no clue.

Quite apart from the reductive aspects of Mickiewicz's approach, it is necessary to remember that he gave his lecture in French, to an audience of foreigners as well as Polish political émigrés. It is not impossible that his paean to the heroic Polish women was a boost to the morale of his compatriots in exile. At the same time, his claims may be seen as a rhetorical strategy of establishing the notion of the superiority of Polish culture and thus shaming the West into action on Poland's behalf. Nevertheless, one cannot help noticing that the women again are being used to promote an ideological project which has little to do with the material conditions of patriarchy.[43]

Even before Mickiewicz's lecture, the story of the patriotic emancipation and empowerment of the Polish women had been repeated and repeated until it gained widespread credence in the West. The underlying concept of Louisa Anne Twamley's untitled poem dedicated to the memory of Plater is a belief that women's "weak, delicate form"[44] is destined for a life of love, sweetness, and elegance rather than the brutality of war. In Poland, however, things are different. "*Poland!* e'en *woman* can change for thee," triumphantly announces the poem's speaker.[45]

Mickiewicz mentioned "many other women" in Poland and Lithuania who had translated patriotic duty into military service.[46] Among Plater's contemporaries there were, for example, Wilhelmina Kasprowicz, Maria Prószyńska, Maria Raszanowicz, and Antonina Tomaszewska.[47] What accounts for Plater's overwhelming resonance in Polish culture, while the other women insurgents retreated into oblivion? After all, Plater made her first appearance in Polish literature—in Konstanty Gaszyński's poem of June 1831—as Maria Raszanowicz's equal.[48] The historical Raszanowicz was an aide-de-camp to Plater, but in the poem they share command as well as heroic status.

According to a chivalric code adopted by the Polish national mythology, there could be no finer way to die than in battle for Poland's liberation. As a palladium of the national cause, Wilhelmina Kasprowicz thus seems more suitable than Plater. Kasprowicz died, at the age of sixteen, on the field of glory, not on the bed of disease. But Kasprowicz's heroic death in battle has not immortalized her. Her martyrdom for liberty has not been preserved by her premature end. The circumstances of Plater's death were quite different. When a military campaign to free Lithuania failed, Plater refused to lay down her arms. In the summer of 1831, she tried to reach Warsaw, but she fell ill and had to seek shelter in a manor near the Polish-Lithuanian border. She died there on December 23. Consequently, Straszewicz found it necessary to mythologize her death by linking it with the surrender of Warsaw to the Russians on September 8, 1831. Plater of the national myth dies of a broken heart on learning of the fall of Warsaw and the end of the insurrection.

The nagging questions return: Why was Plater adopted as the national heroine? How has she secured her place in the Polish pantheon, while her female companions-at-arms vanished into the darkness of history? How was the cultural canonization of Plater possible if public opinion in Poland has not favored the idea of women's military service? The answer lies in a fortuitous set of circumstances.

In the Polish textual production of 1831, when the war with Russia was still being fought, Plater's absence is conspicuous. She appears in only two poems—a fact which baffled the author of a pioneering study of the poetry of the insurrection of 1830–31.[49] After the fall of the uprising, the reluctance to acknowledge Plater's public activity suddenly gave way to her consecration by Polish political émigrés in Paris, particularly in Mickiewicz's poem and Straszewicz's biography.

This secular canonization of Plater coincided with both the formal establishment of the French cult of Joan of Arc and an enthusiastic support for *la cause polonaise*, which swept France in the early 1830s. The Polish insurrection was thought to have prevented Russia's military intervention against France in 1830,[50] and the story of Plater confirmed a belief in the Maid's intercession as a patron of France and a champion of freedom. According to Justin Maurice's "Élégie," Joan of Arc sent Plater to fight for "*la liberté sainte*" and to crush "*l'ignoble barbarie*" of Russia, while heaven turned a deaf ear to the pleas of the invaded Poland.[51] Pierre Simon Ballanche went so far as to hail *la vierge polonaise* as the Maid's double who saved Western civilization from Russian despotism.[52] Michel Pietkiewicz went even further. Plater, he argued, outdid her famous predecessor in every respect:

> Joan of Arc was driven by fanaticism, Miss Plater by her love of her country. Joan of Arc was an anomaly among her sex; our heroine put on a warrior's dress but retained all the tender sentiments of gentleness and humaneness which embellish women. . . . To support the efforts of Joan of Arc, the French had an army; the Lithuanians had nothing.[53]

It did not matter that Plater's own tale was hardly a triumphant one. The three months of her public activity failed to change the course of history, and the glory of banners and trumpets was absent. All of this did not matter because the issue was not historical fact but rather a quasi-magic gesture of repetition. Plater's contemporaries in the West were quick to accept the story of *la vierge polonaise* because it confirmed the model biography of the French heroine, while imbuing it with renewed vitality. The enigma of Plater's military career and the paucity of factual information were an advantage rather than a hindrance. Nothing hampered the process of shaping her biography to fit the myth of her famous tutor. Sometimes Plater's appearance on the European scene was perceived as the Maid's second coming, so to speak. Sometimes Plater was adopted as the Maid's spiritual daughter or *autre Jeanne d'Arc*.[54] In each case, she came to personify a desire for heroic perfection at the time of political uncertainty. To put it differently, Plater's new, ideal biography gave a narrative shape to the ideology which valorized the Maid's patriotic martyrdom.

The cult of Joan of Arc helps to explain Plater's swift rise to prominence as one of the most famous European heroines of the mid-nineteenth century.[55] It also smoothed her triumphal passage into Polish secular hagiography.[56] The Poles blamed the defeat of the insurrection on their male leaders; Plater, like Joan of Arc, answered a deeply felt need for a democratic hero of unflinching loyalty to a patriotic mission.[57] But the role of Plater's spiritual mentor is only part of the answer. The other women insurgents also had the example of the Maid behind them, yet culture's memory of their activities has faded.

Plater owes her spectacular emergence from the obscurity of Lithuania in no small degree to her wealthy and influential relatives Władysław Plater, Cezary

Plater, and Józef Straszewicz.[58] They succeeded in capitalizing on her story to bring the plight of the Poles to the notice of many people who had scarcely heard of it before, and thus to promote the cause of Polish independence in the West.[59]

She owes an even larger debt to Mickiewicz, her fellow Lithuanian. "The Death of the Colonel," written shortly after Plater's death, created a brave and noble figure of unqualified patriotism precisely at the moment when there was, in the wake of the failed insurrection, an ideological as well as therapeutic need for impressive patriotic models. The poem obscures Plater's transgression of gender boundaries by presenting her as a spiritual heir to Stefan Czarniecki and thus an embodiment of what another poet calls the "Polish religion of heroism."[60] Moreover, the poem's emphasis on Plater's piousness suggests that she was carrying on the cause of Poland's freedom with heaven's mandate. It implies that she did not act on her own but was called to accomplish worldly deeds on behalf of God's kingdom on earth.[61]

In other words, Mickiewicz found the right formula to implant Plater in the Polish cultural memory.[62] The main ingredient of this formula is the miraculous appearance of a woman turned warrior and leader at a time when the need for an extraordinary leader was acutely felt. Consequently, Mickiewicz's poem has had an incalculable effect on Plater's afterlife. She is still seen as a man-made, rather than self-made, woman. Without Mickiewicz, so the argument goes, she would have been relegated to obscurity, together with other Polish women warriors, precisely because her transgression of gender identities was so radical.[63]

But the fortuitous set of circumstances which accounts for Plater's posthumous fame involves more than the cult of the Maid, the efforts of the Polish mythmakers in Paris, and the need for a national hero beyond reproach. The puzzle of Plater's persistence in the Polish cultural memory requires additional theorization.

Unlike her kindred spirits Kasprowicz, Prószyńska, Raszanowicz, and Tomaszewska, Plater did not come from the impoverished gentry. She was a countess descended from one of the oldest and most powerful aristocratic families in Lithuania. Whether she was able to raise a regiment entirely on her own or was in command of the troops in any official capacity pales next to the fact that as a countess she commanded respect and was held in high regard. Her standing in society helps to answer the tricky question of how it was that she managed to overcome Polish culture's amnesia despite the odds against her. At the same time, her social status has made her sacrifice seem larger: she was a wealthy countess, but she abandoned a life of leisure to free her country from the Russian yoke.

Plater was almost certainly a virgin. Like her social position, however, the concept of virginity which she embodies has been disregarded. At best, it has been taken for granted or brushed aside as something a little piquant but insignificant. Plater was also a Lithuanian, in the sense that she was born in Vilnius and raised in what once constituted the Grand Duchy of Lithuania. Her virginity and her Lithuanian origins would not have been sufficient to valorize her over Kasprowicz, Prószyńska, Raszanowicz, or Tomaszewska, who also were Lithuanian and chaste. Yet in the context of the other circumstances, these two aspects of Plater's story make her a woman ideally suited for the role of a national heroine. As a virginal Lithuanian countess, she has been a godsend to Polish culture.

Chastity, of course, was the touchstone of female virtue. Hence the moral significance attached to Plater's perfection rests on her intact sexuality. Yet there is more at issue than virginity understood as one of the principal constructs in patriarchal cultural practices. The crux of Plater's story is her signal chastity, which is essential not only to her identity as a positive heroine, but also to her position in the Polish pantheon of national heroes.

In fact, the question "Was she really a virgin?" is beside the point because Plater's virginity is a two-way process, so to speak. On the one hand, her chastity is a sign of her undivided devotion to the cause of Poland's freedom. She has substituted love of country for would-be pleasures of the flesh. Like her French mentor, she has married her homeland. Her virginity thus sanctions and sanctifies her mission by linking her to Joan of Arc conflated with the Virgin Mary, known to the Poles as the Queen of Poland and an intercessor on its behalf. On the other hand, culture returns the favor to Plater by bestowing virginity on her as a badge of patriotic sacrifice, civic virtue, and heroic perfection. She becomes a virgin (or "the virgin hero" in Mickiewicz's poem) precisely by virtue of her extreme, "unwomanly" patriotism.

But Plater's virginity is also politically useful. It represents the ethical purity of the Polish struggle for independence from foreign domination. Moreover, her virginal integrity had an enormous, if not directly acknowledged, symbolic power for the people of the old Polish-Lithuanian Commonwealth, which had been rent asunder by foreign aggression.[64] While Joan of Arc is a personification of France, Plater has not been identified with Poland. Nor is Plater a symbol of Polish national identity, which, after the dismemberment of the Polish-Lithuanian Commonwealth in 1795, was defined by the symbolism of Christ's crucifixion. But Plater's physical intactness, juxtaposed to the violated and dismembered body of the Commonwealth, stands for the pre-1795 union of Poland and Lithuania. In short, her inviolate body is a metaphor of moral good as well as an urgent political symbol of national integrity, a projection of future restoration and unity.

3

Plater's legacy in Polish literature consists of Wacław Gąsiorowski's novel, five poems,[65] and seven plays.[66] The poems and the novel have been a sporadic subject of scholarly and critical discussion, but the fascinating persistence of the Plater figure in Polish drama has gone unnoticed.[67] Plays, of course, are written to be seen, not read. They are to be experienced as a communal event—in the company of other spectators, not in the seclusion of home or library. By the very nature of the theatrical medium, the presence of Plater in drama has the immediacy that other kinds of textual production lack.

My reading of these plays begins by placing them in the textual environment of two sets of dramas from which Plater herself is absent, but her example is invoked in a variety of contexts. One set features her spiritual daughters in the position of protagonist. In the other set, the characters of women soldiers are superfluous to the dramatic action. All these works—I will call them Plater plays—belong to a popular genre. They are second- or third-order works which make no pretense of intellectual complexity. But to grasp the processes which shape a cultural tradition, it is necessary to consider the whole stock of textual production—major as well as minor works.

The Plater plays delight in well-known character stereotypes and cliché-ridden plots. They may seem to confirm the assumption that popular theater seeks to reach the widest approval by supporting preconceptions, not by subverting them. Yet these plays are also fond of extravagant theatrical surprises and unpredictable twists of action. They share a fascination with everything strange and unusual that can arouse our curiosity. They take advantage of the fundamental stuff of theater: reversals of the natural order, transsexual disguise, mistaken identities.

In almost all the plays, Poles live under foreign occupation.[68] They are subject to the invaders' illegitimate rule, which depends on forced submission. Seen in this perspective, the female characters' determination to abrogate the destiny of womankind and to join the military is the ultimate expression of their patriotism. Behind this determination there is always the authority of Plater's model—even when her story is not invoked. When Jadwiga in Stefan Kiedrzyński's *Engaged on a Battlefield* announces her decision to defend home and homeland in the Polish-Soviet War of 1920, the Lieutenant immediately recognizes the precedent: "I can tell this is an old Polish home" (14).[69] As a self-appointed custodian of gender identities, however, he tries to replace the Plater model with one that carries patriarchy's stamp of approval: "There's a lot of other work women can do. This work is just as important" (15).

As the Lieutenant's response suggests, the women's rejection of the female mode of life and their aspiration to enter the traditional sphere of men may also be seen as a demand for gender equity and therefore as a challenge to patriarchy's usurpations of power. Is the patriarchal prohibition on women's military service—and thus on their broader aspirations—at work only in those plays in which the figure of a woman soldier is superfluous? Do the other Plater plays perform acts of sabotage by inscribing an order of values at odds with patriarchal ideology? Do they fulfill the feminist demand for works which would "provide *role-models*, instill a positive sense of feminine identity by portraying women who are 'self-actualizing, whose identities are not dependent on men'"?[70] As usual, no simple answer will suffice.

Bronisław Bakal's *The Battle of Łowczówek*, Witold Bunikiewicz's *The Uhlan Songs*, and Zygmunt Nowakowski's *A Rosemary Twig* distance themselves from Plater's model of female patriotism. Women in these plays are barred from the traditionally male sphere of war. Their role in the patriotic enterprise is merely auxiliary. They stir men to action and raise their spirits. They feed them and dress their wounds. They sweeten the life of national heroes when their exploits are done. In *The Uhlan Songs*, a veteran of the 1863 insurrection goes so far as to suggest that women should do military service because Poland needs soldiers to win the war. But the three young women in the play are content to fence and to shoot at a target as a way of killing time while they wait for young men to return from war.

All three plays take place during World War I. Their spatial arrangements are not a mere backdrop for the stage action but an icon of ideological strategies. *The Uhlan Songs*, set in a patriarchal Polish manor, refuses to grapple with the issue of women in the military by enclosing would-be women soldiers in the domestic circle. *The Battle of Łowczowek* and *A Rosemary Twig*, set outside the confines of home and family, accept the challenge and engage in strategies of marginalization, which are more ingenious—and thus more persuasive—than the approach adopted in *The Uhlan Songs*.

In a moment of near-slapstick in *The Battle of Łowczówek*, Jagna, a young peasant woman, runs in. She has put on her father's suit and has escaped parental authority to join Józef Piłsudski's Polish Legions. The precedent of Plater is her claim to legitimacy: "Emilia Plater could serve in the army, and so can I!" (16). Jagna's future is to be decided at headquarters. A male soldier predicts that the Legions will take her on as a nurse, and she gladly accepts this likely reassignment to a more acceptable role for women. She disappears from the play, assuming a position in the back of a soldiers' column. She marches "in a funny way" because her oversized trousers restrain her freedom of movement (16). We are left with a titillating image of a female clown in drag who at any moment may lose her pants. It is obvious that this broad farcical effect aims to make light of Jagna's aspirations. A woman in man's clothing is an impostor not meant to be taken seriously.

It may seem that Jagna's role is not, after all, limited to providing comic relief mixed with sexual innuendo. When she walks away, her father declares: "If they take her on, I'll sign up as well. I can't be too old yet. They must take me on! Come what will!" (17). But before we rush to congratulate Jagna for mobilizing her father to action, we must wait for the conclusion of his monologue. Her grandfather, we find out, fought the Russians in the 1863 insurrection. "Nothing came out of it," says her father, "but maybe this time—who knows?" (17). While Jagna identifies with Plater, he carries on the cause of Poland's independence with a posthumous mandate of his own father. It is unthinkable that Jagna might have been inspired by her grandfather's precedent, and her father by the example of Plater. Each gender has its own model of patriotism, and the two models must be kept separate—and unequal. The moral authority of the male model remains intact, while the Plater model is prevented from legitimizing Jagna's attempt to overstep gender boundaries.

The opening scene of *A Rosemary Twig*, one of the most popular patriotic plays on the Polish stage, reveals a different strategy of keeping women in their place. The action is set in August 1914 outside a recruitment office in Oleandry near Cracow. An unnamed young woman in men's clothing rushes out of the office. She wanted to enlist in the Polish Legions, but she has balked at the codes of male behavior, which require would-be soldiers to undress in public. She gives vent to her frustrated sense of justice. She sobs and stomps her feet. While men look on, the nurse Sława controls the young woman's outburst and dispatches her to parental jurisdiction.

The incident, soon overshadowed by the pageantry that fills the action of *A Rosemary Twig*, may appear insignificant. But its strategic placement at the very beginning of the play suggests that something important is at issue. To warn female spectators against an ambition such as the young woman has entertained, the scene allows them to test the limits of the permissible. Whether or not a woman can perform martial duties becomes irrelevant beside an insidious appeal to the female audience's sense of dignity. No self-respecting woman, the scene suggests, would want to subject herself to the humiliation of undressing in front of a male crowd.

At the same time, a patriotic play such as *A Rosemary Twig* cannot afford to antagonize women and men when both sexes must work together for the national cause. Therefore the male characters are spared any direct involvement in the episode. The young woman, who has attempted to transgress gender boundaries, withdraws voluntarily. Her explosion of pent-up emotion confirms an assumption about the weakness of the female constitution and thus plays directly into the hands of patriarchal criteria of the feminine. The task of controlling the impostor falls to another woman, one whose occupation, by patriarchal standards, is more appropriate to the female sex.[71] Sława restores the male prerogative by returning the young woman to silence and absence. She performs the job with aplomb and earns the men's praise. They are quick to note that she was charming even as she shouted at the young woman. To be accepted, in other words, a woman must conform to the patriarchal idea of femininity. Sława is rewarded with marriage to the play's hero; the young woman vanishes, and we know nothing more about her. She does not even have a name to be left behind, while the nurse bears the telling name of Sława or glorious fame.

The Battle of Łowczówek and *A Rosemary Twig* do not ignore women's patriotic aspirations, but they successfully eliminate complications. They give comfort by providing a simple image of the patriarchal order whereby an occasional impostor is assigned to the periphery of the dramatic action and true women patriots put their "natural" nurturing faculties in the service of the national cause.[72]

At first sight, the second group of plays privileges Plater's spiritual daughters by featuring them as leading characters. They are Anusia in Antoni Stefan Ździebłowski's *A Heroine of the Insurrection of 1863*, Zosia in Zygmunt Reis's *Love of a Rifleman*, Jadwiga in Stefan Kiedrzyński's *Engaged on a Battlefield*, and Terenia in Bolesław Kazimierz Stefański's *The Recruit Miss*. Almost all of them fight in the national cause—Anusia in the anti-Russian insurrection, Zosia during World War I, Jadwiga in the Polish-Soviet War of 1920. Only Terenia is spared a battle engagement because Poland of the mid-1930s is not at war. What, then, is the role of "the recruit miss" in times of peace and independence? What ideological need does she serve?

Terenia puts on a man's dress as a prank, but the events take an unexpected turn and she is considered a recruit. Through this misunderstanding, she discovers what it means to be a soldier and she likes it. She thus puts detractors of the Polish army to shame. It is obvious that she stands for a masculinist idea of Poland dependent on military strength and established order. But the play unwittingly subverts its ideological project because Terenia threatens the very order she appears to uphold. "If Poland had only citizens who think like you," says an impressed officer to Terenia, "it would have been the most powerful country in Europe" (57). This message carries more than it says because the audience knows what the officer does not—that the recruit is a woman in disguise. The play thus comes dangerously close to advocating women's military service. Judging by Terenia's example, Polish women are better citizens and patriots than many Polish men.

Zosia in *Love of a Rifleman* and Jadwiga in *Engaged on a Battlefield* not only join the army, but their presence in the troops is determining since they save soldiers, including their future fiancés, from certain death. Zosia and Jadwiga come from families which uphold the patriarchal rule that it is not proper for a woman to bear arms. Yet the two women refuse to follow society's ready-made decisions and insist on making their own choices. Zosia runs away from home, and her acting talent is her passport to the Polish Legions. A suitor she has rejected tries to intervene. Zosia does not have parental permission, he informs a recruiting officer. But the soldiers, who are present at the conversation, reply: "Homeland is our first mother" (50). Jadwiga, on the other hand, dutifully seeks the permission of her grandfather, who is her guardian. She wins his support through her persuasive appeal to the patriotic tradition. After all, the grandfather, a veteran of the 1863 insurrection, must concede that in times of national need, women "put on men's clothing and nobody was offended" (16–17).

In *Love of a Rifleman* and *Engaged on a Battlefield*, social resistance against women's military service is overruled by Poland's political circumstances. At the same time, the participation of women is seen as more than sufficient proof that the Polish struggle for independence has been sanctioned by God. As Jadwiga's grandfather points out, "The Good Lord hasn't forgotten about Poland if such brave women are born in this country" (9). Zosia and Jadwiga are thus joined with their fiancés under the patriotic auspices of the national cause—and not because all a woman needs is a good husband. When the war is over, however, the women's military prowess, fearlessness, and presence of mind are brushed aside. In times of peace, both plays make it clear, women must resume their proper role—the maternal role of procreation. *Love of a Rifleman* goes a step further. Zosia is to give birth to a spiritual heir of Piłsudski in order to ensure the continuity of male—rather than female—heroism. Both *Love of a Rifleman* and *Engaged on a Battlefield* succeed only too well in reinforcing patriarchal ideology. What links them to *The Uhlan Songs, The Battle of Łowczówek,* and *A Rosemary Twig* is an essentialist idea that feminine and masculine faculties are different and should stay that way.

In this group of plays, only *A Heroine of the Insurrection of 1863* dispenses with the conventional closure of marital engagement. Anusia does not retreat into private life—but merely because a profligate nobleman she loves has committed suicide. The melodramatic plot is awkwardly entangled with a patriotic one. Early in the play, the villain tries to rape Anusia and to buy her from her drunken guardian. A detachment of insurgents appears at exactly the right time to save her. Anusia thus joins the insurrection merely to escape the machinations of the villain.

Jerzy, the commander of the detachment, assigns to her the traditional role of a nurse, but she answers that she is ready to fight for Poland until the last. Jerzy is impressed with Anusia's pluck, and by act 3 they share the command. Her transgression of gender boundaries, however, does not extend to matters of dress. She is the only one of Plater's spiritual daughters who obeys society's prohibition on cross-dressing when she takes up a martial vocation.[73]

Melodramas, of course, thrive on family secrets, mistaken identities, and sudden reversals of fortune. In Ździebłowski's play, these standard devices are adapted to the demands of ideological exhortations. Anusia finds out that she is a countess, not a peasant, but she gives up her wealth because it has been tainted with corruption and social injustice. When the insurrection fails, she takes on a "fight for the education and betterment of the people" (134). Consequently, one may read the play as a struggle in which humane feminine qualities ultimately supersede inadequate masculine values. Less apparent outside the context of Polish culture is the fact that the play reinvents the Plater figure as a Positivist heroine who refuses to equate the defeat of the uprising with passivity and translates heroic virtue into civic responsibility. When Anusia exchanges, with an overarching conviction of personal mission, the insurgent's saber for the teacher's lectern, her heroic exploits are not dismissed or belittled. They are, so to speak, a required qualification for the new job because they confer on her a special moral authority. They make her a figure of virtue among the play's corrupt and cowardly aristocrats.

Ostensibly, Ździebłowski's melodrama carries a democratic idea: men and women can be penetrated with the same fire of heroic virtue and infused with the same light of civic ideals. But the play does not admit the possibility that an ordinary peasant woman might rise to a position of wisely exercised power solely through her innate qualities of personality. If there is to be a woman leader, she must be well-born.

Plater herself appears in Wanda Brzeska's *Emilia Plater*, Tadeusz Konczyński's *Emilia Plater*, Tadeusz Orsza Korpal's *Emilia Plater: The Maidens of 1831*, Janina Sedlaczek's *Under a Woman's Banner*, and Władysław Winiarski's *Still Another Grave*. In these works, she is not a woman who has usurped the masculine status in the social hierarchy. The plays try to avoid the issue of Plater's gender transgression by drawing on the ready-made image of a heroine of national mythology. Konczyński's, Korpal's, and Winiarski's works point rather insistently in the direction of Plater's canonization by Straszewicz and Mickiewicz. Winiarski's play goes so far as to combine the imagery of Straszewicz's biography with that of Mickiewicz's poem. Plater of *Still Another Grave* dies—as in Straszewicz's account—of a broken heart when she hears that Warsaw has fallen into Russian hands. She is mourned—as in "The Death of the Colonel"—by peasants who have gathered around her body.

But Winiarski's is the only play in which we see Plater on her deathbed. In the other works, she is always a leader ablaze with patriotic ardor. Her fearlessness is rousing and makes soldiers follow her. She is repeatedly compared to a tempest or a thunderstorm which will wipe out the Russian oppression.[74] Her place in the world of these dramas is most apparent in the closing scene of Sedlaczek's play, where she is the only person on horseback. She towers above the other characters as she leads them to battle. She is godlike because she surpasses human standards.

On closer scrutiny, however, these standards turn out to be patriarchy's criteria of femininity. Plater does not join masculine qualities to feminine principles. Rather, she carries the former in her female—imperfect—body, or she transcends her sex altogether. On the one hand, she bears "a hero's soul in a woman's body" (*Still Another Grave*, 29). On the other hand, she is a "pure angel" or "the glorious virgin," an appellation which alludes to the Virgin Mary (*Under a Woman's Banner*, 4; Korpal's *Emilia Plater*, 71). Or, as an old soldier says to Plater: "Your hand is white and girlish, but you are strong and holy" (Korpal's *Emilia Plater*, 46). To put it differently, the plays involve a moral judgment which may be expressed as follows: "women unfortunately *are* women, and . . . their ideal condition is attained by rising above themselves."[75]

To tame Plater's signifying power, she has been turned into a monument. She is redefined so as to be reappropriated to the patriarchal order as a disembodied, otherworldly ideal. Her superiority becomes an inverted form of sexism intent on keeping women in a subservient position. Other women characters in the plays cannot avoid defining themselves against the standard Plater represents—only to realize that they will never match her valor, her independent spirit, her charismatic leadership. They do not question why it is so. They simply resign themselves to their inevitable inferiority. Jadwiga in Sedlaczek's play meekly offers to serve the national cause as a nurse, but this possibility is closed to Rózia in Winiarski's play. Jędrek, an insurrectionist engaged to Rózia, asserts: "Peasant women don't go to war!" (22). Rózia tries to contradict him by invoking the example of Plater, who is recuperating in the village. Yet in the very next sentence she accepts Jędrek's verdict: "Oh, really? Isn't Captain Plater getting ready to go? But if you have to go, go with her. I, a poor woman, can offer only my happiness to Poland, while you give up everything—love and life!" (22). In Korpal's play, Mrs. Abłamowicz admires Plater and feels ashamed that she herself has stayed at home rather than join the fight for Poland's freedom. Maria Raszanowicz, Plater's aide-de-camp, reassures Mrs. Abłamowicz that her decision is legitimate. The women soldiers, she explains, have violated the social norm only because foreign oppression has driven them to such desperate measures.

The pairing of Plater with women such as Mrs. Abłamowicz indicates that although the plays try to avoid the issue of gender transgression, they cannot escape it. They anticipate that among their audiences there will be women trapped in conventional gender roles, and that a confrontation with the Plater figure may be ridden with anxiety. Consequently, the plays are eager to meet or reflect expectations of what women are really supposed to be. As the conversation between Raszanowicz and Mrs. Abłamowicz makes evident, part of the ideological project of these plays is to reassure their female audiences that men and women have a notably different character, different mode of behavior, and, particularly, different social place and function. The plays do not dare to diminish the precedent of the heroine whose position in national mythology is undisputed, but they vigorously defend the dichotomy between masculine and feminine. Plater's high example is to be revered by other women but never duplicated. Thus the figure of Plater becomes restrictive. She is a model of patriotic virtue that reasserts the old, patriarchal order in new terms.

The only exception is Brzeska's play, or so it seems. Intended for school theaters, it features an all-female cast. We see Plater in her ancestral manor on the eve of the insurrection. Her companions, women of the old as well as young generations, would like her to conform to the patriarchal standards of female behavior. Young women should be merry. Marriage is the purpose of women's life. When the country is in danger, "all that a woman can do is to weep and pray" (93). As Plater defends her "otherness" (obcość) she emerges a champion of women's rebellion against the social and sexual code (91). She rejects the idea of marriage and any possibility of personal happiness when there is no happiness in her country under the foreign yoke. In a moment of patriotic ecstasy, she yearns for a spiritual marriage to another woman—Poland. This union, she believes, can be accomplished only through the extinction of earthly life while serving the national cause. She arms herself with her ancestors' saber and declares: "I believe in Poland, therefore I believe in myself!" (93). The idea of independent Poland instills self-confidence in her. It also inspires her young companion to renounce the pleasures of life and to follow her into the traditionally male realm of warfare.

Plater's breathtaking rhetoric makes her, one may say, a kind of proto-feminist—strong, independent, self-reliant. Thus it is easy to overlook the significance of chronological manipulations in the play. It collapses and condenses different time frames in order to move the arrest of Plater's cousin forward in time. The historical Michał Plater was imprisoned for his patriotic activity in 1823; in the play, his arrest and putative exile to Siberia coincide with the outbreak of the insurrection in November 1830. Michał Plater is present in this all-female drama only indirectly, through a story by the young woman. But it is his example that prompts Emilia Plater to translate her vague forebodings and longings into a determination to take up arms. Ostensibly a tribute to Emilia Plater's independent spirit, the play is in fact a paean to the martyrdom of her male cousin.

The plays accept the precedent of Plater—and channel her energy into a host of different ideological projects. They provide her with roles to play, with qualities to personify continuously and publicly, as an actor in the theater of political and social crises. In Sedlaczek's play of 1895, reprinted in Chicago at the height of Polish immigration,[76] the Plater story validates the claim that Poland is morally superior to the materialistic West because only Polish women put Patria before pleasure. The Plater figure becomes useful in the play's exhortations against "the deadly poison" of the loss of heart, which leads Poles to betray patriotic ideals and to abandon Poland for America (10). In a manner reminiscent of Żurawski's lecture of 1911, Winiarski's *Still Another Grave*, published a year later, presents Plater as a heroine of the people who has commanded a peasant regiment in the insurrection. The play, aimed at peasant audiences, affirms the ideology of social solidarity—a reassuring myth of mutual allegiance between social classes. We see a patriarchal village community where peasants dutifully serve their masters, the masters just as dutifully care for the peasants, and all of them protect the ailing Plater from Russian eyes. The mutual concord nurtures national loyalty: the village has sent its best men to fight for the cause of Poland's independence.

Plater's biography has been organized to suit a variety of ends and molded into a bearer of different ideologies. She is a figure that is always polyvalent, varying with the historical context in which she occurs. Or, to be more exact, she is less a character than a kind of cipher or space which at each moment culture fills with readings of its own. Her eminent position in Polish cultural mythology has not led to a weakening of traditional gender divisions, but rather to a reinforcement of patriarchal notions of femininity. It was on the other side of the Atlantic, in Margaret Fuller's *Woman in the Nineteenth Century*, that she was adopted as a role model rather than a talisman—only to meet with the indignant reproof of many American readers.

Notes

1. As Toril Moi has pointed out, one of the patriarchal strategies of keeping women in their place is to impose "certain social standards of femininity on all biological women, in order precisely to make us believe that the chosen standards for 'femininity' are *natural*. Thus a woman who refuses to conform can be labeled both *unfeminine* and *unnatural*." *Sexual/Textual Politics: Feminist Literary Theory* (London: Routledge, 1991), p. 65; Moi's italics.

2. For a biography of Emilia Plater in English, see Józef Straszewicz, *The Life of the Countess Emily Plater* (New York: John F. Trow, 1842), p. 37. His book originally appeared as *Émilie Plater, sa vie et sa mort* (Paris: L'Editeur, 1835).

3. Straszewicz, *The Life of the Countess Emily Plater*, p. 37. Bouboulina commanded a fleet during the Greek struggle for independence in the 1820s.

4. Ibid., p. 166. Straszewicz does not mince words about the reasons why Plater's trip to Vilnius was unsuccessful: "she forgot that she was a woman, and that men affect an exclusive monopoly in politics, courage, and wisdom. Her sex excluded her from that confidence which her enterprising character and extensive designs ought to have secured to her" (165).

5. Wendy Martin, "The Feminine Mystique in American Fiction," in Florence Howe, ed., *Female Studies II* (Pittsburgh: KNOW, 1970), p. 33.

6. Marcia Holly, "Consciousness and Authenticity: Towards a Feminist Aesthetic," in Josephine Donovan, ed., *Feminist Literary Criticism: Explorations in Theory* (Lexington: University of Kentucky Press, 1989), p. 38. The assumption that feminist literature should present positive role models for the female audience is a view held by many feminists. For example, Elaine Showalter has deplored Virginia Woolf's lack of sensitivity to the ways in which women draw strength from their experience. *A Literature of Their Own: British Women Novelists from Brontë to Lessing* (London: Virago Press, 1982), p. 285. Likewise, Patricia Stubbs has criticized Woolf for making "no coherent attempt to create new models, new images of women" in her novels. *Women and Fiction: Feminism and the Novel, 1880–1920* (Brighton: Harvester Press, 1979), p. 231.

7. In the spring of 1985, the Omaha Magic Theatre presented *Mud*, written and directed by Maria Irene Fornes, at the Women's Theatre Festival in Boston. During a public discussion after one of the performances, women in the audience took Fornes to task for closing the play with the heroine's suicide. None of them was willing to admit that such an ending might prompt some viewers to imagine how Mae's life could have been different.

8. Moi, *Sexual/Textual Politics*, p. 8.

9. Holly, "Consciousness and Authenticity," p. 40.

10. Ibid., p. 38.

11. Moi, *Sexual/Textual Politics*, p. 45; Moi's italics.

12. Ibid.

13. During World War II, there was a women's infantry battalion named after Emilia Plater in the Soviet-supported Polish army. See Stanisława Drzewiecka, *Szłyśmy znad Oki* (Warszawa: Ministerstwo Obrony Narodowej, 1985).

14. The most thorough and illuminating discussion of these symbols can be found in Józef Bachórz, "O Emilii Plater i 'Śmierci pułkownika' (refleksje sceptyka)," *Prace Historycznoliterackie* 2 (1973): 41–53, and Bogdan Zakrzewski, "'Ach, to była dziewica . . .' O Mickiewiczowskiej Platerównie," in *"Palen dla cara." O polskiej poezji patriotycznej i rewolucyjnej XIX wieku* (Wrocław: Zakład Narodowy imienia Ossolińskich, 1979), pp. 7–34.

15. Adam Mickiewicz, "Śmierć pułkownika," in *Dzieła* (Warszawa: Czytelnik, 1955), vol. 1, p. 357. For an anonymous English translation, see "The Death of the Colonel," *Harper's New Monthly Magazine* 10 (January 1855): 279.

16. Bolesław Limanowski, "Emilia Platerówna. Szkic biograficzny," in *Szermierze wolności* (Kraków: Książka, 1911), pp. 1–26; Kazimierz Żurawski, *Dziewica-bohater. Życiorys Emilii Platerówny, kapitana 1 kompanii 25 pułku (1 litewskiego) piechoty liniowej wojsk polskich 1831 roku* (Lwów: Koło Towarzystwa Szkół Ludowych imienia Emilii Plater, 1913); Felicja Boberska, "O Polkach, które się szczególniej zasłużyły Ojczyźnie w powstaniu listopadowym," in *Pisma* (Lwów: n.p., 1893), pp. 29–59. An early version of Limanowski's essay was published in 1861 in the Lvov *Dziennik Literacki* under the pseudonym of Janko Płakań. Boberska's article originated as a lecture which she gave in Lvov on November 28, 1880. Żurawski's account was first presented as a public lecture in Lvov in December 1911.

17. In both accounts, the cousins confide their plans to Plater, and she offers to help them.

18. "However, she remained compassionate and tender of heart, and local peasants often benefited from her sympathy and help." Boberska, "O Polkach," p. 49.

19. Ibid., p. 48.

20. Ibid., p. 49.

21. Ibid.

22. Janina Sedlaczek, *Pod sztandarem kobiety* (Poznań: W. Simon, 1895), p. 3. I will discuss this play in part 3.

23. Mary Fleming Zirin's letter of April 14, 1993, to Halina Filipowicz. For a cogent discussion of Durova's place in Russian culture, see M. F. Zirin, "Translator's Introduction: Nadezhda Durova, Russia's 'Cavalry Maiden,'" in Nadezhda Durova, *The Cavalry Maiden: Journals of a Russian Officer in the Napoleonic Wars*, trans. M. F. Zirin (Bloomington: Indiana University Press, 1988), pp. ix–xxxvii.

24. This belief was codified by Mickiewicz in a lecture he gave in French in 1842. See "Wykład XXX," trans. Leon Płoszewski, in *Dzieła*, vol. 10, pp. 378–80.

25. Margaret Fuller, *Woman in the Nineteenth Century* (Columbia: University of South Carolina Press, 1980), p. 34.

26. Ibid., pp. 36, 33. The promotion of Plater to the rank of colonel indicates that Fuller was familiar with the poem by Mickiewicz, whom she later met in Paris. Her account of Plater's participation in the insurrection draws on Straszewicz's biography, which was in Elizabeth Peabody's library in Boston. Fuller applauds Straszewicz for taking Plater's story out of a "domestic circle" and making her a public figure (35). She accepts his "homage" to Plater at face value and attributes it entirely to "a brotherly devotion," selfless and generous (35). The issue of power involved in men's making of women, so to speak, does not enter Fuller's discussion. This is a point to which I will return later.

27. Ibid., p. 159.

28. A letter dated 13 March 1845, in *The Letters of Margaret Fuller*, ed. Robert N. Hudspeth (Ithaca: Cornell University Press, 1987), vol. 4, p. 59.

29. See Józef Bachórz, "Panna Plater czyli kłopoty Amazonki," *Literatura*, October 23, 1975, p. 9.

30. See Bachórz, "Panna Plater czyli kłopoty Amazonki" and "O Emilii Plater i 'Śmierci pułkownika.'"

31. See Wojciech Goczałkowski, *Wspomnienia lat ubiegłych* (Kraków: Nakładem autora, 1862), vol. 2, pp. 17–18.

32. Ignacy Domeyko, *Moje podróże. Pamiętniki wygnańca*, ed. Elżbieta Helena Niec (Wrocław: Zakład Narodowy imienia Ossolińskich, 1962), vol. 1, p. 70.

33. Bachórz, "O Emilii Plater i 'Śmierci pułkownika,'" p. 35. See also "Panna Plater czyli kłopoty Amazonki," p. 9.

34. Bachórz, "O Emilii Plater i 'Śmierci pułkownika,'" p. 34, and "Panna Plater czyli kłopoty Amazonki," p. 9. Assumptions behind his argument are not unlike those that underlie folktales about Bouboulina, which still circulate on her native island, Spetses: "They say . . . that she was so unattractive she had to seduce her lovers at pistol-point." David Howarth, *The Greek Adventure: Lord Byron and Other Eccentrics in the War of Independence* (New York: Atheneum, 1976), p. 42.

35. See Bogdan Zakrzewski, "Emilia Plater," in Zofia Stefanowska and Janusz Tazbir, eds., *Życiorysy historyczne, literackie i legendarne* (Warszawa: Państwowe Wydawnictwo Naukowe, 1980), vol. 1, pp. 189–206, and Dioniza Wawrzykowska-Wiercioch, *Sercem i orężem ojczyźnie służyły. Emilia Plater i inne uczestniczki powstania listopadowego 1830–1831* (Warszawa: Ministerstwo Obrony Narodowej, 1982), pp. 128–266.

36. Boberska, "O Polkach," p. 49.

37. Ibid., p. 59. See Halina Kozłowska-Sabatowska, *Ideologia pozytywizmu galicyjskiego 1864–1881* (Wrocław: Zakład Narodowy imienia Ossolińskich, 1978), p. 159. For studies of the origins of Positivist ideology in Poland, see Barbara Skarga, *Narodziny pozytywizmu polskiego (1831–1864)* (Warszawa: Państwowe Wydawnictwo Naukowe, 1964), and Janusz Maciejewski, *Przedburzowcy. Z problematyki przełomu między romantyzmem a pozytywizmem* (Kraków: Wydawnictwo Literackie, 1971).

38. See Boberska, "O Polkach," p. 59.

39. Żurawski, *Dziewica-bohater*, p. 46.

40. This ideology, popular in Poland after the failure of the 1863 insurrection, sought to maintain the existing order of class structure.

41. See Limanowski, *Szermierze wolności*, p. i. This ideology of the Polish Socialist Party (PPS) was contested by Rosa Luxemburg and Julian Marchlewski, who put class struggle over the struggle for national independence and discredited PPS members as "Polish chauvinists." Henryk Wereszycki, *Historia polityczna Polski 1864–1918* (Wrocław: Zakład Narodowy imienia Ossolińskich, 1990), p. 124. See also Kazimiera Janina Cottam, *Bolesław Limanowski (1835–1935): A Study in Socialism and Nationalism* (Boulder: East European Quarterly, 1978).

42. Mickiewicz, "Wykład XXX," pp. 379–80. Mickiewicz is here echoing Straszewicz's assertions in *The Life of the Countess Emily Plater*, pp. 28–29, 34–35.

43. It should be added that six years later, in his "Skład zasad" ("A Set of Principles"), an ideological declaration of the Polish Legion in Italy, Mickiewicz granted women equal rights. Yet while he went on to elaborate on the rights of Jews, his formulation concerning women's rights remained vague despite widespread debates over women's suffrage at that time. For an expanded version of Mickiewicz's postulate of equal rights for the Jews, see Adam Mauersberger, "Objaśnienia wydawcy," in Mickiewicz, *Dzieła*, vol. 12, p. 331.

44. Louisa Anne Twamley, "From Verses to the Memory of the Countess Emilia Plater," in Straszewicz, *Emilie Plater*, p. 345.

45. Ibid., p. 346; Twamley's italics.

46. Mickiewicz, "Wykład XXX," p. 380.

47. Biographical essays about Raszanowicz and Tomaszewska appeared in Józef Straszewicz, *Les Polonais et les Polonaises de la Révolution du 29 Novembre 1830* (Paris: A. Pinard, 1832–36), no page numbers. The volume also included a short version of his biography of Emilia Plater.

48. See Konstanty Gaszyński, "Wiersz z okoliczności wejścia w szeregi walczących panien Emilii Platerówny i Marii Raszanowiczówny" ("A Poem on the Occasion of Emilia Plater and Maria Raszanowicz's Joining the Ranks of Insurgents"), in Zakrzewski, *Palen dla cara,* p. 39.

49. Janina Znamirowska, *Liryka Powstania Listopadowego* (Warszawa: Kasa imienia Mianowskiego, 1930), p. 146. One of the poems was by Gaszyński, the other, "Na obchód 29 listopada, urządzony 29 lipca w Warszawie" ("On the Anniversary of the Events of November 29, Celebrated on July 29 in Warsaw," 1831), by an anonymous author.

50. A discussion of the Russian threat to France in 1830 can be found in Władysław Zajewski, ed., *Powstanie Listopadowe 1830–1831. Dzieje wewnętrzne. Militaria. Europa wobec powstania* (Warszawa: Państwowe Wydawnictwo Naukowe, 1990), pp. 427–567. For illuminating accounts of the popularity of Plater in France during the 1830s, see Maria Straszewska, "Powstanie listopadowe w polonicach francuskich (na marginesie melodramatu *Les Polonais*)," *Przegląd Humanistyczny* 5 (June 1961): 21–38, M. Straszewska, *Życie literackie Wielkiej Emigracji we Francji 1831–1840* (Warszawa: Państwowy Instytut Wydawniczy, 1970), and Zygmunt Markiewicz and Tadeusz Sivert, *Melpomena polska na paryskim bruku. Teatralia polskie we Francji w XIX wieku* (Warszawa: Państwowe Wydawnictwo Naukowe, 1973).

51. Justin Maurice, "Élégie," in Straszewicz, *Émilie Plater*, pp. 337, 339.

52. Pierre Simon Ballanche, "Préface, " in Straszewicz, *Émilie Plater*, p. xiii.

53. Michel Pietkiewicz, *La Lithuanie et sa dernière insurrection* (Bruxelles: H. Dumont, 1832), pp. 112–13.

54. Ballanche, "Préface," p. xiii.

55. Zakrzewski attributes Plater's posthumous career in Europe primarily to the precedent of Joan of Arc. See "Emilia Plater," pp. 197–98, and "'Ach, to była dziewica . . . ,'" p. 9. A measure of Plater's European popularity is the translation of Straszewicz's biography into Swedish (in 1837), English (in 1842), and Italian (in 1863). Unlike Joan of Arc, however, Plater has not been declared a saint, and no efforts have been undertaken to consider her for beatification or canonization. See Jerzy Mrówczyński, ed., *Polscy kandydaci do chwały ołtarzy* (Wrocław: Wrocławska Księgarnia Archidiecezjalna, 1987). I am grateful to Janusz Wróbel for this bibliographic reference.

56. The Maid's precedent is directly invoked in Gaszyński's "A Poem on the Occasion of Emilia Plater and Maria Raszanowicz's Joining the Ranks of Insurgents" and in Antoni Edward Odyniec's poem "Smug kowieński. Zdarzenie prawdziwe" ("The Kovno Meadow: A True Story," 1832). In Mickiewicz's "The Death of the Colonel," both the creation of a folk heroine and the phrase "the virgin hero" carry echoes of the Maid. For a different interpretation, see Bachórz, "O Emilii Plater i 'Śmierci pułkownika,'" pp. 43–44. He argues that Mickiewicz is silent about Plater's foreign predecessors, such as Joan of Arc and Bouboulina, because he wants to lock her story in the native realm.

57. For a similar view, see Bachórz, "O Emilii Plater i 'Śmierci pułkownika,'" pp. 50–53, and "Panna Plater czyli kłopoty Amazonki," p. 9. However, he does not mention Joan of Arc in this context. The only French example cited in his discussion of models of female patriotism is the allegory of freedom in Eugène Delacroix's famous painting of 1830, *Liberty Guiding the People*.

58. Bachórz and Zakrzewski attribute only minor importance to their efforts, although Fuller's *Woman in the Nineteenth Century* and her correspondence provide evidence to the contrary.

59. For example, Wladysław Plater was the editor and publisher of *Le Polonais: Journal des Intêrets de la Pologne* in Paris. Maurice's "Élégie" first appeared in that journal in 1834. *Histoire d'Émilie Plater, héroine de la Pologne* (1832), published anonymously in Bordeaux, has been attributed to Cezary Plater.

60. Kazimierz Tetmajer, *O żołnierzu polskim 1795–1915* (Oświęcim: Naczelny Komitet Narodowy, 1915), p. 99.

61. A contrast with Gaszyński's poem is striking. He emphasizes that Plater and Raszanowicz are "daughters of valiant Lithuania," and not agents of a heavenly mission. In Bachórz's misreading of Gaszyński's poem, Plater and Raszanowicz personify God-sent angels. See "O Emilii Plater i 'Śmierci pułkownika,'" p. 36.

62. This proposition is pivotal to Bachórz's argument in "O Emilii Plater i 'Śmierci pułkownika.'"

63. For a sampling of such beliefs, see Wawrzykowska-Wiercioch, *Sercem i orężem ojczyźnie służyły*, pp. 246–47.

64. For example, Limanowski points out that Plater represents "the vital importance of Lithuania" for the Polish struggle for independence. *Szermierze wolności*, p. i. Dezydery Chłapowski, one of the commanders of the Lithuanian campaign in 1831, also asserts the ideological and political significance of Lithuania, although he does not mention Plater in this context: "Lithuania has been the crux of our independence." *Pamiętniki* (Poznań: Nakładem synów, 1899), vol. 2, p. 112. It should be added that Limanowski, in his *Dzieje Litwy* (*History of Lithuania*, 1895), cites the leading role of Lithuanians such as Emilia Plater and Tadeusz Kościuszko in the joint Polish-Lithuanian struggles for independence as an argument, in Cottam's words, "to counteract the Russian viewpoint of the Polish-Lithuanian connection, that is, that the historic lands of Lithuania had closer ties with Russia than with Poland." Cottam, *Bolesław Limanowski (1835–1935)*, p. 194.

65. Besides the poems by Gaszyński, Mickiewicz, Odyniec, and an anonymous author, there is also Ferdynand Kuraś's "Platerówna (w siedmdziesiątą rocznicę śmierci bohaterki)" ("Miss Plater [On the Seventieth Anniversary of the Heroine's Death]," 1901). For a text of this poem, see Żurawski, *Dziewica-bohater*, pp. 47–48.

66. I have not been able to locate one of these plays, Eustachy Czekalski's *Emilia Plater*, completed in 1917. Moreover, only one scene of Adam Znamirowski's drama appears to be extant. See *Emilia Plater* (act 2, scene 4), *Ilustrowany Tygodnik Polski* 18 (November 28, 1915): 286. Wawrzykowska-Wiercioch mentions Ludwika Broel-Plater's play *Wybrana* (*The Chosen Woman*). See *Sercem i orężem ojczyźnie służyły*, p. 259. However, *The Chosen Woman*, published in 1903 and staged in 1913, deals only with Joan of Arc.

67. The seven plays about Plater seem paltry next to dozens of dramas about the leading male heroes in the national pantheon, Tadeusz Kościuszko and Józef Poniatowski. But the statistics of textual production are, of course, relative; one may question why Plater has not appeared more frequently in poetry and fiction. Abroad, the most famous play about Plater was Charles Prosper's *Les Polonais: Événement historique*, which had a successful run at the Cirque Olimpique in Paris in 1831. Plater is also the heroine of a one-act love comedy, *L'héroine polonaise ou l'insurrection en Lithuanie*, written in French by the Polish exile J. O. Gliński and published in Havre in 1837.

68. The only exceptions are Kiedrzyński's and B. Stefański's dramas.

69. For complete references, see the bibliography following the notes.

70. Cheri Register, "American Feminist Literary Criticism: A Bibliographical Introduction," in J. Donovan, ed., *Feminist Literary Criticism*, p. 20. Register is here quoting Martin, "The Feminine Mystique in American Fiction," p. 33.

71. For example, Henryk Golejewski, a participant in the insurrection of 1830–31, vehemently juxtaposes Plater to Urszula Piłsudska, who assisted with the wounded. He writes: "When there is Piłsudska, the true Polish woman and patriot, don't talk to me about the Plater kind and *tutti quanti*. An hour's worth of Piłsudska's work did more good than their charlatanic pursuits of the Muscovites, which contributed nothing to the public cause." Those "female Don Quixotes," concludes Golejewski, "renounced their female vocation and character." His implacable hostility toward Plater and the other women insurgents allows us, more than a century later, to grasp the extent of their defiance against patriarchal ideology. *Pamiętnik*, ed. Irena Homola, Bolesław Łopuszański, and Janina Skowrońska (Kraków: Wydawnictwo Literackie, 1971), vol. 1, p. 401.

72. The belief in the nurturing qualities of women is, of course, an accepted patriarchal notion which has been conceptualized as a universal law of nature. As Toril Moi notes, this assumption has reemerged as one of the cherished concepts of feminism. See "Introduction," in Toril Moi, ed., *French Feminist Thought: A Reader* (Oxford: Basil Blackwell, 1987), p. 8. This particular manifestation of patriarchal as well as feminist essentialism has been contested, for example, in Elisabeth Badinter, "Maternal Indifference," trans. Roger DeGaris, in *French Feminist Thought*, pp. 150–78.

73. The play, first staged by an amateur troupe in New York City in 1894, was addressed to Polish immigrants, most of whom were of peasant descent. Anusia's male costume might have been offensive to their sense of a divinely ordained order as well as decorum.

74. See Korpal, *Emilia Plater*, p. 113, and Konczyński, *Emilia Plater*, p. 5.

75. Mary Ellmann, *Thinking about Women* (New York: Harcourt, Brace and World, 1968), p. 67; italics in the original.

76. See Janina Sieniaczek, *W obozie* (Chicago: Polish American Publishing Company, ca. 1913). I have not been able to determine why the author's name has been changed. Sloppy proof-reading may have been a reason.

Plays Cited

If a play has been staged, the year of the première is given in brackets.

Bakal, Bronisław. *Bitwa pod Łowczówkiem.* Warszawa: I. Rzepecki, 1938.

Brzeska, Wanda. *Emilia Plater.* In Maria Ojerzyńska, ed., *Powstanie listopadowe*, pp. 85–93. Poznań: Zjednoczenie Młodzieży Polskiej, 1927. Published under the pseudonym of Eminus.

Bunikiewicz, Witold. *Piosnki ułanskie.* Lwów: Wydawnictwo Polskie, 1919. [1917]

Kierdrzyński, Stefan. *Zaręczyny pod kulami.* Warszawa: I. Rzepecki, 1938. [1920]

Konczyński, Tadeusz. *Emilia Plater.* Warszawa: Biblioteka Groszowa, ca. 1933. [1933]

Korpal Orsza, Tadeusz. *Emilia Plater. Panny w r. 1831.* Miejsce Piastowe: Towarzystwo św. Michała Archanioła, 1937.

Nowakowski, Zygmunt. *Gałązka Rozmarynu.* London: Światowy Związek Polaków z Zagranicy, 1945. [1937]

Reis, Zygmunt. *Strzelecka miłość.* Miejsce Piastowe: Towarzystwo św. Michała Archanioła, 1933.

Sedlaczek, Janina. *Pod sztandarem kobiety.* Poznań: W. Simon, 1895.

Stefański, Bolesław Kazimierz. *Panna rekrutem.* Lwów: Odrodzenie, ca. 1937. [1936]

Winiarski, Władysław. *Mogiła więcej.* Kraków: G. Gebethner, 1912. Published under the pseudonym Marian Ładysławski.

Ździebłowski, Antoni Stefan. *Bohaterka z Powstania 1863 roku.* Chicago: W. Dyniewicz, 1893. [1894]

FOUR

The Landscape of Recollection

Tolstoy's *Childhood* and the Feminization of the Countryside

PAMELA CHESTER

> If one seeks in our painters' canvases the freshness of Turgenev's mornings, the scent of Tolstoy's hay, or the precision of Chekhov's description, one is inevitably drawn to the conclusion that, among all the Russian landscape painters . . . Levitan is alone in rising to the level of these great poets.
> —Diagilev's obituary of Levitan in *World of Art*, 1900 (cited by Bazarov, *Landscape Painting*, 152)

THE LANDSCAPES OF nineteenth-century male artists, whether rendered in paint, in verse, or in prose, in England or in Russia, often represent a nurturant, "feminine" Nature in all her pastoral fertility. Lev Tolstoy, in his *Childhood* (1852), describes the countryside of central Russia as an almost paradisiacal setting for a little boy's first experiences of the world. He was certainly not the first to do so: William Wordsworth's *The Prelude* (1799–1805), an autobiography in verse, also describes idealized scenes of his country childhood. Even in works as apparently disparate as the landscapes of John Constable and Isaak Levitan, the subject is gentle rural vistas of their motherlands.[1] And just as Tolstoy's and Wordsworth's literary works are autobiographical, Constable returned over and over to paint the areas around his birthplace in Suffolk. Each of these is literally a landscape of recollection, an artistic representation of scenes from childhood; each refers to past time, lost and then regained through the exercise of memory. The case of Levitan is more complex, because of his own complicated position vis-à-vis the landscape, but at a minimum he resembles Constable in that many of his canvases focus on the modest lyrical beauty of rural vistas. I would argue that the remembered is always to some degree the imagined, and that Levitan, barred from possessing land because he was a Jew, therefore provides the clearest example of the created "memory" of a native landscape.

In each of these four cases, whether writer or painter, whether or not they directly linked their boyhood reminiscences to the countryside they depict, documentary evidence makes it clear that a feminine presence hovers over, even blurs with, the scene, so that the landscape itself is feminized. This nostalgic urge to identify the childhood garden with Eden, and to conceive of the loss of union with the feminine Other as expulsion from paradise, might appear to be a natural, even a universal, human response to a changing countryside. However, the very obviousness and banality of this observation, like the continued currency of clichés of Mother Earth and Mother Russia,[2] invite further investigation. Margaret Homans has observed that "the mother's absence is what makes possible and makes necessary the central projects of our culture" (2); that is, "[f]or the same reason that women are identified with nature and matter in any traditional thematics of gender (as when Milton calls the planet Earth "great Mother"), women are identified with the literal, the absent referent in our predominant myth of language. From the point of view of this myth, the literal both makes possible and endangers the figurative structures of language" (4).[3] For the male artist, then, the death or loss of the mother is a precondition for the creation of art. Further, "he must transmogrify the lost maternal presence into 'Mother Nature,'"[4] a process which is exemplified in all four of these men. Homans focuses chiefly on the analysis of texts by women writers, but similar questions about this conflation of woman and nature need to be posed about male artists as well. All four of the men considered here, although separated so widely in time and space, treat landscape in very similar ways, binding together the feminine and the earth to define a pleasing shape for the Self.

In the case of Tolstoy, and of Wordsworth, Constable, and Levitan as well, the landscape, whether verbal or visual, in fact constitutes a form of autobiography, a highly abstract self-portrait. Of course, the canvases of these painters are not in any literal sense self-portraits, any more than the landscape descriptions of the writers are directly self-descriptive. Yet the feminized pastoral scene, whether rendered in oils or in prose, serves as a painted mirror, the male artist's depiction of a Lacanian "M/Other" who by virtue of her difference reflects back to him that image of his childhood Self which he wants to see.[5] While this is by no means the result of direct influence among these artists, it is certainly no accident.

For each of these artists, when the landscape itself takes on something of the character and function of the beloved feminine figure, Nature is constructed as maternal provider. She offers him soothing, morally uplifting, uncritical acceptance, a safe sensuality without the complications of mature sexuality (always a Tolstoyan dream), and a return to unity and wholeness. This natural world may even hold out the answer to another central concern of Tolstoy's, a promise of keeping death and dissolution at bay: Time and the linear development of history are contradicted and perhaps undone by the earth's ageless "feminine" cycles of dissolution and new growth. Within the stasis of a landscape, space becomes preeminent over time, offering a foretaste of eternity.[6] The painted landscape by definition has very limited resources for the depiction of time. A verbal landscape description, by contrast, is caught in a permanent tension between the static spatial dimensions of the scene and the necessarily time-bound nature of narrative. In both, however, the very act of recollection, the exercise of memory, serves to cheat Death by preserving the vanished scene not only in the subject's consciousness, but in the relative timelessness of the text or painting.

Painter or writer, each suffuses his images of the countryside with the even, nostalgic light of lyricism. Critics including Cohen, Coe, and Wachtel have demonstrated quite convincingly that such a depiction did in fact become something of a standard in the works of the literary canon, particularly in Russian Childhoods.[7] However, these analyses explicitly or implicitly assume that no distinction can be made between male and female autobiographers of childhood,[8] and often conclude that this emotional constellation is indeed peculiarly Russian.[9] Among studies of men's texts which, unlike Cohen, Coe, and Wachtel, show some awareness of gender issues, Richard Gustafson's very insightful study of Tolstoy includes an excellent analysis of the trilogy, including a passage on the importance of childhood's "paradisical garden" and its link to maternal love.[10] Yet even though Gustafson states directly that "the loving, caring mother whom one does not know is the constant model for Tolstoy's God" (14), he still follows Tolstoy himself in failing to explore the problematics of statements such as "His quest for perfection, the Kingdom of the *Father*, returns him to his *mother's* embrace" (14; my emphasis). I will return in my conclusion to the difficult and complex question of how, or if, the Russian tradition differs from the British, and focus here on the impact of gender on the landscape.

There is good evidence that the earliest Russian autobiographies of childhood were written by women.[11] In fact, some women writers, debarred from many aspects of their culture's discourse, created a rival tradition of an anti-Edenic childhood garden.[12] In the present study, however, I limit myself to a reading of selected landscapes of Lev Tolstoy and a brief comparison with those of William Wordsworth, John Constable, and Isaak Levitan. A comparison of men's literary texts, and men's paintings, within a context which acknowledges their gender and does not erase women's writings from the broad background of the study, reveals something about the gender dynamics at work in their art and contributes to a fuller picture of the artistic process. The major focus is how and why gender, space, time, and memory are interconnected in Tolstoy's depictions of his native landscapes.

Tolstoy's Garden

Although memoirs of childhood are often the fruit of mature reflection on a relatively distant past, Tolstoy (1828–1910) published *Childhood*, his first literary work, just after his twenty-fourth birthday. In this first section of his trilogy *Childhood, Boyhood, and Youth*, although it has often been read as a "pure" autobiography, the young writer in fact blends "auto-psychological" elements with purely invented material, as well as episodes and relationships observed in a neighbor family, the Islavins (1: 305).*

Clearly, Tolstoy believed that his own experience as a male child of a Russian gentry family could easily be generalized into a universal picture of human development: his working title for the tetralogy he initially envisioned was *Four Ages of Development* (1: 305). Tolstoy objected strenuously when he discovered that his

*All citations from Tolstoy's writings are taken from the complete edition in 90 volumes (*Polnoe sobranie sochinenii*, Moscow, 1928–58) and cite volume and page numbers. The term "auto-psychological" was coined by Lidiia Ginzburg to describe Tolstoy's trilogy, in *O psikhologicheskoi proze* (Leningrad, 1971), p. 314.

editor had in fact published the anonymous work (signed only with the initials L. N.) under the expanded title *The Story of My Childhood* (1: 305). He protested, "What does anyone care about the story of *my* childhood?" (Tolstoy's emphasis).[13] In his diaries (e.g., March 7, 1851) and letters, he himself referred to the work in progress as a novel, a *roman* (1: 305); he had set out to create a work of fiction, albeit with strong autobiographical elements, and chose to cast the whole narrative in what Wachtel terms "pseudo-autobiographical" form[14]—that is, his hero has his experiences, but not his name.

Every aspect of *Childhood* represents a conscious artistic decision; this is a carefully crafted construct. This is true even in his handling of facts from his family history, but it can be seen still more clearly in the few purely fictional elements in the trilogy. Foremost among his inventions is Maman; Tolstoy lost his mother before the age of two and had no conscious memory of her (34: 349). Yet he felt so strongly about the rightful power of the mother that he centered the whole emotional world of childhood around the portrait of Nikolen'ka's ideally self-immolating, loving mother. Tolstoy needed to incarnate her so that he could then kill her off at the appropriate point in his young hero's development, when her memory could serve as his moral guide in later life. *Childhood* is less the chronicle of an entire epoch than an account of a single epochal moment which marks childhood's irrevocable disappearance: the death of the mother.

The first chapter of *Childhood* opens on a day specified both according to the official calendar (the Julian calendar then in use throughout the Russian Empire, which lagged twelve days behind the West by the nineteenth century): "On August 12, 18. . . ." (1: 3); and according to the child's own interior and idiosyncratic reckoning: "three days after my tenth birthday" (1: 3). Woven through this framing chronotope is Nikolen'ka's depiction of place, the home where he has lived for the first decade of his life, a Russian country house on an estate which has belonged to his family for several generations. Not surprisingly, nature plays a prominent role in his childhood world, as it did for so many subsequent male autobiographers in Russia.

Childhood contains a wide variety of landscape descriptions. However, one scene becomes particularly important, and is repeated twice, in chapters I and XXII. This landscape of recollection, centered on the manor house and its surrounding gardens and fields, takes on a heightened temporal and emotional resonance because it represents a composite picture. Unlike the scene of some specific episode of the child's life (e.g., the fields and forests where the family members hunt and picnic before their separation in Chaps. VI–IX), this is a view the child has looked at repeatedly, and probably recalled repeatedly. Therefore it is generalized, almost as if it were polished by repeated handling, and has taken on heightened emotional content.

Appropriately, in the first chapter, even when the narrator, his older self, is describing the view from inside his schoolroom, the child's viewpoint and perceptions dominate:

The final wall was taken up by three windows. Here is what the view from them was like: directly under the windows was a road, on which every pothole, every pebble, every rut was long since familiar and dear to me. Beyond the road was a clipped linden *allée*, from beyond which here and there one could see a wattle fence. Across the *allée* one could see a meadow, with a threshing floor on one side and forest opposite it; far off in the forest one could see the watchman's hut. From the window on the right one could see part of the terrace, on which the grown-ups usually sat before dinner. It happened that while Karl Ivanych [their German tutor] was correcting a page of dictation, you would look in that direction, see Mama's dark head, someone's back, and faintly hear talk and laughter there. You would get so annoyed that you couldn't be there too, and you would think, "*When* will I be grown up, stop doing lessons, and always sit not at my dialogues but with those whom I love?" Annoyance would pass over into sadness, and God knows why or about what, you would plunge so deeply into thought that you wouldn't even hear Karl Ivanych scolding about the mistakes. (1: 7)

In the early lines of this description, the speaker emphasizes only the spatial dimensions of the scene. He begins in the immediate foreground, with the wall of the house and the frames of the windows. He then moves systematically deeper and deeper into the field of the picture, moving outside the house to the road beneath the windows, then beyond it, crossing the *allée* and moving behind the woven fence, across the meadow which lies beyond it, and into the depths of the forest. Even this inanimate collection of places, plants, and objects calls up a powerful emotional response in the speaker; after all, even the potholes and pebbles on the road are "dear to" him, with the present-tense verb implying that these feelings, although first experienced in the past, are unchanged in the present.

At the end of the landscape description, the narrator presents the true emotional center of the scene. The first human figure to appear in the landscape is the child's mother, who, although she is situated spatially at the extreme right margin of the field of view, triggers a chain of reflections which are powerful enough to abstract the child entirely from his temporal and spatial surroundings. He passes through a series of emotional states, from annoyance to deep sadness to an almost trancelike meditative state. He returns to a consciousness of the present moment only in the final lines of chapter I, when the tutor puts on his dress coat and summons the children to the drawing room to say good morning to their mother.

Tolstoy's handling of time in this passage, reflected in his combining of past and present verb tenses and his use of iterative forms, blurs a series of ostensibly discrete and specific memories into a universalized, remembered scene; and their emotional resonance is correspondingly deeper as well. Only the final episode of leaving the schoolroom actually represents progress along the narrative's temporal axis, and significantly enough, this event advances the action of the story (such as it is) without revealing anything about the child's inner world.

Tolstoy's agenda, even in this very early attempt at literary composition, emphasized not the springs of the plot mechanism but the psychological states of his characters;[15] therefore the action of the story, if related in its baldest outlines, is astoundingly simple. The twenty-eight chapters of *Childhood* form a carefully crafted

whole. Chapters I through XIV take place in the countryside, which is morally (although not legally) the "world of the mothers," dominated by Maman in company
with her old nurse Natal'ia Savishna, Nikolen'ka's sister Liuba,[16] her French govern-
ess Mimi, and Mimi's daughter Katia. The function of linear time in the book, such
as it is, is to carry the hero and his older brother, in the company of their father and
his male servants, off to the "world of the fathers" in Moscow. The elapsed time in
the first half of *Childhood* is exactly two days, although free-ranging digressions
into reminiscence broaden the picture so much that the reader is hardly aware of
the tightly limited time frame.

Chapter XV, by contrast, serves as a sort of hinge, situated as it is just past the
midpoint of the text; here the voice of the older narrator dominates, and he describes an emotionally dense "interior of recollection" analogous to the landscape
of recollection in chapter I, and with Maman once again at the center.

In the later chapters of *Childhood*, the hero's rural roots are effectively severed,
first by distance and then by death. Even when he and his brother rush back with
their father from the city to the village in time to see their mother on her deathbed,
they remain grounded in the urban world of Moscow. Yet the hero Nikolen'ka can
recover what he has lost through the exercise of memory.

Chapter XXII describes the final crisis of an eventful day in Nikolen'ka's city
life.[17] In honor of their grandmother's name day, the brothers must appear at a children's ball, intended in part to polish their social graces. Nikolen'ka is entrapped
into dancing the mazurka with an unattractive young princess, and in his inexperi-
ence and agitation he loses his composure midway through a difficult figure. His
father cuts in on him:

> "Il ne fallait pas danser, si vous ne savez pas!" said the angry voice of my father
> above my ear, and pushing me away slightly he took the hand of my lady, took a turn
> with her in the old-fashioned way, to the loud approbation of the onlookers, and
> brought her back to her place. Just at that moment the mazurka ended.
> "Lord! Why do you punish me so horribly!"
> . . . .
> Everyone despises me and always will . . . the road to everything is closed to me: to
> friendship, love, honor. . . . It's all over! Why did Volodia make signs to me, which
> everyone could see, and which couldn't possibly help me? Why did that repulsive prin-
> cess look at my feet like that? Why did Sonechka . . . she is a darling; but why was she
> smiling at that moment? Why did Papa blush and grab me by the arm? Was even *he*
> ashamed of me? Oh, this is horrible! If Mama[18] were here, she wouldn't have blushed
> for her Nikolen'ka. . . . And my imagination flew far away in search of that dear image.
> I remembered the meadow in front of the house, the tall lindens of the garden, the
> clear pond over which the swallows circle, the blue sky on which transparent white
> clouds stood motionless, the fragrant cocks of fresh hay, and many other peaceful,
> joyful recollections were flying in my agitated imagination. (1: 72)

Since the child has left the country estate permanently, in both physical and
emotional terms, it is only fitting that he should now look in from the outside at
the house and landscape where he spent his childhood. His viewpoint is correspondingly broader than when he looks out the window in chapter I, taking in

features which are entirely absent from the earlier description, such as the meadow, hayfield, and pond. The sky now comes in for fairly detailed comment, expanding the child's horizons into a whole new realm: whereas in chapter I he was closed in by the walls of the house, his gaze now takes in the high sunlit clouds and heavens.

As before, the scene is marked by the products of human labor; for example, the freshly mown hay neatly stacked into haycocks emphasizes that this is no "virgin" land[19] but a fertile realm which, when seeded and cultivated by man, brings forth good fruit. Yet no human figures appear anywhere in this remembered landscape, where the process of conflation serves to universalize and idealize the scene. Where laborers do appear in *Childhood*, like the reapers in the hunting scene in chapter VII (which is only a memory, rather than the memory of a memory!), they are happy, picturesque rustics content with their lot; in fact, some serfs, including the old housekeeper Natal'ia Savishna and the pilgrim Grisha, far from being degraded by their enslavement, even rise above the moral level of their owners.

This unpeopled landscape in chapter XXII is all the more striking since in chapter I the description of the view from the schoolroom windows ends with the child looking at his mother and other adults, gathered on the terrace and absorbed in their own social circle. Further, Nikolen'ka explicitly states at the beginning of this landscape description that he is going in search of the "beloved image" of his mother. He conjures instead the image of the Russian countryside, and this in itself proves powerful enough to restore his emotional equilibrium. Whereas he begins in a mood of despair and radical isolation, he ends on a note of serenity and joy.

Indications of time and place have been stripped away, even more fully than in the first description of this landscape vista. Earlier on the same day, when Nikolen'ka was upset and overwhelmed by the social demands of his new life, he retreated behind his grandmother's armchair, that is, behind the mother of his mother (chapter XVIII). In chapter XXII the episode begins with a sort of emotional brutalization carried out by his father, and at the point where the son cries out to God, he is clearly still in the ballroom of his grandmother's home, surrounded by the movements of the dancers. The division of the text by the full line of dots is Tolstoy's own device to indicate the sort of emotional break which the child undergoes at this moment. All the closing lines of this chapter are distinguished from what immediately precedes them in a variety of ways.

First, the narration shifts sharply. Unlike the events of the name-day party, which the adult narrator relates using past-tense verbs and direct quotation both for his father and for himself as a child, the last lines of chapter XXII are offered in the present tense, without quotation marks or any other attribution. Suddenly the reader has access to the inner dialogue of the little boy as he/it existed on that November day in his eleventh year of life. Nikolen'ka can "see" (at least in imagination) a locus which is physically distant, filling in those features which have emotional weight (the *clear* pond, the *transparent* clouds) without regard to a single physical locus and perspective, which in chapter I was provided by the rigid framing of the windows. Certainly we have no idea where in the ballroom he is standing during these meditations. The childhood landscape has likewise been entirely purged of temporal and spatial specificity; although the ball takes place in November, the child's mental landscape is abstracted into an eternal sunlit summer of memory. And it may be worth noting that the word used for the "image" which the child desperately seeks (*obraz*) is also the Russian word for an icon. As in a holy artifact, spiritual and moral power now inheres in the landscape of rural childhood. The place of the mother who soothes, guides, and restores her child has been filled by the land itself. The task of maturation, true to the Romantic tradition, is to reclaim the lost wholeness of childhood innocence, to return to the true self, to the right relations with Creation which characterize the noble savage.

Wordsworth's Vale

It is clear that Rousseau, especially his *Confessions*, had an impact on Tolstoy's conception of childhood and of the childhood garden in particular, but Tolstoy did not choose to reproduce this model in detail. A closer parallel exists in another important early modern European autobiography of childhood: *The Prelude* (written 1799–1805) of William Wordsworth (1770–1850). Like Tolstoy, and unlike Rousseau, Wordsworth viewed childhood as a separate and crucial era in human development, and he devoted this entire work to his own childhood, boyhood, and youth. *The Prelude* begins with a look at a rural agrarian scene like the one where the writer spent his childhood:

> Oh there is blessing in this gentle breeze,
> A visitant that while it fans my cheek
> Doth seem half-conscious of the joy it brings
> From the green fields, and from yon azure sky.
> Whate'er its mission, the soft breeze can come
> To none more grateful than to me; escaped
> From the vast city, where I long had pined
> A discontented sojourner: now free,
> Free as a bird to settle where I will. (Book First, ll. 1–9)

As in Tolstoy's *Childhood*, the city figures as corrupt and corrupting, unhealthy; the cityscape blocks all access to the sublime horizons which the landscape of childhood offers both to the eye and to the spirit. And as in chapter I of *Childhood*, the adult narrator's mental gaze soon reaches back through time and space to the landscape surrounding the childhood home; he sees it first with the mind's eye:

> [. . .] Many were the thoughts
> Encouraged and dismissed, till choice was made
> Of a known Vale, whither my feet should turn,
> Nor rest till they had reached the very door
> Of the one cottage which methought I saw.
> No picture *of mere memory* ever looked
> So fair; and while upon the fancied scene
> I gazed with growing love, a higher power

> Than Fancy gave assurance of some work
> Of glory there forthwith to be begun,
> Perhaps too there performed. (Book First, ll. 70–80; my emphasis)

Recollection is not a "mere" reminiscence: it serves actually to carry the poet back into the childhood landscape. Only later does he travel through physical space from the corrupt urban world to the site of his happy and innocent infancy:

> [...] as a Pilgrim resolute, I took,
> Even with the chance equipment of that hour,
> The road that pointed toward the chosen Vale. (Book First, ll. 91–93)

Instead of a scene of primordial wilderness and pristine nature like those prized by such English Romantics as Turner, here Wordsworth, like Tolstoy, valorizes the agrarian scene, where evidence of human labors and even of the technology of the day serves only to add to the charm of the scene. Just as Tolstoy refers indirectly to haymaking and to threshing, Wordsworth pictures the millrace which human labor has constructed along the stream:

> [...] the bright blue river passed
> Along the margin of our terrace walk;
> A tempting playmate whom we dearly loved.
> Oh, many a time have I, a five years' child,
> In a small mill-race severed from his stream,
> Made one long bathing of a summer's day; (Book First, ll. 285–90)

Far from spoiling the view, this (admittedly preindustrial) alteration of untamed nature forms an integral part of the landscape and in fact enhances the illusion of the scene's stability and its temperate, nurturant embrace of the writer.

Perhaps more important and more striking is the way Wordsworth's landscape of recollection, like Tolstoy's, merges with and takes its moral force from the nurturing female figures of the author's childhood world:

> That one, the fairest of all rivers, loved
> *To blend his murmurs with my nurse's song*,
> And, from his alder shades and rocky falls,
> And from his fords and shallows, sent a voice
> That flowed along my dreams [...]
> [...] that composed my thoughts
> To more than infant softness, giving me
> Amid the fretful dwellings of mankind
> A foretaste, a dim earnest, of the calm
> That Nature breathes among the hills and groves. (Book First, ll. 270–74,
>   277–81; my emphasis)

It is precisely this blend of Nature's impact and human childrearing which results in "The Growth of a Poet's Mind," as Wordsworth subtitles his autobiography.[20]

Constable's Country

Wordsworth's treatment of landscape has often been compared in the critical literature with the "domestic sublime" so central to the canvases of John Constable (1776–1838). Many writers have seen a kinship between the verbal and the visual art of the great English Romantics; most often Wordsworth is paired with Constable, just as the more exotic Coleridge is linked with Turner. Further, the critic Karl Kroeber has observed specific links between the autobiographical *Prelude* and Constable's paintings of his native Stour Valley. He points out that Wordsworth's "spots of time" (Book Twelfth, l. 208) are analogous to the "charged spots" in Constable's visual art.[21] Ann Bermingham in her study of Constable's pictorial effort at "mapping the self" (87ff.) picks up Kroeber's point, saying that "by their organization [they] suggest a temporal coherence between the momentary and the eternal."[22] She adds that Kroeber fails to "note the role the horizon plays in imposing a unity suggestive of divine order" (219); this linkage has been made, however, by James Twitchell.[23] He argues that a heightened attention to the meeting of earth and sky "was one of the new focuses of romantic sight" (38), and that "this new panorama was both the cause and the result of the rapid establishment of an aesthetic category distinct from the beautiful, the majestic, and the picturesque—the sublime. [. . . There is a] psychological component of the subliming process, for as the 'eye' goes up to the horizon, the 'I' goes to the threshold of elevated consciousness. [. . .] The sublime separates, or rather mediates between, the conscious and the 'mystical'" (ix). In his view, "thanks largely to Wordsworth, the sublime was becoming a psychological event capable of moral significance; it was being transformed to the *sacred*" (61; my emphasis).

An important commonality of the English Romantic Wordsworth and the Russian realist Tolstoy is that for both, consciousness is central. After all, as Twitchell points out, "the real source of sublimity was not in Nature but within the perceiver" (61); and yet this perception promised to "span the abyss between inner and outer, and outer and 'the Beyond'" (11). Kroeber notes that (like conventional constructions of the Feminine) "the sublime transcends the logical" (57).[24] The high summer sky of chapter XXII of *Childhood* is not unlike the paintings of Constable, which show an increased attention to the horizon line, and to the high clouds and sky itself, especially after the death of his beloved wife in 1827. Figures 1 and 2 show the same scene painted before he met his future wife and after her death. In the later painting, the tree in the foreground is blasted, the scene darker, the sky portrayed with greater dynamism—as if closer to her heavenly abode. And Constable, like Tolstoy, repeatedly depicted the landscape of recollection, the vista framed by the windows of his father's house as well as external views of buildings which were to be part of his patrimony.

Although not an aristocrat like Count Tolstoy, John Constable was also born into a relatively wealthy landowning family. His father was determined to bring John into the family's prosperous miller's trade. Only his own perseverance and the intervention of influential family friends eventually secured for Constable the opportunity to escape from his childhood landscape, that is, to study at the Royal Academy. His return to the family lands, and his canvases depicting his patrimony and his native Stour Valley reveal his attachment to this landscape of his childhood and his intention to claim this patrimony not in commercial terms but in his art: "His rebellious retreats became symbolic recoveries as well" (Bermingham, 96 and passim).

Constable's landscape, like Tolstoy's, was also suffused by the image of a beloved woman, although in this case an adult heterosexual attachment: in 1809 he fell in love with the beautiful Maria Bicknell, the granddaughter of a wealthy and stiff-necked pastor who was the Constables' neighbor in East Bergholt. They married only in 1816, Constable's fortieth year. The fact that these fields had been the scene of their courtship lent them a recollected female presence which became the reigning genius of the place. In his letters to Maria, Constable refers repeatedly to his memories of her as bound up with the landscape itself: "From the window where I am now writing, I see all those sweet fields where we have passed so many happy hours together."[25] This vista became the subject of at least two very different paintings, the first in 1802, long before his relationship with Maria had blossomed; the second, clearly a landscape of recollection (Fig. 3), was painted in 1815, a time when Constable thought Maria might be lost to him forever because of family opposition to their marriage. "It is a commonplace of Constable scholarship," says Bermingham, "to note the coincidence of Constable's falling in love with Maria Bicknell and the emergence of his mature artistic style" (101); and she demonstrates convincingly that this linkage of woman and landscape, far from being coincidental, contributed to that very intensity of emotional, autobiographical content which gives Constable's art such power. His work for the Royal Academy exhibition of 1812, "A Water-Mill: Flatford Mill, Suffolk," grew from his almost obsessive repetition of views of his father's commercial property. It reached its final form, however, only when, as he wrote to Maria, he had "tried Flatford Mill again, from the lock (whence you once made a drawing)" (*Correspondence* 2: 54). Of this connection Bermingham observes, "The sketches are in this sense retrospective and allowed Constable in Maria's absence to imagine what she had once seen and to infuse that vision with the emotion stirred by this process of imagining. In this way the sketches' various orderings of the charged spots suggest a superimposition of present retrospective meaning on the past. [. . .] The collapse of past into present conflates two distinct historical moments into one moment, a moment, moreover, that as a result of the fusion must always remain an ideal" (132–33).

In other words, Constable in the early 1800s followed virtually the same path as Tolstoy forty years later in his pursuit of fusion with a feminine presence, and for both the outcome held out the promise of eternity, of escape from time and its relentless march toward death. They reconfigure their patrimony, and with it the authority of the fathers, regendering the fatherland as the motherland, and

Figure 1. John Constable, *Dedham Vale*, 1802 (17 1/2 × 13 1/2 in.). Victoria and Albert Museum, London.

replacing the flawed moral authority of masculinized society with an ideal Feminine, which is, after all, only "natural."

All the multiple, highly realistic details of the scene simultaneously serve an idealizing trend in their art. And for Tolstoy, as for Constable before him, the artist's recollecting consciousness is paramount: "the past becomes the presence to consciousness of consciousness itself" (Bermingham, 133), offering an artistic

Figure 2. John Constable, *Dedham Vale,* exhibited at the Royal Academy, 1828 (57 1/8 × 48 in.). National Gallery of Scotland, Edinburgh.

solution to the problem of subject-object relations which Homans calls one of the "central questions of Western metaphysics" (1). The technique of pastiche is here used both visually and temporally, and in both verbal and visual art, since the artist combines pieces not just of different scenes but of different *recollected* scenes. This idealization serves also to raise its object above the flow of linear time.

Figure 3. John Constable, *Golding Constable's Flower Garden*, 1815 (13 × 20 in.). Ipswich Museums and Art Galleries, Ipswich.

The Vanishing Countryside

Another important parallel in the societies contemporary to these artists suggests itself: in both cases the landscape itself was threatened. In late eighteenth- and early nineteenth-century England, when Wordsworth and Constable were active, the countryside was undergoing rapid and drastic changes. In response to the demands of a growing empire, the rural agrarian economy was put under pressure to produce crops more abundantly and efficiently. Landlords began to enclose with hedges and walls the lands which previously had been held in common by the village for grazing, and to cultivate these newly hedged fields by more intensive methods. One result was obviously the disappearance of the familiar shape of the rural landscape; another was the impoverishment of significant portions of the rural yeomanry, who could no longer sustain their livestock or get access to the land and water which had been available to them under the old gentry families' aegis (Bermingham, 9–11 and passim). With the advent of industrialization, factories and mills scarred and often polluted the land, and workers in these new enterprises were subjected to a longer and harsher daily regime. The resulting social dislocation was seen as one aspect of the changing rural landscape, of the decline of the moral and physical conditions of daily life. Simultaneously, gentry families who for generations had lived on and actively managed their estates were now increasingly living year round in the great urban centers, removing another source of mediation, organization, and protection of the poor, sick, and indigent from rural society (Bermingham, 75). Although she does not point out this connection, Bermingham's analysis implies that women's informal charitable support of the needy was disrupted by these changes, and was only imperfectly replaced by government bureaucracies such as poorhouses. The loss of a familiar rural topography, and particularly of a clear, unobstructed view of the horizon, naturally enough, came to represent these larger losses which were occurring in the countryside.

The situation in Tolstoy's Russia, although by no means identical, offers many parallels. Until the Emancipation of 1861, the great majority of peasants were enserfed, tied to their owners' lands and forced to work for them directly or to pay them with a portion of the produce of their labors. At about the same time, the Industrial Revolution was also making its belated way into the Russian countryside (Bradley, 9). As in England, it had become fashionable for wealthier aristocratic families to live in the two capitals, Moscow and St. Petersburg, for as much of the year as they could afford. Manufacturing plants were built not in city centers but on the outskirts of urban areas, or in rural areas chosen for development by the rising class of merchants and entrepreneurs (Bradley, 16), and therefore were an obvious intrusion on the face of the countryside. Especially after the serfs were liberated, the villages began to empty as able-bodied young men and women sought the short-term rewards of a factory paycheck.[26]

Tolstoy's "remembered" world of the 1830s, sketched in the early 1850s, represented a declining, or at least threatened, order. Although the irrevocable changes of the 1860s still lay in the future, Russian society and especially the intellectual elite of which Tolstoy was a member was well aware that the old ways of life would soon disappear. Tolstoy, like the British artists of the early nineteenth century (Bermingham, 10), valorized a whole series of social elements precisely at the moment when socioeconomic development was marginalizing them. The rural landscape devoted to agrarian pursuits was being disfigured, reshaped to meet the demands of an industrializing nation; women's lives were being degraded by the removal of able-bodied male laborers from the family group, or the women themselves were uprooted from the countryside and set down in the squalid atmosphere of early industrial slums (Bradley, 36). Both in Europe and in Russia, art produced ideal "remembered" images of both a personal and a national past which had in fact never existed in such pristine and sunlit glory. Tolstoy, Wordsworth, and Constable all stood to lose financial, political, and social power as the old world faded away. However, their deeper emotional need to hold on to the landscape of childhood is dramatized by the parallels between their art and the paintings of Levitan.

Levitan's Adopted Motherland

As the face of Russia's cities and countrysides changed in the 1860s and 1870s, landscapes became more prominent on the canvases of Russian painters.[27] Like other artists of the Wanderers group, Isaak Levitan (1860–1900) captured agrarian scenes;

Figure 4. Isaak Levitan, *Vladimirka*, 1892 (79 × 132 cm.). Tret'iakov Gallery, Moscow.

some could almost serve as illustrations for some of Tolstoy's prose works. Given the striking differences in their personal histories, this similarity cannot be explained by direct connections between experience and art; or to put it another way, Levitan's landscapes are even more obviously imaginative creations than Tolstoy's.

Unlike the aristocratic Tolstoy, who fictionalized circumstances by which he was in fact surrounded (and which he would lose in a new social order), Levitan fabricated his own adoption by Mother Russia. He was born in what is now Lithuania, in a small village in the northwest corner of the Russian Empire; as the son of a poor Jewish railway employee, he was not ethnically Russian. Like both Wordsworth and Tolstoy, Levitan was orphaned early; he came to Moscow as a young teenager, seeking admission to the Academy of Painting and Sculpture. He is represented by his friend Paustovskii in the *povest'* "Isaak Levitan" as becoming the protégé of the painter Savrasov, but also as suffering vicious anti-Semitic slurs at the hands of tavern waiters and of academy faculty, who refuse him the silver medal he has rightfully earned for his senior project and grant him only a diploma as a teacher of drafting (3: 535).[28] Because he was a Jew, Russian law codes not only barred him from owning land; his right to reside in Moscow was also precarious. Once as a teenage art student and again when he was at the height of his success, he was summarily ordered out of the city (3: 532; *Letters*, 303, 309).

It may offer some indirect reflection of Levitan's own state of mind that in Paustovskii's representation of Levitan a repeated theme is his longing for womanly comfort embodied in the natural world. During his early exile to Saltykovka, after

Figure 5. Isaak Levitan, *Golden Autumn*, 1895 (82 × 126 cm.). Tret'iakov Gallery, Moscow.

his first expulsion from Moscow, Paustovskii depicts a Levitan infatuated with the female voice which he hears singing at the adjoining country house: "Levitan hid from the vacationers, longed for the nocturnal songstress, and painted sketches" (3: 533). By the end of the summer, in his account, "longing for motherly, sisterly, womanly love had entered Levitan's heart, and never left him until the final days of his life" (3: 534–35). Paustovkii imbues the whole landscape with unattainable feminine tenderness. When Levitan seeks relief from his recurrent depressions in tramping the countryside with his hunting rifle, Paustovskii tells us, "on such days nature alone replaced a beloved human being in his life—she soothed him, stroked his brow with the wind *as if with a maternal hand*" (3: 538; my emphasis)! Another interesting aspect of this rather dreadful sentimentality is that Paustovskii, writing in 1937, was producing an acceptably sanitized and victimized Levitan for inclusion in the Soviet canon: Levitan's luminous representations of an impossibly beautiful Mother Russia were accepted as iconic in Stalin's USSR even more than in his own day.

In spite of this ostensibly nurturant landscape, Levitan, like Tolstoy, was obsessed with suicidal thoughts. Where Tolstoy limits himself to simply describing his state in *Anna Karenina* and "A Confession," reporting that he (or his alter ego Levin) actually had to avoid handling rope for fear of hanging himself, and to give up hunting so as not to be tempted into shooting himself (23:2), Levitan attempted suicide at least twice.[29] Paradoxically, out of his personal history of darkness, loss, and grief, Levitan crafted the image of a loving Mother Russia, melancholy perhaps, often caught at transitional moments such as sunset or autumn, but ultimately glowing with golden vesper light, embodying the womanly tenderness which Levitan had largely missed in his own biography. Some of his landscapes, like the famous *Vladimirka* (Fig. 4), painted in 1892, show a brooding leaden sky; more striking, though, even here, is the enormous serene vastness of the central Russian plain, and particularly of the sky and clouds arching above them. The trees on the horizon mark a distant garden, like Tolstoy's lindens in chapter XXII of *Childhood*, and even the tiny figure of a woman pilgrim pausing at a roadside shrine[30] suggests the folk piety of Grisha, Tolstoy's "fool for Christ" (chapters VIII–X). Like Tolstoy's landscape in chapter I, Levitan's *Vladimirka* possesses an enormous depth of field, drawing the eye far in, to the horizon line. The road which gave the picture its name, as well as the diverging footpaths, emphasizes this movement into the far background of the canvas.[31] This motif of strong receding diagonals recurs in almost all of Levitan's mature work, sometimes in the shape of the Volga River, sometimes as a wooden bridge, sometimes via the perspective of receding birch trunks in a luxuriant grove of trees.

Even as Levitan's health deteriorated, and his fatal heart defect asserted itself, the predominating colors of his palette were warm and radiant. Golden sunlight dominated such canvases as *Golden Autumn* (Fig. 5), painted in 1895, and even the work which remained unfinished at his death. Significantly, Levitan's intended title for this final work was the ancient name of the Russian land: he ostensibly confessed this desire to glorify his reluctant motherland to Anton Chekhov, saying that "he want[ed] to synthesize his impressions of Russia in a single monumental image, which would embody his rapture at the powerful and majestic beauty of his native nature. He dream[ed] of painting this picture with such power and conviction that with the last strokes of his brush it would be possible to call it simply 'Rus'" (Prytkov, 41).

The Horizon and the Sublime

This attention to distant horizons which mark a sort of threshold to the luminous realm which lies behind the sky links Levitan and Tolstoy to British artists, both visual and verbal, who had chosen similarly sublime themes for their depictions of the rustic landscape and its far horizon some half-century earlier. These "Romantic horizons" served as the markers of a liminal zone, where quotidian reality could touch the higher moral and spiritual realities which give meaning to human existence. British and American critics involved in analyzing these works have overlooked, however, the gender dimensions common to all of these works of art. The vanishing rural landscape, like Eden itself, like the unattainable Sublime on the other side of the horizon, like the Feminine which these male artists paint on the Lacanian mirror so that they can gaze into it to examine their own difference, all are manifestations of the Other which they set out to master in their creations. The mother figure which orphans such as Tolstoy and Levitan project onto the countryside is equally evanescent and unreal, shaped by the longing for a return to perfect union with another being.

Cyclical Time and Historical Time

It is no accident that the figure of the feminine, most often of the mother, hovers so close over the countryside of Russian depicters of boyhood, and for that matter over their Western forerunners. The landscape of recollection, whether painted in prose or in oil, provides a dam in the flow of historical time. As Julia Kristeva points out in her article "Women's Time," linear time is associated with journeys: "time as departure, progression and arrival—in other words, the time of history" (192).[32] In *Childhood*, Nikolen'ka's movement from Petrovskoe to Moscow, from childhood to boyhood, represents linear time. Opposed to this forward drive which carries him inexorably from his mother's realm into his father's, super-imposed on the road (and largely dominating it in *Childhood*) is the cyclical time of nature and mother which rules the rural society. And as the landscape description of chapter XXII makes clear, this time which marks the passing of the seasons, the times of birth and death/regeneration, is far closer than historical/modern time to what Kristeva calls epic time, that is, to eternity. Women are associated with timelessness, with eternity, with the immortality which comes with the unending regenerative powers of nature; but as Kristeva points out,

> The fact that these two types of temporality (cyclical and monumental) are traditionally linked to female subjectivity in so far as the latter is thought of as necessarily maternal should not make us forget that this repetition and this eternity are found to be the fundamental, if not the sole, conceptions of time in numerous civilizations and experiences, particularly mystical ones. The fact that certain currents of modern feminism recognize themselves here does not render them fundamentally incompatible with masculine values. (192)

Without entering into feminism's current debate over essentialist views of femininity, we can say definitely that these male artists chose to construct the feminine, and especially the maternal, along the lines which Kristeva describes. In the case of Tolstoy, it is important to add that the essentially mystical nature of his spirituality lends him an openness to this "type of temporality" and so, unexpectedly, tempers his misogyny by bridging some of the distance between him and the feminine Other.

In a slight extension of this description of time, Kristeva points up the fact that "this linear time is that of language considered as the enunciation of sentences (noun + verb; topic-comment; beginning-ending), and that this time rests on its own stumbling block, which is also the stumbling block of that enunciation—death" (192). Male artists who, like Constable, Tolstoy, and Levitan, suffered from recurrent melancholia, and in the case of the latter two from suicidal tendencies, have bound up the image of earth and mother as an antidote to the terrifying darkness of nonbeing, into a shield against death. In her essay "Stabat Mater," Kristeva refers to the cult of the Virgin Mary as the "resorption of femininity with the Maternal" and asks, "Could it be that such a reduction represents no more than a masculine appropriation of the Maternal [. . .]?" (163). This term could easily be applied to these feminized representations of Mother Earth and especially Mother Russia. Further, this idealized Maternal also offers an escape from the Death in which linear time inevitably culminates: "Mary was contrasted with Eve, life with death" (165). By restricting the notion of the feminine to a maternal figure (or in Constable's case, to the chastely loving wife), Eve could be blocked from her transgression, the Fall could be prevented, and the Edenic state of union would never be lost to Man—at least within the bounds of the work of art. In fact, I would argue that the repeated emphasis on "unity" and "at-one-ness" (Cohen, 23; cf. Gustafson's emphasis on "at-onement" [28]) in male autobiographies of childhood represents the desire to be carried back to a point prior to death's appearance; immortality is, after all, the prelapsarian Edenic state before Eve's transgression cut humankind off from the Tree of Life.

Interestingly enough, Wachtel, in his analysis of Tolstoy's trilogy landscapes, approaches this same point, but does not carry it through to its logical conclusion: "For Tolstoy, nature defies time and space; its beauty, which changes at every season but always returns, recalls a time before the child understood the meaning of death and decay" (53). I would argue that Tolstoy's nature, particularly in his landscape of recollection, valorizes space at the expense of time, in defense against that very death which so terrified him; this spatial irreducibility becomes an integral part of the scene's icon-like stasis, and thus of its moral and spiritual efficacy. These patterns, as Gustafson emphasizes, run through all of Tolstoy's fiction and nonfiction. Given the enormous energy Tolstoy devoted to his own struggles with questions of sexuality and gender, questions such as those raised in this essay can be used to reexamine his later works as well.

Conclusion

There are, of course, some male autobiographers, and even pseudo-autobiographers, who have described a non-Edenic countryside (or a reversal of the linkage of mother and nature: Aksakov, for example, learned to love the rural landscape in hunting and fishing with his father; his citified mother found the outdoor life repellent). Their existence only makes the predominance of Edenic men's Childhoods all the more striking. By contrast, women rarely describe their childhood garden in such paradisiacal terms. Seen in the light of a gendered comparison, the Girlhoods of writers such as Marina Tsvetaeva (1892–1941), or Nadezhda Durova (1783–1866), where she depicts her mother's strictures and violence, or Sophia Kovalevskaia (1850–1891), hobbled by her mother's inappropriate expectations, are not anomalies to be explained away by their political agendas or their lack of artistic pretensions.[33] They form a part of a continuum, a countertradition of women's anti-Edenic childhoods which runs almost unacknowledged beneath the dominant male representations of human development. Women's autobiographical "landscapes" with their evidence of a countertradition logically offer the next stage in our study of Russian literary childhoods, an analysis all the more urgent as we try to discern the place of Russian autobiography in the comparative European picture.

It would seem that critics such as Cohen, Coe, and Wachtel are correct in saying that the myth of the Edenic childhood garden is even more prevalent, and more intense, in Russian men's writings than in those of their European contemporaries. The link of land and mother is correspondingly stronger in Tolstoy than in Wordsworth, who dilutes his mother's influence by describing nurse and sister, or in Constable, whose mother is never absent from his childhood experience[34] and whose longed-for feminine Other is his wife. The experience of lack, of orphanhood, corresponds to a heightened anxiety about the feminine, and often to idealized representations of mother and motherland. The vanishing landscape and the dying mother each possess an exaggerated purity in the works of these male artists. In this aspect of autobiography, the author's gender inclines him to paint a stable Feminine whose remembered image can buffer the Self against change, uncertainty, and perhaps even death, an image which few women autobiographers choose to echo.

Notes

This essay owes its inception to the work of Roger Anderson and Paul Debreczeny on visual and verbal art; in developing my ideas, I have profited from the careful criticism of Sibelan Forrester, Jehanne Gheith, and Alison Hilton. Revision of this essay has been supported by a fellowship from the National Endowment for the Humanities.

1. I refer specifically to "motherland" because this is the aspect of their country and countryside which these artists emphasize. In Russian, the native land can be referred to either as *rodina*, motherland (from the root *rod-*, meaning birth/nat-/gen-), or as *otechestvo*, fatherland (from the root *otets-*, meaning father). Although nearly synonymous, the latter may connote the state, the governmental unit, while the former emphasizes the beloved birthplace without regard to politics. In English, of course, the term "motherland" is rarely used; but interestingly enough, the word "patria" (about whom generations of British schoolboys have been taught that "dulce et decorum est/ pro patria mori") derives from the root *patr-*, father-, yet its grammatical gender is feminine.

2. See, for example, Joanna Hubbs's influential study *Mother Russia: The Feminine Myth in Russian Culture* (Bloomington: Indiana University Press, 1988).

3. In this section of *Bearing the Word: Language and Female Experience in Nineteenth-Century Women's Writing* (Chicago: University of Chicago Press, 1986) Homans is referring to the psycholinguistic notions elaborated in France by Jacques Lacan, and to their feminist revision by such thinkers as Luce Irigaray and Julia Kristeva. In this view, itself a revision of Freudian theory, the child develops figurative or symbolic language, and thus access to the rational discourse of the Father, only when he (!) breaks the Oedipal bond to the mother, who remains in the literal or semiotic realm and thus by her very nature (!) is excluded from the culture's dominant discourse. Homans differs from the French in introducing the American reviser of Freud, Nancy Chodorow. In this "American" version of human psychosexual development, both the male and the female child gain access to the figurative realm, although their different relationship to the mother necessarily means that the female's relation to figurative language will always be ambivalent.

4. Stimpson makes this observation in her foreword to Homans's *Bearing the Word*, p. ix.

5. Homans points out that Lacan's views are set out particularly fully in "The Mirror Stage" and "The Signification of the Phallus"; see Jacques Lacan, *Ecrits: A Selection*, trans. Alan Sheridan (New York: Norton, 1977), pp. 1–7, 281–91. She adds that the work of revisionist feminist critics has become equally

important, since it is the reception of Lacan's ideas which underlies much of the interesting recent work on women's texts and issues of gender (291, n. 10). My own study of Tolstoy and landscape has profited especially from Charlene Castellano's use of Lacanian notions in her unpublished work on poetry and still life "Portraying the Woman in Joseph Brodsky's 'Nature Morte.'"

6. Kristeva's analysis of "women's time" is very useful in this regard, and I will return to this point later.

7. Cohen refers repeatedly to the importance of the countryside in the childhoods he discusses, and of the mother in Tolstoy, but draws few connections among the works in his unpublished doctoral dissertation, "The Genre of the Autobiographical Account of Childhood—Three Test Cases: The Trilogies of Tolstoy, Aksakov, and Gorky" (Yale, 1973). Coe, whose term "Childhood" I adopt and adapt, emphasizes the importance of the mother, which with a flippant misogyny he treats as a sort of morbid obsession ("Mother Russia and Russian Mothers," *Proceedings of the Leeds Historical Society, Literary and Historical Division* 19, pt. 6 [1984]: 44–67; see especially the section "Notes," pp. 44–45 and passim); he refers repeatedly to the natural world in which the action takes place, but does not explicitly note the linkage of mother and nature. In *The Battle for Childhood: Creation of a Russian Myth* (Stanford: Stanford University Press, 1990), Wachtel rightly asserts the centrality of these themes: "The perfection of the mother and the healing power of nature will become two of the central myths of gentry childhood" (55). Yet he devotes surprisingly little space to an exploration of the implications of his observation, and never explicitly links the two categories.

8. Wachtel, *The Battle for Childhood*, p. 226, n. 16: "It is interesting to note that gender does not seem to make any difference in gentry accounts of childhood. Male and female autobiographers recount the same myths and describe the same sort of situations. This is perhaps a function of the fact that up until approximately the age of ten, boys and girls seem to have been treated more or less equally." This is contradicted by the internal evidence of *Childhood* itself, where Liubochka, the hero's sister, seems to have been educated separately from her brothers and since early childhood. Coe's study of more than six hundred Childhoods led him to remark that there was no "revealing differences between men and women" (276). Cohen, writing in the early 1970s, makes no reference to questions of gender at all; however, his bibliography does include one extremely obscure female autobiographer, Kosterina, in a list of twenty, which would seem to imply that he felt male and female authors should be treated without distinction (213–14).

9. Coe devotes a whole section of his monograph on "comparative mythology of childhood" to "Mother Russia and the Russian Mother" (44–59); Wachtel asserts repeatedly that this is a "Russian myth" (title page and passim).

10. See Richard Gustafson, *Tolstoy: Resident and Stranger* (Princeton: Princeton University Press, 1986), p. 29, also pp. 27–52.

11. Mary Zirin's gender-sensitive study of Russian autobiographical texts has pointed up the early and distinctive contributions of female writers to the "Childhood" subgenre; but this work was essentially discounted in one recently published study of the subject. I would like to thank Mary Zirin for generously sharing her unpublished paper "Forgotten Beginnings: Early Depictions of Russian Girlhood—Nadezhda Durova, Avdot'ia Panaeva, and Nadezhda Sokhanskaia" (1989); it has now been published in somewhat revised form under the title "Butterflies with Broken Wings?: Early Autobiographical Depictions of Girlhood in Russia" in the collection *Gender Restructuring in Russian Studies: Conference Papers—Helsinki, August 1992* (Tampere: Slavica Tamperensia 2, 1993). Wachtel dismisses the earlier version in a note (217, n. 56), even though all three authors discussed here had published autobiographies before Tolstoy came on the scene. In fact, Panaeva's "Semeistvo Tal'nikovykh" ("The Tal'nikov Family") meets Wachtel's criteria to be classified as a pseudo-autobiography.

12. I lay out the evidence for this position in my study of Tsvetaeva's autobiographical prose, *Marina Tsvetaeva's Anti-Eden: The Genesis of a Woman Poet* (in progress).

13. Wachtel, in *The Battle for Childhood*, claims that this letter to Nekrasov was written but not sent. In fact, although an early draft of the letter was not sent and remains in Tolstoy's archive at the Lenin Library, Nekrasov's archive contains a second version, evidently rewritten after a cooling-off period of several days. Here Tolstoy tones down many of his criticisms but repeats the exact phrase included in the original: "Komu kakoe delo do istorii *moego* detstva?" (cited PSS 1: 333).

14. Wachtel coined this term to describe works such as Tolstoy's, which clearly contain a good deal of autobiographical material, although the author distinguishes himself from his first-person narrator by assigning the hero a different name (3). The distinction is a useful and interesting one, especially in studying autobiographies of writers. An interesting side issue, however, is that an exclusive concentration on this subgenre neatly frames out the majority of women's texts. To my knowledge, only Avdot'ia Panaeva and Evgeniia Tur among Russian women writers have written pseudo-autobiographies; among the works of English women writers, Charlotte Brontë's *Jane Eyre* would in fact fit Wachtel's criteria.

15. Gustafson's discussion of "Recollective Consciousness" covers many of these issues in some depth (see p. 278, for example).

16. It is interesting that Tolstoy, whose own sister was named Mariia, has chosen to call Nikolen'ka's sister Liubov', which means in Russian "Love."

17. In the second half of *Childhood*, Tolstoy had already abandoned his plans for a strict two-day time scheme, although the greater part of the action still occurs on two days in Moscow, just as chapters I–XIV represent a total of two days in Petrovskoe. The first day is the grandmother's name day in November, not long after their arrival, which is marked by gift giving and a religious service in the morning, a series of visits in the afternoon, and a children's ball in the evening. The second day is in April, when the boys' father receives the letter about his wife's mortal illness. This second chain of events covers several days, and extends from the boys' departure from Moscow through their mother's death and burial and on through their return to the city, bearing the bad news to their grandmother. The narrator stretches the time frame still further to take in the death of Natal'ia Savishna a year later, since emotionally this event belongs to the world of childhood, which ends when the mother figures die.

18. Significantly, at this moment of stress, Nikolen'ka refers to his mother not with the French word *maman*, as he usually does, but with the affectionate Russian diminutive *mamasha*. This contrasts sharply with his father's linguistic behavior, who delivers his rebuke not in the child's mother tongue but in French, and in the formal second-person plural at that!

19. Susan Layton's treatment of the "virgin" borderlands of Russia in "Eros and Empire in Russian Literature about Georgia" (*Slavic Review* 51, no. 2 [Summer 1992]: 195–213) offers interesting parallels with the native landscapes discussed here. She argues:

> For Russians, the valleys of Georgia approximated Eden. [. . .] Such notions of Georgia as a plentiful garden had definite erotic overtones, connoted in the phrase "virgin land." The pastoral idea of a green paradise on earth holds forth the promise of an easy life and tremendous gratification in exchange for relatively little work. Pastoralism thus entails the wish to experience the land as a nurturing female who creates for the individual a warmly satisfying, comforting environment. (206)

For the four men considered here, of course, the overtones are of "safe" maternal sexuality, which within limits is an even more nurturant and abundant provider than the eroticism of a nubile and available maiden.

20. For a fuller discussion of Wordsworth's childhood, and of his relationships with female caregivers, including mother, nurse, and sister, see Homans's discussion in *Bearing the Word*, especially chapters 2 and 6.

21. Karl Kroeber, *Romantic Landscape Vision: Constable and Wordsworth* (Madison: University of Wisconsin Press, 1975), pp. 3–28.

22. Ann Bermingham, *Landscape and Ideology: The English Rustic Tradition, 1740–1860* (Berkeley: University of California Press, 1986), p. 219.

23. James Twitchell, *Romantic Horizons: Aspects of the Sublime in English Poetry and Painting* (Columbia: University of Missouri Press, 1983).

24. Gustafson's discussion of Tolstoy's treatment of the sky (mainly in his novels rather than in the trilogy) (282 and passim) chimes interestingly with much of this discussion of the English Romantics; his emphasis on the artist's consciousness (see especially the section on "Recollective Consciousness," pp. 277–337) has much in common with them as well.

25. John Constable, *Correspondence*, ed. R. Beckett, L. Parris, C. Shields, and I. Fleming-Williams, 7 vols. (Ipswich, Suffolk, 1962–75), 2: 78.

26. Joseph Bradley, *Muzhik and Muscovite: Urbanization in Late Imperial Russia* (Berkeley: University of California Press, 1985), p. 26.

27. Konstantin Bazarov, *Landscape Painting* (London: Octopus Books, 1981), p. 150. Kroeber observed the same order of development in English Romanticism: "poets [. . .], more adventurously than painters of the time, explored interactions between the mind and nature" (59). The time lag between Wordsworth's *Prelude* and Constable's mature landscapes is roughly twenty years, while Levitan's *Vladimirka* postdates the publication of *Childhood* by precisely forty years. I can offer no explanation for this phenomenon as yet, and have found no evidence to suggest a direct link between the British and the Russian artists, or between the Russian wanderers' interest in the landscape and the prose landscapes of such writers as Tolstoy or Turgenev. By contrast, Constable, Turner, et al. knew the poets well and sometimes used poetry as captions for their paintings at exhibitions—cf. Malcolm Cormack, *Constable* (Oxford: Phaidon Books, 1978), p. 190.

28. See Konstantin Paustovskii, "Isaak Levitan," in *Sobrannye sochineniia*, vol. 3: *Povesti* (Moscow, 1982), pp. 530–49; cited by volume and page hereafter. It may be added that the chronicle of Levitan's life in the volume of his *Letters* offers a more complex and slightly less horrific version of these events in Isaak Levitan, *Pis'ma. Dokumenty. Vospominaniia* (Moscow: Iskusstvo, 1956), pp. 23–24.

29. Once by hanging and once by shooting (Chekhov, *Letters*, I: 106–107, cited by Prytkov in *Chekhov i Levitan* [Moscow, 1946], p. 6; Levitan, letter to Dr. Langovoi, July 13, 1895, held by Manuscript Division of Tretiakov Gallery, cited by Prytkov, pp. 32–33; and *Letters*, pp. 304 [1885], 311 [1895]).

30. These details are drawn from the memoirs of Kuvshinnikova, Levitan's mistress, who was with him on the day he first stumbled on and sketched this scene (*Letters*, pp. 170–71).

31. Like Constable, Levitan includes a concealed temporal dimension in his painting by choosing a scene with historical significance: his subject here is the road which political prisoners were forced to travel en route to Siberian exile or hard labor. Thus the scene was habitually interpreted by Soviet critics as a social commentary, since Russia's revolutionaries were deemed to constitute her "bright future," her new horizons.

32. Julia Kristeva, *The Kristeva Reader*, ed. Toril Moi (New York: Columbia University Press, 1983).

33. Wachtel, *The Battle for Childhood*, p. 227, n. 28: "That the decision to describe childhood in negative terms was part of a specific ideological stance can be seen in the case of at least one famous 'nihilist,' the mathematician S. V. Kovalevskaia. [. . .] I, of course, would interpret Kovalevskaia's tendency to remember the negative aspects of her childhood not in terms of her tendency to 'self-dramatization' [as her biographer did—P.C.], but rather as an expression of her desire to repudiate her gentry past and the myths associated with it." Here, the critic's unwillingness to add gender to this picture prevents his giving a more accurate sense of Kovalevskaia's place in the Russian literary tradition.

34. At least, she is not physically lost to the child. Their correspondence reveals, however, that she largely yielded to her husband in questions of John's education and career, although she seems to have been more inclined to support his artistic ambitions than her husband ever was. This would serve as a neat illustration of the Lacanian scenario, where the powerful father intervenes to break up the closeness of mother and child and insist on his own primacy in the family group. Thus, Constable lost his mother not literally but figuratively.

FIVE

Modernism vs. Populism in Fin de Siècle *Ukrainian Literature*

A Case of Gender Conflict

SOLOMEA PAVLYCHKO

Marking an Epoch

THE CHARACTER OF the Ukrainian *fin de siècle*, perhaps the most interesting period in the national culture, has never been thoroughly analyzed. This is a key period for understanding many of the problems that arose in the twentieth century, above all the problem of Ukrainian modernism. I use the term "modernism" to delineate the attempt at aesthetic and stylistic modernization of Ukrainian artistic culture around the turn of the century. This attempt polemicized with the populist model which had taken shape along with the literature of the written popular Ukrainian language, and which by the end of the nineteenth century was established as a complete artistic system.[1] Among the challengers of populism, I will highlight two figures whose names are connected with revolutionary changes in Ukrainian literature at the end of the nineteenth century: Lesia Ukraïnka (1871–1913) and Ol'ha Kobylians'ka (1863–1942).

The modernist opposition to populism at the turn of the twentieth century was the first attempt to move away from the dominance of that cultural norm. The discussion it evoked slowly grew into a deep conflict, not between generations of artists, but rather between artistic convictions. Moreover, the conflict was marked by gender: it is no accident that it was the women writers, Ukraïnka and Kobylians'ka, who attempted to bring down the dominant ideology in the sphere of culture. Their opponents—who met modernism, intellectualism, and European-ism with caution, prejudice, or outright hostility—were almost exclusively men. Ukraïnka and Kobylians'ka enriched their culture both aesthetically and politically, and the last aspect should be especially emphasized. The linguistically eccentric letters of Lesia Ukraïnka and the stylistically brilliant stories of Ol'ha Kobylians'ka reveal a process of radical redefinition of self in protest against patriarchal culture. And although the conflict was painful, and technically the "modernists" were defeated, it nonetheless testified to a certain maturity of Ukrainian culture, the complexity of its discourse, and the polyphonic nature of its artistic thought. Indeed, the anti-populist ideology and the new artistic aesthetic of the end of the nineteenth century were not marginal phenomena from the point of view of the next one hundred years. Analogous attempts were made in the 1920s, 1940s, and 1960s, each carrying with it the imprint of a corresponding stage of literary development. One might say, paraphrasing Jacques Derrida, that the marginal appeared to be central in Ukrainian literature of the period.

In autumn of 1898, nationally minded Ukrainian intellectuals marked the celebration of the 100th anniversary of Ivan Kotliarevs'kyi's epic poem "Eneïda," the first literary work in modern Ukrainian, and of twenty-five years of scholarly and literary activity by the literary patriarch Dr. Ivan Franko. The tone of the jubilee celebrations in Kiev (in eastern Ukraine, under Russian subjugation) and L'viv (in western Ukraine, then part of the Austro-Hungarian Empire) showed the extent to which Ukrainian literature at the time was dominated by a conceptual model that can be called "traditional-populist." Franko himself envisioned artistic creation as a workaday routine, ennobled by the writer's sense of obligation and concern with the topics of the day. The major function of the literature of a divided and socially underdeveloped people—a people without its own state—had to be in that literature's service to the people, in assertion of that people's national and human rights.

It would be a misinterpretation to view populism as a monolithic phenomenon. It was a system or hierarchy of styles, a system of views with many individual models, a system inclined to development and modification. On the level of artistic forms and styles, populism prescribed

> a particular gravitation toward traditional, old, or autonomous artistic structures (the baroque, burlesque), toward the active production—with the goal of self-preservation—of a romantic-populist ideology, toward the absorption and strengthening of didactic and ethnographic forms of creativity, and toward the use of conversational (chiefly low-style) language and not the written literary language, etc. (Hundorova and Shumylo, 55)

This pseudo-explicit and pseudo-realistic expression was actually superficial and always accompanied by mythmaking. Populism is not only patriarchal (its deepest characteristic) but also mytho-patriarchal. For example, the root of Panteleimon Kulish's populism lay in the idealistic myth of the community, the folk, the "national" individual (soul), and, of course, the national woman. The patriarchal system was completed and secured precisely "with the help of an ideal female creature" (Hundorova, 16), in a series of impersonal, romantic female figures, the first of which was Kvitka-Osnov'ianenko's Marusia. Populism was constructed "in the formation of a culture (as of a cult) with the aid of mythologizing thinking" (ibid.).

At the turn of the century, however, new currents were flourishing in the European literatures. In Ukraine, especially in the western region of Galicia, Czech and Polish "modernism" was spreading. Gerhart Hauptmann, Maurice Maeterlinck, Arthur Schnitzler, and Anatole France (to name just a few) were increasingly popular. Therefore, an acute question of choice faced every aspiring Ukrainian writer. On the one hand, populism advocated service to the people, however one understood "the people," be it the peasant class, or everyone who worked, or the whole nation. On the other hand, writers were devoted to art and culture. The most cultured and most inclined toward aesthetic search understood that populism as an ideology restricted culture—it was ruinous for culture. At the same time, populism had an enormous innate appeal. Defending oneself against populism, trying to ignore the political circumstances of one's work—particularly when, in the East, it was illegal to write in Ukrainian—was not only difficult but absurd. This dilemma produced an ambivalence among Ukrainian writers, a constant internal doubt which was only natural on both sides of the debate.

————

ONE OF THE FIRST SIGNS of literary change was Lesia Ukraïnka's address in late 1899 at the Kiev Literary Society (Kyïvs'ke literaturne tovarystvo), "Ukrainian Writers in Bukovyna" ("Malorusskie pisateli na Bukovine"). Ukraïnka was twenty-eight, but since her literary debut at thirteen she had acquired considerable authority. Dr. Ivan Franko himself (in his role as literary arbiter and judge) had analyzed and praised her work in a long article the year before. She was the Wunderkind of Ukrainian culture, daughter of the writer and feminist Olena Pchilka and niece of the political émigré Mykhailo Drahomanov. Ukraïnka's writing defended the Europeanization of Ukrainian culture and advocated a broad program of translation from other languages and integration of European values into Ukrainian spiritual life. Her speech in 1899 congratulated Ol'ha Kobylians'ka, among other writers of a new generation and a new aesthetic. Ukraïnka not only evaluated Kobylians'ka's works positively; she also unequivocally alluded to the restrictions of populism, using the controversial word "modern."

Ol'ha Kobylians'ka was the first in Ukrainian literature to write about the intelligentsia for the intelligentsia, in a completely new psychological style. She was eight years older than Lesia Ukraïnka, though she began publishing later. In 1899 Kobylians'ka was the author of two long feminist stories and several short stories, including the controversial "Valse mélancolique." From their first appearance, her works were variously perceived. Their reception and the polemics around them testify to the cultural conflict which marked the Ukrainian *fin de siècle.*

"Modernism" that did not aspire to destroy the deep patriarchal cultural canon and its idealizing mythology remained on the level of superficial aesthetic experiments and applied itself fully only to the modernization of populism. The evolution of Hnat Khotkevich, who made his debut in 1898, or the silence of Vasyl' Stefanyk from the beginning of this century, ran along these very lines. It was instead the women—Ukraïnka and Kobylians'ka—who rose up not only against the formal characteristics of populism, but also against the patriarchal model of culture which underlay those characteristics.

This was not a mere intellectual exercise. Ukraïnka and Kobylians'ka acutely sensed the neglect accorded them in comparison with men. The structure of society foresaw no place for them, they had no chance at a formal career, traditional marriage did not attract them, and thus, without anything, they had nothing to lose. Expanses of freedom opened beyond the bounds of social structure—intellectual freedom based on education and an orientation toward Europe, creative freedom centered on the priority of art, freedom of political thought, and, finally, the ideals of personal freedom and feminist liberation, in contrast to women's general lack of rights in society.

Conflicted Reception

Although Lesia Ukraïnka and Ol'ha Kobylians'ka fundamentally valued intellectual knowledge, neither was able to obtain a systematic education, and each had to learn by herself. Both suffered terribly from the inadequacy of their formal education and regretted the lack of a university education, though they were extremely learned for the time. Both judged themselves rigorously and noted that the lack of regular criticism was a great defect of Ukrainian literature. Both had complex relationships with their milieux. This often resulted in unjust condemnation of Kobylians'ka and silence toward Lesia Ukraïnka, and both women faced a lack of understanding and were later canonized on the basis of lesser works. Both had unhappy personal lives and suffered terrible illnesses, but neither was afraid to challenge social norms in life as well as in literature: Lesia Ukraïnka lived for some time in a common-law relationship (with Klymentii Kvitka), while Ol'ha Kobylians'ka, after a long, painful affair with Osyp Makovei, never married.

In literature, both writers emphasized professionalism and condemned dilettantism, amateurishness, and lack of literary technique. In poetry, Ukraïnka most valued a command of technique. The "Westernizing" of Kiev's younger generation was for her the principal sign of this professionalism. She considered herself part of it, and she was very much its chief ideologue. Kobylians'ka valued technique and style in prose above all. The two writers loved each other's artistry and were well aware of their exceptional place in the Ukrainian literary tradition. Ukraïnka wrote to Kobylians'ka at the beginning of their friendship, "You are an artist. In our public this is not valued very highly, but I love it above all. Es lebe die Kunst!"[2] (Ukraïnka 1970, 516). "Artistry," "art," *Kunst* were watchwords signifying opposition, and opening onto a future of deep communion.

The place of Ol'ha Kobylians'ka as the leader of a new school of Ukrainian literature at the turn of the century is completely assured, but Lesia Ukraïnka stands, as it were, outside movements and schools. She is the third cult figure in Ukrainian literature—after Shevchenko and Franko—because of her poetry, mainly that part of it which corresponds to Franko's ideal of a poetry of struggle, or, to paraphrase the poet herself, "word-armament." However, aside from the politically programmatic and patriotic poetry, her legacy also included philosophical dramas, which she considered the most important part of her oeuvre, as well as prose, essays, and translations, which she worked on throughout her life and often considered more significant than her own poetry.

Translations (of works by Heine, Hauptmann, Byron, and Polish and Russian authors) played a special role in Lesia Ukraïnka's system of values. They served to broaden the narrow framework of Ukrainian culture and gave an alternative to populism, which sought its basis solely in internal cultural tradition. When

Ukraïnka was only eighteen, she wrote to her uncle Mykhailo Drahomanov, a political émigré who decisively influenced her Europeanism.

> Europeanism has recently begun to spread among young Kievans: they are beginning to learn European languages and are getting interested in European literature. Proof of this might be that we (the young people) have conceived a plan of publishing a whole series of translations of the best works of European and Russian authors. (Ukraïnka 1970, 97–98)

Under Drahomanov's influence, Ukraïnka developed broad democratic views on culture, social order, and nationality. She was an intellectual and cosmopolitan, impatient with provinciality or restrictions of culture. She saw no place for herself among the Ukrainophilic, nationalist, populist intelligentsia. Correspondingly, the populists viewed her with suspicion. She wrote about this to Drahomanov:

> It was in vain that they reproached me for cosmopolitanism in this affair; my cosmopolitanism stays with me, and the patriotism of the nationalists remains with them, and that's the end of it. Perhaps I will indeed suddenly turn out to be a traitor—then I will be very happy. (1970, 244)

Lesia Ukraïnka traveled a great deal, mainly in western Europe, from one doctor to another, seeking treatment for tuberculosis first of the bones and joints, then of the lungs. Her first encounter with western Europe in 1891 had an enormous effect on her.

> My first impression was as if I had arrived in some different world—a better and freer world.
> Now it will be even more difficult in my own country than it was before. I am ashamed that we are so enslaved, that we are in chains and sleep in them peacefully. Thus did I awake, and it is difficult for me, and sorrowful, and painful. (1970, 136)

In contrast to Ukraïnka, who lived under Russian subjugation, Ol'ha Kobylians'ka had grown up in Europe. Her homeland was southern Bukovyna, part of the Austro-Hungarian Empire. However, this part of Ukraine was cut off not only from the cultural centers of Europe, but even from the cultured Ukrainian region of Galicia, with L'viv at its center. Kobylians'ka had no opportunity to travel, and this added to her sense of isolation. She was raised in a German environment, which deeply influenced her creative work. Her first short stories from the early 1880s (still unpublished) and the intimate "Diary" were all written in German. The first drafts of her novels *A Person* (*Liudyna*; written 1886 and published 1894) and *The Tsarevna* (*Tsarivna*; written 1888–93 and published 1895) were also written in German. The Ukrainian versions are filled with German quotations, epigraphs, and imagery, and are inspired by German literature, in particular by the ideas of Friedrich Nietzsche.

Kobylians'ka came by her native Ukrainian with difficulty at the beginning of her literary career. Therefore, no Ukrainian critic would refrain from reproaching her for her dependence on German culture—at best with respect to language, and at worst with respect to thematics, ideology, and psychology. Ukraïnka alone saw this trait not as a shortcoming but as an advantage. When the two writers began to correspond in May 1899, Ukraïnka noted in her first letter to Kobylians'ka:

> the Galician critics reprimand you on account of Germany, but I think that your salvation was in this Germany. It led you to recognize *world* literature, it transported you out into the broader world of ideas and art—this simply leaps out at one, when one compares your writing with that of the majority of Galicians. . . .
>
> It is a good thing that you came to our literature through the German school, and not through the Galician-Polish one. . . . It does not matter that you learned our literary language late—instead, you *learned* it, while the others straight away *thought that they knew*. (1970, 482–83)

Another letter to Kobylians'ka elaborates: "If, for example, Dr. Pavlyk knew that I praise you for your Germanism and urge you on to [read] Russian things, then he would blow up at me! So I think I will tell him—I like to scandalize my compatriots from time to time" (ibid., 486). She kept her word and wrote to Mykhailo Pavlyk, the well-known publicist, maintaining that Kobylians'ka's work was saved rather than destroyed by "the Germanism." She compared Kobylians'ka with "patriot-writers, who write for patriot-readers" to the patriots' detriment, adding, "think about it yourself: who is exotic? She with her Germanism, or they with their 'Ukrainianism?'" (490).

As Kobylians'ka's critics continued to harp on her "Germanism," some decided that she could not be called a Ukrainian writer. A broad dialogue about what was appropriate and inappropriate for Ukrainian literature—whether only folk life could be the subject of Ukrainian literature, or whether the life of the intelligentsia was also a suitable subject—entwined with the polemic that developed over Kobylians'ka's story "Valse mélancolique" in 1897 and 1898. The three heroines of that story were called "creations of purely European culture" (*Ol'ha Kobylians'ka,* 42), too European to be wholly adequate for Ukrainian literature. Kobylians'ka could be pleased with such accusations of "foreignness" and un-Ukrainianness and wrote: "Preserve me, O Lord, from being a Galician-Ruthenian author" (5: 324). But she mourned that even her defenders seemed to consider that "my Ruthenianness in my writings is completely German" (5: 338).

For a while Kobylians'ka maintained cordial relations with Osyp Makovei, the literary critic, publisher, and populist prose writer; this grew into love around 1897. After his marriage, the relationship broke off. His wife was beautiful, well-off, and traditional in her views—as befitted an important publisher and "Galician-Ruthenian author." Over the course of several years Makovei played the role of teacher and confidant for Kobylians'ka, although they were complete antipodes in their work. She subconsciously understood this and was often harshly critical of his writings. The few letters that have survived, and Makovei's articles on Kobylians'ka, give the impression that he feigned understanding rather than actually comprehending her. The affair was doomed by the fact that she, as a writer and as a person, fit poorly into the dominant cultural norms he represented. However, in 1898 they were still close friends, and it was to him that Kobylians'ka confided her indignation over unjust criticism of her first publications. Makovei repeated her comments on her own work almost verbatim in his positive article about her. The affirmative tone of his article is unique for the time; other critics tended to approach Kobylians'ka's work with prejudice: "Narration in the form of a maiden's diary for more than 400 pages—Brrr! I thought to myself, looking through this book" (Hrushevs'kyi 1898a, 174, reviewing *The Tsarevna*). Serhii Iefremov's colossal article in *Kievskaia starina* in 1902, "In Search of a New Beauty" ("V poiskakh novoi krasoty),[3] stands out as the most aggressive denial of Kobylians'ka's literary persona, but it was not unique in its condemnation.

> The fact of the matter is that in all areas of intellectual life we have so few workers [. . .], and every purposeful waste, even if it is of one's own personal powers, is not simply recklessness and carelessness, but already a crime against our native country and people. (119)
>
> Mrs. Kobylians'ka [. . .] has created a dangerous, anti-social tendency in literature which will lead weaker minds astray and which will not pass, indeed is *not* passing without leaving its mark. (120)

Besides Makovei, at this stage (before appearance of *The Land* [*Zemlia*]) only Lesia Ukraïnka understood and unconditionally supported Kobylians'ka, though she did criticize her on particular points. Ukraïnka was later somewhat frightened by the new tendency toward "rusticism" in Kobylians'ka's works at the beginning of the twentieth century, but she came to see that this "rusticism" did not mean glorification of the rural village, but rather its demystification. In fact, Ukraïnka so strongly identified with Kobylians'ka's position that her health suffered after she read Iefremov's brutal rejection of Kobylians'ka—an indirect criticism of Ukraïnka's support for the Bukovyna writers and the new direction in Ukrainian literature which they represented.

Even so virulent a populist as Iefremov would think twice before criticizing Lesia Ukraïnka more directly. Franko had canonized her in an article published in 1899, setting her poetry next to Shevchenko's. However, he mentioned only the poetry that corresponded to his ideals, and he used telling terms of gender:

> reading the soft and neurotic or coldly pedantic writings of the contemporary young Ukrainians and comparing them with those works that are lively, powerful, and daring, moreover comparing them with the likes of the simple, sincere words of Lesia Ukraïnka, one involuntarily thinks that this sickly and weak young lady is perhaps the only man in all of modern Ukraine. (Franko 1981, 31: 270–71)

The "writings of the young Ukrainians" of course refer to "modernism" or the "new school," which are never directly named, although the discussion assigns them two possible roles—namely, the neurotic and the esoteric.

Franko dismissed Lesia Ukraïnka's dramas in a single line, asserting that they did not measure up to her talent. Incontestably, they did not fit the concept of "word-armament." However, Ukraïnka considered these dramas the center of her creative work. Critics either treated them negatively, as with *The Blue Rose* (*Blakytna troianda*), or paid no attention to them. Ukraïnka commented much later, in 1911: "my dramas belong precisely to those things that are 'lauded, but not read' (Rusova, for example, read nothing that she was reviewing)" (Ukraïnka 1970, 847 and 850). Franko, as I have already mentioned, did not even consider it necessary to review them.

Critical reception of Lesia Ukraïnka and Ol'ha Kobylians'ka thus unequivocally alludes to the conflict between two outlooks and artistic principles. Populism meant Ukrainianness, patriotism, glorification of the village, isolation of culture, conservatism, realism, and depiction of folk life, while modernism, correspondingly, meant Europeanism, cosmopolitanism, intellectualism, openness of culture, democratism, aestheticism, and depiction of the life of the intelligentsia. However, there was still another crucial opposition between these two paradigms—feminine and masculine, the feminist and the patriarchal. All the participants in the literary discourse of the time were completely aware of this.

Feminism

Feminist ideas began to spread in Galicia in the 1870s. The need for equal rights for women became part of the complex of new, revolutionary ideas that Natalia Kobryns'ka (1855–1920) set out in the title of her well-known short story "The Spirit of Time" ("Dukh chasu"), written in Vienna in 1883. Kobryns'ka was in the first group of Galician intellectuals that arrived in the Austrian capital to study at the university, or simply to imbibe the European spirit, culture, and new areas of scholarly inquiry.

Kobryns'ka was the central figure in the Ukrainian feminist movement of the time. It was she who founded the Society of Ruthenian Women (Tovarystvo rus'kykh zhinok) in Stanislav (present-day Ivano-Frankivs'k) in 1884, with the help of Franko and Pavlyk. Immediately after this she began preparation of an almanac, which she published with Olena Pchilka (Lesia Ukraïnka's mother) in 1887 as *First Garland* (*Pershyi vinok*). Franko and Pavlyk warmly greeted its appearance in the press.

The pieces by the editors are of the greatest interest among the essays, articles, and belletristic works by and about women in *First Garland*. There is a set of articles by Kobryns'ka on the woman's question and a novel by Pchilka, *Women Friends* (*Tovaryshky*), written à la Turgenev, about two young Ukrainian women studying at the Faculty of Medicine at the University of Zurich—a subject the author defined as "about the emancipation of womanhood" (Kobryns'ka and Pchilka, 358). A pair of poems by Lesia Ukraïnka, who was sixteen at the time, found their way into the almanac. However, a story by Kobylians'ka, "Lorelei" ("L'oreliai"), the first variant of *The Tsarevna*, was kept out on the advice of Franko, who assisted in preparation of the almanac.

The feminist ideas of Lesia Ukraïnka did not always lie on the surface, as was the case with Kobryns'ka, or even with Kobylians'ka's early work. Two main positions emerge in Ukraïnka's views: one is that feminism seems natural and needs no supporting proof; the other, that the position of women is miserable and demands struggle. All the figures in Ukraïnka's plays—from Liubov in *The Blue Rose* to Oderzhyma, Boiarynia, Kassandra, and Mavka—are variations on the theme of women's tragedy: betrayal in relationships with women, women's solitude, women's patriotism that is sometimes deeper than men's, and dramatic feminine devotion to truth. (See Weretelnyk for further discussion of this subject.)

The first Ukrainian feminist critical article was written by Lesia Ukraïnka. Her "New Vistas and Old Shadows ('The New Woman of Western European Belles-Lettres')" ("Novye perspektivy i starye teni ['Novaia zhenshchina zapadnoevropeiskoi belletristiki']") was published in 1900, in Russian, in the Saint Petersburg journal *Life* [*Zhizn'*]. At the same time, she expressed skepticism about the exclusively feminine literary publications that Kobryns'ka propagated. Ukraïnka did not support this sort of "separatism."

The works of Ukraïnka and Kobylians'ka unequivocally show that they both saw and strove to represent the deep gender conflict in society. It is interesting that one of Ukraïnka's first letters to Kobylians'ka discussed Galician men, with whom "one cannot . . . feel free. . . . Among the Galicians I sense some strange, difficult relationship toward women: they all either look down at us from on high, or else look up to us from below, but for them to look at us as equals is impossible!" (486). Ukraïnka was not surprised that "Galician minds" had not influenced Kobylians'ka, and that Kobylians'ka did not trust the "Galician progressives" when they expressed their empathy for woman.

Of course, she was right. The Galician progressives were never constant or even sincere in their support of the feminist movement. At a deeper level there remained a concealed fear of the subversiveness of feminism, a desire to set the movement within the bounds of "decency," to control it with an authoritative male hand; this, in fact, is to some degree what Franko, Pavlyk, Makovei, and others managed to do. Makovei betrayed a deep fear of feminism: in an unpublished letter to Kobylians'ka, trying to give reasons for their separation and to soften it, he writes:

> In 1950 some savage feminist will write in your biography, "Osyp Makovei played an integral role in Kobylians'ka's life. This blockhead thought that he could satisfy a woman with friendship. He even wrote something about her—and completely favorable—and he was interested in her work, but nonetheless when his dull head could not lift itself to higher attestations of friendship, he left such a burning love behind for . . ." (this will be published in 1950). . . .
>
> Where are you, O feminist of 1950? If only I knew where you're prowling in the world and whether you're already here, I would find you and give you a good drubbing straightaway. (Makovei)

The early works of Kobylians'ka that frightened men, programmatically feminist (*A Person, The Tsarevna*) and inherently feminist ("Uncultured," "Nature," "Valse mélancolique"), impressed Lesia Ukraïnka. Few understood them as well as she did. Her own short story "Pity" ("Zhal'"), dated in 1890 on the basis of correspondence, was in its way a variation on the same plot as *The Tsarevna*, only more severe and more realistic. Ukraïnka's heroine, the companion of a rich aristocratic woman, does not happily marry the son of her mistress, but instead kills the aristocrat because of her cruelty.

Kobylians'ka's *A Person* was dedicated to Kobryns'ka and was undoubtedly written under the influence of her "Spirit of the Time." In 1894 Kobylians'ka was one of the founders of the Society of Ruthenian Women in Bukovyna (Tovarystvo rus'kykh zhinok na Bukovyni). Her address "On the Idea of the Women's Movement" ("Deshcho pro ideiu zhinochoho rukhu") of that same year was published by Pavlyk. Her first two long stories, *A Person* and *The Tsarevna*, treat a feminist subject. The center of attention in both is a woman smothered by middle-class life who enunciates feminist ideas and fights for her human rights. The first work narrates the defeat of such a woman, but the second shows her victory—in the end she marries for love and even becomes a writer.

Ol'ha Kobylians'ka's heroines are intelligent people with principled convictions gained from books. Reading is their only consolation in the oppressive petty-bourgeois atmosphere of the provincial middle class. They prefer to read Western, German literature, and trust books and book learning more than their own surroundings, which provide neither freedom, nor logic, nor intelligence. All this crystallizes in the maxim "A free person with intelligence—this is my ideal" (Kobylians'ka, 1: 227).

Natalka in *The Tsarevna* not only reads, she also tries to write. At first she sets out her thoughts on the rights of women, then she begins to write artistic works. Intellectual experiences take on an emotional life: "having read J. Stuart Mill, I cried. From that point on I read with doubled intensity. The realization of my low level of education weighed on me and humiliated me greatly. I set for myself the goal of somehow gaining a higher education" (Kobylians'ka, 1: 123).

In the beginning, Kobylians'ka set forth feminist ideas in a fairly linear fashion. Her stories, especially *The Tsarevna*, seem in parts more like essays than works of belles-lettres. Natalka's life in *The Tsarevna* also outlines a feminist position. She leaves her relatives, supports herself independently by serving as the companion of a rich widow, and sews on consignment. She refuses to marry someone she does not love—and even someone she does love.

Kobylians'ka was well aware of the originality of her female protagonists: "my merit lies in the fact that . . . side by side with the contemporary Marusyas, Hanusyas, and Katrusyas can stand women of European character, who are not especially Galician-Ruthenian" (5: 322). Beside this, her women lacked the romantic, populist impersonality of female characters in masculine populist literature. Kobylians'ka transformed Nietzscheanism in a rather original way, portraying strong women and feeble men. In her first two novels all the men, excepting Marko, are negative characters.

The best of these male characters, the student-medic in *A Person*, is "a boring pedant, . . . spiteful" (1: 75), and moreover inclined to alcoholism. Another, a forester, is an uneducated he-man who lives by his basest instincts. In *The Tsarevna* the socialist Oriadyn "befouled himself with his impotence" (1: 181). Although Kobylians'ka's male characterizations were less daring than the female ones, and more schematic, the very attempt to show a man who was inadequate in his social role was a serious challenge to the patriarchal norm.

One further point: The women protagonists of both Ol'ha Kobylians'ka and Lesia Ukraïnka share a certain pattern of behavior that is peculiar to them. They strive for true, free love, but on the other hand they fear it; they want—and then do not want—to love. Liubov flees from Orest in *The Blue Rose*; Natalka pushes Oriadyn away in *The Tsarevna*. This is a fundamental fear of any relationship with a man, a terror of patriarchal confines. The model repeats countless times, reflecting a subconscious terror—not only of the characters, but also of their authors—in the face of inequitable relationships with men. One alternative to this is the relationship between women described in "Valse mélancolique," discussed below.

Analyzing Kobylians'ka's work in her address "Ukrainian Writers in Buko-vyna," Lesia Ukraïnka indicated: "Subsequently, she significantly cooled to femi-nism, perhaps because it became for her an 'outlived moment,' and the idea itself of women's equal rights appeared to her to need no theoretical proofs" (Ukraïnka 1977, 8: 69). Kobylians'ka herself came to consider her first works programmatic even earlier, in 1895. "For me the woman's question is a point that has been over-come, and from now on I won't even write programmatic novels on the order of *A Person*, for example. Also, I do not want to serve two masters, that is, an agenda and poetry" (Kobylians'ka, 5: 283).

Posing the question in this way did not mean a denial of feminism, but rather its deeper aesthetic achievement. Literature as art was broader than any single con-cept, whether populist or feminist, and it could not be solely the vessel of that concept. Nonetheless, the feminist idea remained one of the underpinnings of anti-populism.

Anti-Populism

In one of her formulations of her literary role and calling, Lesia Ukraïnka wrote: "I cannot give up the thought that my work, or, as it were, 'calling,'[4] is Ukrainian literature and that it is free in every sense of the word; well, such a 'call-ing' can bid one go far" (1970, 381).

"Liberty" (*volia*) represented a challenge to aesthetic canons, stylistic recipes, cultural isolation, national oppression, political despotism, and the like. Populism was a form of dependence, limitation, canonicity. Anti-populism was the logical consequence of Europeanism, intellectualism, high culture, and a rational rather than mythologizing view of Ukrainian reality. Thus, liberty, which included the idea of equality between the sexes, necessarily came into conflict with populism at every level. However, Ukrainian critics almost never mentioned Ukraïnka's acute denial of literary ethnographism or national theater, nor Kobylians'ka's wearisome declarations about the unpleasant, exasperating impotence of her native people.

These views were too out of step with the accepted images of the self-consciousness and self-valuation of the Ukrainian writer.

Lesia Ukraïnka was interested in folklore and collected folk songs, like every Ukrainian writer of her time without exception. However, her view of them was unique. She did not transfer ethnographic leanings into her original writings, but rather looked at ethnography from the point of view of literature: "I cannot help but look at folk poetry through a 'literary' lens, and perhaps it is because of this that I love our lyric songs so much" (1970, 170).

Ukraïnka sharply challenged excessive populism in culture, whether in the novels of Nechui-Levyts'kyi or in the theatrical works of Sadovs'kyi and Saksahans'kyi: "For God's sake, don't judge us on the novels of Nechui, for you would have to condemn us completely without cause. At the very least, I do not know a single intelligent person in Nechui's novels. If one were to believe him, than all of Ukraine would appear to be a dunce" (1970, 156).

Ukraïnka emerged as a playwright largely as a result of her dislike of folk theater. She liked various styles of contemporary European theater (Ibsen, Hauptmann, Maeterlinck), and she translated and popularized these authors. Her rejection of populist theater came to some extent from her mother, who wrote to her daughter in 1894–95: "Those deadheads have to think something up, because the public is beginning to comprehend that Sadovs'kyi and *tutti quanti* are simply stupid, and the public is already too annoyed by their lambskin hats to applaud" (1970, 286; see also 308).

Olena Pchilka was nonetheless an ambivalent figure. On the one hand, she conjured up resonantly populist pseudonyms for herself and her daughter.[5] On the other hand, she was an educated person with a European orientation, and a feminist. She saw education and knowledge as indispensable for better service to the people—for the modernization of populism. At the same time it is clear from the example of her views on populist theater, among others, that for Pchilka education modeled cultural behavior.

Returning to Lesia Ukraïnka, we note one of her letters to Drahomanov:

> Someone also complained that I hide from "folk" themes while I compose with folk language, that I climb into "belles-lettres land" and "intellectualize." But here the whole problem is certainly that I understand the words "populism," "literariness," and "intelligentsia" differently than my critics do.... Here in Ukraine these eternal polemics will never end, and how can they end when the combatants do not understand each other? (1970, 123)

Reading Ol'ha Kobylians'ka for the first time, Ukraïnka understood that she had found an interlocutor who posed an even more decisive and uncompromising challenge to traditionally populist views. She was not mistaken. Kobylians'ka, steeped in Nietzscheanism, formulated her disenchantment with the Ukrainian folk (*narod*), which was bereft of inner energy and power for struggle. A strong heroine would want to belong to a strong people. However, her people were oppressed, colonized, resigned. For this reason Natalka in *The Tsarevna* says:

"I hate . . . the uniform, mournful-sick smile on the pale faces of our people. We have all grown weak from sorrow for the past; and the sorrowful melody that reverberates in our souls and that we understand so well has lulled all of our energies into impotence. Isn't it so? Ah," she finished sadly, "it is so. I too am a daughter of the Ruthenian-Ukrainian people." (Kobylians'ka, 1: 215)

This feebleness of the folk—"a melancholy sadness, which is inscribed in everything, and upon which this unfortunate people reminisces" (1: 401)—wells up in some of Kobylians'ka's characters, as in the heroine of *Nature*. The other side of this weakness is the heroine's inherent sexual urge toward power. She loves physical power, although she herself does not exercise it, and reduces it almost to a cult: "Physical strength and beauty meant a lot to her, and although she rarely 'loved' anyone, all the same, handsome, strong men were pleasant to her" (1: 411). The cult of power, of course, does not sit well with feminism, but the discovery of physical pleasure, about which we will speak below, does.

The Land (1902), Kobylians'ka's central work, has often been considered a return to the populist theme and a critique of private ownership, since it depicts brother killing brother over land. Land appears as a terrible power which enserfs and brutalizes people. Culture exists at the opposite pole. Only landless Anna has some chance of breaking free from the land and moving nearer to culture. In this sense she is the main character of the work. However, the all-encompassing, murderous dependence on the land, characteristic for all the other characters of the novel, destroys her life too.

In terms of populist culture, *The Land* was a revolutionary work. First, it showed that life in the village lacked harmony, and so argued against the patriarchal, populist myth of the entire culture. The work demystified and demythologized critical understandings that were all sacred to the populist contingent—the ideal nature of the community and the natural person (the Ukrainian villager), the ideal nature of women (mentioned above). Kobylians'ka was the first to assert that the romantic purity of interpersonal relations and family harmony in the village was a myth. Violence, instinct, sexual passion, and incest ruled in the village; neighbors lived in mutual suspicion and ill will, and parental tyranny verged on bestial savagery. Human nature, not constrained or refined by culture, was abominable when human relations were deformed by patriarchal norms.

Sexuality

Beside this, *The Land* is filled with eroticism. It confirms that life in the village has little of the sexual puritanism described by Kvitka-Osnov'ianenko. Ol'ha Kobylians'ka was not only the first psychologist in Ukrainian prose, but also the first to touch upon sexuality as an experience and as a problem. Her heroines are conscious of the human body, sensuality, and physical necessities that might conflict with spiritual needs and intellectual abilities. Thus, Olena Liaufer in *A Person* marries not for love but because of material difficulties, against her feminist principles. However, she chooses a young forester, whose masculine body attracts her.

Interest in the physical side of sensations was motivated largely by feminism. Among the legitimate and organic rights of a woman was the right to satisfaction from a physical relationship with a man. This process in women (becoming aware of one's attraction to another's body, desire for physical contact, and actual sexual contact) was of the utmost interest to Kobylians'ka the psychologist. Feminism challenged male chauvinism by gazing where the populist was afraid to look.

The short story "Nature," written in 1887 in German, published in 1895 in Stuttgart and then in 1897 in Ukrainian, has the first scene of physical love in Ukrainian literature. It plays on a familiar model, with an educated woman from the middle class and a coarse Hutsul[6] who considers his passion a witch's provocation. They differ in class, culture, status—in everything, but they are united by physical attraction, instinct, and nature.

Nature is the first symbol of eroticism in the works of Kobylians'ka. The second such symbol is music, "fettered passion." Quite often music appears as a euphemism for erotically tinged sensation. Music arouses sexual fantasy, which might become a sharp physical sensation of orgasmic character, as in the scene in *A Person* where a Chopin étude, the "Impromptu phantasie," causes an ecstatic state bordering on neurosis. The heroine once heard this music during a confession of love. Then, "it had been a deep-welling force, a powerful, uplifting force that knows no obstacle, which is frightened by nothing, which, while laying down a new road, tears everything from itself and often destroys what laws and custom and time built up with difficulty." Now, the same music recalls that state of being in the heroine:

> The music now snatched up the young girl in its embrace. She began to laugh nervously, quietly, quietly and yet so fully that her entire supple figure trembled. An exclamation broke from her mouth, but she pressed her hands to her face even harder, she ground her teeth together, she wanted to be calm. . . . O, God, calm! . . .
> A little later she lay motionless with her exhausted head against the spine of the divan and moved only to cover her eyes with her hand. (Kobylians'ka, 1: 72)

Music's movement and rhythm, resonating with the vibration of the aroused body, stimulate or substitute for physical love in Kobylians'ka's intellectual heroines: "I drink and become intoxicated by it [music], as by the caresses of a living being, so to speak" (1: 155). Music is often described as a physical partner. The musical background of "Valse mélancolique" unambiguously underlines the sensual nature of the relationships binding the three female protagonists of the story.

The critical reaction—exclusively male—to this aspect of Kobylians'ka's work was predictable. Makovei commented on "Nature" and "Uncultured" with Aesopian language, hinting at what he would not risk discussing: "This is a rather sensitive business, and in our social circles especially one does not talk explicitly about the needs of the flesh" (Makovei 1899, 45). He even gently criticized Kobylians'ka for placing greater emphasis on love than on social freedom for women. Iefremov, the ardent populist, broached the topic of sexuality in his article "In Search of a New Beauty" with all the pathos of the male chauvinist. For him it was all simply "filth," unacceptable in such a serious arena as literature. He cited no convincing example of this "filth"; he only raged. His logic was that the cult of beauty is the cult of love:

> the cult of love turns into a cult . . . of the naked body, of course mainly female. . . . And this, if you please, was inevitable [. . .]: if the *entire* meaning of life is located only in beauty and in sexual love, then sooner or later this beauty and love will hinge on one point—simple sensuality and the most naked pornography. (Iefremov, 110)

Iefremov's analysis is perhaps the sharpest manifestation of the populist's terror when faced with sexuality. His storming indicates the true reason for the hostility that male populist critics displayed toward Kobylians'ka: her extraordinarily open—for Ukrainian literature—depiction of and sensitivity to eroticism.

Lesia Ukraïnka had a completely different, though unpublished, reaction. She liked "Valse mélancolique," "Uncultured," and "The Battle" ("Bytva") best among Kobylians'ka's stories of the 1890s. About "Uncultured" she wrote:

> I did not expect from an Austrian Ruthenian woman such sincerity and the daring with which both character and situations are portrayed. While I read, from time to time I would think: Bravo! Miss Kobylians'ka! Es lebe die Kunst! Es lebe die Freiheit! You must chide your "dobrze wychowani" countrymen,[7] because they have not gotten used to the fact that a woman, even though a writer, could screw up her courage to undertake "such as this."[8] Do not think, though, that I see "such as this" in your "Un-cultured." In my opinion there is nothing untoward in it. (1970, 508)

Mykhailo Mochul's'kyi, in 1907, was perhaps the only critic to acknowledge that "O. Kobylians'ka preaches free love in a very delicate manner, retaining artistic tact" (*Ol'ha Kobylians'ka*, 149).

"Valse mélancolique" was unique in Ukrainian literature for its portrayal of the relationship of three women: Sophia, a pianist, Hannusya, an artist, and Marta, the narrator. Marta refers to each of the others simply as "woman" and idolizes both of them. All three live in an atmosphere of music and painting, isolated from society and ignoring society's norms. However, this short-lived idyll is destroyed when the musician dies, having played her favorite waltz one last time, after learning that her relatives have refused her the money for study at the conservatory in Vienna.

For Kobylians'ka, the story is not about the cruelty of the world, which ultimately serves the dramatic dénouement in the *fin de siécle* style. Rather, the essence of the story is its relationships or, more precisely, the tragic love relationships outside traditional bounds. The musician was disillusioned in her relationship with a man, and she remembers it with hatred. The artist does not even admit the possibility of relationships with men—she sees only humiliation in them. This despair over the spiritual potential of men ("There is a type of love in women . . . which a man will never understand. For him it is too broad to comprehend" [Kobylians'ka, 2: 389]) engenders female separatism. Feelings meant for someone of the opposite sex are expressed to a woman, the only person capable of receiving and valuing them.

It is not surprising, then, to read:

> The artist fell in love with her, as a man would, and almost suffocated her with her sincere feelings, which seemed to the very being of the other one—Sophia—stormy and overly expressed.
>
> But I quietly prayed for her.
>
> Hannusya found new beauty in Sophia every day. She worried over her appearance as she would over a child. She combed her long, silken hair. [. . .] I, for my part, loved her without "conditions." No, I loved them both. (2: 383)

Typical for European culture of the time were elements such as the beauty of youth and of death, thoughts and feelings on the limits of permitted morality, the neurotic sensuality of the heroine, and the sensual nature of the text itself, in the spirit of a Chopin étude. All this set "Valse mélancolique" in the cultural context of the Viennese stories of Arthur Schnitzler or portraits by Gustav Klimt. By virtue of its protagonists' character, its style, and its inherent ideas, "Valse mélancolique" became a manifesto, high point of a new style and a type of artistic thought that was discordant with traditionalist populist thought.

Personal Relations

"Valse mélancolique" was written three years before Ol'ha Kobylians'ka met Lesia Ukraïnka. However, from their correspondence one can trace analogous relations between the two women writers, in mutual sympathies, spiritual closeness, and emotional tension. Unfortunately, aside from a single letter from Kobylians'ka to Ukraïnka, only Ukraïnka's letters to Kobylians'ka have been preserved.

As mentioned above, the correspondence began in May 1899. The initial letters, written in Ukraïnka's typically intense style, treat mainly literary affairs and events. Ukraïnka's style changed significantly after she met Kobylians'ka in the Carpathian Mountains in 1901. Thereafter, her businesslike, amicable tone became emotional and even intimate; this contrasted with her previous letters to Kobylians'ka, and even more with her letters to other people. In the later correspondence an esoteric, idiosyncratic language appeared; one could say that these letters are her most enigmatic works.

All the letters are written in the third person, rather than the first person, and exclusively in the masculine gender. The masculine gender appears primarily in the way Ukraïnka and Kobylians'ka refer to themselves: "someone" and "someone" (*khtos'* for both correspondents), or "someone white" (*khtos' bilyi* for Ukraïnka) and "someone black" (*khtos' chornen'kyi* for Kobylians'ka).[9] This use of the third person can confuse a reader today, but along with the general style it masks quite daring passages and declarations. For example, the phrase "someone loves someone" (*khtos' kohos' liubyt'*), a cipher for "I love you," ends almost all the letters.

Other cliché greetings are used no less frequently: "Liebe, liebste Wunderblume!" ("Dear, dearest wonder-flower").

The homoerotic element in the letters underlines the growth of the writers' professional and personal friendship. On the one hand, the two women considered themselves partners in aesthetic questions, and this partnership was equivalent to opposition to everything propagated by Franko, Makovei, et al. On the other hand, they drew even closer together because both had already experienced personal tragedies in relationships with men.

Lesia Ukraïnka arrived in Chernivtsi in 1901 after a difficult loss. Her friend Serhii Merzhyns'kyi had died of tuberculosis in March. Their affair began in the summer of 1897 in Yalta. From January 1901 until his death, Ukraïnka lived in Minsk, taking care of the dying Merzhyns'kyi's every need. In particular, he did not hesitate to dictate love letters to another woman, Vira Kryzhanivs'ka-Tuchaps'ka. All of this undermined Ukraïnka's health. In May 1901, a relation wrote to Kobylians'ka: "Lesia buried her dear friend; this in and of itself is such a great sorrow. . . . For two months she did not leave the side of the sick man, and he died in her arms. After the burial she suffered a very severe nervous attack" (Ukraïnka 1970, 537). Ukraïnka's relatives hoped that her trip to Bukovyna would help her put the tragedy behind her. Her relationship with Klyment Kvitka was just developing. In the future, she would live with him in a common-law marriage, despite her family's resistance, and later would formally marry him. At this earlier period she still treated him like a good friend and wrote to Kobylians'ka:

> Although someone [i.e., Ukraïnka][10] is now great friends with Mr. Kvitka and has fraternal relations with him, he [Ukraïnka] still cannot talk with him [Kvitka] about every topic, because some topics might irritate Mr. Kvitka, he being a man and nervous, and others might only be understood by a woman, and of the age of someone [Ukraïnka] and also someone [Kobylians'ka], because younger women (happily for them) do not understand everything. (1970, 560)

In 1901 Ol'ha Kobylians'ka broke off relations with Osyp Makovei. In a letter written much later (the only one from her to Ukraïnka that survives), she speaks about the influence of these relations on her life and attitudes toward men:

> She [Kobylians'ka] spent some time with her whole soul on a young man named Ostap Luts'kyi, but she stopped having faith in him. Os(yp) Makovei killed any faith she had in men, and she already has no faith even in Luts'kyi. Makovei himself is miserable. He married a very coarse type. He would like to draw closer to her [Kobylians'ka] again, but she *no longer wants it.* (Ukraïnka 1970, 831)

The meeting in 1901 brought the two women emotionally closer, as the following passages from Ukraïnka's letters unambiguously show:

> *2 August 1901, from Burkut:* And if now both someone [Ukraïnka] and someone [Kobylians'ka] were here, they would go out together on the Cheremosh, as on this dark, very dark night, and they would listen to the gurgling of the water [. . .], and

they would recall silently, not saying a word, all the worst and all the best of their lives. Their views and their hands would meet in the darkness and it would be so very quiet in spite of the river's gurgling . . . and then someone [Ukraïnka] would return to his house already less saddened. (1970, 558)

24 August 1901: . . . someone [Ukraïnka] was nasty and lazy, and did not want to write anyone letters, although he very often thought about someone [Kobylians'ka] and wanted to talk with someone, and most of all wanted to sit down half-undressed on that someone's bed, as someone in a scarf under a comforter who wants partly to sleep, but also partly does not want to sleep, and who has dark eyes with golden sparkles. If only someone knew that someone (white) needed someone to support his soul, because that someone's soul often happens to be quite beaten down. (1970, 560)

5 November (continuing a letter dated 20 October) 1901: Someone [Ukraïnka] now and forever loves someone [Kobylians'ka] likewise and wants to "incline the heavens" to someone, but sometimes he does not know how to write as he would want: a sour stomach, a headache, various superfluous thoughts get in the way. Thus, someone writes so blandly in a way, apathetically, entirely not the way that he thinks about someone, that he loves someone. But if he were now with someone, then he would not need to sit and dab this pen over the paper. Rather, he would lie down next to someone and would make hypnotic gestures at someone, and perhaps would say little, but on the other hand would say more than this incompetent letter. (1970, 573)

19 December 1901 (New Year's Day, 1902, New Style Calendar): Someone [Ukraïnka] would like to kiss someone [Kobylians'ka], and caress someone, say much, and gaze much, and think much. (1970, 582)

20 March 1902: . . . someone loves someone (this is the latest thing). (1970, 610)

3 October 1902, from Kiev: And someone [Ukraïnka] loves someone [Kobylians'ka], and never gets angry at someone, and never got angry, and never will get angry . . . [someone] kisses someone and gazes and so forth, and so forth . . . and still so forth. (1970, 636)

With time the letters become more restrained; however, a unique style remains, where phrases in the spirit of "O, you, my priestess of beauty and purity" sound completely natural. In one of Ukraïnka's last letters to her friend, written in Egypt at the end of 1912, she wrote: "someone and also someone *die gehören zusammen* [belong to each other]. Someone loves someone" (1970, 860). When she died, her mother, Olena Pchilka, wrote to Kobylians'ka, "I know that you not only respected her as a talented writer, but that you *loved* her. She also loved you very much. There truly was some sort of spiritual affinity between you" (1970, 878).

The bisexual affections of the women writers and corresponding depictions of lesbian caresses were not exceptional for early modernist culture. However, Ukraine with its particular circumstances did not, and indeed could not, shelter a bohemian artistic milieu like the Parisian avant-garde salons, where such things were tolerated and embraced. In this way the United States and Britain were similar to Ukraine—for example, Renée Vivien (Pauline Tarn), one of the first lesbian poets of the twentieth century and also one of the first twentieth-century expatriate writers in Paris, could change her whole identity when she came to Paris in 1898 (Annan, 11–22). Nonetheless, the setting and development of these themes in "Valse mélancolique" and the loving correspondence between Lesia Ukraïnka and Ol'ha Kobylians'ka were organic phenomena of their time.

Finale

In 1906, as the political situation in Russia grew especially acute and the tsarist government became more repressive, Lesia Ukraïnka wrote from Kiev to Kobylians'ka:

> Does someone [Kobylians'ka] know that one of his fiercest critics (S. Iefremov) has been in jail (as a "political") since Christmas, and now he has gotten ill with tuberculosis and is in the prison hospital, and they say that things are very bad for him. This fate has overtaken many people, and who knows therefore if this country will ever exist. . . . And still *pendant*: the one (H. Kohtkevych) who was so censured along with you by that critic is now in emigration (also a "political") after all the troubles—this means that now the "idealists" along with the "non-idealists," the "realists" along with the "decadents," the "exotics" along with the "workadays"—have all been made equal. (1970, 774–75)

And in truth, the tsarist regime did not stop to analyze the aesthetic or political divergences of the Ukrainian intellectuals it was persecuting. It was not interested in their dilemma of choice between service and art, nor in the complexes, fears, dreams, and doubts connected with that dilemma.

In 1912 Serhii Iefremov published his first *History of Ukrainian Literature* (*Istoriia ukraïns'koho pys'menstva*), in time to present it to Lesia Ukraïnka. He wrote admiringly of her poetry, but deemed the dramas not worthy of broader analysis. His characterization of Ol'ha Kobylians'ka was somewhat softer in tone, although without substantial revision of his 1902 critique. Later, Iefremov's views came to undergird the socialist canons of the history and theory of Ukrainian literature. However, he himself was arrested in 1929 for anti-Soviet activities and perished in the GULag in 1939.

In 1913 Lesia Ukraïnka died, in terrible pain from tuberculosis in multiple organs. Ol'ha Kobylians'ka lived until 1942, although her literary talent peaked at the turn of the century. By 1910 she had become a cult figure for "Young Muse" (Moloda muza), a group which united the new generations of Ukrainian poets. Franko, who died in 1916, fought against them with all the might of his polemical pathos.

Ukrainian feminism, which had such vocal resonance at the end of the nineteenth century, had no champions during the modernist experiments of the 1910s and 1920s. There were no writers who proposed to analyze the relationship between the sexes in terms of the conflict between them. The question either was not posed at all, or else it was dominated by a masculine approach—usually under a neopopulist, neopatriarchal scheme. Sexuality, and especially sexuality from a woman's point of view, returned for a long time to the realm of the taboo.

———

THIS STUDY SHOWS that Ukrainian modernism was *not* deprived of gender, as the majority of scholars have surmised—never having delved into the topic. On the contrary, it had direct, genetic links to gender. In the context of Ukrainian *fin de siècle* literature, things feminine and things feminist became both a cause and a symbol of modernity. Women writers of this pivotal period rejected and replaced the patriarchal reified images of women that had dominated the national literature in the nineteenth century; they also smashed the myth of the eternal passivity and weakness of women and the eternal activity of men. They placed everything in doubt—from fundamental social norms to linguistic traditions. Ukrainian modernism and the Ukrainian *fin de siècle* were in no way exceptional phenomena. Analogous processes—though in somewhat more pronounced forms—developed in European and American literatures (Gilbert and Gubar).

The creative careers of Lesia Ukraïnka and Ol'ha Kobylians'ka testify unequivocally to a crisis of traditional Ukrainian masculinity. Their female protagonists—new, autonomous, self-sufficient, and strong women—had no corresponding male partners. The more openly this thought was expressed, whether in stories or in plays, the greater the fear it aroused in men. The perception of personal danger spilled over into patent hostility among critics of Kobylians'ka and Ukraïnka, or into the purposeful silence which fills the critical texts of this period—the masculine, populist criticism which laid down the aesthetic canons of culture for decades to come. The apparent victory of populism, however, proved illusory. Today it is clear that modernism, with its feminine face, belongs among the central phenomena of Ukrainian literature.

Translated by Rob de Lossa

Notes

1. For the sake of my argument, I will define "populism" as a sociopolitical movement multifaceted in its theoretics, but with one underlying characteristic: belief that service to the "people," a concept variously understood, should be the inherent *raison d'être* of culture (including art) and society (including politics). The term will be discussed and refined below.

2. *Trans. note:* German, "Long live art!"

3. *Trans. note:* This is in Russian, as were all other Ukrainian scholarly works published at this time in the Russian Empire. Tsar Alexander II's Ems Ukase in 1876—reinforcing and broadening the Valuev Circular of 1863—banned publication of all Ukrainian-language texts except for belles-lettres and historical documents, and prohibited the import of Ukrainian-language texts from abroad, use of Ukrainian in schools, and use of Ukrainian in theatrical presentations. It included directives to remove Ukrainophile teachers from schools in the Ukrainian provinces and to maintain a majority of ethnic Russian teachers there. The Ukrainian language had already been banned from the churches. Later (1881) provisions allowed the publication of Ukrainian-language dictionaries, as long as they were in the Russian and not the Ukrainian Cyrillic alphabet. Stage performances in Ukrainian were allowed only if approved by the provincial authorities. There was no such ban on the Polish language in the Russian Empire. Also, there was no such ban against the Ukrainian language in the western part of Ukraine (including the cities of L'viv and Peremyshl'), which at that time formed part of the Austro-Hungarian Empire.

4. *Trans. note:* Here Ukraïnka gives the Russian word *prizvanie,* "calling, vocation," within her Ukrainian text.

5. *Trans. note: Pchilka* means "Little Bee." *Ukraïnka* means "Ukrainian woman." Their real names were Ol'ha Petrivna Kosach-Drahomanova (Pchilka) and Larysa Petrivna Kosach (Ukraïnka).

6. *Trans. note:* The Hutsuls are a Ukrainian ethnic group living in the Carpathian Mountains; they are the people featured in Sergei Paradzhanov's film *Shadows of Forgotten Ancestors.*

7. *Trans. note:* Es lebe die Kunst! Es lebe die Freiheit! *German:* Long live art! Long live freedom! The comment "dobrze wychowani" (Polish "well educated") refers to the fact that Kobylians'ka's part of Ukraine was long under Polish influence, so that many Ukrainian intellectuals became Polonized (as opposed to the many Russified Ukrainian intellectuals in the East).

8. *Trans. note:* Ukraïnka here parodies the Galician intellectuals who will not even name female sexuality, referring to it only by innuendo.

9. *Trans. note:* Ukrainian "someone" (*khtos'*) is grammatically masculine, though it can have both masculine and feminine referents.

10. Bracketed material in quotations hereafter will be the translator's.

Works Cited

PRIMARY SOURCES

Kobylians'ka, Ol'ha. *Tvory.* 5 vols. Kiev: Derzhavne vydavnitstvo khudozhn'oi literatury, 1962–63.
Makovei, Osyp. Letter to Ol'ha Kobylians'ka, August 11, 1901. Dept. of Manuscripts, Institute of Literature, Academy of Sciences, Ukraine. Fond 14/340.
Ukraïnka, Lesia. *Khronolohiia zhyttia i tvorchosty.* New York, 1970.
———. *Zibrannia tvoriv u 12-ty tomax.* 12 vols. Kiev: Naukova dumka, 1975–79.

SECONDARY SOURCES

Annan, Pamela J. "'Drunk with Chastity': The Poetry of Renée Vivien." In *The Female Imagination and Modernist Aesthetic,* ed. Sandra Gilbert and Susan Gubar, 11–22. New York: Gordon and Breach, 1986.
Franko, Ivan. *Literaturno-naukovyi vistnyk* 21, no. 2 (1903): 114–19.
———. *Zibrannia tvoriv u p'iadesiaty tomakh.* 50 vols. Kiev: Naukova dumka, 1976–86.
Gilbert, Sandra M., and Susan Gubar. *No Man's Land: The Place of the Woman Writer in the Twentieth Century.* Vol. 2: *Sex Changes.* New Haven: Yale University Press, 1989.
Hrushevs'kyi, Mykhailo. 1898a. Review of *The Tsarevna. Literaturno-naukovyi vistnyk* 1, no. 3 (1898): 174.
———. 1898b. "Vidchyt na Naukovij Adademiï 1 lystopada 1898 na pam'iatku 100 rokovyn "Eneïdy."" *Literaturno-naukovyi Vistnyk* 4, no. 11 (1898).
Hundorova, Tamara. "Pohliad na 'Marusiu."" *Slovo i chas* 6 (1991): 15–22.
Hundorova, Tamara, and Natalia Shumylo. "Tendestsiï rozvytku khudozhn'oho myslennia (pochatok XX st.)." *Slovo i chas* 1 (1993): 55–66.
Iefremov, Serhii Oleksandrovych. *Literaturno-Krytychni statti.* Kiev: Dnipro, 1993.
Kobryns'ka, Natalia Ivanivna, and Olena Pchilka, eds. *Pershyi vinok.* L'viv, 1887.
Ol'ha Kobylians'ka v krytytsi ta spohadakh. Kiev: Derzhavne vydavnitstvo khudozhn'oi literatury, 1963.
Weretelnyk, Roman. "A Feminist Reading of Lesia Ukraïnka's Dramas." Ph.D. dissertation, University of Ottawa, 1989.

PART II

THE TWENTIETH CENTURY

Wooing the Other Woman

Gender in Women's Love Poetry in the Silver Age

SIBELAN FORRESTER

WOMEN HAVE ALWAYS been present in Russian love poetry—if only as addressees. From the eighteenth century on, Russian women also wrote and published poetry which often expressed the suffering and apprehension of romantic relationships. It was in the Silver Age, lasting roughly from 1895 to 1925, that women poets began more actively to express female desire in literary discourse. The lasting or renewed popularity of such writers as Anna Akhmatova and Marina Tsvetaeva[1] definitively brought the rhythms of female language from the margins of discourse into the canon of high-culture Russian poetry. At the same time, the tradition that formed during the Silver Age, still largely dominated by men and men's language, required some adaptation from women who wrote in it. Although Russian allows and even (in some forms) requires a speaking subject to reveal his or her gender, the resources of the language itself were limited by its traditional use and scope. How much could these writers create and maintain difference within a discourse that still figured them as others and their words as responses to the dominant male discourse?[2] This essay examines a selection of poems by Zinaida Gippius, Poliksena Solov'eva, Marina Tsvetaeva, and Sof'ia Parnok, and in particular their love poems addressed to women. Although until the Revolution all these women lived in relative privilege,[3] with the education and leisure necessary to form durable poetic identities, their love poems to women stand doubly outside the standard of the time: written by women, and deviating from the heterosexual plot normative in Russian literature. The past and present homophobia of many parts of Russian society (not to mention our own) has meant that writing which raises these issues is often ignored or repressed, sometimes even by its own authors. In addressing some of these issues, I hope to contribute to discussion of the workings of gender in Russian poetry, and hence in Russian society.

Poets of the Silver Age took themselves very seriously and claimed a leading position in their culture; the Silver Age rejected the genre preferences of Russian realism without abandoning its writerly agenda. This exalted position conflicted with the expectation that respectable women would remain in the private sphere of home and family, rarely or never venturing into public discourse since doing so would render them at once "public women." A woman's personal emotions and experiences were coded as the private domain of the men who protected her virtue rather than as the stuff of poetic revelation. This tradition was modified by the *fin de siècle* interest in gender issues and the writer's freedom to perform gender in ways that might not be normative in society. In a printed poem, after all, only the signature remains of all the body that wrote the poem and the voice that recited it. At the same time, propriety exerted strong pressure against any expression of lesbian sexuality in public discourse, where it was either criminalized or medicalized. Laura Engelstein documents the persistent association of lesbians with prostitutes (sexual criminals) in the first decades of the twentieth century.[4] Given this context, the poems serve as examples of the negotiation of complex difference in one literary tradition.

I

Women of the Silver Age learned to read, write, and value poetry within a pre-existing tradition created mostly by men. Earlier women's works (in poetry and prose, as well as less privileged genres such as journalism, children's books, and autobiographical/historical memoirs) had been largely forgotten or displaced from the canon,[5] and as new female poets read and wrote, they addressed almost exclusively male poets and texts written from a man's point of view.[6] To clarify the nature of this tradition, I suggest a reading of a well-known poem by Aleksandr Pushkin (1799–1837), "Ty i vy."[7]

Ты и вы

Пустое *вы* сердечным *ты*
Она, обмолвясь, заменила
И все счастливые мечты
В душе влюбленной возбудила.

Пред ней задумчиво стою,
Свести очей с нее нет силы;
И говорю ей: как *вы* милы!
И мыслю: как *тебя* люблю!

1828

By a slip of the tongue she replaced empty *vy* with heartfelt *ty* and woke all the happy daydreams in [my] infatuated soul. I stand before her pensively, I lack the strength to avert my eyes from her; and [I] tell her, "Aren't you [*vy*] a dear!" and [I] think, "How I love you [*ty*]!"[8]

This lovely poem, tracing a game of pronouns that can hardly be reproduced in English,[9] creates an evocative picture of the role of language in lovers' discourse and the tension between public speech and private, inner language. The assumption that lyric love poetry primarily expresses deep, individual emotion cannot address the role of the love poem as a published model for behavior in society and for the love poems of later generations of poets.[10] Pushkin's position in Russian poetry, whether he is described as the greatest Russian poet, Russia's first great poet, or the father of Russian poetry, guarantees that no Russian can grow up intending to be a poet without knowing his words—even if some poets and movements later reject them. Though in his own day and for years after his death Pushkin was often seen as a troublesome rebel, by the height of the Silver Age he had become a primary and normative authority for both writers and critics.[11] The poem "Ty i vy" offers two things to this study: first, its gestures demonstrate the construction of gender in a lyric poem; second, it succinctly illustrates the workings of the Russian poetic tradition within which women have come to voice.

One level of the meaning of Pushkin's poem is already familiar to many American students of Russian, given its pedagogical use explaining second-person pronouns. Pushkin calls *vy,* the formal pronoun, "empty," since it expresses the polite distance that educated speakers of Russian at the time assumed in speaking to strangers. *Ty,* on the other hand, is "heartfelt," since it is used with close friends and relatives; the switch from *vy* to *ty* between former strangers is charged with meaning, and in this poem it suggests an admission of love. *Vy* is rendered empty by its very safeness, while *ty* is the form of inner truth, not always spoken aloud but living in the poet's secret thoughts and, he hopes, in the thoughts of the woman he loves. The formal *vy,* like other plural forms in Russian, tends to blur the language's gender distinctions, requiring plural past-tense verb forms or, as here, short-form adjectives with plural endings (*kak vy mily*). Calling a woman *vy* thus leaves her gender ambiguous, keeps it at a respectful distance, whereas calling her *ty* allows or requires language that expresses her gender.[12] Changing from *vy* to *ty* (as a slip of the woman's tongue) would grant the speaker the right to dwell familiarly on her gender, and this gives the accidental switch a sexual charge. Loving intimacy is acceptable within the speaker's own thoughts (*kak tebja ljublju!*), but it cannot be spoken aloud. It is ironic, then, that the gender of the poem's speaker is not revealed within the poem: were it not for the highly authoritative signature of Pushkin, grammatically the poem might be uttered by a woman. As Antonia Gove points out in a study to which I return below, the predominantly male and heterosexual tradition of Russian poetry leads the reader to assume a male speaker and female addressee in a love poem unless led by grammar or other indicators of gender to do otherwise.[13]

This reading, however, neglects to point out that the *woman* in the poem is not *ty* or even *vy* at all. These pronouns appear in the poet's reported speech, one level "below" the poem's address to its readers. On this level, *she* is identified in the third person.[14] The true addressees of the poem are the single reader (*ty*) and the plural reading public (*vy*), who in Pushkin's time could be described with a masculine plural (as *gospoda,* gentlemen) that subsumed its female members. The only person whose location remains the same if we shift from the situation narrated in the poem to the poem's active presence in the Russian literary tradition—the person who bridges the private scene described in the poem and the public act of publication—is one whose gender is not explicitly given in the poem, the "I" who signs his work "Aleksandr Pushkin." In this way, a poem which represents the most intimate linguistic relations turns out to be a public presentation of that intimate relationship and of objectified desire. Recalling the care with which Petr Grinev in Pushkin's novel *Kapitanskaia dochka* (*The Captain's Daughter*) conceals the name of his beloved Masha, one could argue that "cloaking" the beloved woman behind the third-person pronoun is a way of protecting her from public exposure in a world (eighteenth- or nineteenth-century alike) where naming a woman could cause her shame and disgrace. On the other hand, reducing any woman to an unnamed "she" turns her into all women, and thus Woman, representative of a category rather than an individual. The effect of the woman's concealment in anonymity is voyeuristic: we watch her along with the poem's speaker, and we hear, of all the words that she might have spoken in conversation, only the one word which defines the poet/speaker's position. The woman's perspective in the poem resides in a slip of the tongue, whose meaning must be interpreted for us by the poem's speaker. We see not her choice but his desire. The poet displays his love for a certain unnamed woman to the reading public, inviting them to read and repeat the words; when that poet is the foremost poet of his day, the display becomes a normative demonstration of the heterosexual romance. Future readers inherit the message that the poet controls the discourse of sexuality: whether or not he was correct in interpreting his beloved's pronoun choices, it is he who describes and codifies the encounter for all time.[15] If he expresses a certain bewilderment at the power that language can have in the mouth of a woman, this is because he chooses to present his reaction in this way. Thus a primary function of the poem is to model the relationship, to outline the shape of the private, intimate life of love in the public sphere of published poetry.

This poem also demonstrates the importance of love poetry in the Russian poetic canon, parallel to the centrality of romantic interest in Russian novels (the word *roman* in Russian, taken from the French, means both a novel and a love affair), which had more explicit pretensions to analyzing and correcting society. Lyric love poetry, especially if memorized by the literate part of society, serves as a tool for social modeling, while the position of men in literature and society at large ensures that most of it will be written from a male perspective.[16] Such grammatical inscription of the heterosexual romance could place additional pressure on later poets, who might wish to participate in the poetic tradition without duplicating these gender relations in love poetry of their own.

II

Zinaida Gippius (1869–1945), the most prominent woman among the Symbolists, chose to use a masculine speaker because she wanted to write *kak chelovek, a ne tol'ko kak zhenshchina* (as a person, not only as a woman).[17] This statement suggests that female language, like a female body, obscures some gender-neutral inner reality that is better expressed by masculine language. A famous 1905 drawing by Lev Bakst shows Gippius dressed like a page in elegant man's attire, slouching so that her body reveals no feminine characters besides her luxuriant hair.[18] Most widely reproduced pictures of Gippius show her in women's clothes, and so Bakst's picture is particularly powerful because it embodies the transvestism of her poetry. Transvestism in life, as in written language, can be subversive and liberating for a woman, as Sandra Gilbert suggests in her essay "Costumes of the Mind: Transvestism as Metaphor in Modern Literature";[19] in fact, if one counts pictures of the young Tsvetaeva wearing *sharovary* in Koktebel',[20] then all four of the poets I treat here left pictorial evidence of cross-dressing that underlines the subversive treatments of gender in their poetry.[21] Since Gippius signed her poetry with her own name, rather than with one of the masculine pseudonyms she used for critical articles, the dual presence of male language and female name kept the tension of her gender identity present on the page.[22] I would suggest, however, that in some cases Gippius's use of male language and male poetic tradition results not in subversion but rather in reinscription of women's subordinate gender roles.

Gippius's assumption that a *person* would use a man's language agrees with Roman Jakobson's description of masculine gender in Russian as unmarked (opposed to the marked feminine).[23] Sandra Gilbert and Susan Gubar, from another angle, describe the masculinist consequences of equating poets with priests,[24] a poetic stance very like that of the Neo-Romantic Russian Symbolists.[25] In poetry which foregrounds a self and that self's searchings and experiences, Gippius's "I" has plenty of chances to reveal its gender. Antonina Gove's valuable "Gender as a Poetic Feature in the Verse of Zinaida Gippius" finds that about half of Gippius's poems containing singular first-person speakers have unspecified gender, while about 45 percent have masculine speakers. Only a tiny percentage of the poems have a feminine first-person speaker, and none of those can be equated unambiguously with the poet's own persona.[26] In Russian poetry, as elsewhere, male sexuality was accepted both as universally human and also as symbolic of more elevated desires and yearnings, and Gippius's desire to write "as a person" seems to accommodate the idea that male sexual desire for a female addressee[27] symbolizes something greater than untranscended, perhaps insurmountable, female sexuality.

The assumption that an ungendered, androgynous person would use male language is exploited in Gippius's well-known 1905 poem "Ona," which begins by describing that "She" as a disgusting, inhuman creature who cannot be escaped or divorced. In the first stanza, especially, "She" sounds like a smothering wife or mother:

В своей бессовестной и жалкой низости,	In her unscrupulous and pathetic baseness,
Она как пыль сера, как прах земной.	She is grey like dust, like the ashes of the earth.
И умираю я от этой близости,	And I am dying from this closeness,
От неразрывности ея со мной.	From her inseparability from me.

Although the ensuing stanzas show this feminine presence more as an animal of female gender, the sense that "She" is a distinct individual, if not a person, strengthens the horrifying effect of the final revelation that "She" is the speaker's soul (*dusha*), grammatically feminine, from which the only possible escape (no doubt for the superior, grammatically masculine spirit, *dukh*) must be death and disincarnation. The soul of Gippius's male speaker is not a constitutive part of him, but is alienated from his true being by the stress placed on its feminine gender. This contrasts strikingly with Parnok's reference to her soul in a poem discussed below.

The poem "Potselui" ("The Kiss") provides a somewhat extreme case of masculinization in Gippius's speaker and stereotypical femininity of her addressee in an erotic context.

Поцелуй   The Kiss

Когда, Аньес, мою улыбку   When, Agnes, I move my smile
К твоим устам я приближаю,   Closer and closer to your lips,
Не убегай пугливой рыбкой,   Don't run away like a skittish fish,
Что будет—я и сам не знаю.   What will be—I myself don't know.

Я знаю радость приближенья,   I know the joy of the approach,
Веселье дум моих мятежных;   The cheer of my rebellious thoughts;
Но в цепь соединю ль мгновенья?   But will I unite the moments into a chain?
И губ твоих коснусь ли нежных?   And will I touch your tender lips?

Взгляни, не бойся; взор мой ясен, Look at me, don't be afraid; my gaze is clear,
А сердце трепетно и живо.   And my heart is tremulous and lively.
Миг обещанья так прекрасен!   The moment of promise is so splendid!
Аньес . . . Не будь нетерпелива . . . Agnes . . . Don't be impatient . . .

И удаление, и тесность   Both distance and crowdedness
Равны,—в обоих есть тревожность. Are equal—in both there is anxiousness.
Аньес, люблю я неизвестность,   Agnes, I love uncertainty,
Не исполнение,—возможность.   Not the realization—the possibility.

Дрожат уста твои, не зная,   Your lips tremble, not knowing
Какой огонь я берегу им . . .   What sort of fire I save for them . . .
Аньес . . . Аньес . . . Я только края Agnes . . . Agnes . . . I'll only touch
Коснусь скользящим поцелуем.   The edge with a slipping kiss.

1903

"Potselui" shows Gippius's technical skill in its fine crafting and appears in recent Soviet and Russian editions of her work.[28] Furthermore, through its masculine speaker the poem refutes the idea that men are interested only in sexual fulfillment; instead, it argues that anticipation is the truly valuable part of sexual experience.[29] This resembles other Symbolist writings privileging anticipation over the dirty realization of sex.[30]

This poem is at least in part a stylization and probably is meant to be funny. This is already clear in the phrase *puglivaia rybka* in the first stanza, which deftly draws a young woman who is both eager for a kiss (her lips pursed like a fish's) and scared of it. The non-Russian name An'es (French Agnès), which lacks the standard Russian feminine noun ending -*a*, is repeated five times in five stanzas, and repetition may defamiliarize it as a name, letting the reader recall that etymologically it means "lamb." (Indeed, it bears a phonetic as well as etymological resemblance to the Russian word for lamb, *iagnenok*, as well as the high-style Slavonic form for a sacrificial lamb, *agnets*.) The associations here include Christian ones: a lamb is pure, an ideal sacrificial victim; like Christ, a sacrificial lamb wipes away the sins of the one making the sacrifice. However, a lamb grows up to be a sheep, an animal famous for following wherever it is led. So Agnes is at once an innocent lambkin and a representative of the herd sexual instinct that draws humans from the heights of desire and anticipation into the murky ocean of sex and procreation.

This is where the poem becomes less amusing. In her eagerness to display the (male) speaker's refinement and freedom from the first steps of the traditional course of heterosexual romance (marriage, sex, children, dirty diapers), Gippius assigns the addressee, Agnes, the silent and objectified role that women so often play in narratives of male sexual development and fulfillment. In the first stanza Agnes is a skittish virgin who flees the speaker's kiss (her lips are painted with the elevated word *usta*, but the speaker's own lips are even less fleshly, described metonymically as "my smile"), as if fearing that the kiss might lead farther than it should. Later in the poem she is redrawn as waiting impatiently for the speaker's kiss, assuming that love and sexual attraction lead to a fixed set of behaviors. Her silence and stereotypical expectations serve to set off the eloquence and novelty of the speaker: her behavior is funny, but once the narrator reaches his point, the joke ends and the reader is left to learn and admire.

This is not to say that Gippius sets out to degrade and objectify the woman in this poem. Instead, her choice of masculine language, and hence the male role in a love poem addressed to a woman, leads in this case to manipulation and objectification of a female addressee, real or imagined. It is also the case that reading the poem as the words of a (butch) lesbian who speaks with masculine language changes its implications, undoing the assignment of untranscended sexuality to women though perhaps retaining its loaded presentation of femininity versus masculinity. This alternative reading would suggest a kind of sexuality that differs indeed from what the poem's addressee, Agnes, may have generalized from experience and the habits of heterosexual love.

A very different treatment of gender emerges in Gippius's beautiful poem "Ty," analyzed by both Gove (393) and Olga Matich,[31] where the genders of speaker and addressee shift as the speaker expresses mystical love for the moon. The gender of words alternates in each line of the poem along with the crossing rhyme; the first and third lines of each stanza, containing masculine nouns and adjectives, end with feminine rhymes (´_), while the second and fourth lines, containing feminine nouns and adjectives, end with dactylic rhymes (´__) as if to suggest the "third-sex" androgyne's transcendence of dualistic gender. The fourth and final stanza brings the speaker's own gender into the pattern, and the alternation becomes more rapid:

Ждал я и жду я зари моей ясной,	I [masc.] waited and I wait for my clear dawn,
Неутомимо тебя полюбила я . . .	I [fem.] have come to love you tirelessly . . .
Встань же, мой месяц серебряно-красный,	Arise then, my silvery-red moon [masc.]
Выйди, двурогая,—Милый мой—	Emerge, two-horned one [fem.],—My dear
Милая . . .	[masc.]—Dear [fem.] . . .

The two Russian words for the moon, *luna* and *mesiats*, respectively feminine and masculine in gender, allow such a fluctuation. The speaker, whose identity is more fluid than in "Potselui," uses both *Zhdal ia* and *poliubila ia* to describe his/her actions. This stresses that the pronoun *ia* itself is not linked to either human gender, and suggests that gender resides at the level of the earthly actions and traits expressed through verbs and adjectives, the grammatical categories where gender is labeled. Though often personified, the moon is nonetheless far above the fishy lips and sheepy sexual behaviors of human society; as Matich points out, Aristophanes associated it with androgynes,[32] ideal and variously sexed beings who were severed from one another because the gods envied their happiness. Obviously, Gippius is strongly interested in gender (Gove's article offers ample proof), but one of her most significant artistic challenges to the fixity of gender occurs in a love poem written not to a human being but to a satellite. When as in "Potselui" she writes a rather traditional love poem, the female addressee is confined to traditional silence and manipulation in service of the male speaker's self-revelation; she is neither liberated nor represented by the "person" writing the poem. This hints at the linguistic weight of a poetic tradition of poems with male speakers and female addressees which Gippius receives into the bargain along with adoption of a male speaking position and Symbolism's Romantic image of the poet.

Such poetic transvestism can enrich the variety of gender patterns in a literary tradition only if readers know (and know widely, beyond the poet's intimate sphere of acquaintance) that a woman is writing. Like the body concealed behind Gippius's page costume, her feminine signature gives the masculine "costume" of her speaker's gender new meaning. (This differs from the famous case of Nadezhda Durova, who successfully maintained a masculine identity during the Napoleonic Wars: Durova's game would have been up if too many people had found out, as her military career required her to pass for a man, albeit a young one.)[33] The signature is crucially important for many of Gippius's poems, if we want to appreciate their subversive potential; otherwise some, such as "Potselui," merely reinscribe the gender structures of dominant discourse.

III

Like her friend Zinaida Gippius,[34] Poliksena Solov'eva (1867–1924) consistently wrote poems with a masculine speaker and masculine grammatical forms in the first person. The Symbolist image of the poet-as-priest or -troubadour at the feet of the Beautiful Lady (*Prekrasnaia Dama*), inherited from the Romantics, may have encouraged Symbolist women poets to use male forms more often than non-Symbolist female contemporaries, though this question needs further study. Solov'eva signed her poems and visual artworks with the pseudonym "Allegro," which expressed her background in music along with, perhaps, reference to the quick passing of human life on earth.[35] This pseudonym does not reveal the poet's gender—indeed, it reveals no gender at all, seeming from Russian morphology to read as an adverb. The title page of the 1905 collection *Inei* (*Hoarfrost*) gives Solov'eva's real name above her pseudonym,[36] making the pseudonym an addition to her name rather than a replacement for it. Readers were evidently well aware of Solov'eva's gender; critics read her work on that basis, stressing its "feminine" qualities.[37]

Solov'eva not only let herself be photographed in telling garb; she had a life-long love relationship with Nadezhda I. Manasseina, who collaborated with her in editing children's books and one of the best journals for children of the time (*Tro-

pinka [*The Path*]). Several of Allegro's poems are dedicated to Manasseina. Her poetic use of masculine forms by a first-person speaker serves both to reveal and to conceal the lesbian poet's identity. This information, like discussion of Gippius's sexuality, has been suppressed by some scholars, or alluded to only tangentially (there is more information about Solov'eva's relationship with Manasseina in Simon Karlinsky's biography of Marina Tsvetaeva than in either Pachmuss's short biography of Solov'eva or the brief outline provided in *Tsaritsy muz*, a Soviet publication including some of Solov'eva's work),[38] and with less apparent justification: Gippius's sexuality might be as difficult to summarize as her philosophy,[39] but Solov'eva spent most of her adult life with the woman euphemistically identified as "the wife of a Moscow doctor." (I will return below to the issue of excising biographical information viewed as sinful or unmentionable.)[40]

Although many of the poems in the collection *Inei* have masculine speakers, in others the reader may assume out of habit that an indeterminate speaker is masculine. Some poems, addressed to grammatically feminine entities such as death (*smert'*, p. 37) or the red glow of dawn and sunset (*zaria*, p. 61), personify their addressees. The explicitly masculine speaker of "Vecherniaia zaria" ("The Evening Glow") addresses the sunset in its final two stanzas:

Скажи, зачем же ты так много мне сулила,	Tell me, for what purpose did you promise me so much,
Там, за деревьями, до полночи горя,	There, beyond the trees, burning until midnight,
И золотом обет несбыточный чертила,	And you traced in gold a vow that was not to be,
Моя прекрасная, неверная заря!	My splendid, unfaithful sunset!
Но на тебя роптать не стану, золотая,	But I shall not complain against you, gold one,
Обман твой, ясная, по прежнему люблю	Your deception, clear one, I love just as before
И, сердцем о твоих обетах вспоминая,	And, recalling your vows with my heart,
За ложь прекрасную тебя благословлю.	I bless you for the splendid lie.

Here, despite the typical Symbolist preference of anticipation over reality, the sunset glow figures in terms that recall false female lovers throughout poetry; she is unfaithful but splendid, she promises to return but does not, and she belongs to the speaker (*Moia*) because of the power of [his] love and desire.

In the same collection, however, one poem refers to Allegro's own love relationship, and its tone is noticeably different:

Помнишь, мы над тихою рекою	Remember, we walked along the quiet river
В ранний час шли детскою четой,	At an early hour, like a pair of children.
Я—с моею огненной тоскою,	I—with my fiery longing,
Ты—с твоею белою мечтой.	You—with your white dream.
И везде, где взор мой замедлялся,	And everywhere, wherever my gaze lingered,
И везде, куда глядела ты,	And everywhere, wherever you glanced,
Мир, огнем сверкая, загорался,	The world flamed up, sparkling with fire,
Вырастали белые цветы.	White flowers grew up.

Люди шли, рождались, умирали,	People went, were born, died,
Их пути нам были далеки,	Their paths were far from us.
Мы, склонясь над берегом, внимали	We, leaning over the bank, attended
Тихим сказкам медленной реки.	To the quiet tales of the slow river.
Если тьма дышала над рекою,	If gloom breathed over the river,
Мы боролись с злою темнотой:	We would fight with the evil darkness;
Я—моею огненной тоскою,	I—with my fiery longing,
Ты—своею белою мечтой.	You—with your white dream.
И теперь, когда проходят годы,	And now, when the years are passing by,
Узкий путь к закату нас ведет,	A narrow path leads us towards the sunset,
Где нас ждут не меркнущие своды,	Where unfading vaults await us,
Где нам вечность песнь свою поет.	Where eternity sings us its song.
Мы как встарь, идем рука с рукою	As of old, we go hand in hand,
Для людей непонятой четой:	For people a misunderstood couple;
Я—с моею огненной тоскою,	I—with my fiery longing,
Ты—с твоею белою мечтой.	You—with your white dream.[41]

1905

This poem opens the second section of *Inei* on p. 100, the point at which the drawings become less frequent and the poems denser (this poem is the first one in the book to be printed entirely on the "back" side of a page); this links it with one other poem in a similarly stressed initial position, "Inei" ("Hoarfrost"), which opens the collection and is dedicated to "N. I. M." (Manasseina's initials). Thus both the dedicatory poem and the poem that opens the "poetic" rather than "visual" part of the volume seem to address the same "thou," Manasseina. This is one of a small body of poems in which Solov'eva openly discusses her relationship with her companion, and biographical background offers an essential explanation of why the couple is "not understood." The poem resembles many of Allegro's other lyrics in the subdued and unobtrusive position of its "I"—she tends to subsume the first-person singular in the first-person plural. Dominance of the "we" shapes this evocation of a couple's progress through life, perhaps to recognize the fact that Allegro would not be writing as she does without her partner. However, the lack of any first-person verbs or adjectival forms conceals the speaker's gender, so that while not explicitly feminine, she/he is no more than implicitly masculine.[42] The masculine gender of the speaker in many other poems in *Hoarfrost* serves as camouflage for this poem:[43] any reader ignorant of Solov'eva's personal life may assume that her words to a feminine addressee express "universal" masculine love for some embodied eternal feminine, or that "thou" here is the speaker's soul. However, the two main characters in the poem are associated with nouns which are feminine in gender, *toska* and *mechta*, repeated three times like a musical refrain; the difference, if any, between two femininities appears in the variant feminine instrumental endings, *-oiu* as opposed to *-oi*, which alternate through the dark-sounding refrain (*Ia—s moeiu ognennoi toskoiu, / Ty—s tvoeiu beloiu mechtoi*). As a couple, too, they are *cheta*, a grammatically feminine entity.

The other in this poem is a full equal of the speaker, but the two are incomprehensible to others, including even readers of the poem that reproduces the relationship for public view. The speaker and her companion walk the path of life together, but there is no suggestion of love or (heaven forbid) sex: the only contact, besides "hand in hand," is visual, through *vzor* (gaze) and the verb *gliadet'* (to glance). It is as if the relationship itself is not merely a relationship, but rather a symbol of something higher, unearthly, and perhaps therefore "unnatural" and incomprehensible to limited earthly beings. Between Russian society's patriarchal values[44] and the Symbolist emphasis on transcendent rather than earthly reality, this may be as close as Solov'eva cared to come to embodying a love relationship in poetry.

IV

Marina Tsvetaeva (1892–1941) is the best known of the poets I am reading here, and this fame may reflect not only her outstanding poetry but also the fact that she, unlike the other poets here, addresses most of her love poetry to men.[45] In this way, her work is more obviously connected to the love poetry of nineteenth-century Russian women. At the same time, some scholars have downplayed or ignored Tsvetaeva's relationship with Sof'ia Parnok, or have argued (with or without an attempt at textual basis) that it was a passionate friendship with no sexual component. While poetry's value does not depend on the writer's biography, censoring a writer's life or works from the point of view of any kind of morality, and in Tsvetaeva's case out of residual fear of the Soviet literary bureaucracy, is questionably productive.[46] This is all the more true given Parnok's importance in Tsvetaeva's poetic development; even the careful Anna Saakiants grants that the poetry to Parnok takes a sudden quantum leap over what Tsvetaeva was writing before the two women met.[47]

The cycle of poetry written during Tsvetaeva's relationship with Parnok and entitled "Podruga" ("The Girlfriend" or "The Woman Friend," 1914–16) is widely accepted as a most unusual poetic event in Russian literature, a lesbian cycle.[48] However, it is in fact the only body of love poetry to a woman in Tsvetaeva's opus and remained unpublished in her lifetime.[49] With very few exceptions (among her earliest poems), Tsvetaeva consistently uses a female first-person speaker in her poetry, but the gender of her addressee in the poems of "Podruga" varies: of the seventeen poems in the cycle, seven use *Vy*, the capitalized, formal plural form of "you;" six poems, mostly later ones, address a feminine singular *ty*; one uses *ona* ("she"), and three do not specify the gender of their addressee. Thus the cycle offers two new variations on the gender patterning used by Gippius and Allegro, who wrote love poems to women with masculine or unspecified speakers. Tsvetaeva writes love poems as a woman to an addressee who is sometimes a feminine singular "thou," sometimes a formal "you" whose feminine gender emerges from the context.

Since some of the poems in the cycle "Podruga" have been treated in more depth than others, I will examine the seventh poem:

Как весело сиял снежинками	How merrily your—grey, [and] my—sable
Ваш—серый, мой—соболий мех,	Fur shone with snowflakes,
Как по рождественскому рынку мы	As we searched the Christmas market

Искали ленты ярче всех.	For the brightest ribbons of all.
Как розовыми и несладкими	How I stuffed myself with pink,
Я вафлями объелась—шесть!	Unsweet waffles—six!
Как всеми рыжими лошадками	How I grew sentimental in your honor
Я умилялась в Вашу честь.	At all the chestnut horses.
Как рыжие поддевки—парусом,	How the ginger peasant weskits—like a sail,
Божась, сбывали нам трапье,	Swearing, tried to sell us rags,
Как на чудных московских барышень	How the stupid peasant women
Дивилось глупое бабье.	Wondered at the eccentric young ladies from Moscow.
Как в час, когда народ расходится,	How at the hour when the people scatter,
Мы не хотя вошли в собор,	Without meaning to we went into the cathedral,
Как на старинной Богородице	How you stopped your gaze
Вы приостановили взор.	On an old-fashioned icon of God's Mother.
Как этот лик с очами хмурыми	How that image with the sullen eyes
Был благостен и изможден	Was full of blessing and emaciated
В киоте с круглыми амурами	In the icon-case with the round Cupids
Елисаветинских времен.	From the times of Empress Elizabeth.
Как руку Вы мою оставили,	How you let go my hand,
Сказав: "О, я ее хочу!"	Saying, "Oh, I want her!"
С какою бережностью вставили	With what care you placed
В подсвечник—желтую свечу . . .	A yellow candle—in the candlestick . . .
—О светская, с кольцом опаловым	Oh worldly hand, with the ring
Рука!—О вся моя напасть!—	Of opal!—Oh all my misfortune!—
Как я икону обещала Вам	How I promised to steal the icon
Сегодня ночью же украсть!	For you that very night!
Как в монастырскую гостиницу	How, like a regiment of soldiers,
—Гул колокольный и закат—	—A rumble of bells and sunset—
Блаженные, как имянинницы,	Blissful, as if it were our nameday,
Мы грянули, как полк солдат.	We burst into the monastery guesthouse.
Как я Вам—хорошеть до старости—	How I swore to you—to get more beautiful—
Клялась—и просыпала соль,	Until old age—and spilled the salt,
Как трижды мне—Вы были в ярости!—	How three times—you were furious!—
Червонный выходил король.	The king of hearts came up for me.
Как голову мою сжимали Вы,	How you squeezed my head,
Лаская каждый завиток,	Caressing each curl,
Как Вашей брошечки эмалевой	How the flower of your enamel brooch
Мне губы холодил цветок.	Chilled my lips.
Как я по Вашим узким пальчикам	How along your narrow fingers
Водила сонною щекой,	I drew my drowsy cheek,
Как Вы меня дразнили мальчиком,	How you teased me calling me a boy.
Как я Вам нравилась такой . . .	How I pleased you like that. . . .
Декабрь 1914 г.	December 1914

The poem uses *Vy* for its addressee, the formal pronoun capitalized to indicate respect, and the gender of that *Vy* does not appear until the third stanza, where both speaker and addressee are identified by a "stupid" third party as *baryshni*, young, presumably unmarried women. The speaker's gender, on the other hand, is clearly revealed in verb forms as feminine, which is not the case in every poem of the cycle. It may seem odd that a poem describing such intimate contact uses formal second-person forms, which conceal or deemphasize the addressee's gender, but the cycle as a whole shows little physical contact between the speaker and the addressee. The pronoun may reflect the discomfort of such a relatively frank and erotic description, holding the addressee at a distance from the speaker.[50] On the other hand, Tsvetaeva and her husband, Sergei Efron, used *Vy* over the whole course of their relationship (they married in 1912).

This poem reveals examples of the gender play that Diana Burgin has noted in her reading of Tsvetaeva's whole cycle to Parnok.[51] Peasants are identified by their reddish garments, *poddevki*, worn by men but feminine in gender; the peasant women are summed up with the derogatory neuter collective *bab'e*. The speaker and her addressee are first *baryshni* ("young ladies"), then *imenninitsy* ("name-day girls"), both feminine in gender; then they are compared to *polk soldat*, a regiment of soldiers, whose arrival at the monastery would threaten the safety and chastity of the religious community inside. The speaker is teased for being like a boy at the end of the poem, but in the sixth stanza her addressee not only desires the Mother of God (depicted on an icon), but carefully inserts a (potentially phallic?) yellow candle into a candleholder below the icon with her arousing, ringed hand. Here, as elsewhere in this cycle, the practice of writing love poetry to a woman seems to increase Tsvetaeva's awareness of gender in language, both as a marking feature in her own first-person discourse and as a means for developing conflicts in her poetry.[52]

The lack of a socially determined power differential in a relationship between two women of the same generation means that control could be contested and renegotiated, a more or less playful process that influenced the genders associated with either lover in the poetry.[53] Being like a boy allows a lover to reproduce gender difference without the kind of fixed position of dominance claimed by adult men. Gender difference, here performed rather than "natural," produces the otherness needed for erotic contact (or conflict), what Diana Fuss has called "the crucial sense of alterity necessary for constituting any sexed subject, any subject as sexual."[54] Moreover, a boy and a woman are constant contestants in power: as an adult she holds authority over him, but he will grow up to assume power in the patriarchal system. The performative and shifting nature of this gender borrowing appears in the poem as both figures avoid fixity in either pole of masculinity or femininity.

At the same time, teasing the speaker for being like a boy (which, the speaker adds, pleased the addressee) resonates with other poems in this cycle and in Tsvetaeva's earlier poetry so as later to undermine the desirability of such a poetic relationship. One early poem from her first book, *Verchernii al'bom* (*The Evening Album*), "Malen'kii pazh" ("The Little Page"),[55] shows the grief of a little boy whose love for an unappreciative woman ends in his suicide. Knowing French, Tsvetaeva may have connected the masculine *pazh* with its feminine homonym, *page*, to conclude that in a love affair between a younger man and an older woman, it is the woman who inscribes her text on the younger man (her blank page, so to speak), marking his life with the narrative she has chosen. Tsvetaeva refers to the "Spartan child" in the fourteenth poem of her cycle,[56] based on Karolina Pavlova's 1854 poem "My stranno soshlis',"[57] which she read with Parnok; unlike the earlier poem, Tsvetaeva's does not allow her addressee to share the pain and stoicism of the child. Pavlova's poem was itself written to a younger man, Boris Utin, whom she met when she was forty-seven, twenty-five years his senior. In the fifth poem of the cycle "Podruga,"[58] Tsvetaeva's speaker calls herself "Your little Kay" after the boy hero of Andersen's fairy tale, referring to another powerful woman who would control the boy's destiny. A couple similar to all these is prominent in Tsvetaeva's mature poetry, but there the poet takes the more rewarding role of the older woman.[59] The paradigm of a younger man and an older woman offers ways of imagining a relationship between two women, but Tsvetaeva later adapts it to poetic treatment of heterosexual desire.

Tsvetaeva's effort to cast herself as an innocent and even a boy in the cycle of poems to Parnok contrasts with Parnok's 1915 poem "Devochkoi malen'koi,"[60] where the child/addressee (presumed to be Tsvetaeva) is explicitly and even stereotypically feminine—happy about a new outfit or a slipper—but also easily shaped by the older lover (*No pod udarom liubvi ty—chto zoloto, kovkoe!* [But under the blow of love you are malleable, like gold!]). Perhaps it is this power to transform and shape the soft and precious beloved that leads Parnok, after the passion of lovemaking, to take on the role of mother, gazing on the sleeping girl with tender and protective love. Tsvetaeva too eventually refigures her lover as mother rather than corrupt older seducer, in the 1916 poem "V ony dni ty mne byla, kak mat',"[61] especially the first two stanzas:

В оны дни ты мне была, как мать,	In those days of yore you were like a mother to me,
Я в ночи тебя могла позвать,	I could call you in the night,
Свет горячечный, свет бессонный,	Feverish light, sleepless light,
Свет очей моих в ночи оны.	Light of my eyes in those nights of yore.
Благодатная, вспомяни,	[You,] full of grace, recall
Незакатные оны дни,	Those days of yore without sunset,
Материнские и дочерние,	Maternal and daughterly,
Незакатные, невечерние.	Without sunset, without evening.

The third and fourth stanzas of that poem continue the gentle, lulling tone of the first two, and any discomfort with the informal pronoun is neutralized (along with the erotic excitement) by replacing the heterosexual model of older woman and younger man with the relationship of mother and daughter, where age displaces gender difference. The psychology here resounds oddly with Tsvetaeva's much later prose work "Lettre à l'amazone,"[62] which justifies a younger woman's need and desire to leave her older lesbian lover as the natural wish for adult life (that is, a man who will give her children), the natural expectation that a daughter will grow up and leave her mother's house. Since Tsvetaeva never published the cycle "Po-druga," publication of "V ony dni" in its chronological place in *Versty I* (minus its original dedication to Parnok) narrowed the range of possible readings for anyone unaware of her biography from twenty-two to twenty-four. Love between women was still a risky topic in public discourse, and protective Aesopic language could as always obscure a poem's significance.

Tsvetaeva's opus includes no other love poetry written unambiguously to a woman. The poems written during Tsvetaeva's relationship with Sonechka Holli-day, which some scholars have called a lesbian infatuation, portray a young woman loving men (albeit unhappily), as do the dramatic roles which Tsvetaeva wrote for Holliday.[63] It appears that, after her relationship with Parnok, Tsvetaeva's interest in love between women, and the discourse this love creates, received artistic expres-sion only in prose ("Pis'mo amazonke," "Povest' o Sonechke"). Traces of Parnok in Tsvetaeva's poetry also appear, again, in the works where the speaker plays the role of older woman to a younger man, perhaps presenting herself as an unusual or even unlikely woman, but never again speaking a woman's love for her female ad-dressee.

It is highly significant that the cycle "Podruga" was not printed during Tsve-taeva's lifetime—in fact, it was first printed in its entirety as an appendix to S. Poliakova's 1979 edition of Parnok's poetry, published in the United States. Tsve-taeva frequently rededicated her love poems to men, but there was no way to make this cycle acceptable within the tradition, not even under the title "Oshibka" ("The Mistake"), which Tsvetaeva considered, and she was understandably as concerned with her stature in her own community as with the survival of her works. The cycle as a whole remained unpublished for more than sixty years after its writing, and its absence limited its influence on other readers and poets. The poetic heirs of the cycle "Podruga," Diana Burgin argues, are the late lesbian love cycles of Sof'ia Parnok.[64]

V

Sof'ia Parnok (1885–1933) was born before Marina Tsvetaeva, but her later blooming as a poet and continuing love poetry to women lead me to place her last in this otherwise chronological sequence.[65] Until quite recently, Parnok seemed to be forgotten. In part this reflected her internal exile in the Soviet Union: Parnok re-mained there after the Revolution but could not make a successful poetic career under the new regime; unlike Akhmatova, she did not outlive the worst excesses of the regime that repressed her. She was also careless with her papers, so that much of her work was scattered or lost even before her death.[66] However, her apparent lack of concern with later status or publication also freed her, toward the end of her life, to write definitely homoerotic poems despite the weight of the heterosexual tradition in Russian poetry. Burgin goes so far as to argue that Parnok consciously inscribed a lesbian life in her work,[67] quite an achievement for the time.

Early in her career, Parnok wrote a series of tastefully erotic Sapphic styliza-tions.[68] One of these, "Ty dremlesh', podruga moia" ("You doze, my [girl]friend"),[69] recalls the poem "Devochkoi malen'koi," based on the fragment of Sappho it takes as an epigraph, where Parnok adds the role of mother to relations with a less mature lover.[70] Other poems of the time use Sappho's enabling example to link lesbian sexuality with a community of female poets,[71] so much so that Parnok stresses the poetic value of the school of Sappho more than its sexual meanings. In various poems the speaker imagines herself a reincarnated woman from that school, or one who should have been born then but came too late.[72] Sappho and the Sapphic tradition underlie some of Parnok's best later work, providing ways to assume a position of power vis-à-vis her own literary tradition. The fact that these poems can be read as stylizations of the Greek makes their homoerotic content less shocking for readers accustomed to the strongly heterosexual Russian poetic tradition.

Even earlier, Parnok expressed desire for women of her own time, in a way that rejects the literary plots and roles created for women by men:[73]

Журавли потянули к югу.	The cranes have reached towards the south.
В дальний путь я ухожу.	I leave for a distant path.
Где я встречу ее, подругу,	Where will I meet her, the (girl)friend,
роковую госпожу?	the fateful lady?
В шумном шелке ли, звонких латах?	In loud silk, in ringing armor?
В кэбе, в блеске ль колесниц?	In a cab, in the gleam of chariots?
Под разлетом бровей крылатых	Under the flight of winged eyebrows,
где ты, ночь ее ресниц?	where are you, night of her lashes?
Иль полунощные бульвары	Or else the boulevards of midnight (lands)
топчет злой ее каблук?	are trampled by her wicked heel?
Или спрятался локон ярый	Or the furious lock has hidden
под монашеский клобук?	under a monastic hood?
Я ищу, подходя к театру,	I seek, walking up to the theater,
и в тиши церковных стен—	and in the quiet of church walls—
не Изольду, не Клеопатру,	not Isolde, not Cleopatra,
не Манон и не Кармен!	not Manon and not Carmen!
1 августа 1915. Святые Горы	August 1, 1915, Sviatye Gory

In the original Russian, the poem's speaker is not identified by any explicit grammatical marking of gender. Like Solov'eva, Parnok writes this love poem in a voice that readers might take as a man's. The final stanza, however, hints at future directions of Parnok's love poetry as it explicitly rejects the love plots men have created for heroines such as Isolde, Cleopatra, Manon Lescaut, and Carmen—plots revolving around men and deadly to the women. Parnok's imaginary fatal woman is granted unusual possibilities: she may be a society lady in rustling silks, but she may also wear ringing armor, like the amazon that recalls another ancient community of women.[74]

Parnok's poems to Tsvetaeva have received some scholarly attention because of Tsvetaeva's literary prominence,[75] but it is Parnok's last two poetic cycles that most freely depict the poet's love for another woman. I will examine one poem from that period:

Седая роза

Ночь. И снег валится,
спит Москва . . . А я . . .
Ох, как мне не спится,
любовь моя!

Ох, как ночью душно,
запевает кровь . . .
Слушай, слушай, слушай!
Моя любовь:

Серебро мороза
в лепестках твоих.
О седая роза,
тебе—мой стих!

Светишь из-под снега,
роза декабря,
Неутешной негой
меня даря.

Ну, что ж, умри,
          умри теперь,
моя душа,
          мой бич, мой зверь.

С тобой была я на краю,
с тобой бродила я в раю.

16–17 июня 1932

The Gray-Haired Rose

Night. And snow tumbles down,
Moscow sleeps . . . And I . . .
Ah, how I don't feel like sleeping,
My love!

Ah, how stuffy it is at night,
[my] blood begins to sing . . .
Listen, listen, listen!
My love:

The silver of frost
is in your petals.
O gray rose,
my verse is—to you!

You give off light from beneath the snow,
rose of December,
giving me the gift
of inconsolable languor.

Well then, die,
          die now,
my soul,
          my scourge, my beast.

With you I was on the edge,
with you I wandered in paradise.

June 16–17, 1932

This poem is the nineteenth in Parnok's final cycle, "Nenuzhnoe dobro" ("Unneeded Goods"),[76] dedicated to the physicist Nina Vedeneeva (1882–1955) and first published in the United States in 1979. It is not as erotically explicit as some of Parnok's Sapphic stylizations from the late 1910s: in the cycles devoted to Vedeneeva, explicit erotic details are given in a jocular tone, as in "Moia liubov'!" ("My love!") and "Glaza raspakhnuty . . ." ("[Your] eyes are open wide . . .").[77] Nonetheless, as Poliakova and Burgin have argued, Parnok's final cycles are highly unusual in Russian poetry since they treat the forbidden topic of lesbian love.

The whole cycle "Nenuzhnoe dobro" is dedicated to Vedeneeva, so the reader may assume that she is the *ty* in this poem too. The poem includes no past-tense verbs for the second person, but the nouns identifying the addressee, *liubov'* and *roza*, are both feminine in gender. These words are so typical of love poetry, in Russian as in others, that they work to equate the addressee (the speaker's beloved) with the speaker's own emotion (love). The poet's emotional response to a real addressee is intimately linked with her ability to create and define that addressee in writing, through the rhythmic song of (grammatically feminine) blood. These positive feminine nouns (plus night and Moscow) are covered by snow in the first and fourth stanzas and frost in the third stanza; both *sneg* and *moroz* are masculine in gender. These two markers of whiteness and winter bring a whole range of symbolic possibilities: age (the frost in the rose's petals as the beloved's gray hair, or Parnok's own advancing years at forty-seven), winter as the season of ending and death, and perhaps even the postrevolutionary censorship which hindered the poet's creative activity. Snow buries things and renders them inaccessible, withering them if they bloom out of season. The speaker herself, finally, is marked as feminine only in the verb forms of the last stanza, precisely where she evokes the most meaningful events of the past after calling for death.[78]

As Burgin points out in "After the Ball Is Over,"[79] Parnok's whole cycle dwells on the pain of love that comes too late in life—hence, her gray-haired rose is a rose of December. The stress on age and untimeliness here, too, shows in this poem's dating (as published) on June 16–17, the beginning of summer, when it is highly unlikely that the snow mentioned in the poem could really be falling outside, even in Moscow. The poem's internal landscape contrasts strongly with the date appended to it, making the frost on the rose's petals all the more easy to identify with the lover's gray hair, especially as the word *sedaia* is used of people more than of objects. A woman's description of her own or her beloved's grayness suggests an "unattractive" aging that subverts the youthful freshness typical in poetry's images of loved and loving women.[80] Parnok's final two cycles praise her beloved's youthful appearance, but she does not see her as an unformed young woman on whom a poet can inscribe whatever she pleases.

Once Parnok evokes her December rose, she tells it to die, calls it "my soul" (feminine in gender) but also "My scourge, my beast." The negative words (*bich* and *zver'*) are masculine in gender, as if to equate that with pain and devouring, and perhaps also linking the scourge and beast with the snow of the first stanza and the frost of the third.[81] Parnok's stanzas change shape here, too, from four-line units which irregularly alternate trochaic trimeter with two-beat iambic lines in crossing rhyme, through the transitional fifth stanza, to the longer final rhyming couplet in iambic tetrameter.[82] Love and its addressee pass through these rhythmic and verbal alterations as if to prepare for the violence of approaching death. Burgin's point that the cycle shows foreboding of death clearly applies in this poem. The identity of the "you" ordered to die includes even the "I" herself.

Evocation of paradise in the poem's final line ("With you I wandered in paradise") brings in a wide range of associations. These include Adam and Eve, the original human inhabitants of paradise, the forbidden fruit of the biblical story which is so often associated with sexuality, and thus the typical equation of lesbian sexuality with sin and even with demonic forces. In another late poem, Parnok takes on the role if not the name of Adam by calling Vedeneeva her "gray Eve" and inviting her *v nash greshnyi rai* (into our sinful paradise).[83] In "Sedaia roza," however, the addressee (who acquires "masculine" identity in the negative words "scourge" and "beast") could hold Adam's place, since *ia brodila* marks the speaker as the feminine member of the couple, maybe the one who first tempted her companion to sin. Adam also invents and applies human language, as the speaker and addressee not only wandered through paradise but named the things they found there. This reading subversively locates a lesbian couple and their fall from innocence into sexual knowledge at the source of human history and culture. This poem, though, shows the end rather than the beginning, compounding the bitterness of the final stanza.

The penultimate poem of the same cycle as it is published, "Pomnish' koridorchik uzen'kii," offers an even greater series of transformations, granting the addressee more freedom from the defining energy of the speaker's love and emphasizing the speaker's own powerlessness.

Ты помнишь коридорчик узенький в кустах смородинных? С тех пор мечте ты стала музыкой,[84]	Do you remember the narrow corridor in the currant bushes? Since then to [my] dream you've become music,
чудесной родиной.	a miraculous homeland.
Ты жизнью и смертью стала мне— такая хрупкая— и ты истаяла, усталая, моя голубка! . .	You have become life and death to me— so fragile— and you melted away, tired, my dove [dear]! . . .
Прости, что я, как гость непрошенный, тебя не радую, что я сама под страстной ношею под этой падаю.	Forgive me that I, like an uninvited guest, don't make you glad, that I myself often fall beneath this passionate burden.
О, эта грудь неутолимая! Ей нету имени . . . Прости, что я люблю, любимая, прости, прости меня!	Oh, this insatiable breast! It [she?] has no name . . . Forgive me that I love, beloved, forgive, forgive me!
5 Февраля 1933	February 5, 1933

This poem is dated about six months before Parnok's death on August 26, 1933. Like Solov'eva's "Pomnish', my nad tikhoiu rekoiu," it begins by questioning whether the addressee remembers, since the poet's emotional geography and history are private, not shared by others, and vulnerable to loss from memory. This addressee moves through several transformations (*muzyka* [music]—*rodina* [homeland]—*zhizn'* [life]—*smert'* [death]—*golubka* [pigeon / dove], and finally the substantivizable adjective *liubimaia* [beloved], all feminine in gender though varying between nominative and instrumental case), which underline both her significance for the speaker and her own freedom to change rather than be fixed in a narrative. The transformations move toward greater autonomy—the "daydream" (*mechta*) is largely under the dreamer's control, but music is external to its listener, while the "homeland" is a complex outward embodiment of the beloved who began as the speaker's fantasy. The speaker compares herself to an uninvited guest, masculine in gender as in the proverb the line recalls (perhaps, in context, to stress her unwelcomeness additionally), but the same stanza reveals her feminine gender with the word *sama* (myself): masculine forms enter through nouns, lending a gender flexibility to the verbal and adjectival feminine forms that the speaker herself motivates. The speaker's regret at her inability to change might, as in "Sedaia roza," convey an inability to keep pace with the transformations of her beloved, since only death will intervene to solve the problem of her "passionate burden." The last line, *Prosti, prosti menia!* (Forgive, forgive me!), also carries the sense of "farewell," expressed with the imperfective imperative of the same verb (*proshchai*).

Poliakova and especially Burgin have pointed out the influence of Tsvetaeva's cycle "Podruga" on Parnok's last cycles. If Parnok productively linked poetry and lesbian love through Sapphic stylizations (some of which date from her relationship with Tsvetaeva), where fragments of Sappho's verses are woven into the poems, then it is natural that both Tsvetaeva's poems to her and her own earlier poems would serve as ennabling subtexts for Parnok's later work, including the final cycles. As far as lesbian love poetry went, not much else was available. Parnok's cycles went unpublished until 1979, meaning that for decades her most striking love lyrics were not widely available to readers and poets. Parnok's last cycles face and largely overcome the paucity of models for the kind of poetry she was writing and the burden of assembling and establishing the context of her own work. Her poetry, which could enrich the range of models for relationships and social behavior in the genre of lyric poetry, was suppressed by the collectivizing and patriarchal ideological discourses of the Stalinist period and by the Russian tradition's renascent rejection of homoerotic content in literature. This last comment should suggest that if any of the poems cited here seem less "classic" than Pushkin's lyric, this may be in part because they express points of conflict in the dominant tradition and reveal its underlying contradictions rather than fitting within it seamlessly.

VI

These poems, read together, show considerable flexibility in the use of gender in women's love poetry to female addressees. At least four options are available: writing as a man to a woman, writing as an indeterminate speaker to a woman, writing as a woman to an indeterminate addressee, and finally, most novel and difficult of all, writing as a woman to a woman. The variety of solutions to the problem of introducing new gender relations into a literary tradition further illustrates the point that gender in language is not at all the same thing as biological sex.[85] By clothing her speech in shifting indicators of gender, a Russian poet can project a variety of textual bodies in differently gendered combinations. Although a woman writer's own biological sex may lead her to question and disrupt the naturalness of the traditional gender system, gender that emerges in a poem results from the writer's performance, her choice of linguistic garb. A lesbian love lyric goes even further, to reveal the limits of the heterosexual tradition of the language in which it is written. Judith Butler discusses the effect of this kind of performance in destabilizing accepted ideas about the nature and meaning of gender. "There is no 'proper' gender, a gender proper to one sex rather than another, which is in some sense that sex's cultural property. Where that notion of the 'proper' operates, it is always and only *improperly* installed as the effect of a compulsory system."[86] The availability in Russian of gender-marked language which allows "cross-

dressing," and the number of important poets who have practiced such transvestism, make gender in Russian poetry particularly rich and problematic. Calling
into question the naturalness of a gender structure that marginalizes women also
points up the arbitrariness of signs of gender in language—and vice versa. Language is used every day and reflects society's habitual relations, but its conventions
work differently on the page: the system is at once controlling and malleable. Published and public writing preserves the writer's name and gendered language rather
than the sexed body. The excess effect of gender as constructed with Russian grammar shapes the tradition, or else eases one out of the tradition if those female
pronouns make one's writing seem too individual, not sufficiently universal.

In addition to the resources of the Russian language, poets work to find poetic
and textual ancestors who can help to convey impulses from the biographical
world into the literary tradition. In the rich poetic exchange between Tsvetaeva and
Parnok, Tsvetaeva attempts a gesture of closure by writing Parnok in the role of
mother,[87] so as to be her heir and inheritor and to outlive her. Parnok, in Burgin's
reading, at least, not only takes Pavlova as her great-grandmother but eventually
refigures the earlier relationship in order to make Tsvetaeva her mother in turn, or,
in a final gender blur, the being whose seed allows the poet to conceive fruits of her
own.[88] The terms of biological kinship underline a desire to leave poetic progeny,
to live on beyond the narrow circle of people who happen to hear poems recited
or to read them in handwritten copies. Given gendered language's function as a
mask and/or expression of lesbian sexuality, Gippius and Solov'eva got love poems
addressed to women into print more easily: their male speakers and masculine
grammatical forms let their work be read as "universal." Parnok and Tsvetaeva,
whose homoerotic lyrics were mostly unpublished in their own lifetimes, inscribe
rich performances of gender in their love poetry. The risks of writing "outside" a
tradition increase in proportion to how far "outside" one is, and the risks are both
personal and professional: a writer who is not published and read has truly died to
her tradition without leaving any heirs. On the other hand, poems that we know
and read can continue to seduce us.

Notes

I would like to thank Diana Burgin, Pamela Chester, and my colleagues the Flaming Bitches
for their very helpful comments on this text.

1. Akhmatova and Tsvetaeva did not enjoy untroubled access to readers, and the works of
each were eclipsed for a time (for stylistic as well as political reasons). However, poets never forgot
their work, and it served both before and after their "rehabilitations" to inspire and support
younger generations of writers.

2. Compare, for example, the directions given to readers who aspired to poetic culture in the
journal/catalogue of a popular *fin de siècle* publisher:

> For reading à deux the selection is much broader than for reading in company. À
> deux I understand to mean, of course, "him" and "her." "He" is supposed to read. Not,
> it is true, because she cannot read better, but somehow it has been settled that he
> always reads.

(The reason for this convention, the author goes on to speculate, is that reading poetry aloud requires more attention than merely listening; women keep their hands busy with needlework, whereas men would have no such compensatory activity and so their attention would wander while listening.) Pl. Krasnov, "Kogda i gde chitaiut nashikh poètov," *Izvestiia knizhnykh magazinov Tovarishchestva M. O. Vol'f* 4, no. 7–8 (April–May 1901): 84.

3. "Relative," of course, to the vast majority of Russian women. These women were not all from aristocratic families and faced different, variously difficult circumstances during their lives, especially after the Revolution.

4. Laura Engelstein, *The Keys to Happiness: Sex and the Search for Modernity in Fin-de-Siècle Russia* (Ithaca and London: Cornell University Press, 1992). Diana Burgin makes essentially the same point in "After the Ball is Over: Sophia Parnok's Creative Relationship with Marina Tsvetaeva," *Russian Review* 47 (1988): 427: "Little distinction has ever been made—least of all during the fin-de-siècle period—between literary depictions and/or stereotypes of lesbians, courtesans, prostitutes, and other feminine 'idols of perversity.'"

The postrevolutionary period depicted lesbians as upper-class decadent perverts: the healthy freshness of proletarian culture would presumably cleanse Russia of unnatural vices, along with the literary work that expressed them. Thus, although lesbian relationships were not criminalized as male homosexual activity was, their assignment to the realm of "mental illness" was hardly conducive to a vibrant presence in literary life.

5. Here I define "the canon" loosely, to mean the authors and literary works that were reprinted, anthologized in textbooks (*khrestomatii*) to be read and even memorized by schoolchildren, and referred to in public and in private by the shapers of public discourse.

6. This is more true of Gippius and Solov'eva than of Parnok and Tsvetaeva: not only did Parnok and Tsvetaeva grow up able to read Gippius and Solov'eva, but the Symbolists' project of discovering and reevaluating neglected nineteenth-century poets made several earlier Russian women poets more available to readers in the 1910s. Akhmatova was aware of Anna Bunina, to whom her family was distantly connected, calling her "Russia's first poetess" in one fragment of autobiographical prose (included by way of introduction to Anna Akhmatova, *Stikhi i proza* [Moskva: Iskusstvo, 1989], p. 7). Parnok and Tsvetaeva discovered Pavlova and other poetic predecessors in the early to mid-1910s, and this discovery significantly influenced their poetic and emotional relationship. At the same time, familiarity with these women's work was not part of their early educations; it came after they had already begun to write poetry.

7. Aleksandr Pushkin, *Polnoe sobranie sochinenii v desiati tomakh*, vol. III (Moscow-Leningrad: Izd. Akademii nauk SSSR, 1949), p. 60. The poem was written in 1828.

8. Here and elsewhere all translations from Russian are mine and strive for literal accuracy rather than poetic effect.

9. For this reason I will use the Russian forms in quotes throughout this section. The word "thou," etymological equivalent to *ty*, sounds formal to many speakers of English because of its archaism and association with biblical texts and canonical literary works (Shakespeare and the like). Thus, "you" is the only adequate translation for both *ty* and *vy* in contemporary standard English, as it is for the comparable *tu* and *vous* in French.

10. The role of artistic representation in structuring sexuality and related social relationships is stressed by Tessa Boffin and Jean Fraser: "If sexuality and representation are mutually constituted, then it cannot be possible to discuss them as two discrete entities, one existing before the other. Representations do not merely reflect sexuality but play an active role in its production. Sexuality is always mediated and it is through representations that our bodies, and our fantasies, come to be sexually organized." "Introduction," in *Stolen Glances: Lesbians Take Photographs*, ed. Boffin and Fraser (London: Pandora Press, 1991), p. 10.

11. The importance of this authority seems especially marked for writers who, intentionally or not, fall outside the critical norm and reappropriate Pushkin in poetry or prose for their own purposes—good examples are Tsvetaeva (discussed briefly in Barbara Heldt, *Terrible Perfection: Women and Russian Literature* [Bloomington: Indiana University Press, 1987], pp. 100–102) and later Maiakovskii (the 1924 poem "Iubileinoe"). The "Silver Age," commonly accepted to name

the period, points to the earlier and nominally superior Golden Age as its model and origin. For more detailed examinations of the interrelationship of the two periods, see Gasparov, Hughes, and Paperno, eds., *Cultural Mythologies of Russian Modernism: From the Golden Age to the Silver Age* (Berkeley: University of California Press, 1992).

12. In Russian the six persons (first, second, and third in both singular and plural) are marked by distinct conjugated verb forms in the present and future tenses which do not reflect gender. In the past tense, however, Russian verbs collapse into only four forms: masculine, feminine, and neuter singular, and the gender-ambiguous plural. This means that the first- and second-person singular (like the third) provoke masculine or feminine singular forms in the past, even though the first- and second-person pronouns themselves are not marked for gender. Compare, for example:

		1st	2nd	3rd persons	
past-tense verbs	masculine:	я был	ты был	он был	(I was,
	feminine:	я была́	ты была́	она́ была́	thou wast,
	plural:	мы бы́ли	вы бы́ли	они́ бы́ли	etc.)
short-form adjectives	masc.:	я добр	ты добр	он добр	(I am kind,
	fem.:	я добра́	ты добра́	она́ добра́	thou art
	pl.:	мы добры́	вы добры́	они́ добры́	kind, etc.)

13. Antonina Filonova Gove, "Gender as a Poetic Feature in the Verse of Zinaida Gippius," in *American Contributions to the VIIIth International Congress of Slavists*, vol. 1: *Linguistics* (Columbus, Ohio: Slavica, 1978), p. 388.

Readers may sense gender in elements of a text other than the strict grammatical marking of verbs, adjectives, and other parts of speech. I have heard from both Russians and Americans who read Russian that they "know" a poem in Russian was written by a woman even when the author has used grammatically masculine forms to refer to herself. This sense would parallel the possibility of identifying a writer's sex in English, with grammatical gender marking far more limited than in Russian or many other languages, and where the existence and nature of a distinctly "women's language" are therefore open to debate. Since this "sense" for a writer's gender is more difficult to quantify and analyze than explicit grammatical signs of gender, however, I will not address it in this essay. It is worth noting that the possibility of revealing feminine gender through other means, while at the same time "masking" it with masculine grammatical forms, offers options for Russian women who wish to convey anything besides stereotypical "femininity" and normative heterosexuality in their writing.

14. *Ona* (She) in the first stanza, and *nee* (her) and *ei* (to her) in the second (genitive and dative forms of the feminine singular pronoun *ona*).

15. Catriona Kelly points out that Anna Akhmatova's lyric "I kak budto po oshibke" (1909), part II of the two-poem cycle "Chitaia Gamleta," picks up this scene and treats it from the female point of view, while at the same time responding to Hamlet from the point of view of Ophelia. Kelly, *A History of Russian Women's Writing, 1820–1992* (Oxford: Clarendon Press, 1994), p. 211.

16. I would speculate that men reading a poem where the "I" is masculine and the "you" feminine, through the force of grammar, read from the position of the speaker ("I") rather than that of the addressee (even if men are arguably the genuine addressees of such a poem as in Pushkin's poem above), while women reading the poem assume the role of "you" and the position of the speaker's love object. This is suggested not only by the theories of Pl. Krasnov, but also by the way poets such as Akhmatova and Tsvetaeva treat Pushkin and other great male poets in their writings, a topic beyond the scope of this study.

17. Her explanation thus stresses the wish for full poetic seriousness. The statement has often been quoted; I cite it from Temira Pachmuss, *Zinaida Hippius: An Intellectual Profile* (Carbondale: Southern Illinois University Press, 1971), p. 17.

18. See, for example, Sergei Makovskii's *Na parnase serebrianogo veka* (Munich: Izdatel'stvo Tsentral'nogo Ob"edineniia Politicheskikh Emigrantov iz SSSR, 1962), following p. 86. Makovskii

himself describes Gippius as "similar to an androgyne," with narrow hips and not even a hint of breasts (ibid., 89). The attraction of Bakst's portrait, however, depends on the kind of gender uncertainty that Marjorie Garber describes in *Vested Interests: Cross-Dressing and Cultural Anxiety* (New York: Harper Collins, 1993), esp. pp. 9–11. Cross-dressing, says Garber, causes a crisis of category, undermining binarism by indeterminacy, the impossibility of assigning the cross-dressed person easily and immediately to one of the two genders normative in our society.

19. Sandra M. Gilbert, "Costumes of the Mind: Transvestism as Metaphor in Modern Literature," in *Gender Studies: New Directions in Feminist Criticism*, ed. Judith Spector (Bowling Green, Ohio: Bowling Green University Popular Press, 1986), pp. 70–95.

20. For an example, see *Tsvetaeva: A Pictorial Biography*, ed. Ellendea Proffer (Ann Arbor: Ardis, 1980), pp. 42–43.

21. Solov'eva appears wearing a shirt, tie, and jacket in the photograph given in Temira Pachmuss, trans. and ed., *Women Writers in Russian Modernism: An Anthology* (Urbana: University of Illinois Press, 1978), following p. 176. If Pachmuss's (non-)treatment of Gippius's and Solov'eva's sexuality is any indication, one supposes that she would have preferred to show Solov'eva in a dress, if a picture were available. Sof'ia Parnok wears a jacket and tie in some of the later photographs included in *Sobranie stikhotvorenii*, ed. S. Poliakova (Ann Arbor: Ardis, 1979), pp. 15–16. See Elizabeth Wilson, "Making an Appearance," in Boffin and Fraser, *Stolen Glances*, p. 54: "By the early twentieth century, male dress for women was clearly associated, at least in France, with lesbianism." In Russia as well, many women in this period used male attire to identify themselves as (butch) lesbians.

Full-face portraits such as these could not have been made without the subject's consent and cooperation (the same applies to Bakst's drawing of Gippius). By sitting still for the camera or the artist, these women agree to include cross-dressing among their public and publishable images.

22. Even the poet's signature, if it consists only of the last name with one or two initials (a format often used in Russian), need not convey the writer's sex, since Gippius, like Parnok, is a non-Russian name without the gender marking one sees in Russian names such as Solov'eva or Tsvetaeva, with their indicative feminine -*a* ending. Gippius could, after all, have used only her husband's name, Merezhkovskii, which was often appended to her own name in book catalogues—just as Tsvetaeva could have prolonged her brief practice of signing the gender-eliding "Efron" after her marriage.

23. Roman Jakobson, *Shifters, Verbal Categories and the Russian Verb* (Cambridge, Mass.: Harvard University Press, 1957), p. 6.

24. Sandra M. Gilbert and Susan Gubar, "Introduction," in Gilbert and Gubar, eds., *Shakespeare's Sisters: Feminist Essays on Women Poets* (Bloomington: Indiana University Press, 1979), p. xxi.

25. Jane Taubman points this out usefully in *A Life through Poetry: Marina Tsvetaeva's Lyric Diary* (Columbus, Ohio: Slavica Publishers, 1988), p. 8.

26. Gove, "Gender as a Poetic Feature," p. 381.

27. Ibid., p. 382.

28. For example, "Potselui" is one of ten poems by Gippius included in *Tsaritsy muz* (Moscow: Sovremennik, 1989). To put that in context, this edition of women poets up to 1917 gives twenty-two poems by Evdokiia Rostopchina, twenty-nine by Karolina Pavlova, and fourteen by Solov'eva; even Vera Figner, better remembered (and justly so) for her achievements outside of the realm of poetry, has nine selections. The editors of the collection must see "Potselui" as more representative of Gippius's work, or perhaps more acceptable, than her other prerevolutionary poems.

29. Gove, "Gender as a Poetic Feature," p. 383.

30. Such as, for example, the scenes with the boy Sasha in Fedor Sologub's novel *Melkii bes* (*The Pretty Demon*), which Ol'ga Matich discusses in "Androgyny and the Russian Silver Age," *Pacific Coast Philology* 14 (1979): 44, along with other Silver Age androgynes.

31. Matich cites the poem in "Zinaida Gippius and the Unisex of Heavenly Experience," *Die Welt der Slaven* 19–20 (1974–75): 103–104, and in "Androgyny and the Russian Religious Renais-

sance," in *Western Philosophical Systems in Russian Literature*, ed. Anthony Mlikotin (Los Angeles: University of Southern California Press, 1979), p. 169.

32. Matich, "Zinaida Gippius and the Unisex of Heavenly Existence," p. 103, and "Androgyny and the Russian Religious Renaissance," p. 169.

33. See Nadezhda Durova, *The Cavalry Maiden: Journals of a Female Russian Officer in the Napoleonic Wars*, trans. Mary Fleming Zirin (Bloomington: Indiana University Press, 1989). After her military career, Durova, who reportedly used masculine forms to refer to herself in her speech, wrote her memoirs with feminine language with the first person, perhaps to foreground the constant tension in her imposture.

34. The friendship between Gippius and Solov'eva lasted until Solov'eva died in Moscow in 1924 (Pachmuss, *Women Writers*, p. 176).

35. The word "allegro" certainly does not describe Solov'eva's poetic work; it is more largo.

36. Poliksena Solov'eva (Allegro), *Inei. Risunki i stihki* (St. Petersburg: T-vo R. Golike i A. Vil'borg, 1905), title page. I suggest that "Allegro" is not the sort of pseudonym that a man would use; Russian men have used pseudonyms that cry out pseudonymity (for example Gor'kii [the masculine adjective "Bitter"], Belyi [the masculine adjective "White"]), or pseudonyms that take over the functions of their original names (Kornei Chukovskii), but rarely pseudonyms that seem chosen to avoid the question of gender (compare Mikhail Tsetlin, "Amari"—"A Marie," referring to his wife).

37. Examples are cited in Pachmuss, *Women Writers*, pp. 176–77; for example, a critic in *Russkoe bogatstvo* (*Russian Wealth*) notes "some original, delicately sad, and femininely graceful coloring, which is typical of her art in general" (ibid., p. 176).

38. Simon Karlinsky, *Marina Tsvetaeva: The Woman, Her World, and Her Poetry* (Cambridge: Cambridge University Press, 1986), p. 53.

39. Matich states baldly that Gippius "was either bisexual or frigid," not much of an improvement on Pachmuss's stately avoidance of the issue. "Androgyny and the Russian Silver Age," p. 45.

40. Noel Riley Fitch illuminates the difficulties of addressing anyone's (homo)sexuality in a work about "something else," in "The Elusive 'Seamless Whole': A Biographer Treats (or Fails to Treat) Lesbianism," in *Lesbian Texts and Contexts*, ed. Karla Jay and Joanna Glasgow (New York: New York University Press, 1990), pp. 59–69.

41. Pachmuss gives another translation of this poem in *Women Writers*, pp. 189–90. Although, as I pointed out, Pachmuss ignores Allegro's lifelong relationship with Manasseina, including this poem in her selection of translations indicates that she does recognize its importance in the poet's whole opus. I cite the Russian text from *Inei*, p. 100.

42. I speculate that writing a personal love poem made Solov'eva less willing to don the masculine linguistic garb she often uses elsewhere. On the other hand, in line 5 the speaker refers to a noun of masculine gender, *vzor*, with the associated masculine forms of possessive pronoun and verb, *vzor moi zamedlialsia*, while the addressee is consistently surrounded only by feminine forms.

43. Out of fifty-nine poems in the collection *Inei*, twenty have definitely masculine speakers, twenty-four have first-person singular speakers of indeterminate gender, and fifteen do not use any first-person singular forms; none have feminine speakers. Altogether, that means about 34 percent of the poems have a masculine speaker, while 66 percent have indeterminate speakers. The percentages of Solov'eva's entire opus should be compared with the numbers Gove obtains for Gippius. The lower percentage of definitely masculine speakers suggests that Solov'eva does not stress those grammatical forms (past-tense verbs, adjectives, etc.) that reveal gender, perhaps that her work as a whole is more impersonal than Gippius's.

44. For example, Tsvetaeva later describes this couple in negative terms in her "Lettre à l'amazone" (1932–34), a response to Natalie Clifford Barney's advocacy of lesbianism; Russian translation "Pis'mo k amazonke (Tret'ia popytka chistovika)," trans. K. Azadovskii, *Zvezda* 2 (1990): 187. After her death, as her poetic work slowly began to reappear in the Soviet Union and abroad, Tsvetaeva's love poems appeared in print more frequently than their percentage in her

opus would indicate. Moreover, these editions preferred poems that are stereotypical even in their presentation of a heterosexual relationship. One example is "Vchera eshche v glaza gliadel" ("Yesterday he still looked [me] in the eyes") from a series called "Pesenki" ("Little Songs") that is clearly not intended as a statement by Tsvetaeva's own poetic persona, but which was the only original poem published during Tsvetaeva's life in the Soviet Union after her return from Paris (in *Stikhotvoreniia i poèmy*, vol. II, p. 288; notes on p. 401); its speaker is devastated after her male lover has left her. Another is "Popytka revnosti" ("An Attempt at Jealousy"), the longest of Tsvetaeva's four poems included in *The Heritage of Russian Verse* (intro. and ed. Dimitri Obolensky [Bloomington: Indiana University Press, 1976]), whose speaker castigates her former lover for his bad taste in women in terms that condemn him less harshly than his new lover.

46. The Tsvetaeva heirs and scholars to whom this comment refers hoped to protect her reputation in the Soviet Union by suppressing or downplaying anything too sexy or political—since keeping her "clean" made it possible to publish more poetry and continue scholarly work on her oeuvre. Like all choices between two evils, this results in unfortunate distortions.

47. First, she was engaged in a passionate relationship with a poet, which channeled her emotional energy further into poetry and provided a qualified critic, strongly interested in her poem's depiction of their relationship. Moreover, Parnok apparently introduced Tsvetaeva to Karolina Pavlova and other women poets (see the 1915 letter where Tsvetaeva asks her sister-in-law to pick up books by Pavlova and Rostopchina, which she had left at a friend's house, cited in Anna Saakiants, *Marina Tsvetaeva: Stranitsy zhizni i tvorchestva (1910–1922)* [Moskva: Sovetskii pisatel', 1986], p. 81), and so raised for her the question of women's language and writing in Russian. Trips with Parnok into the Russian provinces, one of which is described in the poem cited here, caused or coincided with a new interest in folk language and genres, which gave Tsvetaeva an important source of women's voices, expressions, and speech rhythms. All of these factors (self-criticism and critical attention, poetry by earlier Russian women, and Russian folk genres and language) were crucial in Tsvetaeva's formation as a poet.

48. Diana Burgin, Simon Karlinsky, and Sof'ia Poliakova are among the scholars who concur with this assessment. At the same time, one should be wary of projecting current attitudes back seventy or eighty years. Indeed, I suspect that differing definitions of the term "lesbian" are responsible for much of the debate over the nature of Tsvetaeva's relationship with Parnok.

49. Svetlana El'nitskii argued persuasively, in a paper read at the Tsvetaeva Centennial Symposium in Amherst, September 1992, that Tsvetaeva's 1921 poem "Bessonnitsa" ("Insomnia"), dedicated to Tat'iana Skriabina, is in fact a continuation of the earlier poetic dialogue with Parnok. However, this poem is the only example in Tsvetaeva's later poetry.

50. Although the contact described is nothing shocking to a reader today, this is the only poem in the cycle to be so frank. The rest of the cycle treats the beloved and her body more visually; often that body is addressed through its parts—as here, when we see a close-up of the addressee's hand—which the speaker strives to interpret like pieces of a puzzle.

51. Burgin, "After the Ball Is Over," pp. 427ff.

52. Probably the best-known example is the poem "Tsar'-Devitsa," whose patterning of gender roles is explored in Gerry Smith's article "Characters and Narrative Modes in Marina Tsvetaeva's Tsar'-Devitsa," *Oxford Slavonic Papers* 12 (1979): 117–34, and Jerzy Faryno's book *Mifologizm i teologizm Tsvetaevoi ("Magdalina"—"Tsar'-Devitsa"—"Pereulochki")*, Wiener Slawistischer Almanach, Sonderband 18 (Wien, 1985), pp. 111–256.

53. In part of her important study of the poetry and relationship between Tsvetaeva and Parnok, Sof'ia Poliakova seems anxious to code Parnok as the butch and Tsvetaeva as the femme in their relationship. *Zakatnye ony dni: Tsvetaeva i Parnok* (Ann Arbor: Ardis, 1983), p. 54.

54. Diana Fuss, "Inside/Out," introduction to *Inside/Out: Lesbian Theories, Gay Theories*, ed. Fuss (New York and London: Routledge, 1991), p. 7.

55. Marina Tsvetaeva, *Stikhotvoreniia i poèmy v piati tomakh* (New York: Russica, 1980–83), vol. 1, p. 22.

56. "Est' imena, kak dushnye tsvety," ibid., p. 185.

57. Karolina Pavlova, *Polnoe sobranie stikhotvorenii* (Moskva: Biblioteka poèta, 1964), p. 153.

58. "Segodnia, chasu v vos'mom," in Tsvetaeva, *Stikhotvoreniia i poèmy*, vol. I, p. 179.

59. Examples would be Tsvetaeva's later cycles of poems written to Aleksandr Bakhrakh ("Chas dushi," "Naklon," "Rakovina," in *Stikhotvoreniia i poèmy*, vol. III, pp. 87–90) and Anatolii Shteiger ("Stikhi sirote," ibid., pp. 192–96).

60. Parnok, *Sobranie stikhotvorenii*, pp. 141–42.

61. Tsvetaeva, *Stikhotvoreniia i poèmy*, vol. I, p. 225; the poem is dated April 26, 1916, by most accounts after the end of Tsvetaeva's relationship with Parnok.

62. Tsvetaeva, "Pis'mo amazonke," esp. pp. 185–86.

63. Moreover, of the dramatic roles not written for Holliday, Henrietta from "Prikliuchenie" ("An Adventure") does indeed first appear in man's clothing as Henri, and did once fight a duel over a woman, but the audience sees her mainly in her interactions with the nicely heterosexual Casanova, who only in the final scene calls her "Platonova rodnaia polovina!" ("My dear Platonic half!"). Tsvetaeva, *Teatr* (Moscow: Iskusstvo, 1988), p. 165.

64. Burgin, "After the Ball Is Over," p. 438: "Some of the fruits of Parnok's late and best verse can be seen, in part, as blossoms from Tsvetaeva's seed."

65. The best survey of Parnok's life and work is Diana Burgin's *Sophia Parnok: The Life and Work of Russia's Sappho* (New York and London: New York University Press, 1994).

66. If nothing else, the huge industry of Pushkiniana must have convinced every Russian poet from the Silver Age on that a certain level of success was bound to create lively interest in one's biography, writings, and other relics.

67. Burgin, "Sophia Parnok and the Writing of a Lesbian Poet's Life," *Slavic Review* 51, no. 2 (Summer 1992): 214: "the life Parnok created in her lyrics for herself and for her readers is a consciously conceived, albeit unnamed, lesbian existence, politically as well as spiritually aware of other lesbian existences in history, myth, art and life."

68. Karla Jay, in her book *The Amazon and the Page: Natalie Clifford Barney and Renée Vivien* (Bloomington: Indiana University Press, 1988), p. 63, points out that in the *fin de siècle* period, "Love between women was evidently tolerable, even piquant, to the public taste if the lovers wore chitons."

69. Parnok, *Sobranie stikhotvorenii*, p. 146.

70. Ibid., p. 141.

71. I point out the political consequences of this use in Sibelan Forrester, "Prijevod kao reinkarnacija: Očuvanje razlike u tekstualnim tijelima" ("Translation as Reincarnation: Preserving Difference in Textual Bodies"), trans. Tihana Mrsić and Sanja Matešić, *Književna smotra* (Zagreb) 26, no. 91 (1994): 68–73.

72. See, for example, "Tak na drugikh beregakh, u drugogo pevuchego moria," in which a maiden sitting by the other sea imagines herself completing Sappho's songs and dreams. Parnok, *Sobranie stikhotvorenii*, p. 147.

73. Ibid., p. 134.

74. See the "triptych" "Penfesileia" ("Penthesileia"), first published in *Rozy Pierii*; Parnok, *Sobranie stikhotvorenii*, pp. 147–48.

75. This is especially true of Poliakova's *Zakatnye ony dni*.

76. In Parnok, *Sobranie stikhotvorenii*, pp. 254–55; on p. 328, Poliakova provides some variant readings of the cycles' order and components.

77. Ibid., p. 247 and p. 242.

78. Burgin points out that the last two stanzas were added several months after the first four, explaining their very different tone and also the final dating in a season when snow cannot be a realistic detail. *Sophia Parnok*, pp. 297 and 300.

79. Burgin, "After the Ball Is Over," pp. 440–41.

80. Compare here Tsvetaeva's own stress on her golden hair in her youth and her admiration for Parnok's reddish "helmet" of hair in the cycle "Podruga" with the poetic use she makes of her own premature grayness in 1921–22. Her late poem "—Pora! dlia ètogo ognia" (*Sochineniia y dvukh tomakh* (Moscow, 1988], vol. 1, p. 330, dated Jan. 23, 1940), like Parnok's poem here, indicates that it is somehow monstrous for an old woman ("a mountain of fifty Januaries") to be

in love or even interested in love.

81. This suggestion would seem not to apply to the masculine-gendered *moi stikh* (my verse) in line 3, but that is not necessarily so: if the poet's pride in her verse turns to bitterness at its uselessness, the verse can come to be seen as a harmful parasite, assuming the shape of the thing it covers as does frost on a rose, and like frost or snow threatening to sap the vitality of the reality it is based on.

82. Pamela Chester has pointed out to me that the startling change in rhythm may reflect the irregular heartbeat that foretold Parnok's imminent death.

83. "Dai ruku, i poidem v nash greshnyi rai!" Parnok, *Sobranie stikhotvorenii*, p. 254.

84. My thanks to Diana Burgin for pointing out to me the error in the line on p. 256 of Parnok, *Sobranie stikhotvorenii*.

85. Gove makes essentially the same point; "Gender as a Poetic Feature," pp. 379–81.

86. Judith Butler, "Imitation and Gender Insubordination," in Fuss, *Inside/Out*, p. 21.

87. Compare the similar but more subtle process as Tsvetaeva appropriates the position of Akhamatova's heir, mentioned in my "Bells and Cupolas: The Formative Role of the Female Body in Marina Tsvetaeva's Poetry," *Slavic Review* 51, no. 2 (Summer 1992): 240.

88. In Parnok's case, in particular, this dynamic was complicated further by her inability to have children, due to illness.

SEVEN

Mothers and Daughters

Variations on Family Themes in Tsvetaeva's *The House at Old Pimen*

NATASHA KOLCHEVSKA

And then here are those who were given poetry in their cradle, and who know that if there is nothing left, there is still the world of language. I take the risk of saying that these people answer nothingness . . . poetically. They are people who at the very moment of struggle, of encounter with historical disasters, work on language, transform it, work it, garden it, graft it. They are masters of the signifier. Language is their universe and with it they build a little house that is a palace. It is of no surprise that one finds that work on the signifier is formed among people who staked their tents in language: Rimbaud, Lispector, Tsvetayeva, Celan and others.

—Cixous, 132

IN 1934, IN the last decade of her life and at a point when she had practically stopped writing poetry, Marina Tsvetaeva constructed such a house in *The House at Old Pimen*, the longest and most complex of her childhood memoirs.[1] While it is attentive, like her other autobiographical pieces ("Khlystovki," "Mother and Music," "The Devil," "My Pushkin"), to the young Marina's childhood conflicts and to the adult Tsvetaeva's attempts to understand and give artistic form to unresolved issues in that childhood, *The House at Old Pimen* stands somewhat apart from these. As I shall discuss below, by focusing on a surrogate family, the Ilovaiskiis, and the house in which they dwelled, Tsvetaeva shifts from the rich psychological self-probing of the other childhood memoirs to a mythified, lyricized critique of the cultural and social norms of late empire Russia, and of their effects on several generations of Russian women, including her own. In the adult narrator's consciousness, the Ilovaiskiis can be read as a surrogate for the social and psychological conflicts of that family, a palimpsest on which she will write the tale of her own coming to creativity and consciousness. Parallels both physical (her mother, like many of the Ilovaiskiis, died an early death of tuberculosis) and psychological (particularly, as I will show, in the authoritarian relations of parents to children, and in the cruelty of maternal love in the two families) are transformed into a meditation on the nature of love and family, on the emotional disfigurement of both men and women by the patriarchal system, and on the impact of this family's tragedy on Tsvetaeva's sense of herself as a mother and a poet.

Tsvetaeva's skepticism about the traditional, organized forms of feminism ("There is no female question in art—there are female answers to human questions") has been duly noted by her biographers (e.g., Karlinsky, Taubman).

Nevertheless, *The House at Old Pimen*'s interest lies precisely in its negotiation by one *woman* writer of essential human questions. Through the prism of the young girl's emotions and the adult writer's reconstruction of those emotions thirty years later, the narrative explores the multiple meanings of patriarchal structures, matrilineal bonds, and their significance for a woman writer.

As with other major Russian poets, the boundary between life and writing was always a fluid one for Tsvetaeva, and any analysis of her writing will be incomplete if it does not address the particular conjunction of historical and biographical moments in her personal and literary lives. At the risk of overdetermining the genesis of this particular text, I will suggest several that seem the most relevant.

The House at Old Pimen was written "on command," so to speak: Tsvetaeva's editor at *Contemporary Notes*, a major émigré journal and the most consistent publisher of her prose, requested additional pieces in 1932. Tsvetaeva, as always short of money—she was essentially her family's sole support—agreed, though reluctantly.[2] Certainly, in part this was a practical decision based on her awareness that Russians have always been avid consumers of memoirs and biographical writing, and therefore memoirs would be more marketable. In addition, she could read these at the poetry evenings that she organized in Paris—largely single-handedly— once or twice a year. The early 1930s were also an emotionally difficult time for Tsvetaeva: in 1932, the year that she turned forty, she learned of her half-brother's death—from tuberculosis, like the subjects of her narrative—in the Soviet Union; death and loss also left their mark in the relatively large number of memoirs that she wrote about dead or distant fellow poets and artists (Voloshin, Belyi, Mandel'shtam). Of equal significance for her personal life, these years saw a gradual estrangement between Marina and Ariadna, her older and only surviving daughter. Tsvetaeva had poured all her desire for the creation of a matrilineal line of artistic geniuses into her talented child, and by many accounts treated her more as sister than as daughter. While there are seemingly few parallels between the harsh, unloving mothers of *The House at Old Pimen* and Tsvetaeva's own experiences as a mother to Ariadna, it is plausible that this rupture compelled her to examine the darker sides of motherhood.

Reading Tsvetaeva's letters from the years before her return to the Soviet Union in 1939, I was struck by her growing sense of exclusion from that culture which she had grown up believing she would inherit, and of pessimism and contemplations of death and suicide. In 1934, Tsvetaeva writes of a felt need "to write a testament [*zaveshchanie*] . . . not to dispose of objects—I have nothing—but something that I need so people will know about me: an explanation [*raz"ias-nenie*]. To settle accounts" (115). There is a sense in much of her prose from this period of "settling accounts," through the more direct forms that prose may offer over poetry, with her familial and cultural predecessors. As I shall demonstrate, in *The House at Old Pimen* this desire to "settle accounts" translates itself into a dual trajectory. By challenging received truths and tackling "big" questions—in other words, by writing "like a man" in this text Tsvetaeva confronts a public image, created to a large extent by male critics and readers—that artistic aristocracy that shaped Russian cultural taste—of a hysterical woman and mannered, "decadent" writer. Conversely, by writing as a woman, by speaking for the women in her text, she fills in, brings to public attention, what had been that "empty space" inhabited by unknown, silent women who stir in the background of prominent men, who are assumed to have no story of their own.[3]

Like much of Tsvetaeva's prose, *The House at Old Pimen* is difficult to categorize generically.[4] As a work of experimental, modernist sensibility, it merges elements of autobiography and family chronicle, fact and fiction, social commentary and individual psychology, mythifying lyricism and historical analysis, biographical fact and poetic fiction. *The House at Old Pimen* is based on a wide variety of discursive strategies that rely for their effect on the speaker's ability to establish a highly personal and emotional dialogue with her reader and with the subjects of her story. In what she characterizes as an "involved, co-creative reading," Sibelan Forrester points out that Tsvetaeva "as an author ... is not an authority but a provocation to further thought, feeling, and artistic experimentation" (481, and fn. to 485).[5] In a later comment that is essential to understanding Tsvetaeva's expectations for her narrative, Forrester adds that Tsvetaeva does not write only for a male audience (although in patriarchal society, men traditionally control "official" responses to texts and the parameters of literary authority) but "for any reader," and "the female reader is invited to identify with the female speaker, to assume herself the position of subject rather than object" (485). In contrast to traditional autobiography, there is no sense of authorial growth and development in *The House at Old Pimen*: the tale of the Ilovaiskiis—by turns nostalgic and angry, but always passionately involved, subjective—is told directly, by a mature adult whose interpretation, to quote Elizabeth Bruss, "invests the past and the self with coherence and meaning that may not have been evident before the act of writing itself" (46). It is precisely the speaker's highly emotional, intimate, and discursive language that gives birth to this text. As Barbara Heldt points out: "Our sense of the author's self comes to us directly through the style; there is no coherent exposition of a life-view as it developed. . . . Rather, the past is judged by a self already formed and in a uniquely acute tone of voice. The text itself becomes the only truth" (98).

As is the case for many women autobiographers, the narrator's subjectivity, through which she establishes the right to define her text in terms of her relationships to the subjects of her narrative, is a central structural principle in *The House at Old Pimen*. Heldt's comment, that "[b]y choosing a style of highly-mannered subjectivism when not talking ostensibly about herself, Tsvetaeva is declaring her freedom from conventions of objective narration" (98), is well taken. Breaking out of what French feminist theorists have called "the forward drive of logocentric certitude and individuality" (Smith, 13), it is deliberately, even ostentatiously, discontinuous, full of gaps and ruptures, subjective comments, intimate disclosures, conscious linguistic searches and word plays, and, perhaps most important, it is intent on involving its reader in the process of discovery and reconstruction of this family chronicle.

There is also a fascinating intertextual aspect to Tsvetaeva's narrative: the discourse in *The House at Old Pimen* relies for many of its facts, though not their mythic reconstruction, on the nine-year (1928–37) correspondence that Tsvetaeva carried on with Vera Nikolaevna Muromtseva-Bunina. Muromtseva was some ten years older and a contemporary and childhood friend of Valeriia Tsvetaeva, the poet's half-sister, and of Nadia Ilovaiskaia, who, as we shall see, was the subject of the young Marina's most intense feelings. In 1931, Muromtseva published her own brief (ten-page) memoir about the Ilovaiskii family, "Near Old Pimen (Church)."[6] Her text is important because it provided Tsvetaeva with firsthand accounts of events that the child Marina, who in fact had little contact with either the Ilovaiskii parents or their children, did not witness herself. For the critic it also serves as a useful tool for analyzing the way that Tsvetaeva reaccentuates the experiences as described by Muromtseva into both a more personal and a significantly more experimental narrative. In one letter to Muromtseva, Tsvetaeva described their two memoirs as "four-handed piano playing." Indeed, the narrative lines of the two texts converge at many points, and Tsvetaeva acknowledges her debt by dedicating the memoir to Muromtseva and closing it with a direct citation from the other woman's memoir.

Muromtseva's family portrait, told compassionately but with an authorial distance that is totally absent in Tsvetaeva's narrative, is that of a rather conventionally patriarchal upper-class Moscow family: an emotionally remote father, absorbed in the world of ideas (historical, anti-Semitic) but out of touch with the new social developments of his time; a sketchily drawn mother ("Aleksandra Aleksandrovna Ilovaiskaia wore an unnaturally serious expression, which did not suit her pleasant face at all; she managed the household with the care of a model housewife" [532]); and beautiful but ill-fated children, in particular Nadia, the older daughter from Ilovaiskii's second marriage. While she remembers no overt hostility between parents and children, Muromtseva recalls their spiritual distance: "In no other family that I knew did I sense such distance between the parents and children, such two mutually exclusive worlds, such a hidden struggle, such an incapability of finding a common language, as in the Ilovaiskiis', in spite of the incessant parental care and filial respect. . . . Their lives were divided in every possible way." (533). What is missing in Muromtseva's text, and so dominant in Tsvetaeva's reconstruction, is the rewriting of this familial drama in terms of patriarchal structures and their consequences for the women of the Ilovaiskii and Tsvetaev families.

Tsvetaeva's *The House at Old Pimen* opens with a dedication: "To Vera Muromtseva—who shares my roots." This simple line announces the structure of Tsvetaeva's ensuing text: the dedication is to a woman, another writer, wife, and mother; the text will explore "common roots," but "roots" themselves signal a public as well as a private dimension: any individual is rooted in familial, historical, cultural, and mythical or religious traditions that shape consciousness and destiny. Similarly, shared roots point to a collective experience, although in this case it is a mediated "literary" collectivity: having scarcely known each other in their youth, in their letters and memoirs the adult Tsvetaeva and Muromtseva construct texts with a common referentiality but different tonalities.

Expanding and mythologizing the "facts" in Muromtseva's memoir, Tsvetaeva re-creates the Ilovaiskii family as a family of tragically grand proportions, victims as well as perpetrators of failed social and personal relationships. But rather than judge and condemn, thereby demonstrating her distance from these failed relationships conveniently bracketed in the past and no longer part of her (as men have often done in writing their life stories), Tsvetaeva's narrative is one of participation, through voice and poeticization, in these relationships. Admitting in a letter to Muromtseva her horror (conceived in both literal and metaphoric terms) at the Ilovaiskii "house," she never attempts to extricate herself from its painful memories. Rather, as my discussion of the central characters of Tsvetaeva's childhood will show, it is a chronicle of what Cixous has called "positive loss," an attempt to recover meaning from tragedy, to examine those secret bonds that will both reveal the specificities of her personal experience and invest them with a coherence and meaning for others.[7]

> An autobiographer who is a woman must suspend herself between paternal and maternal narratives, those fictions of male and female selfhood that permeate her historical moment. This rhetorical woman then is product both of history and of psycho-sexual phenomena: her self-representation reveals both contextual and textual forces of signification. Thus the autobiographer confronts personally her culture's stories of male and female desire, insinuating the lines of her story through the lines of the patriarchal story that has been autobiography. (Smith, 19)

The bulk of Tsvetaeva's childhood memoirs have two related focal points: the young Marina's coming to sexual and artistic awareness, and the complex family relationships—particularly to her mother and other *female* relatives—as reconstructed by the adult writer. With the exception of Grandfather Ilovaiskii, men and boys play a minor role.[8] One of the central questions confronting the reader of these memoirs, then, is why does the "surrogate" grandfather, Dmitrii Ivanovich Ilovaiskii, whom Tsvetaeva, by her own account, had seen on only a few occasions, become the object of some of the strongest emotional and artistic expression in Tsvetaeva's prose? Why does the figure of this elderly reactionary historian, rather than that of Ivan Tsvetaev, by all accounts a benevolent if rather uninvolved father and a culturally prominent figure, fascinate her? Why does she invest the Ilovaiskian house with such portentous and tragic meaning? Finally, what effect does this tale of parental oppression and its conflicting reactions of filial silence and rebellion have on her own quest for legitimacy as a writer and a woman?

For the adult Tsvetaeva, *The House at Old Pimen* is inhabited by a chain of literal presences and literary allusions. The ghosts of Dostoevsky, Saltykov-Shchedrin, and the Belyi of *St. Petersburg* are palpable in the literary text, as are the explicit evocations of Homeric and other Greek myths. These allusions frame the tale of the historical Dmitrii Ilovaiskii and his clan (a succession of two wives and six children), who live at different times in a house on an old Moscow lane that is named for the monk-chronicler St. Pimen, patron saint of historians in Russian culture. The *biological* connection of Dmitrii Ilovaiskii to Marina is nonexistent: he is the father of Ivan Tsvetaev's first wife, who dies of tuberculosis before the age of thirty.[9] Conversely, the *spiritual* connection, through which Tsvetaeva addresses Ilovaiskii in his multiple roles—as family patriarch, historian (always a figure to be reckoned with in Tsvetaeva's writings), and proprietor of this tragic house—is the locus for her tackling of the meanings of male authority for her own creation as a writer and a woman.

Evidence within and outside the text of *The House at Old Pimen* points to Tsvetaeva's intention to write specifically about Dmitrii Ilovaiskii. The two parts of the memoir, "Grandfather Ilovaiskii" and "The House at Old Pimen," carry titles that relate directly to him. In her letters to Muromtseva, Tsvetaeva consistently speaks of the text as "my" or "our" grandfather, referring to the Ilovaiskii women primarily when she has concrete questions to ask her. It is telling that even when she is the most outraged at yet another rejection of some aspect of her manuscript by the editors of *Contemporary Notes*, she frames her indignation at not being able to tell her family chronicle in her own terms as a rejection of Ilovaiskii rather than of the whole of her narrative.[10] She writes to Muromtseva:

> —Well, Vera, our "grandfather" has been chased out again. . . . Why can [the novelist, Fedor] Stepun spend years telling about his wives, fiancées, relatives, etc., while I cannot speak of my only grandfather Ilovaiskii? . . .[11] I would think that the most important thing for an editor is: how is a piece written, i.e., who wrote it, and not who is it about. And it is a big mistake to think that my memoirs of, let's say, a famous literary personage are more valuable than those about the setter [dog], Mal'chik, for example. The only important thing is the degree of my enthusiasm for my subject, which is at the heart of its secret and power (secret power).
>
> I have the feeling that literature is in the hands of some kind of illiterates. (438)

Indeed, the shorter, first part of her narrative, rendered through the child Marina's eyes, is dominated by the powerful figure of this Methuselah-like patriarch. Dmitrii Ilovaiskii, who is treated in Muromtseva's memoir as an irrelevant anachronism, becomes in Tsvetaeva's reconstruction a complex and contradictory figure: rigid, always solitary, an insomniac, he thrives into healthy old age while his first wife and two children, and two of three children from his second marriage, die early, tragic deaths from tuberculosis: "Everything in this house was dying, everything except death. Except old age. Everything: beauty, youth, charm, life. Everything in this house was dying except Ilovaiskii" (220). Analytically, she sees in him a conflation of parental and masculine authority who, as a reactionary, anti-Semitic[12] historian and the author of several textbooks widely used in tsarist *gimnazii*, controls texts; who, as husband and father, controls his wife's and daughter's sexuality; and who, as owner of the house on Old Pimen Lane and trustee of the Tsvetaev house on Three Ponds Lane, controls the property and the lives of both these families.[13] Nonetheless, the text is full of appeals for forgiveness and compassion for Ilovaiskii's Olympian fate as the patriarch of a family doomed by the gods.

Through the important metaphoric identification of grandfather (*ded*)/house (*dom*)/neighborhood (*kvartal*) (all masculine nouns in Russian), old Ilovaiskii becomes an archetypal symbol of an ancient, coercive, patriarchal order that predates and runs deeper than enlightened thought and progressive social policies can penetrate. Perhaps most important for Tsvetaeva's purposes, in *The House at Old Pimen* it is an order that silences its women, denying them access to the masculine domains of ideas and agency, thereby controlling their search for and identification with new readings and meanings.

Although Tsvetaeva visited the house on Old Pimen Lane only once, several years after the narrative's emotional climax in Nadia's death, in her imagination the house and its master are linked through a complex cluster of physical and mythic qualities. Both are immobile and isolated: the house, mired in a "sleepless garden," with its heavy "Godunovian" vaulted walls, and windows with their stacks of back issues of *Kremlin*, the journal Ilovaiskii published, as Tsvetaeva puts it, "for a readership of one," "not allegorically but physically cut off . . . visitors and inhabitants from God's light and world" (220).[14] Like its master, it is a house of "silent prohibitions and orders" (217). In its very floor plan, with the parents' light and spacious bedrooms *above* their children's damp, dark quarters, the house makes concrete the oppressiveness of a social order that protects its adults while destroying its children.[15] As Tsvetaeva's entire narrative shows, women and children who enter this house leave it "stretched out" [e.g., dead—NK].

Tsvetaeva's response to Ilovaiskii's role in his domain is alternately conciliatory and harsh. Forgiving him on the human plane, she places his and his family's fates squarely at the mercy of the Fates. She detects, to her own surprise, a bond of mutual respect between the old man and her mother. Perhaps most important for her own development as a writer, she acknowledges his ability to include the telling detail that she incorporates into her own explanation of art's purposes: "Once, opening his textbook, the following note, at the bottom of the page, in small print, caught my eye: 'In the Pontian swamps Mithridates lost seven elephants and an eye.' An eye—I liked that. Lost but preserved. I assert that that eye is a work of art. For what is all art but the finding of lost things, the immortalization of loss?" (219).[16] Nonetheless, her assessment of Grandfather Ilovaiskii as an agent of the dominant patriarchal social and cultural order is significantly harsher. By not recognizing women as creators and bearers of ideas as well as of children, as creatures of spirited minds as well as of beautiful bodies, as generators as well as subjects of texts, Grandfather Ilovaiskii cuts them off from any fulfillment of their creative possibilities and consequently allows them to die, either literally, as with his daughter Nadia, or spiritually, as is the case for his wife. Significantly, the one daughter to survive this tragic destiny, Ol'ga, must die figuratively for her father by eloping with a young man of Jewish blood and running off to Siberia. Ultimately, Dmitrii Ivanovich and his wife are left alone, bereft of both the children and the property to which they have spent their lives establishing a claim. At the end, the Ilovaiskiis, with their (in Tsvetaeva's eyes) immoral valuation of the house at Old Pimen above life itself, are left fruitless and dispossessed. In a stroke of divine (or literary) justice,

The House at Old Pimen ends with a chilling murder, not, however, of Dmitrii Ivanovich but of his wife: Aleksandra Aleksandrovna is murdered by burglars in 1929 in a basement room (the others having been commandeered by the Bolsheviks) of the house on Old Pimen Lane.

The narrator's reduction, both physical and metaphoric, of Aleksandra Aleksandrovna's domain to a single room in her old house exemplifies Tsvetaeva's reliance on spatial imagery (the "Godunovian" vaults and the house's floor plan, among others) and spatial boundaries.[17] In one of the narrative's most vivid scenes, Grandfather Ilovaiskii sits, Colossus-like:

> in the middle of the ballroom on a bentwood chair, most often without even taking off his big, floor-length fur coat—knowing well the chill of the ground level at Three Pond Lane, since this was *his* house, given by him as a dowry to his daughter Varvara Dmitrievna when she married my father. Grandfather Ilovaiskii never went beyond the ballroom and never sat on the round, green ballroom divan, always on a bare chair in the middle of the bare parquet floor, as if on an island. Poking in the air at the girl as she approached and sat down: "And who is this—Marina or Asia?—Asia. Ah—yes—yes." Without approval, without wonder, or even recognition. . . . We *knew* that he didn't see us. The two-year-old, the four-year-old [girls], and the seven-year-old [boy] knew that we *don't exist* for him. (216; Tsvetaeva's emphasis)

Here and elsewhere, Tsvetaeva transforms an old man's near-sightedness as recorded in Muromtseva's recollections[18] into an essential blindness and ideological self-absorption that limit recognition and authority to his own person and texts.[19] He is unable to distinguish between the two Tsvetaeva sisters, to *name* them, because "the Marina who stood before him—was she five or fifteen—it was no concern of his, since she was not a Mnishek, and he himself had seen eighty winters or more" (218). The reference is to Marina Mnishek, the rebellious Polish noblewoman from the Time of Troubles, a recurring figure in Tsvetaeva's poetry and an important female predecessor to whom she traces her own spiritual bloodline. Here she functions as Tsvetaeva's reproach to Ilovaiskii, who as a historian assigns (false) meaning to the infernal woman and her historical role even as he is blind to the real lives of the women in his own family.[20] Ilovaiskii similarly appropriates his wife, who becomes nothing more than his executive secretary, and invokes the force of his parental and historical authority to control and silence his children, in particular his daughters, as they attempt to live out their own lives, to write their life texts as it were. The identification that Tsvetaeva makes here between the patriarch, his calling, and his children is explicit, and her anger at the social order that creates such a conflation of power can best be summarized in Domna Stanton's words: "the [Victorian] system of private property served to constrain the proliferation of new meanings and readings" (16), e.g., constrained what is the essence of the poet's task.

Nevertheless, Tsvetaeva refuses to make a monster of this figure from her childhood, shifting the horror and blame for the tragic lives of his family onto the mythologized house, a nineteenth-century house of Priam that connives with the Fates to enforce a cruel destiny on its children. She manipulates her narrative through apologies for her own gothic excesses in her description of Grandfather Ilo-vaiskii and, through repeated imaginary dialogues, appeals directly to the reader's compassion for his and his family's fate. As a result, the reader is confronted by the writer's own ambiguous relationship to Ilovaiskii, a figure who is, by her own admission, a symbol of patriarchal power and infallibility (221). A modern reader sees Ilovaiskii as a man who, through his control of property and texts, controlled and silenced the women and children in his life, but Tsvetaeva's reading is more problematic than that, as she acknowledges in a letter to Muromtseva: "There's something touching about the old man. . . . Inhuman, even inhumane, but all on some high note. In general, every absolute provokes trepidation, not fear . . . but it's better in German: 'heilige Scheu' ['holy trembling']. It's useless to judge such a person" (421).[21]

Thus, much as the content of her portrait of Ilovaiskii leads her in one direc-tion, her rhetoric traces an opposite course, a process that Smith, speaking of women's autobiography in general, has characterized as a kind of "double helix of the imagination that leads to a double-voiced structuring of content and rhetoric" (51). Retaining her childhood awe of Dmitrii Ilovaiskii, Tsvetaeva does not fully confront the historical and psychosexual pressures that have left her, a mature poet, still proving her credentials to an audience largely controlled by male critics. She continues to suffer from what Gilbert and Gubar have called the woman writer's "anxiety of authorship," the apprehension that Ilovaiskii's blindness to her as a young girl was justified, as her contemporaries' silencing of her writing now (by their unwillingness to publish her and their demands for what she considered un-justified cuts) makes all too apparent.

Searching for a satisfactory identity to use in mediating the roles of woman and poet in an androcentric world, in *The House at Old Pimen* Tsvetaeva reaches out across time and memory to three women from her childhood who, together with her mother, are essential to her quest for self-definition. As throughout her writings, here Tsvetaeva's tracing of her spiritual and poetic lineage is based less on genealogy (other than her mother, none are blood relatives) than on a concatena-tion of literary and psychological ties that she traces to other poetic, folkloric, historical, or mythic figures.[22] While Grandfather Ilovaiskii is the dominant pres-ence in the first part of Tsvetaeva's narrative, in the second, significantly longer section we enter a world that is populated almost entirely by women, whose re-lationship to the adult Tsvetaeva can be traced through what Svetlana Boym has called the "metaphor of motherhood": the status of each as a daughter and/or mother speaks volumes about socially and culturally defined assumptions regard-ing women's roles and destinies and the ways that women participate as both victims and co-creators in their lives. Each of these women is, like Tsvetaeva her-self, a failed mother or the daughter of a failed mother.[23] Through death, physical or spiritual, each has abandoned her daughter. The speaking subject, through the deliberate and overt insertion of her own subjectivity into the stories of these women and through the strategies of lyricized speech and imaginary dialogues, ef-faces the boundaries between the teller of this tale, her characters, and her (female) readers. The social or historical validation withheld from these three women during their biographical lives is thus restored through the author's text. In turn, for Tsvetaeva the text becomes an act of survival, legitimizing her own rebellious, "against the grain" spirit.

Anya Kroth's argument for Tsvetaeva's dichotomous vision, a vision in which "the relationship between the conceptual poles of each antithesis is not that of radical independence but rather of mutual interconnection" (580), is relevant for understanding Tsvetaeva's pairing of two sets of male/female characters: Dmitrii Ilovaiskii and his second wife, Aleksandra Aleksandrovna, and of their two children, Nadia and Serezha. Dmitrii Ilovaiskii, as symbol of patriarchal power, is joined in his oppressiveness by Aleksandra Aleksandrovna. In Tsvetaeva's mind, both contribute to the children's premature deaths from tuberculosis by their actions as agents for their patriarchal society's valorization of property and authority over familial love and self-sacrifice: for both, loyalty to the couple, as guardians of the house on Old Pimen Lane, is their primary attachment. Leaving that house, even temporarily, to seek treatment for their mortally ill children is unthinkable:

> Wouldn't it be simpler to go to the Crimea? But to the Crimea (the arguments advanced, presumably, by Old Pimen) they cannot go alone: again everybody will fall in love with Nadia, and what if the paragon Serezha is ensnared by some trash? But for mother to go with them would mean dropping everything. Everything—that means the house. The house—that means the trunks. Whom can they be left with? The little German housekeeper? But she's just a baby. . . . How can she cope with the thieving maid, the sly yardman, the drunken cook . . . the entire gang of thieves? And who will pour the tea at Dmitrii Ilovaiskii's scholarly Fridays? (234)

Here the mature speaker's editorial comments blend with Aleksandra Aleksandrovna's fictionalized stream of thought (little Marina was in Italy at the time). A mother's inner monologue of concern for her sick children is transformed, through the attribution to "Old Pimen," into a checklist of domestic concerns, with protection of property—both human and tangible—monopolizing Aleksandra Aleksandrovna's attention. Rather than give her children love, and with it the possibility of life, she remains, like her husband, concerned with property, and her children die, quite literally, from a lack of maternal love.

As Ilovaiskii's right, "executive" hand, Aleksandra Aleksandrovna is the more directly oppressive parent, matching his "blindness" to household and family matters with an all-seeing, ever-vigilant eye, turning his philosophic maxims ("one ought not") into interdictions ("one must not"), so that "physical prohibition became spiritual prohibition" (224). The identification is pervasive: even his "bare chair" reappears as a "hard chair" that little Marina notices Aleksandra Aleksandrovna sitting on after Serezha and Nadia die (230). What emerges is, as Tsvetaeva writes to Muromtseva, "a . . . monster."[24] Adrienne Rich has called our attention to the contradiction between the mother's seeming power in the family and her actual powerlessness,[25] a point that Tsvetaeva reinforces in this symbol of failed maternal love. Because the power relationship is never equal between the two parents (she is, after all, "his right hand"), in spite of many common characteristics their identification is not complete, breaking down along gender lines. With a high level of historical accuracy, Tsvetaeva describes a social order that kept *women* indentured to their households and turned children, as she notes, into "domestic duties" (226), while men remained uninvolved, even as their authority in all domestic and familial matters was reinforced by the legal and economic subordination of women and daughters to their husbands and fathers.[26]

Ultimately, Aleksandra Aleksandrovna is a failed mother not because she, like her husband, allows her children to die, but because even as she loves her son she is unable to love her daughters. While she genuinely mourns her son's death, becoming "his living portrait after his death" (230, also 224)—and the conflation of visual and symbolic is always important in Tsvetaeva's vision—the symbolic language in which her relationship to her daughter is described could not be more different. With time, Aleksandra Aleksandrovna, once a beautiful young woman, becomes the Cerberus-like guardian of the house, and of her beautiful daughter, Nadia. The adult speaker, remembering an episode when she was nine and she and her sister had joined Serezha and Nadia in the Italian village of Nervi, visualizes the mother's two different poses in regard to her children: "I see you. . . . Serezha in the shade of the room and his mother, Nadia in full light, but transected by her mother's shadow. The mother protects [*khranit*] Serezha, but Nadia she guards [*sterezhet*]" (222). In a typical Tsvetaevan stroke, the contrast in maternal attitude is present not only at the semantic level, in the contrast of the two verbs, but also through her manipulation of spatial imagery—while the mother's shadow "encircles" Serezha, it "cuts across" Nadia.

Just after this, Tsvetaeva is reminded of a ghoulish Ukrainian folktale: a young girl is saved by her dead godmother from her real mother, also dead, who wants to bring her into her own fold of unquiet souls. Having told the tale, the speaker, clearly Tsvetaeva, steps in to analyze it:

> When, as always in these cases, I began telling this tale to clarify it for myself and then asking, "What's the point here? Why?" only one of my interlocutors, a woman, said categorically: "It's quite clear, jealousy. Her daughter is her rival." Posthumous jealousy of youth, the unhappy one's jealousy of the happy one, the dead one's jealousy of the living one. And to return to A. A.: the restless passions of a dead woman who had *never* lived. For A.A. had never lived. When, as a young beauty, she married old Ilovaiskii, she married for money and his name, but she received keys on her belt and a cross on her back. According to family stories, he was terribly jealous of her. That hard-necked man loved beauty. (223; Tsvetaeva's emphasis)

Aleksandra Aleksandrovna's rage at herself and her acquiescence in her fate is translated into tyrannization of her daughters—those children who are biologically her heirs. Nonetheless, as the above passage shows, Tsvetaeva, even as she creates this "monster," does not condemn her but rather lays this cycle of maternal self-rage and tyrannization of daughters at the door of a patriarchal order that regards women as property, and beautiful women as particularly precious property that is to be not merely protected but aggressively guarded, for future conveyance from father to husband.

As she does for Dmitrii Ilovaiskii, Tsvetaeva pleads with her reader for compassion for Aleksandra Aleksandrovna. Ultimately, both parents suffer at the hands of a mythically conceived fate that deals its cards blindly. In a sense, theirs is, jointly, a failed parenthood. Nonetheless, Aleksandra Aleksandrovna is, though unwillingly, "a bit [more] of a monster" than her husband because patriarchal society's construction of marriage ruptures fruitful mother/daughter relations.[27] Tsvetaeva's troubled relationship to this circumstance is inscribed in her conflicting attitudes toward Nadia's mother: the young woman who entered into this loveless marriage is both victim of her society's mores, and its agent when it comes to her own daughters. However, even as she tells her tale of the murderous mother, in the next breath Tsvetaeva deflects any condemnation onto patriarchal society's strictures on motherhood:

> And then the children came along—children cut off from her at once by the traditional wall of wet nurses, nannies, nursemaids, governesses, and teachers. . . . How could you get through to your child under these circumstances? How could you fight your way through that whole like-minded and resilient density? . . .
>
> In the meantime, life was ever so gradually reshaping the beautiful young girl. When you know that it will be—never, nowhere—you begin to live here. In this way. You adapt to your cell. That which upon entry seemed madness and lawlessness becomes the measure of things, and the jailer, noticing submissiveness, softens a little, and a monstrous alliance begins, the real alliance of the prisoner with the jailer, of the unloving with the unloved, the molding of *her* in his image and likeness . . . If, in the simplifying mythology of the relatives and servants, Dmitrii Ilovaiskii lived off his children's lives, Aleksandra Aleksandrovna "ate them up" [*zaedala*—an untranslatable pun—; NK]. No, she didn't eat them up. She received no nourishment from their juices, for then these juices would have helped her, which was not the case; she squeezed them with a steely hand, allowing them no passage, so that her female offspring too would not be happy. . . . I suffocated—don't you breathe either.
>
> Monstrous? But isn't such a marriage monstrous? She has herself to blame. But did "she" really know? Did she know what marriage is? Today's women know. Those women of fifty years ago flew into that hell like a moth to the light—headfirst. (223–25)

Narrative authority in this, one of the most penetrating critiques anywhere of the patriarchal, autocratic Russian system and of its impact on women and families, devolves to Tsvetaeva because of her multiple perspectives as mother, daughter, and poet. Analysis crosses over to compassion as the speaker merges private, domestic details with their public resonances. The complexity of Aleksandra Aleksandrovna's commitment to the house at Old Pimen is central to Tsvetaeva's (and the reader's) concern with the internalization by both men and women of the limited "meanings and readings" imposed on them by a patriarchal culture, yet by insisting on the "unconsciousness" of her rage against her own position and that of her daughters, Tsvetaeva assumes a noncondemnatory stance. Nevertheless, the reader is struck by her own rebellion against that order, implicit in her writing this text.

Boym and others have commented on Tsvetaeva's attitudes toward feminine beauty. The poet's readings of the metaphor of beauty are varied and not entirely consistent. In contrast to her physical inscription of herself as a child (always plump and plain, always healthy) or to the silence about her mother's appearance (from which we infer that in her daughter's eyes she was no beauty), the tragic women in the Ilovaiskii house are linked by their physical beauty.[28] While beautiful men, in this case Nadia's brother Serezha, can be an object for Tsvetaeva's adoration and even beatification, feminine beauty results in tragedy. In the case of Aleksandra Aleksandrovna, the desire of the much older Ilovaiskii for a young, beautiful wife results in a loveless marriage, the tragic consequences of which play themselves out on the fruits of that marriage, the children. Beauty is one important symbolic element among a number of links between the other two women in *The House at Old Pimen*: the half-sisters Varvara Dmitrievna and Nadia share the same father, and both die early deaths from tuberculosis.

Although little Marina had never met Varvara Dmitrievna, Ilovaiskii's daughter and Tsvetaev's first wife, who had died before little Marina was born, she appears three times in Tsvetaeva's narrative. Each appearance is accompanied by an overt or covert dialogue, through voice and image, with Tsvetaeva's own mother. Boym's observation, that "a beautiful girl is an object of desire, and a lonely girl is a writing subject" (277, fn. 30), is useful for understanding the juxtaposition of these two women, so dissimilar, yet linked from Tsvetaeva's earliest childhood memories by similar fates—marriages to significantly older men for reasons other than love (a fact that also connects them to Aleksandra Aleksandrovna), and early deaths. Moreover, there is a second important link between them—their mutual interconnection as incarnations of the traditional separation of women as mothers and women as sexed beings. Resurrected in the text entirely through the adult speaker's emotions and imagination, rather than through any firsthand experience (which is the case with all the other personae in her memoir), Varvara Dmitrievna emerges from Tsvetaeva's chronicle as an icon to feminine beauty and desire. Like another (in)famous female figure in Tsvetaeva's eyes, Pushkin's wife, Natal'ia Goncharova, Varvara Dmitrievna is evoked less as a human being than as a compilation of physical attributes, costumes, adornments, and smells.[29]

This juxtaposition of what Cixous has called "[Tsvetaeva's] two mothers . . . one [of whom] gives permission, the other prohibits" (135), hints at a juxtaposition that is given its full articulation in an early passage in the narrative, in which the dead woman's trunks (now her daughter Valeriia's dowry) are rolled out for their annual spring cleaning in the presence of the little Tsvetaeva girls, their mother, and the domestic help. The two mothers "meet," through Tsvetaeva's orchestration of voices across time and memory and elaboration of metaphoric clusters. From her multifaceted, emotionally charged exploration of that relationship, we can trace her negotiation of the many conflicts and resolutions that have shaped the author's own consciousness and self-definition as a writer:

In spring, onto the scene of our green poplared Three Ponds courtyard rolled the leather Ilovaiskii trunks, the dowry of Andriusha's dead mother, the beauty Varvara Dmitrievna, the first love, the eternal love, the eternal longing of my father.

The tiny slipper (that was how we talked when we were children) with the heel as high as the foot was long ("My goodness but her ladyship's feet were teeny!" oh'd Masha the maid), the curve of the black lace, the white shawl, its fringe sweeping the ground, the red coral comb. We never saw things like that belonging to *our* mother, Mariia Aleksandrovna Mein. Corals too: a necklace of seven strands (Mother to two-year-old Asia: "Say it, Asia, say 'coral necklace'"). It would be nice to touch it a minute with your hands. But—you mustn't touch.... And these here with red fire and even wine inside are garnets. ("Say it, Asia, say 'garnet bracelet.' Brace-let."). And here's a coral pin—a rose. Garnets ... granates.... Pomegranates are things you eat.... ("They say the lady was an actress, sang in the theater," Masha whispers to our Baltic nurse-maid. "They say our master grieved awfully without her." "*Dummheiten*," the Baltic nursemaid cuts her off in her deep voice, guarding the honor of the house. "She was just a wealthy daughter, with a wealthy father. And she sang like a bird for her own pleasure.") ... Failles, moires, fermoirs. Jewelry boxes, bandboxes.... That, the way all this smells is patchouli.... Timidly I say to mother: "Mama—how beautiful!"—"I don't find it so. And it has to be taken care of because it's Lera's dowry."—"But what silvery snow!"—"That's naphthalene. So the moths won't eat anything." Napthalene, moths, dowry, patchouli—there's no sense to it, it's just magic. (216–17)

Cixous's two mothers, of "permission" and of "prohibition," come to life through a compact manipulation of imagery and voice: Varvara Dmitrievna emerges, icon-like, as a combination of emblematic physical attributes and personal objects, all unmistakably marked for stereotypical femininity. Her persona here—all vivid heat and vibrant colors, with its literary and operatic allusions to unrepressed female sexuality—is not that of the respectable wife of an upper-class Russian academic but that of a performer dressed in the trappings of feminine beauty.

The dominant physical attribute to emerge from this fragmented portrait is Varvara Dmitrievna's voice, which, as the Baltic nursemaid remarks, she used "for her own pleasure."[30] Mariia Aleksandrovna also appears as a disembodied voice (it is the only sign of her presence in this passage), but hers is markedly, albeit pedantically, maternal. The obverse of Varvara Dmitrievna's, emphatically not "for her own pleasure," it is the voice of the mother, addressed to her daughters, constantly naming, teaching, imprecating. Through a related but different narrative strategy, the lushness of the description of Varvara Dmitrievna is paired with its obverse: a complete absence of any physical description of her mother. We know from "Mother and Music," the most extensive examination of the author's relationship to her mother, that Mariia Aleksandrovna emphatically rejects, as a point of principle, the trappings in those Ilovaiskiian trunks, with all their connotations of femininity, confinement, and entrapment into the patriarchal order. This rejection is a source of tension in the Tsvetaev family: on the one hand, Mariia Aleksandrovna, ever the obedient wife and helpmate, treats her daughter's needs for self-definition with considerable ambivalence, and does her best to prepare her for marriage and motherhood. On the other hand, as Karlinsky observes: "[Tsvetaeva] felt that her mother had given her the love of culture, a contempt for materialistic values, her pride and independence. She saw her mother's life as a tragedy of unfulfilled longings and wasted potential" (23).[31]

Thus, this passage is a striking example of Tsvetaeva's ability to establish discursive authority through a merging of several positions: she is aware of essential differences between the two women and the drama of her two mothers as they vie—one from the grave, the other from behind her wall of duty and responsibility—not for the affection of the father (for it seems neither woman loved Ivan Tsvetaev), but for the attention of little Marina, the child who will give birth to this text thirty years later. In terms of the formation of a young child who will grow into the mature poet, this scene thus unites two antipodal essences: each consciousness—the sensual and the didactic—merges in the adult's re-creation of her earliest sensory and linguistic memories. The final images—the smells of patchouli and of naphthalene—divide along the matrix of images for the two women: patchouli, the sensuous oil of India, and naphthalene, the dry white powder of preservation. As different and dissonant as these two voices are, through the string of images in the last line—"napthalene, moths, dowry, patchouli"—the poet repeats the major themes of her chronicle—patriarchy, maternity, death, memory, female sexuality—ending with a closure through which art asserts its power over remembered experience: the entire scene is "just magic, pure magic."[32] Without the actual objects in Varvara Dmitrievna's "treasure chests," and their naming by Mariia Aleksandrovna, there would be neither sense nor magic, the two elements—the logic of words and the magic of their sounds—of Tsvetaeva's own poetry. The nexus of deficient, unresolved relationships in the historical Tsvetaeva/Ilovaiskii families finds its only possible resolution through their re-creation in this poetic autobiography, which prevails over the constraints of human mortality and personality to produce an enduring artistic document.

The primal symbolism of heat, fire, and the color red used to inscribe Varvara Dmitrievna is repeated for her half-sister Nadia, the daughter of Dmitrii and Aleksandra Ilovaiskii, through the homophonic identification, less obvious in English, of two objects: in Russian, the word for both pomegranates and garnets is the same (*granaty*).

> Here is V. D., the beloved wife of an unloved man, she who loved another man, who released her unhappiness in song under the Neapolitan sun and died after giving birth to her first son—[died] with a half-uttered word on her lips, a bouquet in her hands, dressed-up, decked-out—a clot of blood moving and moving until it reached her heart. V. D., showered with corals, with the still unchilled blush of the south and of her first joy. There she is, waving the end of her coral necklace at the son she is leaving behind. . . .
>
> And—the fog over the Lethe is clearing—no, not an album, not a portrait! Nadia, alive—chestnut-haired and rosy-red, all warm and velvety, like a peach in the sun, in her garnet/pomegranate [*granatovaia*] (Persephone!) cape, which she, in a double gesture of feverish chill, first opens, then closes. (221–22)

The garnet/pomegranate thread that runs between these two women presents another Tsvetaevan variation on the nature of mother/daughter bonds. While never occupying the same narratological space, these two beautiful Ilovaiskii daughters share common fates and behaviors in their biographical lives, leading Tsvetaeva to discover through myth the source of their tragedy, and to reverse the tragedy visited upon the daughter, Nadia, through the creation of her text.

The healthy but "lonely child" and "plain, small girl" that was little Marina fell in love with her physical opposite, a young woman of pre-Raphaelite beauty, literally aglow with the dual fires of passion and disease.[33] Attracted first to her beauty, the young Marina sensed in Nadia that desired Other—a socially and sexually rebellious spirit that sets her, like many of the literary and historic heroines with whom Tsvetaeva identifies, at odds with familial and social authority.[34] The little Marina grows into the poet Tsvetaeva, who, through the emotionally intense lyricism of her text and her transformation of the relationship of the adult Tsvetaeva and Nadia into the story of Demeter/Persephone, restores to Nadia that life taken away by her mother's nonlove. The child—powerless to change anyone's life—could only grieve at Nadia's death, but the poet has the power to incarnate her, through the body of her text, as Aleksandra Aleksandrovna does for Serezha through her body.[35]

In the last third of *The House at Old Pimen*, Nadia's death, the precocious Marina's persistent search for her return, and the mature Tsvetaeva's understanding of her grief at that death are set against earlier discourses on Aleksandra Aleksandrovna's inability to love, and specifically to grieve for, her dead daughter. In a typical Tsvetaevan imagined dialogue addressed both to herself and to her audience, the speaker wonders why her love for Nadia is more important to her now than the love (so important then!) that she had had for Nadia's brother, Serezha:

> Why was it not Serezha that I loved? The repentant love of my early childhood? Why did I reconcile myself to his death, accept it like everyone else did?
> Because Serezha himself made his peace with it, while Nadia did not.
> Because Serezha no longer wanted to live, but Nadia did.
> Because Serezha died completely, but Nadia did not. He went "there" completely, with everything he had inside himself, but Nadia, with everything that was in her—that beat in her—did not depart but remained completely behind.
> And also because, possibly, Serezha's mother grieved *so much* for him, while for Nadia, no one (and I claim this even now), no one did, never. Dear Nadia, what was it that you needed from me? (239)[36]

Several earlier motifs merge here: the androgynous quality of Marina's affections, her valorization of rebels (Nadia) over martyrs (Serezha), as well as the Hadean resonances of the house on Old Pimen Lane. However, Tsvetaeva now shifts her mythifying lens from the generation of the parents to that of the children, and specifically to Persephone, the daughter of Demeter and Zeus, kidnapped by Hades and made Queen of his Underworld, but returned to Earth through her mother's intercession for part of the year. Of the major Greek myths, the story of Demeter and Persephone is the only one to focus on the mother/daughter relationship as a response to the dilemma of human mortality, loss, and separation.[37] A tale of the (partial) restoration of life and of assertion of maternal power over patriarchal powers through the constructive use of anger and grief, within the text it has the same regenerative potential for the doomed house of Ilovaiskii. That potential is thwarted, however, because while the classical text is based on what Marianne Hirsch has described as the "mutual desire for connection" of mother and daughter (5), in Tsvetaeva's tale it is precisely the lack or impossibility of this connection that she laments. Aleksandra Aleksandrovna is *not* Demeter, that profoundly bereaved and elementally angry mother who intercedes and aggressively fights the (male) pantheon of the gods for the return of her daughter from the Underworld. Consequently, the restoration of the (natural) daughter to mother is impossible within a patriarchal structure in which the mother's maternal role as protectress of her children has been replaced by that of guardian of the patrimony.

It remains for the poet, whose mythifying vision sees essential truths as the historian cannot, and disentangles hidden threads in the fabric of family relations that escape the ordinary eye, to uncover the higher truth and secret connections between life and myth, to re-birth in artistic form young Nadia, whose fate is otherwise permanent residence in the Hadean world of oblivion and silence. In this tale of "step" or "surrogate" families, Tsvetaeva now willingly assumes the role of Nadia's surrogate mother. Seeking to heal the fatal breach between biological mother and daughter, she makes her tribute to Nadia the emotional centerpiece of *The House at Old Pimen*. The striking aspect of this passionate outpouring, in which the speaker recounts in detail young Marina's attempts, evocative of Demeter's wanderings in search of her daughter, to literally "find" and "see" Nadia everywhere after her death, is the effacement of boundaries between these two consciousnesses: not only does she express the girl's longing and love for the dead Nadia, but Nadia enables that love to exist through an assertion of her will across the boundaries of biological mortality and social limitation. Nadia, removed from *byt* (everyday reality) by death, draws out of Tsvetaeva the love that can bring her back to life. "Why was it me that you followed," she asks Nadia's shadow, "why did you stand before me and not another among those who, just a short time ago, had followed and surrounded you?" And the poet's response: "Perhaps, dear Nadia, when you saw the whole future from over there, by walking behind me, you walked behind your own poet, the one who resurrects you now, just short of thirty years later?" (239–40).

In the Greek myth, Persephone, though longing to return to her mother, is too helpless to play a role in her own rescue: it is Demeter's grief and wrath that return her daughter to Earth, at least for half the year. But as Laura Weeks cites in her Jungian interpretation of the Demeter/Persephone myth in Tsvetaeva's early poetry, a discussion that stresses the unity of mother and daughter, "the fact that each figure contains the other within herself" (579), may explain the unified power of the two female figures in the fight against the forces of distorting history and obliterating biology. In this passionate dance on the border between life and death, the poet's love, as constituted in the text, returns Nadia from oblivion, while Nadia empowers her with the knowledge of love's transformative power in matters of the heart and of art.

> It's strange. I, who was so unsparing of myself about my looks, so ashamed at my plainness before hers (and Serezha's and every kind of beauty), did not hesitate for one second at the thought: "And what if a beauty such as Nadia, when she sees me, plain and small, doesn't want me?" It's as if I already knew Goethe's line:
> *O lasst mich scheinen, bis ich werde* [O let me be visible until I come into being—NK], and that *werde* means I will come into being there in the form of my soul, that is, I will be just the same as Nadia, and even if I am *not*, even if I'm still in the old shell . . . it means that they don't look at beauty or nonbeauty. It was as if I knew even then what I so invincibly, irrefutably, ineradicably, and triumphantly know now: that there I will get back what was lost. . . . I knew that in *this* love I would have no rivals. (238)

Nadia, the unloved daughter, is brought back to life through the text of her surrogate mother, Tsvetaeva, the writer. Both are transformed by love, so that earthly, time-bound categories of beauty/nonbeauty (traditionally applied to women) give way to a higher, eternal beauty. Loss and separation, while inevitable, become, to return to Cixous's formulation, "positive," legitimizing the existence of both writer and her subject.

How, then, does *The House at Old Pimen* function as Tsvetaeva's "testament," the self-explanation to which I had alluded at the beginning? I would suggest that through her text, Tsvetaeva describes patriarchal reality as experienced by a group of educated, cultured women in late empire Russia, and transforms that description through her own gender-inflected, mythologizing vision. Conceived out of her identification with "Grandfather" Ilovaiskii, and motivated by an attempt to humanize him, her narrative follows a rather different course. It is for the Ilovaiskii/Tsvetaev women—that matrilineal line of which she fears she is the last member—that Tsvetaeva creates a space in the cultural and textual record. Conversely, it is through her passionate and compassionate cathexis (investment of mental or emotional energy in a person, object, or idea—NK) in their stories that she validates the iconoclastic, often transgressive patterns that structure her own writing and life. The analogy between biological and textual daughters that Tsvetaeva draws, particularly through the Aleksandra Aleksandrovna/Nadia relationships, makes it clear that for women (and women writers) to collude with patriarchy's laws is to collaborate in the death of their own—biological and textual—children.[38] Writing forty years before Adrienne Rich's seminal essay "When the Dead Awaken: Writing as Re-Vision," Tsvetaeva anticipated her thoughts: "We think back through our mothers if we are women. . . . Re-vision . . . the act of looking back, of seeing with fresh eyes, of entering an old text from a new critical direction . . . is for us more than a chapter in our cultural history: it is an act of survival" (90–91). For Tsvetaeva, who died by her own hand in isolation and persecution in 1941, this text stands as an act of artistic survival.

Notes

1. I would like to thank the Summer Research Laboratory of the Russian and East European Center at the University of Illinois, Champaign-Urbana, and the University of New Mexico Research Allocations Committee for supporting the research and writing of this essay. My thanks

also to Sibelan Forrester, Pam Chester, and members of the discussion group on Women in Slavic Literatures and Culture at the University of Illinois for their careful reading and many useful suggestions.

2. She writes to Tesková on November 24, 1933: "Emigration is turning me into a prose writer. Of course, prose is *mine* too, and the best thing in the world other than poetry is lyrical prose, but nevertheless behind poetry" (106).

3. See her letter of September 1, 1933, to Muromtseva-Bunina: "What is it we are doing but protecting the past from the present and, I fear, from the future?" *Neizdannye pis'ma*, p. 434.

4. Svetlana Boym aptly describes Tsvetaeva's autobiographical writings as "polygeneric" or "intergeneric" (240).

5. Patricia Sollner, analyzing Tsvetaeva's poetry, comes to a similar conclusion in a discussion of ellipses in her poetry: "The ellipses are part of the strategies Tsvetaeva uses to make direct claims upon her readers' co-creative imagination. . . . By demanding active participation from readers, the poet creates an intimate bond with these readers on many levels—thematic, logical, aesthetic and emotional." Quoted in Taubman, pp. 110–11.

6. Muromtseva-Bunina's memoir was published in the newspaper *Rossiia i slavianstvo* (Paris), no 116, 14 February 1931. It is reprinted in *Neizdannye pis'ma*, pp. 531–41.

7. Cf. Cixous: "Many poets develop a sense of positive loss, like Clarice Lispector, or Anna Akhmatova, in whose poetry we read of something never lost at the very bottom of loss, or Marina Tsvetaeva, in whose texts the stakes are something that she never had. Theirs are all texts of despair, that is of hope" (111).

8. Tsvetaeva generally treats her father with warmth and respect. Cf. King notes on p. 444. Several shorter autobiographical pieces in which her father plays a central role, also from the early 1930s, are distinctly different in content and emotional expression, revealing little of the drama and anxiety of those that focus on her mother or the Ilovaiskiis.

9. Hence, not her *svodnyi dedushka*, or "step-grandfather," as she calls him.

10. Although, as Taubman points out, "like a poem, [Tsvetaeva's] prose pieces were organic structures which could not be easily condensed" (251), Tsvetaeva's letters to Tesková record continuing battles with émigré journal editors who want to abridge her work. She was more successful at preventing editorial cuts in *The House at Old Pimen* than in several of her critical essays.

11. ". . . *my only grandfather*" is, obviously, inaccurate in both its parts: as this text and her biographers show, there was little contact between Marina and Dmitrii Ilovaiskii during her childhood, so that the claim does not stand even on emotional grounds. Grandfather Mein, the father of Tsvetaeva's mother, a benevolent, kindly man and Dimitrii Ilovaiskii's antipode, appears very briefly at the beginning of *The House at Old Pimen*. The fact that he is quickly dismissed from the family drama underscores my point that in her narrative, Tsvetaeva selects family members on the basis of their significance for her mythifying vision.

12. Tsvetaeva's famous line from "Poem of the End": "All poets are Jews" reminds us of her identification of rebels (herself) with other outcasts (Jews).

13. Gilbert and Gubar's gloss on Edward Said's discussion of the connection between the institution of patriarchy and social and literary authority, and of their impact on gender-related issues for the woman writer is crucial to my interpretation of Dmitrii Ilovaiskii's role in *The House at Old Pimen*.

14. All references to *The House at Old Pimen* are from M. Tsvetaeva, "Dom u starogo Pimena," in *Izbrannaia proza v dvukh tomakh*, vol. II (New York: Russica, 1984), pp. 215–45. Translations throughout are mine, although I have consulted J. Marin King's translations as well.

For a recent discussion of Tsvetaeva's juxtaposition of the Kremlin's patriarchal authority with that of Moscow's "feminine" churches, see Forrester, "Bells and Cupolas," p. 234.

15. Cf. Muromtseva-Bunina, in Tsvetaeva, *Neizdannye pis'ma*, p. 532. A more typical, if likely idealized, liberal attitude comes through the comments of the radical journalist N. V. Selgunov: "Children became the first members of the household; they began to get the best, brightest and most spacious rooms"; quoted in Engel, p. 52.

16. In speaking of Tsvetaeva's identification with Pushkin, Stephanie Sandler notes Tsvetaeva's assertion of "her connection to a man of nearly boundless verbal authority" (147). Tsvetaeva responded very positively and strongly to all who commanded authority in their spheres, be they poets such as Pushkin, reactionary historians such as Ilovaiskii, or anarchic rebels such as Emel'ian Pugachev.

17. See Pamela Chester, "Domestic Space and the Inner Landscape in Tsvetaeva's Prose," for further analysis of the function of this and other spatial imagery in her autobiographical prose.

18. Evidently, in her letter to Tsvetaeva, Muromtseva had described Grandfather Ilovaiskii as an obsessive reader and writer who, in his later years was forced to wear two pairs of reading glasses. Cf. *Neizdannye pis'ma*, p. 423.

19. Again, Gilbert und Gubar's argument that male authorship is based on men's use of the "phallic pen" to inscribe their texts on the blank page of the female body is important to this and subsequent observations in my article.

20. Tsvetaeva similarly uses the blindness trope to pass judgment on Ilovaiskii's indifference to the revolution taking place around him and its importance. Interrogated after the revolution about his knowledge of its leaders, in her account, this was Ilovaiskii's reaction:

> The defendant is silent, and we think he didn't understand again, or maybe that he's deaf? And suddenly, with complete indifference: "Toward Le-nin and Trotsky? Ne-ver hea-ard of them." At that point N. lost his composure: "What do you mean! You haven't heard of them? When that's all the whole world hears about! And who are you, once and for all, the devil take you, a monarchist, a Cadet, an Octobrist?" And then *he* lectures [N.]: "And have you read my works? I was a monarchist, and I still am a monarchist. How old, my dear sir, are you? Thirty-one, perhaps? Well, I am ninety-one. In your tenth decade, my young gentleman, you don't make changes." At that point we all burst out laughing. Brave old man! Said with dignity! (243)

Note also that she has added at least three years to Ilovaiskii's age (he died in 1920 at the age of eighty-eight), thus emphasizing his Olympian and Methuselan image.

21. Similarly, Tsvetaeva's mixed emotions come through in her account of Ilovaiskii's interrogation at the hands of the Bolsheviks, quoted above: he emerges as the recipient of his interrogator's admiration.

22. Tsvetaeva's textual dialogues with a range of historical and cultural personae have been analyzed in numerous articles. Perhaps the most complete overview of these can be found in Sibelan Forrester's dissertation, "Marina Cvetaeva's Self-Definition as a Female Poet."

23. Cixous perceptively writes: "For Tsvetaeva, it is not only the separation between men and women, not only impossible love, but also a primal drama, something originary that takes place between life, of which one did not ask anything, and the one who put us in the world, that is to say, the real author or the mother.... people like [the Brazilian writer—NK] Clarice Lispector or Marina Tsvetayeva were born from a tomb. The relation to their mothers, to birth, are failed, so they are painful" (120).

24. On August 21, 1933, Tsvetaeva writes: "AA is turning out to be worse than DI . . . she's a bit of a monster"; in a later letter she worries that the Ilovaiskiis' remaining child, Ol'ga (now living in emigration), might take public offense at this portrait of her mother. *Neizdannye pis'ma*, pp. 419, 451.

25. As quoted in Chodorow, p. 83.

26. Barbara Engel, speaking of the merchant class, notes that "mothers in reaction to the tyranny they themselves experienced, often tried to tyrannize over children in their turn" (10). The Ilovaiskiian household, in its conservatism and parental authority, resembles one typical of Moscow merchants more than one of the liberal intelligentsia.

Another observation from Engel's book is also germane: "Authority over a daughter remained just about the only authority a mother could exercise after the emancipation of serfs. As the old world crumbled . . . many a mother clung to the remnants of her old power by appealing to her daughter's guilt" (68). While Aleksandra Aleksandrovna is of a later generation, this is an apt description of her hold over Nadia, and indicative again of Tsvetaeva's characterization of the senior Ilovaiskiis as reactionary even for late empire Russia.

27. Discussing the connection between maternal giving and maternal love as articulated by Cixous, Domna Stanton writes: "Like 'the Mother Goddess' woman gives/loves in ways that are radically different from proprietary man" ("Difference on Trial," p. 168). Aleksandra Aleksandrovna's "monstrousness" lies in her inability to give/love *as a woman*. One might be tempted to see in Aleksandra Aleksandrovna's symbolic "murder" of Nadia, the daughter who is "beautiful" like her mother, an unconscious gesture of self-annihilation, the mother's only recourse against the patriarchy, a gesture that in death will save her daughter from her mother's fate. The absence in Tsvetaeva's account of any conscious action or emotion on Aleksandra Aleksandrovna's part precludes, at least in my mind, such a reading.

28. It is telling that in Tsvetaeva's re-creation, Nadia's "healthy" but similarly rebellious sister, Ol'ga, is barely mentioned. Ol'ga, plain and plump (like the self-image Tsvetaeva has of herself as a child), ultimately achieves independence from this tragic house by eloping and moving to Siberia. The beautiful Nadia pays the price of an early, tragic death.

29. Note Sandler's comment: "Natal'ia Goncharova is simply the fateful woman, that blank space to which one is drawn, around which all forces and passions collide" (147). Also, see Sandler's comments on Tsvetaeva's image of silent feminine beauty as "a blank space," "a hollow shell" devoid of essence, an analogy that brings us once again to the Gilbert/Gubar model.

30. Note Forrester's observation that "in Cvetaeva's poetics the voice also represents the soul, the singer's own special identity" ("Marina Cvetaeva's Self-Definition," p. 403).

31. The contradictory relations of both mother and daughter are a *locus classicus* of Tsvetaeva scholarship. See, for example, Karlinsky: "Marina Tsvetaeva may have resented what her mother had done to her childhood, but she also stressed how much she owed to her" (23).

32. The biographical similarities between Mariia Aleksandrovna and Aleksandra Aleksandrovna, although not as pronounced as those between Mariia and Varvara Dmitrievna, are worth mentioning. Mariia is clearly the more talented of the two: she gave up a promising career as a pianist at her father's behest, while there is no indication of particular talent in Aleksandra, nor any desire for her daughter to be a talented genius. Less beautiful, Mariia Aleksandrovna is also less intentionally cruel: her love, though overbearing and intolerant of her daughter's real talents, is also one of concern and high expectations. Nevertheless, the two share a common patronymic, and certain essential traits (suppression of the self, a stern and authoritarian attitude toward child-rearing, romantic lovers before their marriages who were deemed unsuitable by their parents), and certain recurrent imagery, particularly having to do with coldness and dryness, is used for both.

33. Cf. letter of August 21, 1933, to Muromtseva: "I always felt a 'secret fire' in Nadia; this is why I loved her so" (*Neizdannye pis'ma*, p. 419). In the same letter, she contrasts this heat to Aleksandra Aleksandrovna's "icy (there can be no worse) mother."

34. Beautiful *and* rebellious, a potential rather than real mother, Nadia shares qualities of all three "mothers." Again, Kroth's observation of the interrelation and correspondence between the poles of various antitheses (581) is germane. Note that Mariia Aleksandrovna was secretly rebellious, urging her daughters to pursue their (often imagined) talents, yet concerned about their marriageability (see Taubman, p. 276, n. 11).

35. In Tsvetaevan glosses on different modes of incarnation, Aleksandra Aleksandrovna becomes her son's "living portrait," Ivan Tsvetaev installs Varvara Dmitrievna's portrait in the salon after Mariia Aleksandrovna's death, and Tsvetaeva "re-embodies" Nadia through her text.

36. Space does not allow me to discuss the androgynous qualities and role reversals in the brother-and-sister pairing of Serezha and Nadia. In general, they incorporate the features discussed both by Kroth and by Gove in their articles in *Slavic Review*.

37. Marianne Hirsch (18, 28–39) perceptively analyzes the Demeter/Persephone myth as a life-affirming alternative to the models presented by other female figures from Greek mythology (specifically Electra and Antigone).

38.   Some readers of this essays have rightly perceived a relationship between Tsvetaeva's textual recuperation of Nadia and her guilt over the death of her own daughter Irina, whom she left
in an orphanage during the Russian Civil War and who subsequently died of malnutrition two
months before her third birthday. While there is nothing in the published correspondence to link
the two, it is psychologically plausible that Tsvetaeva's installation of herself as surrogate mother
to Nadia reflects her own struggle to come to terms with that decision, especially in light of her
deteriorating relationship with her older daughter, Ariadna, during the 1930s.

Works Cited

Boym, Svetlana. "The Death of the Poetess." In *Death in Quotation Marks*, pp. 191–240. Cam-
bridge: Harvard University Press, 1991.
Chester, Pamela. "Domestic Space and the Inner Landscape in Tsvetaeva's Prose." Unpublished
paper read at annual convention of AAASS, November 1992.
Chodorow, Nancy. *Feminism and Psychoanalytic Theory.* New Haven: Yale University Press, 1989.
Cixous, Hélène. "Poetry, Passion and History: Marina Tsvetayeva." In *Readings: The Poetics of
Blanchot, Joyce, Kafka, Kleist, Lispector and Tsvetayeva*, ed., trans., and intro. by V. A. Conley,
pp. 110–51. Minneapolis: University of Minnesota Press, 1991.
Engel, Barbara Alpern. *Mothers and Daughters.* Cambridge: Cambridge University Press, 1983.
Forrester, Sibelan. "Bells and Cupolas: The Formative Role of the Female Body in Marina Tsve-
taeva's Poetry." *Slavic Review* 51, no. 2 (Summer 1992): 232–46.
———. "Marina Cvetaeva's Self-Definition as a Female Poet." PhD Dissertation, Indiana Univer-
sity, 1990.
Gilbert, Susan M., and Sandra Gubar. "The Queen's Looking Glass." In *The Madwoman in the
Attic*, pp. 3–44. New Haven: Yale University Press, 1979.
Gove, Antonina Filonov. "The Feminine Stereotype and Beyond: Role Conflict and Resolution in
the Poetics of Marina Tsvetaeva." *Slavic Review* 36, no. 2 (1977): 231–55.
Heldt, Barbara. *Terrible Perfection: Woman and Russian Literature.* Bloomington: Indiana Univer-
sity Press, 1987.
Hirsch, Marianne. *The Mother/Daughter Plot: Narrative, Psychoanalysis, Feminism.* Bloomington:
Indiana University Press, 1989.
Karlinsky, Simon. *Marina Tsvetaeva: The Woman, her World and her Poetry.* Cambridge: Cam-
bridge University Press, 1985.
Kroth, Anya. "Androgyny as an Exemplary Feature of Marina Tsvetaeva's Dichotomous Poetic
Vision." *Slavic Review* 38, no. 4 (December 1979): 563–82.
Kudrova, Irma. "Voskreshenie i postizhenie." *Neva* 12 (1982): 151–60.
Muromtseva-Bunina, Vera. "Dom u starogo Pimena." In M. Tsvetaeva, *Neizdannye pis'ma*,
pp. 531–41.
Rich, Adrienne. *Blood, Bread and Poetry: Selected Prose, 1979–1985.* New York: Norton, 1986.
Sandler, Stephanie. "Cvetaeva's Reading of Puškin." *SEEJ* 34, no. 2 (Summer 1990): 139–57.
Smith, Sidonie. *A Poetics of Women's Autobiography: Marginality and the Fictions of Self-
Representation.* Bloomington: Indiana University Press, 1987.
Stanton, Domna. "Autogynography: Is the Subject Different?" in *The Female Autograph: Theory
and Practice of Autobiography from the Tenth to the Twentieth Century*, ed. Domna Stanton,
pp. 3–20. Chicago: University of Chicago Press, 1984.
———. "Difference on Trial: A Critique of the Maternal Metaphor in Cixous, Irigaray, and Kris-
teva." In Nancy K. Miller, *The Poetics of Gender*, pp. 157–82. New York: Columbia University
Press, 1986.
Taubman, Jane. *A Life through Poetry: Marina Tsvetaeva's Lyric Diary.* Columbus: Slavica, 1988.
Tsvetaeva, Marina. "Dom u starogo Pimena" ["The House at Old Pimen"]. In *Izbrannaia /proza
v dvukh tomakh* [*Selected Prose in Two Volumes*], vol. II, pp. 215–24. New York: Russica, 1984.

————. *Neizdannye pis'ma* [*Unpublished Letters*]. Edited by G. and N. Struve. Paris: YMCA Press, n.d.

————. *Pis'ma k A. Teskovoi* [*Letters to A. Tesková*]. Prague: Academia, 1969.

————. "The House at Old Pimen." In *Marina Tsvetaeva, A Captive Spirit: Selected Prose*, ed. and trans. J. Marin King. Ann Arbor: Ardis, 1980.

Weeks, Laura D. "'I Named Her Ariadna . . .': The Demeter-Persephone Myth in Tsvetaeva's Poems for Her Daughter." *Slavic Review* 49 (Winter 1990): 568–85.

EIGHT

Angels in the Stalinist House

Nadezhda Mandel'shtam, Lidiia Chukovskaia, Lidiia Ginzburg, and Russian Women's Autobiography

SARAH PRATT

To the memory of Lidiia Ginzburg

NADEZHDA MANDEL'SHTAM'S two volumes of memoirs, *Hope against Hope* and *Hope Abandoned*, portray the author's life with Osip Mandel'shtam and, after his death, her struggle to preserve his poetic heritage.[1] Lidiia Chukovskaia's *Notes on Anna Akhmatova* record the author's almost daily encounters with Anna Akhmatova from 1938 to 1941 and from 1952 to 1962.[2] Lidiia Ginzburg's "Notes of a Blockade Person" describe life during the siege of Leningrad, focusing on the experience of a composite figure created by the author, a certain male scholar designated simply by the initial "N."[3] None of these works is "about" its author in the sense that a traditional autobiography is "about" the author. Each is "about" someone else, yet each functions in significant measure as autobiography.

My hypothesis (and it can be only a hypothesis, given the vast number of existing autobiographies) is that the stretching of the genre by these authors is not so much "idiosyncratic"—based on the peculiarities of a given individual—as it is "eccentric"—reaching outward from the center. Each author creates a palpable tension between the expansiveness of her individual literary gesture and the inward pull of the autobiographical impulse. Much as Victorian women took on the role of "the angel in the house," sacrificing the self for the moral and spiritual well-being of the family (a role that terrified Virginia Woolf, who popularized the term "angel in the house" in one of her essays),[4] these Russian women sacrifice the extreme self-centeredness of the autobiographical genre for the sake of their role as angels in the house of the Russian intelligentsia, for the sake of their function as guardians of its cultural and spiritual well-being. In this constant relation to something outside the self, they provide a realization of the theory of alterity or "otherness" in women's autobiography, which will be discussed below.

Equally as important as the theoretical issues of gender and genre, however, are certain cultural phenomena that affect the autobiographical significance of these works. The Russian concept of the self, for example, is very often a concept of self in relation to others, a self informed by a sense of communality articulated in the terms *sobornost'* (a rather slippery concept of moral unity, usually implying adherence to Eastern Orthodox Christianity) and *kollektiv* ("collective" as a noun, denoting a group with a single sense of identity). In addition, Russian reverence for the Word as a source of moral and cultural value dramatically increases the stature of the self that writes. A writer creates the Word, and the Word in turn transforms the writer into a self worth writing about. Finally, there is the particular cultural role inherited by Russian women of the intelligentsia, a role determined by political and material conditions; by the powerful image of female virtue in Russian literature;[5] and by the religious concept of *kenosis* so prevalent in Russian spiritual life—the achievement of moral worth, even moral power, through denial or emptying of self, through suffering in imitation of Christ.[6]

Some critics, of course, would prefer to dismiss these and other aspects of the ideology of Russianness as "myths" deserving nothing so much as to be dismantled. Yet whatever we call them, and however skeptical some may be about their validity, these ideas have been used by generations of Russians (especially, but by no means exclusively, the intelligentsia) to interpret reality, and have themselves shaped reality. It behooves us, then, not to dismiss them, but to examine their function in the realm of autobiography and elsewhere. Thus what I am writing about here is the intersection of gender, genre, and culture that yields a written version of the self.

In addressing the basic problem of definition, the easiest argument would be that almost anything counts as autobiography these days, for we live in the midst of a critical free-for-all about the nature of the self, the nature of reality, and hence, the nature of autobiography. Yet there are still scholars who are most aptly termed traditionalists, those who define autobiography as an individual's presumably truthful, rational exposition of her or his own life story.[7] And there are those who might be called "literary liberals," who see autobiography as a more flexible, capacious genre ranging from works of fiction, through traditional autobiography, to various forms of diaries, journals, and even scholarly writing.[8] And there are "radicals." These are primarily more extreme feminists, deconstructionists, and materialists of various ideological persuasions. Radical feminists typically perceive the genre of traditional autobiography as an embodiment of patriarchal values, and hence invalid in relation to women. Deconstructionists deny the very concept of the self, some putting the word "self" in quotation marks throughout their studies. "Self" in this sense—in quotation marks—is a literary and historical construct providing little in the way of individual moral or metaphysical significance. Autobiography in this context becomes a genre constructed around a constructed concept of "self."[9]

The works to be treated here might seem to support a deconstructive approach, given the obvious "decentering" of the traditional notion of the autobiographical self and given the obvious shaping of that self by overwhelming historical and cultural forces. Yet what ultimately emerges is not an argument for deconstructive nihilism in relation to the self, but a strongly positive concept of the self and of writing about the self, rooted in the most basic traditions of Russian culture.

Nadezhda Mandel'shtam's memoirs are so well known as to need virtually no introduction. On first reading, the autobiographical aspects are all but overwhelmed by the brilliance of her husband Osip Mandel'shtam's personality, by the fierceness of Nadezhda Mandel'shtam's determination to preserve the poet and his legacy, by the mind-numbing complexity of the experience she portrays, and by the lucid force of her prose.[10] Mandel'shtam (in this study "Mandel'shtam" designates Nadezhda, not Osip) reinforces this initial non-autobiographical impression with statements such as "Thinking about *this* [i.e., Stalinism and its brutal ramifications], I forgot myself and what had happened to me personally, and even that I was writing about my own life and not somebody else's"; or "In writing my first book [the first volume of her memoirs], I excluded myself."[11]

Her portrayal of her husband at times gives further credence to the image of self submerged. "From me, he wanted only one thing," she writes, "that I should give up my life to him, renounce my own self, and become a part of him." She reports that her husband "firmly believed" that if one of them perished, the other would soon follow, and then offers a vignette from their married life, apparently oft repeated, in which her brother says to Osip Mandel'shtam, "Nadia doesn't exist—she is just your echo," to which the poet "gleefully" replies, "That's just the way we like it!"[12]

Yet through all this, the reader eventually begins to sense ambivalence and signs of a self so strong that neither Osip nor Nadezhda Mandel'shtam can suppress it. In the statement above, for example, in which Mandel'shtam says she forgot that she was writing about her own life, she is at the same time underlining the fact that she actually was writing about her own life. Or, in an example fraught with obvious ambivalence, she describes her own unobtrusive behavior when her husband talked with Akhmatova or other poets: "One thing I can say to my credit is that I was always able to sit and listen quietly, not trying to assert myself or constantly butting into the conversation like so many wives." Then, however, the cost of this humble stance becomes clear, as she adds with a typical combination of rancor and self-irony, "I must say, I regard this as a great virtue. Why was I never given a prize for it?"[13]

As soon as one begins to recognize these small eruptions of Mandel'shtam's self, that self comes to loom ever larger. Several of the most powerful autobiographical elements of the memoirs are so obvious as to be easily overlooked. The clear and frequent articulation of Mandel'shtam's own point of view is one of these. To be sure, she devotes the major portion of the text to her husband, his views, his poetry, but very, very often she first makes the reader aware that herself is the source and, more important, the interpreter of the information. She prefaces many a discussion with an introductory phrase such as "I have now found the reason that . . . ," or "But I understood well enough that. . . ."

Even more important, the memoirs are governed by Mandel'shtam's own emotional chronology, a chronology in which time always flows toward the central event, her husband's arrest and death.[14] This emphasizes the power of her purposefully subjective stance first of all by demonstrating her ability to tamper with a basic aspect of "normal" reality, and secondly by focusing on the events that made her into a writer. The death of the poet Osip Mandel'shtam brings on the birth of the writer Nadezhda Mandel'shtam, something that the memoirs will not let us forget.

And finally, given the overt personal bias of the memoirs, and the fact that the titles *Hope against Hope* and *Hope Abandoned* were suggested to a greater or lesser degree by Mandel'shtam herself, one surely can argue that the bilingual pun on "hope," in Russian *nadezhda*, represents a claim to Nadezhda Mandel'shtam's pivotal position within the text.[15] These volumes may not take the form of traditional autobiography, but there is too much "Hope" in them for one to maintain that they are not in large measure autobiographical.

Chukovskaia's *Notes on Anna Akhmatova* constitute a similar phenomenon realized in different form. Again an intelligent, articulate woman devotes a major portion of her life to a brilliant, needy, and occasionally selfish poet. She serves the poet's cause by acting as a helpmeet in life, by committing the poet's works to memory at a time when written manuscripts spelled certain danger, and by recording the poet's actions, moods, and utterances.

As a diary organized around short daily entries, however, Chukovskaia's notes are necessarily less coherent than Mandel'shtam's memoirs, organized by theme and emotional chronology. Chukovskaia's work lacks the analytical perspective afforded Mandel'shtam by the passage of time. One senses the all-important texture of Akhmatova's life, but the connectedness and larger significance of events is not yet apparent.

Where, then, is Lidiia Chukovskaia present in the notes? She is obviously present as the editor, as the consciousness that decides what to include and what not to include in the text. She is present in her occasional comments, such as "A gloomy day with Anna Andreevna. One of the gloomiest," or "Anna Andreevna is sometimes amazingly unjust in her judgments."[16] Moreover, she is present in the introductions and appendixes to the volumes, segments written some years after the notes themselves, which not only offer factual information about relevant people and events, but also allow Chukovskaia to shape the reader's perspective on them.[17] It is also from these sections that the reader learns about major aspects of Chukovskaia's own life. One could indeed argue that the introductions and appended material provide yet another set of valuable, if fragmented, memoirs. In any case, they provide a distinctive counterpoint to the tightly focused main line of the text, like the second voice in a fugue balancing and enriching the main melodic line.

Lidiia Ginzburg's "Notes of a Blockade Person" are the most anomalous of the works treated in this study. These notes of a blockade survivor deal less with the facts and physical reality of the siege of Leningrad than with affiliated metaphysical and social-psychological issues, or, as stated by Boris Gasparov, with "questions of the essence of being."[18] Moreover, unlike the works of Chukovskaia and Mandel'shtam, these notes have neither a first-person narrator nor a real human being as their textual object. The faceless, omniscient narrator uses analytical discourse that would be cold if it were not for an underlying sense of identification with, even love for, the city and the whole people, the *narod*, under siege. "N," the ostensible protagonist of the notes, is, in the words of the author, a "composite, conditional person," a figure dependent on the notes for his very existence.[19]

In the course of the notes, N gets out of bed, looks out the window, fetches water from the basement, carries out a pail of slops, goes to his job in an editorial office, eats dinner in a cafeteria, stands in line, seeks shelter from enemy shelling, and goes to bed. He is, at various times, cold, warm, malnourished and very hungry, malnourished and moderately hungry. He engages in no dramatic actions and provides no quotable quotes. He has no name and almost no gender. He is designated by the pronoun "he," but he functions as a generalized human being, not a specifically male being. In terms of Russian semantics, he is not a "blockade man" (*blokadnyi muzhchina*) but precisely a "blockade person" (*blokadnyi chelovek*).[20]

Perhaps N's most striking limitation is the fact that he is absent from much of the text. The pattern of the first page is typical. Ginzburg introduces N as he wakes up one day during the spring of 1942 and then very quickly moves from the description of N's individual zeal in following the progress of the war to a discussion of the general hunger for information. The grammatical forms shift from the third-person singular "he" to the first-person plural "we," as the narrator says about the opening beeps of the radio signal, "We had never heard a more forlorn sound." From "we" Ginzburg moves to the still-broader concept of "people"—"And people stood by the radio with bated breath"—and from "people" to an impersonal form of generalization: "This compulsive thirst for information was terrifying."[21] She further documents the desperate need for information with a description of the way people would cast themselves at anyone returning from the front and drive the returnees to distraction with seemingly endless incomprehensible questions. This leads to an analysis of the motivation behind the eccentricities of blockade behavior, an analysis in which Ginzburg's use of the abstract, substantivized participles "the one being questioned" (*rassprashivaemyi*) and "those who were asking" (*sprashivaiushchie*) shows just how far the text has come from the particulars of N's life to the realm of generalized intellectual discourse.

> The one being questioned [*rassprashivaemyi*] would get angry at the incomprehensible queries. Because what those who are asking [*sprashivaiushchie*] really wanted to know was not at all what they were asking about. They wanted to know what it's like when there's a war, what it would be like....
>
> This sense of not knowing was the distinguishing characteristic of the first days of the war....[22]

Here and throughout the notes, N's individual experience serves as a point of departure for quintessentially Ginzburgian analysis. It is a form of analysis strikingly similar to that in Ginzburg's own literary studies *On Psychological Prose* and *On the Literary Hero*, in which she examines such issues as the formation of character through the word. It is also similar to the analysis of human behavior and the function of literature in the various editions of her selected works.[23] N does exist as a literary fact, but his existence is repeatedly supplanted by the consciousness and method of his creator—so much so that the "blockade person" of the title is clearly as much Ginzburg herself as the more obvious figure of N.

Stepping back to look at all of these sets of memoirs, Mandel'shtam's *Hope against Hope* and *Hope Abandoned*, Chukovskaia's *Notes on Anna Akhmatova*, and Ginzburg's "Notes of a Blockade Person," one can see a common pattern. In each case, the author takes on the apparent task of writing about someone else. And in each case an autobiographical element flows like a subterranean stream beneath the surface of the prose, nourishing the visible growth above. At times the life-giving water of the author's self seeps to the surface little by little. At times it bubbles up dramatically, even flooding the surface. Whatever its degree of visibility, it is always there.

Such combinations of autobiographical presence with orientation toward an "other" have given rise to the theory of alterity or "otherness" in women's autobiography. In short, the theory holds that women autobiographers tend to establish their identity by means of a relationship to someone or something outside the self, whereas male autobiographers typically project a whole world dominated by a single self. In explaining this phenomenon, Mary G. Mason notes that "the egoistic secular archetype that Rousseau handed down to his Romantic brethren in his *Confessions* presents an unfolding self-discovery where characters and events are little more than aspects of the author's evolving consciousness," whereas in women's autobiography, "the self-discovery of female identity seems to acknowledge the real presence and recognition of another consciousness, and the disclosure of female self is linked to the identification of some 'other'"[24]

Mason identifies the prototypes for women's autobiography in the life writings of two fourteenth-century mystics, Julian of Norwich and Margery Kempe, and two seventeenth-century figures, Margaret Cavendish the Duchess of Newcastle and the American Puritan poet Anne Bradstreet. From these examples, she extrapolates four paradigms of alterity within women's autobiography: autobiography in which a man's selfhood emerges (1) in relation to one other autonomous being (Margaret Cavendish's relation to her husband); (2) in relation to a single transcendent being (Julian of Norwich's relation to God): (3) in relation to two others (Margery Kempe's complex relation to God and her husband); (4) in relation to a collective (Anne Bradstreet's relation to the Puritan community of which she was a part).[25]

The notion of finding the self through something outside the self finds particular resonance in the culture of Russian Orthodoxy, in which recognition of the divine kernel within another brings one that much closer to the Divinity, and hence that much closer to one's own true, God-given identity. For example, that pivotal figure in Russian culture and autobiography the Archpriest Avvakum quotes Abba Dorotheus's exhortation, "Strive to be united with one another; inasmuch as one is truly united with another, so much is he united with God."[26] A figure closer to the contemporary world, the Orthodox priest and scholar Pavel Florenskii, maintains that "a creative transition from one's self-containedness into the realm of 'the other' and a real discovery of oneself in that other" constitutes a victory over identity and a fundamental truth expressed in the dogma of consubstantiality.[27] A later reworking of a similar notion is, of course, Bakhtin's concept of the dialogic imagination, in which an author achieves wholeness of vision by giving full voice to "others," which is to say to the fictional characters of his created universe. In terms of specifically female characters in Russian fiction, the positive function of other-orientation blends with the general function of kenosis, as Russian heroines typically preserve the self through selflessness.[28]

The exemplars provided by Mandel'shtam, Chukovskaia, and Ginzburg support Mason's argument in general, but fit the particulars of her scheme only with certain alterations. First, whereas Mason's prototypes show obvious autobiographical intent, with each author consciously placing herself at the center of her work, Mandel'shtam, Chukovskaia, and Ginzburg are ambiguous in this respect, since the most apparent motive in each case is to write about someone else. Another scholar of women's autobiography, however, Julia Watson, builds on Mason's theory of alterity and goes beyond it to identify autobiographical significance in texts more like the ones we are dealing with. She notes that some women's autobiographies "masquerade as the life of another in which the writing 'I' is presented as only a kind of connective tissue. Yet the reader's experience of an autonomous voice narrating a life may be the strongest where the self is apparently suppressed"[29]

A second refinement of Mason's theory for our present purpose stems from the fact that the Russian authors each partake of at least three of Mason's paradigms of alterity, rather than fitting neatly into a single category. Each author evokes an image of self in relation to a single autonomous being: Osip Mandel'shtam, Anna Akhmatova, and the fictitious N, respectively. Each relates to a transcendent power, not the transcendent God of Julian of Norwich and Margery Kempe, but the transcendent power of Russian culture embodied in the Word. And each relates to the collective of the Russian intelligentsia and, on occasion, to large segments of the Russian people as a whole.

As is often the case, Nadezhda Mandel'shtam provides a brilliant articulation of relevant issues. She entitles the first chapter in her second volume "The 'Self'" ("*Ia*" in quotation marks), and the third chapter "We" ("*My*" also in quotation marks). In these segments Mandel'shtam provides a theoretical statement of the relation between the self and other, expressing a particularly Russian and, if Mason, Watson, and others are right, particularly womanly relation to the collective. Perhaps reflecting the Russian Orthodox position outlined above, she asserts:

> Individual identity is dependent on the world at large, on one's neighbors. It defines itself by reference to others and becomes aware of its own uniqueness only when it sees the uniqueness of everyone else.
> ....
> I am entirely convinced that without . . . . a "we," there can be no fulfillment of even the most ordinary "I," that is, of personality. To find fulfillment, the "I" needs at least two complementary dimensions: "we" and—if it is fortunate—"you."[30]

In another instance, Mandel'shtam writes specifically about herself, here counting both Osip Mandel'shtam and Anna Akhmatova as formative others in her life: "If my life had any meaning at all," she says, "it was only because I shared the tribulations of Akhmatova and Mandel'shtam and eventually found myself, my own true self, through my closeness to them."[31]

Thus Mandel'shtam defines herself in relation to both a single "other" and a dual or collective "other," but the overarching motivation for her writing and for her life is the ultimate "transcendent other" of the Russian intelligentsia, the Word, the repository of moral and cultural value that makes life possible. "What was it [that kept us going]," she asks rhetorically, "but faith in the value of poetry and its sacramental nature?"[32] Mandel'shtam preserves the Word as it is embodied in the works of her husband, and the Word, for its part, preserves her. The cause of her husband's poetic legacy gives her reason to live in a time of unrelenting mortal danger. But more than that, in her attempt to preserve the Word in her memoirs, Mandel'shtam herself becomes a creator of the Word. She not only establishes a canonical identity for her husband, but consciously affirms the validity of her own role, defining herself as a person, as a writer, and as a contributor to the life spring of Russian culture.[33] Just as in the Russian Orthodox tradition an icon painter or the author of a saint's life can achieve his own true and sacred identity because he has comprehended and re-created the divinity of his subject,[34] so Nadezhda Mandel'shtam achieves her own true identity as a creator of the Word because she has comprehended and re-created the essence of the Word of another.

Mandel'shtam's own summation from the chapter entitled "The 'Self'" puts all of this in perspective—her relation to a single other and to others, her relation to the transcendent cause of poetry, and her acute consciousness of the value and rightness of her own role: "if the verse I have preserved is of some use to people, then my life has not been wasted and I have done what I had to do both for the man who was my other self and for all those people whose humane, that is human, instincts are roused by poetry."[35]

In Chukovskaia's *Notes on Anna Akhmatova*, alterity functions in a similar fashion as the author both loses and finds herself in her relations with Akhmatova and with the Word represented by Akhmatova. Chukovskaia explains that the nightmarish quality of Stalinism—the arrest and disappearance of her husband, the constant threat to family and friends—diminished her sense of the reality of her own individual life, so that her sense of continuing human reality, and hence her diaries, came to focus more and more on her meetings with Akhmatova:

> With every day . . . my fragmentary notes became less and less the re-creation of my own life, turning instead into episodes from the life of Anna Akhmatova. In the middle of the spectral, chimerical, and murky world that surrounded me, she alone seemed to be not part of a bizarre dream, but reality. . . . She was something real beyond a doubt, something certain and trustworthy amidst all that wavering uncertainty.[36]

For these women of the intelligentsia, the Word constituted a primary, possibly *the* primary, aspect of reality. The very existence of Akhmatova therefore provided emotional succor and psychological stability at a time when other manifestations of reality were so terrible as to fall beyond the realm of normal human comprehension. For example, when Chukovskaia learns that her husband is indeed dead more than two years after his disappearance at the hands of the secret police, Akhmatova's reading of her own verses restores some sense of the joy that makes life possible. Chukovskaia writes:

> She recited again for me the poems about death, and then one that I had never heard, "The Reseda Plant Smells of Water."
> And again from that well of grief came a sensation of such happiness that I could hardly bear it. I understand Pasternak: if this exists, it is truly all right to die.[37]

In another instance, Chukovskaia describes a permutation of reality reminiscent of Andrei Belyi's Petersburg, as the physical reality of Leningrad disappears behind the force of Akhmatova's poetry. Chukovskaia has just memorized some new verses to prevent them from being lost.

> I left her apartment late. I walked along in the darkness, trying to remember the poems. I had to recall them immediately, from beginning to end, because I couldn't part with them. . . . I remembered everything, word for word. But for all that, when I was washing and getting undressed before going to bed, I couldn't remember a single step I had taken. How had I passed the sign for "Engaging Science"? How had I crossed Nevskii Prospect?
> I had walked like a sleepwalker, but instead of the moon, it was the poetry that had led me onward, and the world was absent.[38]

Chukovskaia's recognition of Akhmatova's power to restore and transform reality prompts her to see in Akhmatova something beyond the living person. "Akhmatova's fate," she says, "is something greater than even her own individual identity."[39] This "something greater" is precisely Russian literature, a fact that Chukovskaia articulates parenthetically after describing a conflict over vacation passes between Akhmatova and an obnoxious secretary from Litfond: "(Oh, how grateful I am that Akhmatova knows exactly who she is, and that, preserving the dignity of Russian literature, which she represents in some invisible court of law, she never takes part in the general fray.)"[40]

Having recognized Akhmatova as the personification of Russian literature, Chukovskaia both implicitly and explicitly recognizes her own moral obligation to take on the role of the guardian of Russian literature. She writes of her dilemma as to how to preserve the Word and the Poet, a potentially self-contradictory task in those lethal times. Her use of the words "criminal," "treason," and "damnation" conveys the sense of both her own moral imperative and the political risk involved: "Should I write down our conversations? Wouldn't that mean risking her life? Should I not write down anything about her? That would also be criminal." And again: "To forget Requiem, even a line of it, would be treason on my part. But to write it down would be worse than treason: it would be damnation."[41]

When Chukovskaia commits herself to this sacred task, she becomes, like Mandel'shtam, an arbiter of the poet's canon, both the actual canon of verses which otherwise might not have survived, and the canonical biography of the poet. Indeed, each volume of Chukovskaia's notes includes a section of some thirty pages of Akhmatova's poetry entitled "Poems by Anna Akhmatova (those without which it would be difficult to understand my notes)." Chukovskaia legitimately makes Akhmatova's Word an integral part of her own text, just as it was an integral part of her own life,[42] and she becomes a creator of Russian culture herself, as her own Word contributes to the culture's continuity and value.

Lidiia Ginzburg's "Notes of a Blockade Person" in some sense only mimic the alterity of Chukovskaia's notes and Mandel'shtam's memoirs, for Ginzburg's "autonomous other" is the fictitious and anonymous N. Yet like Akhmatova and Osip Mandel'shtam, N acts as a catalyst for a text that ultimately has much to say about the author's own self. As an individual character who eats breakfast, goes to work, seeks shelter from German shelling, and ruminates on the significance of events and conditions, N serves as a focal point for the larger reality portrayed by Ginzburg. As a composite figure, he allows Ginzburg to go beyond her own individual life while still preserving the genre's traditional claim to life experience. Moreover, precisely because he is a composite figure, N himself embodies the "collective other" and the notion of the social bond so crucial to Ginzburg's thinking.[43]

While the "collective other" through which Chukovskaia and Mandel'shtam establish their identity is limited generally to the Russian intelligentsia or, in its broadest terms, to lovers of Russian poetry, Ginzburg's "collective other" includes people who read little, if at all. She establishes her identity not only within the confines of the wartime intelligentsia, but as a Leningrader, one among many people from all walks of life caught in the siege, as a particle of the whole *narod* struggling against the German invaders.[44] Thus, after reporting a conversation between a dressmaker and her customer about prerevolutionary ladies' fashions and the cut of the dress to be made, Ginzburg concludes that for all their trivial concerns amid the rampant tragedy of the blockade, these women, by going about their daily lives as best they can, are "fulfilling the historical function of *Leningraders*."[45] They are heroes. They, like N and like Ginzburg herself with her own daily concerns, are part of the vital force that keeps the city alive.

In another instance, Ginzburg articulates her belief in the significance of the "collective other" within a discussion of Remarque's novel *All Quiet on the Western Front*. She concludes that the bitter irony of the title—the text of a bulletin on the day the novel's hero is killed—reflects a kind of Western individualism, or as she puts it, "individualistic pacifism," alien to the Russian collective mentality:

> People of those years (especially Westerners) did not want to understand that social life is a mutual social bond (otherwise it is nothing but oppression and coercion). But we knew that when any of us was killed by one of Hitler's artillery shells, somewhere someone would say about that same day: "Leningrad, under enemy fire, continued to live its usual life, carrying on business as usual." Moreover, everyone here would say, "*We* have surrounded Kharkov, *we* have taken Orel."[46]

As with Chukovskaia and Mandel'shtam, the most significant "other" in relation to which Ginzburg establishes her own identity is the "transcendent other" embodied in the Russian Word. From the beginning, however, Ginzburg uses the

Word to shape and verify reality, a function recognized only secondarily by Chu-kovskaia and Mandel'shtam, who claim preservation of poetic legacies as their primary interest. In this vein, Ginzburg's notes open with a reference to Tolstoy's *War and Peace* as a test of reality and moral validity:

> During the war years people read *War and Peace* eagerly—to check on themselves (not to check on Tolstoy, whose ability to transmit real life no one doubted). And the reader would say to himself: So, this means I've got it right. This is how it really is. Anyone who had the strength to read in Leningrad during the blockade eagerly read *War and Peace*.
>
> Tolstoy had the final say about courage, about a person engaged in the common task of a people's war.[47]

Toward the middle of the notes, Ginzburg considers the nature of the Word again, this time in a comprehensive analysis of the function of conversation, which then provides the context for the numerous conversations recorded in the text. To put it briefly, Ginzburg sees conversation as "ersatz freedom" for a person subjected to the laws of the material world, as the "murky prototype of art," and as a "power-ful means of self-affirmation, an assertion of one's own worth."[48]

This notion of the creative power of the Word, its function as a shaper of re-ality, a binding force of human society, and a creator of self-identity, is ultimately as important an element in the notes as the descriptions of life during the siege. And it is by no means a separate issue, for it is the reality of the blockade that evokes, even necessitates, verbal response. The notes close with an almost Bakhtin-ian statement of the creative power of the word as deed—*postupok*. The blockade becomes a symbol for the imprisonment of consciousness, and the Word becomes the heavy artillery in the battle to break through the circle. It becomes a deed that will restore the necessary social, psychological, and ethical bonds of human society.

> The circle is blockade symbolism for consciousness locked within itself. How can one break out of it? . . . How can one break the circle with a deed? A deed is always a recog-nition of common bonds. . . .
>
> Those who write, like it or not, enter into a conversation with something outside the self. Because those who have written, die, but that which they have written, with-out asking them, remains. . . .
>
> To write about the circle means to break the circle. One day or another it is a deed. In the abyss of lost time, it is something found.[49]

It is no accident that Ginzburg's notes begin and end with statements about the Word. Indeed, the notes are not ordinary notes, but "meta-notes," notes about notes, notes about the Word. The figure of N and the siege of Leningrad serve as catalysts for the narrative, but the notes are ultimately less a story of their osten-sible protagonist N and less a story of the blockade than they are a story of Lidiia Ginzburg and her relation to the Word.

For Ginzburg, as for Mandel'shtam and Chukovskaia, the role of the angel in the house of the Russian intelligentsia does involve a "denial of self," if "denial of self" denotes a literary focus on something other than the unmediated, self-

referential impressions of the authors themselves. But this is by no means the dimi-
nution of self that threatened Virginia Woolf and her Victorian forebears, for it is
at the same time an enhancement of self. As these Russian women "denied the self"
in preserving the Word and experience of others, they became creators of the Word
themselves, and they themselves came to embody the highest values of Russian
culture.

———

JUST AS RUSSIA and its culture exist midway between East and West, so a truly
Russian form of autobiography should exist somewhere between Eastern forms of
nihilism of self and Western individualism, or between deconstructive distrust of
selfhood and romantic, Freudian fixations on selfhood.[50] The post-Reformation,
and especially the post-Freudian, West posits a human being, most often a male
human being, as a creature continually aware of an individual self and in search of
complete self-realization. While the Western man's soul may be fraught with passions and he may ultimately make an irrational leap of faith, his autobiography
generally emphasizes the rational analysis and exposition of his life.[51] And in all
this, he is generally assumed to be the representative of an important segment of
humankind. Women's contributions to this genre, characterized by rational individualism and a single, self-reflexive vision, have been limited. In many cases the
limitation stems from cultural assumptions about, and the reality of, women's roles
in society. In others, however, the limitation may have more to do with the nature
of the established genre, which, if Mason, Watson, and other feminist scholars are
right, simply does not provide a suitable literary vehicle for the life experience of
most women. In the introduction to their book *Life/Lines: Theorizing Women's
Autobiography*, Bella Brodzki and Celeste Schenk sum up the situation as follows:

> The tradition of autobiography beginning with Augustine had taken as its first premise
> the mirroring capacity of the autobiographer: *his* universality, his representativeness,
> *his* role as a spokesman for the community. . . . No mirror of *her* era, the female auto-
> biographer takes as a given that selfhood is mediated: her invisibility results from her
> lack of tradition, her marginality in male-dominated culture, her fragmentation—
> social and political as well as psychic. . . . [T]he female autobiographer has lacked the
> sense of radical individuality, duplicitous but useful, that empowered Augustine and
> Henry Adams to write their representative lives large. A feminist reconstruction of
> women's autobiography, against the backdrop of twentieth century philosophical ques-
> tioning of the self, can begin to use autobiography for the fertile ground it is.[52]

In Russia, where the individualistic tenets of the Reformation and the ego-
oriented concerns of Freudian psychology have yet to take hold, where rationalism
in the Western sense has never been an intrinsic aspect of the culture, where philosophical questioning of identity is endemic—indeed, something of a national
pastime—the whole notion of the self, and hence the notion of autobiography,
takes on a different coloring. Women's autobiographies, while still rare, nonetheless exist within an arena of widened generic possibilities because of the close
relation between the "other"-orientation frequently found in women's life writing,

and the tradition of self-realization through identification with something beyond the self characteristic of Russian Orthodoxy, Russian Marxism, and the Russian ideology of the Word.

I leave you, then, with a series of questions: What *is* the quintessential Russian autobiography? Can it be that the quintessential Russian autobiography is not "about" its author? And can it be that the quintessentially Russian autobiography has been—or will be—written by a woman?

Notes

I would like to thank the Institute for the Study of Women and Men in Society at the University of Southern California for supporting the research for this essay.

1. Nadezhda Mandel'shtam, *Hope against Hope* and *Hope Abandoned*, trans. Max Hayward (New York: Atheneum, 1970, 1974). The Russian versions are *Vospominaniia* (New York: Izdatel'stvo imeni Chekhova, 1970) and *Vtoraia kniga* (Paris: YMCA, 1972). In subsequent notes, references to the translated versions quoted in the text will be given first; the analogous page number from the Russian version will follow in brackets. I occasionally revise the Hayward version slightly for the sake of greater clarity in the given context.

2. At present, these are available only in Russian. The translations here are my own. See Lidiia Chukovskaia, *Zapiski ob Anne Akhmatovoi*, vol. 1 (Moscow: Kniga, 1989), vol. 2 (Paris: YMCA, 1980).

3. The translation of Ginzburg's Russian title, "Zapiski blokadnogo cheloveka," is problematic. A literal rendering as "Notes of a Blockade Person" sounds stilted in English, yet I have chosen to keep this awkwardness, for it is precisely the notion of a generalized human being combined with the concept of a blockade, psychological as well as military, that motivates the work. The translations here are my own, with reference to Jane Gary Harris's unpublished translation. I am grateful to Professor Harris for letting me use her manuscript, and to Professors Harris and Irina Paperno for sharing their understanding of the "Notes" and of Ginzburg in general. See Lidiia Ginzburg, "Zapiski blokadnogo cheloveka," *Neva* 1 (1984): 84–108; also included in Lidiia Ginzburg, *Literatura v poiskakh real'nosti* (Leningrad: Sovetskii pisatel', 1987), pp. 334–92, and *Chelovek za pis'mennym stolom* (Leningrad: Sovetskii pisatel', 1989), pp. 517–78, along with an addendum, "Vokrug 'Zapisok blokadnogo cheloveka,'" pp. 579–606. Lidiia Ginzburg was a Leningrad literary scholar and student of the Formalists, and should not be confused with Evgeniia Ginzburg, whose memoirs entitled *Krutoi marshrut* could also fall under the rubrics of this study but are not treated because of space limitations.

4. "The Angel in the House" is the title of a popular Victorian poem by Coventry Patmore idealizing domestic life. In her essay "Professions for Women," written in 1931 but published only in 1942 after her death, Virginia Woolf transforms the Angel into a negative phantom who seeks to keep women from having minds of their own or undertaking serious "men's" tasks such as writing. Woolf maintains that in the end she had to kill the Angel in the House or perish herself as a writer. See Susan M. Gilbert and Sandra Gubar, eds., *The Norton Anthology of Literature by Women* (New York: Norton, 1985), pp. 1383–88; and Virginia Woolf's collection of essays *The Death of the Moth* (1942).

5. For a comprehensive survey of this topic, see Barbara Heldt, *Terrible Perfection: Women and Russian Literature* (Bloomington: Indiana University Press, 1987). For a more specific case study, see the discussion of female characters in Irina Paperno, *Chernyshevsky and the Age of Realism: A Study in the Semiotics of Behavior* (Stanford: Stanford University Press, 1988).

6. See George P. Fedotov, ed., *A Treasury of Russian Spirituality* (Belmont, Mass.: Nordland, 1975); Steven Cassedy, *Flight from Eden: The Origins of Modern Literary Criticism and Theory* (Berkeley: University of California Press, 1990), p. 102, and especially Florenskii's reworking of the concept in terms of cognition, as described on p. 115; Leonid Ouspensky, *Theology of the*

Icon, trans. Anthony Gythiel (Crestwood, N.Y.: St. Vladimir's Seminary Press, 1992), vol. 1, p. 152.

7. See, for example, Francis R. Hart, "Notes for an Anatomy of Modern Autobiography," *New Literary History* 1, no. 1 (Fall 1969): 485–511; William L. Howarth, "Some Principles of Auto-biography," *New Literary History* 5, no. 2 (Winter 1974): 363–81; James Olney, *Metaphors of Self: The Meaning of Autobiography* (Princeton: Princeton University Press, 1972); Roy Pascal, *Design and Truth in Autobiography* (London: Routledge, Kegan Paul, 1960); A. O. J. Cockshut, *The Art of Autobiography in Nineteenth and Twentieth Century England* (New Haven: Yale University Press, 1984); Elizabeth Bruss, *Autobiographical Acts: The Changing Situation of a Literary Genre* (Balti-more: Johns Hopkins University Press, 1976); Karl Weintraub, "Autobiography and Historical Consciousness," *Critical Inquiry* 1, no. 4 (June 1975): 821–48.

8. See, for example, William C. Spengemann, *The Forms of Autobiography* (New Haven: Yale University Press, 1980); Sarah Pratt, "Lidija Ginzburg's *o starom i novom* as Autobiography," *Slavic and East European Journal* 30, no. 1 (Spring 1986): 41–53, and "Lydia Ginzburg and the Fluidity of Genre," in Jane Gary Harris, ed., *Autobiographical Statements in Twentieth Century Russian Lit-erature* (Princeton: Princeton University Press, 1990), pp. 207–16; Lidiia Ginzburg, *O psikho-logicheskoi proze* (Leningrad: Sovetskii pisatel', 1971, reprinted by Khudozhestvennaia literatura, 1977); Estelle C. Jellinek, *The Tradition of Women's Autobiography: From Antiquity to the Present* (Boston: Twayne Publishers, 1986); Mary G. Mason, "The Other Voice: Autobiographies of Women Writers," in James Olney, ed., *Autobiography: Essays Theoretical and Critical* (Princeton: Princeton University Press, 1980).

9. See, for example, Felicity Nussbaum, *The Autobiographical Subject: Gender and Ideology in Eighteenth Century England* (Baltimore: Johns Hopkins University Press, 1989); Sidonie Smith, *A Poetics of Women's Autobiography: Marginality and the Fiction of Self-Representation* (Bloom-ington: Indiana University Press, 1987); Domna Stanton, ed., *The Female Autograph* (New York: The New York Literary Forum, 1984); Paul de Man, "Autobiography as De-Facement," *Modern Language Notes: Comparative Literature* 94, no. 5 (December 1979): 919–30; Louis A. Renza, "The Veto of the Imagination," and Michael Sprinker, "Fictions of the Self: The End of Autobiography," in Olney, *Autobiography: Essays*, pp. 268–295, 321–42; Robert Folkenflik, ed., *The Culture of Auto-biography: Constructions of Self-Representation* (Stanford: Stanford University Press, 1993).

10. In the "Introduction" to *Hope against Hope*, Clarence Brown writes: "the angle of vision is always hers. But for all this, she herself, her person, the externals of her life are strangely absent. Her book is very much the book of her husband." Mandel'shtam, *Hope against Hope*, p. vii. Like-wise, Barbara Heldt states: "Mandel'shtam centers her narrative on her poet-husband, almost effacing herself except as a voice." *Terrible Perfection*, p. 151. I do not believe that these statements are entirely wrong, but that, as will become apparent below, the "angle of vision" and "voice" play a far more significant role than suggested here.

11. Mandel'shtam, *Hope Abandoned*, pp. 3, 11 [7, 15].

12. Ibid., pp. 232, 234 [362, 264].

13. Mandel'shtam, *Hope Abandoned*, p. 452 [506–507].

14. See Charles Isenberg, "The Rhetoric of Nadezhda Mandelstam's *Hope against Hope*," in Harris, *Autobiographical Statements*, p. 201.

15. In the case of *Hope against Hope*, the suggestion may have been indirect. Clarence Brown in his "Introduction" to the volume states that Mandel'shtam "savors the slightly fusty Victorian-ism of some of her idioms. 'Hope against hope' is one of these, which I count so often as I read back through her letters that it has practically become her slogan in my mind" (vii). Max Hay-ward, in his "Translator's Foreword" to the second volume, states directly that the book is "called *Hope Abandoned* in translation at Mrs. Mandel'shtam's request" (vi).

16. Chukovskaia, 2: 167, 127.

17. "Vmesto predisloviia" in volume 1 is dated 1966, and "Nemnogo istorii" in volume 2 is dated 1978–1979.

18. Boris Gasparov, "Tvorcheskii portret L. Ia. Ginzburg," in "Tsel'nost': O tvorchestve L. Ia. Ginzburg," ed. E. Mikhailov, *Literaturnoe obozrenie* 10 (1989): 81–82.

19. Ginzburg, "Zapiski," p. 84.

20. See Gasparov, "Tvorcheskii portret," p. 82.

21. Ginzburg, "Zapiski," p. 84.

22. Ibid.

23. See Lydia Ginzburg, *On Psychological Prose*, trans. Judson Rosengrant (Princeton: Princeton University Press, 1990); Lidiia Ginzburg, *O psikhologicheskoi proze; O literaturnom geroe* (Leningrad: Sovetskii pisatel', 1979). The editions of Ginzburg's selected works are the following: *O starom i novom* (Leningrad: Sovetskii pisatel', 1982), *Literatura v poiskakh deistvitel'nosti*, and *Chelovek za pis'mennym stolom*.

24. Mason, "The Other Voice," pp. 210, 213. See also Mary Grimley Mason and Carol Hurd Green, eds., *Journeys: Autobiographical Writings by Women* (Boston: G. K. Hall and Co., 1979); Germaine Bree, "Autogynography," and Julia Watson, "Shadowed Presence: Modern Women Writers and Autobiography," in James Olney, ed., *Studies in Autobiography* (New York: Oxford University Press, 1988), pp. 171–79, 180–89. It is interesting to speculate as to how this orientation toward the other in women's autobiography might be related to the concept of women's own existence as "other" in the dominant male consciousness, a position articulated, for example, by Simone de Beauvoir in *The Second Sex*, trans. H. M. Parshley (New York: Knopf, 1953).

25. Mason, "The Other Voice," p. 231.

26. Abba Dorotheus was the sixth-century religious writer whose works were published in Moscow in 1652. The citation here is from Priscilla Hunt, "The Inversion of the Icon: The Autobiography of the Archpriest Avvakum and Medieval Orthodox Poetics," in Hunt's study in progress, *Councils of the Heart: The Life of the Archpriest Avvakum*. See also the discussion of Abba Dorotheus and the third redaction of Avvakum's *Life* in Dmitrii Likhachev, *Velikoe nasledie. Klassicheskie proizvedeniia literatury drevnei Rusi* (Moscow: Sovremennik, 1975), pp. 300–301; and Archpriest Avvakum, *The Life Written by Himself*, trans. Kenneth N. Brostrom (Ann Arbor: Michigan Slavic Publications, 1979), note 2, pp. 207–208. I am grateful to Professor Hunt for generously sharing of her understanding of Avvakum's role in the Russian autobiographical tradition.

27. Pavel Florenskii cited in N. O. Lossky, *History of Russian Philosophy* (New York: International Universities Press, 1951), p. 181.

28. Heldt, *Terrible Perfection*, p. 153. For a journalistic treatment of suffering and power in the lives of Soviet women, see Francine du Plessix Gray, *Soviet Women: Walking the Tightrope* (New York: Anchor Books, 1990); and Tatyana Tolstaya's review of Gray's book, "Notes from Underground," *New York Review of Books*, May 31, 1990, pp. 3–7.

29. Watson, "Shadowed Presence," pp. 182–83. The texts Watson has in mind are Gertrude Stein's *The Autobiography of Alice B. Toklas*, Lillian Hellman's "Julia" in *Pentimento*, and Christa Wolf's *The Quest for Christa T.*

30. Mandel'shtam, *Hope Abandoned*, pp. 7, 25 [11, 32].

31. Ibid., p. 232 [362]. Mandel'shtam adds here, "While [Osip] was still alive, incidentally, I had no thought of 'finding myself.' We lived too intensively and too intimately to think of 'searching' for ourselves." In another example further supporting Mason's theory, Mandel'shtam writes: "in general, I had no time for my own 'self,' only for 'them' and 'us,' and an inner pain worse than anything caused by the worst heart attacks. If you lost your self, the sense of life vanished with it. . . . there was no longer any life or sense of life for me, any more than for all the others, but most of us were saved by the existence of someone else, by the thought of a 'you.' Instead of sense, my life had a concrete purpose: not to allow 'them' to stamp out all traces of the man I thought of as 'you,' to save his poetry." Ibid., p. 7 [11].

32. Ibid., p. 8 [12].

33. See Charles Isenberg, "The Rhetoric of Nadezhda Mandelstam's *Hope against Hope*," in Harris, *Autobiographical Statements*, especially pp. 193, 206.

34. See John Baggley, *The Doors of Perception: Icons and Their Spiritual Significance* (Crestwood, N.Y.: St. Vladimir's Seminary Press, 1988), pp. 99–100; Hunt, "The Inversion of the Icon," p. 3.

35. Mandel'shtam, *Hope Abandoned*, p. 11 [15].

36. Chukovskaia, *Zapiski*, vol. 1, p. 8.

37. Ibid., p. 50.

38. Ibid., p. 11.

39. Ibid., p. 8.

40. Ibid., p. 134.

41. Lidiia Chukovskaia, introduction to excerpts from *Zapiski ob Anne Akhmatovoi*, in *Pamiati Anny Akhmatovoi* (Paris: YMCA, 1974), pp. 52–53.

42. This sense of a personal and literary integration was at least to some degree mutual, as suggested by Akhmatova's inscription in Chukovskaia's copy of *Beg vremeni*: "Lidii Chukovskoi—moi stikhi, stavshie nashei obshchei knigoi—druzheski Akhmatova. 7 oktiabria 1965." Chukovskaia, *Pamiati Anny Akhmatovoi*, p. 50.

43. See Sarah Pratt, "Lidiia Ginzburg, a Russian Democrat at the Rendezvous," forthcoming in a special issue of *Canadian-American Slavic Studies* on Lidiia Ginzburg edited by Jane Gary Harris.

44. For an excellent discussion of the Tolstoyan element in Ginzburg's treatment of the *narod*, see Gasparov, "Tvorcheskii portret."

45. Ginzburg, "Zapiski," p. 100.

46. Ibid., p. 85.

47. Ibid., p. 84.

48. Ibid., p. 96.

49. Ibid., p. 108. The historian and humanitarian Dmitrii Likhachev offers a statement on the value of the word that partakes of both Mandel'shtam's notion of the word as a source of moral and even physical strength ("What was it but poetry that kept us going?") and Ginzburg's concept of the word as a source of the continuation of social bonds (but on a smaller scale) during the blockade. Likhachev writes: "Such was the loneliness of every family. . . . And the only thing that could help was poetry, because with a kerosene lantern, only one person at a time could read, one person could read out loud. To read something out loud when thoughts were constantly interrupted by hunger pangs. Only poetry. Only verse, poetry could overpower the sensation of hunger." Dmitrii Likhachev, *Ia vspominaiu* (Moscow: Progress, 1991), p. 196.

50. See Gusdorf, "Conditions," pp. 28–30; Mason, "The Other Voice," p. 235.

51. See Weintraub, "Autobiography and Consciousness," p. 235.

52. Bella Brodzki and Celeste Schenk, *Life/Lines: Theorizing Women's Autobiography* (Ithaca: Cornell University Press, 1988), pp. 1–2.

NINE

Writing the Virgin, Writing the Crone

Maria Kuncewicz's Embodiments of Faith

MAGDALENA ZABOROWSKA

WHEN I RECEIVED a copy of the program of the 1993 Annual Conference on Polish Affairs, "Poland between Two Worlds," I was stunned that it did not feature a single session on women. Six months before, the Polish Seym had passed an anti-abortion bill, and I was sure that a panel about the bill's implications would be one of the highlights of the conference. Perhaps I should not have been surprised that no presentation on Polish women took place, as studies about them continued to be rare even as controversies surrounded the vital issues in their lives: contraception and abortion, divorce, political representation, etc. Despite their central roles in national mythologies, Polish women's voices have been marginalized. As might be expected, feminist or gender approaches to Polish literature are similarly relegated to the periphery of critical discourse. For this reason I shall preface this study of the prominent Polish writer Maria Kuncewicz (1897–1989) with a sketch of the context in which she wrote. Without an understanding of this background, the true power of her writing cannot be appreciated.

Throughout history, women in Poland have been relegated to the social and political margin, as in other European countries, though their importance as upholders of national virtues and supporters of their men has never been underestimated. In the nineteenth century, a crucial period for the development of modern Polish cultural values, Polish women were worshipped in romantic poetry as heroic mothers, chaste lovers, muses, and staunch upholders of the national cause during the period of partitions. After World War II, socialist realist propaganda praised them as sturdy comrades and activists of the new ideology. At present, they are faced with the mutually exclusive perspectives of the church, which demands that they fulfill their ambitions solely through the "natural duties" of motherhood and piety, and of the capitalist market, which tempts them with contradictory images of "businesswoman," "modern housewife," and "femme fatale." Always expected to support their men and their country, to adorn and nurture their families and their churches, Polish women are often the objects of an ideological contest between church and state, but they have rarely been allowed to speak for themselves.[1]

This silencing of women is not surprising in a strongly Catholic country such as Poland. It arises from a paradoxical construction of femininity as both powerless and powerful, a construction especially visible in representations of the Virgin Mary as a mortal woman and a goddess. The Marian cult is central to the religious experience of Catholic Poles; the Mother of God symbolizes both idealized womanhood, meekly serving the Lord, and a divine figure, whom average believers consider nearly as important as the Holy Trinity.[2] An embodiment of divine motherhood and an example of feminine subservience, Mary is seen as close to ordinary people and capable of understanding their mundane problems. Her humanity and femininity let her play the role of people's advocate with God, the remote Father—her divinity is tempered with motherly sympathy and typically "feminine" traits of compassion and forgiveness. Churchgoing Poles have long taken the Virgin's power and divinity for granted, regardless of official church doctrine—a stance which often puzzles Westerners.[3] Poles who were raised Catholic inherit a powerful, romantic nineteenth-century tradition that Poland and its people were chosen to be the "Christ of the Nations," the savior who would redeem Europe "for the millions."[4] Thus Christ's Mother became Mother of Poland, Queen and goddess, who is enshrined and enthroned as the Black Madonna in her sanctuary Jasna Góra, in Częstochowa. This shrine attracts millions of pilgrims from all over the world with its jeweled icon, its long history of miracles and healings, and innumerable votive offerings attesting to the power of the Polish Catholic Goddess.[5]

The Virgin Mary in Poland, like the women of that country, is nonetheless virtually speechless. She stands for feminine power as a cultural and religious figure, but represents powerlessness as a silenced mortal woman who bore a male God. Female worshippers seek strength and endurance, inspired by her superficial passivity and her ambiguous, implicit status as both mortal and divine. In Maria Kuncewicz's late work *Listy do Jerzego* (*Letters to George*, 1988), the Virgin first appears as a voiceless and powerless idol to pray to, but through Kuncewicz's writing she becomes a fellow sufferer who offers wisdom and an eternal power of life and renewal. Kuncewicz presents a dialogic encounter with the deity to whom she prays, but whom she also perceives as a "sister" entrapped in the female body.

In this study, I explore the meeting between the Virgin—the Mother of God—and the Crone, the elderly writer, for it provides a central metaphor for a feminist reading of Kuncewicz's texts. Close examination of *Listy do Jerzego* shows that the encounter illuminates the paradox and mutual dependence of women's power and powerlessness in Polish Catholic tradition. Kuncewicz writes out of her own voicelessness as a Polish writer unknown abroad, and out of her powerlessness as a female Roman Catholic; she gains voice and power by revising church dogma, reinterpreting for herself the man-made Word that narrates her story and the Virgin's. Her text thus traces the women's stories on the body, framed by religion, art, and storytelling. As Kuncewicz's own rich biography shows, her life and career consist of renaming and translating her identities as Pole, woman, writer, intellectual, mother, lover, political refugee, and believer.

Naming the Things That Don't Have Names

For a Polish writer in the twentieth century, being female means belonging to a group that has been silenced as active cultural subjects—resulting in practical invisibility to the rest of the world. Poland itself is often invisible to the "West," and especially to the United States, where James Michener's bestseller *Poland* was written so that "the book's price would not exceed the curiosity of the American reader."[6] To Western eyes, modern Poland usually appears through the images of male heroic narratives, perpetuated by the media and popular writers such as Michener: tales of the cavalry charge against German tanks during the Second World War, documentaries on workers' protests against the Soviet regime, or dissident stories of defection and political exile. In contrast to these narratives, the biography and texts of Maria Kuncewicz project a unique female voice that criticizes and debunks external cultural narratives that define her as woman, author, Polish Roman Catholic, or international refugee. Referring to Michener's Poland in *Listy do Jerzego*, Kuncewicz remarks rather bitterly that personal knowledge of Poland and long residence in the United States mean nothing on the American literary market, which prefers authors who cater to popular tastes over opaque foreigners and their firsthand stories.

Of course, Kuncewicz failed to capture American readers because of many complex factors. Her works explore one of them: the conflict between an individual's perception of the world and that individual's inevitable entrapment in the external social, political, gender, class, and ethnic narratives that "write" all people. Kuncewicz sees herself as "being lived" rather than independently "living." In *Listy*, she explains her continual passion for redefining her story: "[The] need to name things that don't have names still remains. And the participation in senseless performances continues to bother me. Still, when I am writing this, it's not so much that I live, but that 'I am lived'" (LJ, 7).

The confessional character of Kuncewicz's *Listy* makes it an arresting variation on the theme of "being lived." It also closes, like a testament, the impressive list of novels, memoirs, reportage notebooks, short stories, and plays created by this nationally famous Polish writer. Composed as letters to her deceased husband, a series of prayers, and memoirs, *Listy* is a personal document, the writer's farewell to a rich life and an impressive career interwoven with this century's most dramatic and painful historical and political events. Born in Samara, Russia, of exiled Polish parents who brought their infant daughter back to their homeland in 1899, Kuncewicz bore from the beginning the stigma of a "stranger" caught between cultures—the theme of her award-winning first novel, *Cudzoziemka* (*The Stranger*, 1936, 1945).[7] Her flight from the war in Poland in 1939, recorded in *Klucze* (*The Keys: A Flight through Europe at War*, 1948, 1943) and *Zmowa Nieobecnych* (*The Conspiracy of the Absent*, 1957, 1946–50), began an artistic and personal exile lasting nearly twenty years, the major theme of her later autobiographical trilogy, *Fantomy* (*Phantoms*, 1971), *Natura* (*Nature*, 1975), and *Przeźrocza* (*Slides*, 1985). In transition from one culture to another, Kuncewicz kept building her unique literary domain—what she termed "the free-for-all country"—stretching from Poland to France and England, where she lived through the war, to the United States, where she taught at the University of Chicago and where she became an American citizen, before returning to Poland in the late 1960s.

Polish readers have called Kuncewicz's diverse texts psychological, auto-biographical, and deeply moralistic. Czesław Miłosz praises her "detached investigations of human psychology without regard for political commitments" and terms her the "most Western" of Polish women writers of her time because of her "focusing upon the individual."[8] Other studies approach her recording of exile, re-creation of national and international myths, and chronicles of the historical past and present.[9] Since she died in 1989, publications in Poland have reclaimed her travels, immigrant experiences, and involvement in émigré and P.E.N. circles, presenting her as a writer who gave her native sensibility an international dimension; the very traits valued in Poland, however, have often been perceived as "foreign" by readers and reviewers abroad.[10] Besides the international acclaim of *The Stranger*, and in part *The Olive Grove* (1963) and *Tristan* (1974), briefly available in the author's translation, her books in English failed to win lasting interest because of the poor quality of the translations. Hardly anyone in the United States would know today that Kuncewicz received numerous awards in Poland and abroad, and that she even was briefly considered as a nominee for the Nobel Prize in Literature.[11]

Firmly established in the literary pantheon in Poland, Kuncewicz still has rarely been read as a *woman* writer.[12] This blindness to gender issues is unexpected, given an author whose international biography made her a sophisticated witness and recorder of history, a forerunner of such immigrant East European critics and writers as Julia Kristeva and Eva Hoffman. Like these two intellectuals, Kuncewicz was politically involved in the postwar order and deeply invested in exploring her gender subjectivity amid this order. Her writings, created between Eastern Europe and the "West," explore her position as a woman writing herself from within the predominantly Roman Catholic culture of pre- and postwar Poland. "Being lived" where the political and the personal have intertwined into a web of incomprehensible paradoxes, Kuncewicz works out her own semantics of "living" a woman's experience as author and believer. Her almost biblical, insatiable need for "naming things that don't have names" is the driving force behind her art; it emphasizes the dilemma of a writer who must wrestle every day with the expressive inadequacy of language.

In *Listy*, looking at snow-covered trees, the narrator-writer realizes that even now she is unable to capture in words the beauty that surrounds her. "Silence. Such silence cannot exist in any church. This phenomenon is called: winter. How poor is our vocabulary!" (LJ, 46). Comparing silence in the natural woods with silence in a man-made church elicits the superficiality of the way we use language. By emphasizing that we communicate through descriptive approximations of image and sensation, by comparing "natural" and "artificial" silence, she implies a religious faith in her artistic aesthetics. Both language and belief in God demand a leap into narrative structures—cultural story lines—that are prescribed for us as writers, readers, critics, and believers. These prescriptions "write" us as subjects, but once "written" we become objects in the larger designs that inspire infinite interpretation. By thus defining her task as naming, Kuncewicz evokes Adam, the author in Paradise after God has empowered him to name animals, plants, and objects.

However, as her texts prove, Kuncewicz does not see herself as a "New Adam"—the language and power she struggles with are her own creations rather than gifts from the Father. For instance, in her short story "Dom. Wizja przyszłego fin de siècle'u" ("Home: Vision of a Future Fin de Siècle"), two women choose to follow Eve's individualistic curiosity and thirst for knowledge, to run their lives against the rules of the state. After all, the writer's task is not to trust reality but "to construct a fiction that is more real than life," to deal with the fact that "the object of experience is the subject: the native and always alien 'I'—the only crucible, the only material."[13] In a close reading of Kuncewicz's writing, the writer's "I" unfolds, questions, and subverts the clichés defining her. Kuncewicz is an artist of the word who writes with religious conviction, zeal, and passion; she re-creates and rewrites not only herself but also the tradition that formed her, and her self-criticism highlights the complexities and intricacies of texts and cultures.

It is important to remember, however, that Kuncewicz's texts challenge the reader in the deceptive simplicity of her persistence in renaming the obvious, constructing her writings as a seamless hybrid of religious and artistic sensitivity. Any attempt at a critical reading risks being just another venture into the very realm of treacherous language and institutionalized images that her texts try to resist. As a critic who shares much of Kuncewicz's background—religious, national, and linguistic—I argue that we can comprehend her literary vision only once we reconcile ourselves to fragmentation rather than narrative cohesion and to fluidity rather than stability. Perhaps (and this is often the case with involved critical readings) I am reading/writing my own story of growing up female in Catholic and Communist Poland into Kuncewicz's literary journey from youth to old age. Nevertheless, I believe that my personal experiences of Polish Catholicism's construction of female believers can aid understanding of Kuncewicz's literary aesthetics. Looking at her works, and especially the central encounter with the Virgin Mary in *Listy*, I want to emphasize the need to examine Polish literature from a feminist perspective, with that perspective's sharpened attention to how women's lives are "being lived" in texts and in society.

Letters to Herself:
Maria Writing Mary between Religion and Art

[The Lord's Prayer]—a difficult prayer. In the evening I am so tired of this prayer, my dead husband, as if I have been trying to lift your tombstone. The night comes, time of murders, but also of vulnerability, the time of dreams. I long for a breather. I crave to talk with a gentle deity who doesn't know Satan. So: "Ave Maria." The Angel of the Poles seems to be asking about the well-being of the Virgin, the Mother of God's Son conceived not by the body but by the Spirit. In Polish, it isn't the Latin "Ave," welcome. To my Polish ear, the phrase sounds like a question: "Are you well, Maria?" The incomprehensible being is revealed to me as a sister. As a "lady" susceptible to being well or unwell. After such a familiarization with the deity, perhaps it will be easier for me to understand the answer, which I know from the Gospel: "Be it unto me according to Thy word." (LJ, 50)

In *Listy do Jerzego*, Kuncewicz gives a summary of her never-ending quest for a literary and religious aesthetics and for a text that would express the aesthetics fully and communicatively. *Listy* is also a prism for Kuncewicz's artistic development—from early short stories and novels about women's lives to the later autobiographical series fictionalizing her progression through different countries and traditions. That is why she says in her last book of epistles/memoirs, addressed to her dead husband: "[T]hese letters from me to you are turning more and more into a correspondence with myself" (LJ, 68). Bringing into focus Kuncewicz's whole life and career, this self-addressed correspondence serves as a springboard and pivotal axis for my examination of her literary and religious writings.

As a woman defined by the cultural tradition of Polish Roman Catholicism, the narrator of *Listy* must confront her individual concept of faith with official dogma. Her invocation to the Virgin Mary in the quotation that begins this section introduces the complexities of textual and religious visions, which always cross-fertilize in Kuncewicz's works. All through *Listy*, Kuncewicz constructs the image of an old woman praying, tired of life, weary of the ritual, but nevertheless persevering in both despite her aching body, holding on to tradition with weakening strength.

However, the same fragment also projects the old woman's disillusionment with the words of the Lord's Prayer, that invocation to the patriarchal and impalpable God of man-made Christian theology. She desires a more "human" and tangible deity and so turns to "Ave Maria," interpreted as an invocation to the Virgin—Mother of God's Son, Queen of Catholic Poland—and also an encounter with a woman—a sister bearing the same common name, Mary-Maria, a fellow female susceptible to sufferings of the flesh, "to being well or unwell." In this context, Kuncewicz's prayer to Mary becomes an act of bold familiarization through the female body the "sisters" both share. It is daring because the worshipping narrator makes no clear distinction in "rank" between God the Father and His Son's (and thus His Own) Mother, though she knows that Mary has never been considered a "deity" by the authorities of the church. However, in suggesting the possibility of addressing Mary as a "goddess," Kuncewicz's narrator echoes the Polish Marian tradition of the Virgin, Queen and Mother of Poland, who protected her land through centuries of wars and partitions like a beloved child, to be the redeemer of other countries. Therefore, though challenging official church orthodoxy, Kuncewicz's narrator aligns herself with folk and national tradition and validates her people's ways of worship through intellectual and literary reiteration.

This approach to Mary emphasizes her as a woman deity whom the believer creates, as if "in her own (human) image," and thus reflects a larger cultural design which has inscribed the Virgin as product both of Catholic orthodoxy—a disembodied saint—and of many nations' popular beliefs and folk traditions—a worshipped woman/sister/mother. As Marina Warner emphasizes, historical Mary, a woman Kuncewicz wants to identify with, is beyond our grasp. Since the purpose of her existence was to fulfill the Christian God's narrative, her personal essence dissolves in symbols and narratives from other sources. Representations of Mary by all kinds of artists attest to widespread fascination with her human and divine nature.[14]

As an artist of the world, to whom "religion has been coming, only to meet with one act of resistance after another, slowly, like a duty of the conscience rather than a hope for happiness," Kuncewicz's narrator in *Listy* cannot identify with the disembodied male God of the Lord's Prayer:

> To me, a practicing Catholic, God's Son is still elusive, God conceals Himself in His secrets; I can't feel the taste of the body and blood in the Host, I feel an order: "Partake! It is me, the One and Only in the Holy Trinity. Partake of me! Partake of God, who is in heaven and in every place, and who thus should be inside you. Partake of God!" I leave the altar and, while the Host is melting in my mouth, I wait for a miracle.
>
> I have been waiting so since the moment of my first communion, until today, the day before my last rites. Is it that God is making His miracles in ways incomprehensible to me? Is it a miracle that God descends upon me when I am looking at a tree in bloom, not at a monstrance? At the moon, not at a chalice? Would it be a miracle that, without feeling the taste of the Lord's Body and Blood, I try to live as if this taste were familiar to me? (LJ, 31–33)

Her futile wait for a miracle, suspended between two important Catholic rituals bracketing a believer's life, the first communion and the last rites, turns into a period of religious and artistic creativity. By asking herself whether or not she understands her religion, the narrator of *Listy* realizes that she knows what it means to be in a state of grace, even though her experience of this knowledge may not correspond to the orthodox definitions. Kuncewicz's narrator's "grace" is embodied in nature—blooming trees and the moon—rather than in the props of church rituals. By emphasizing the continuity of her discoveries and locating her faith from childhood to old age—from first communion to last rites—she explains the "mystery of faith" in her own terms. The woman in *Listy* sees faith as a process in which she affirms her love for all mysteries and ambiguities, religious and artistic, "for two reasons: 1. fear of truth, 2. worship of poetry which makes truth into something with many meanings, something unyielding to dogmas, unyielding to criteria other than beauty and love" (LJ, 32).

The narrator of *Listy* clearly associates beauty and love, mystery and ambiguity, with her version of Mary. She finds solace in seeing herself and the "lady" as women whose shared carnality can be captured and explained through writing. To the narrator, author of many texts, Mary is also a fellow artist who creates her fate—participates in the divine scenario—with the painful and tragic heroism of one torn between the separate worlds of heaven and earth. Looking at a Polish painting of the Annunciation, the narrator sees an inhabitant of the mortal world, a woman with a basket of knitting at her feet. Yet this ordinary woman is asked to become a vessel for the Holy Spirit and God's Mother, and her submission to God's will is a "tragic act" as she is taken from her familiar environment into the unearthly realms of God's design (LJ, 105). Mary's human tragedy and palpable human fear of the incomprehensible are captured by the talented painter. But to the narrator of *Listy*, this woman who is "being lived" within God's narrative turns into an artist whose feelings at the Annunciation Kuncewicz, somewhat blasphemously, compares to the human power of creativity: "the inspiration which comes to a craftsman, making him into an artist."

Kuncewicz paints Mary as a woman-sister and metaphorically brings her back to earth. The chaste vessel, entered and impregnated by the Spirit, becomes nevertheless a palpable, flesh-and-blood deity, fully able to understand the narrator's prayer. The Virgin in *Listy* is invoked by a female believer who is acutely aware of "being lived" in external social and religious designs, who describes her living between the aching flesh of an old woman and the eternally youthful spirit of an artist. In seeing Mary as deity and woman, caught in divine and earthly scenarios, Kuncewicz not only retrieves the Virgin's body—the sexuality and motherhood the church rejects—but also reaffirms herself as a woman, writer, and believer who dares to create her own artistic and religious vision of faith.

Embodying the Virgin

> I tell you that on the days when the old body bothers me more than usual, it just seems to me that "two moons" equals "two cows" equals "two bombs." In this case, what about such words as Creator, Redeemer, Holy Spirit? Do human words mean anything different in eternal existence? After all, churches, synagogues, mosques, all the earthly houses of supernatural deities are filled with people who crave uniqueness of meaning from human and Divine words. (LJ, 68)

When we read the New Testament, and especially the Gospels, we realize how marginal Mary was to its authors, who mention her a few times as one of the characters in her Son's story (Warner, 3–24).[15] In this context, Kuncewicz's emphasis on Mary as a heroine combines, again, an individual believer's desire for more palpable contact with the deity and popular Marian cults where, as in the sanctuary in Częstochowa, "the crowds of Catholics find an outlet for their hunger for miracles, their passion for demonstrations." However, the narrator of *Listy* does not want to accompany her German friend on a trip to Częstochowa because, "since Luther and Calvin have taken the role of Mother of humankind away from the supernatural Virgin, Częstochowa . . . is only a point on Poland's tourist map" (LJ, 100). Here, Kuncewicz distances herself from the commercialization of Marian worship and from the erasure of the individual in its crowd-pleasing rituals. It is true that for Catholics in Poland Mary serves as intercessor with Christ, her power to beg favors for her "children" growing in inverse parallel to her discrediting in the Protestant tradition, which refused her saintly qualities or power to work miracles. As a public symbol, Mary remains a disembodied and distant icon to Kuncewicz's narrator, who would prefer to ask her namesake about her well-being privately, rather than join the crowds at the sanctuary that has become a profitable tourist attraction. Excessive institutionalized worship has blotted out the woman-sister from the Black Madonna's image. When her friend returns from Jasna Góra, the narrator asks, "'And what about the Black Madonna? What impression did you get of her?' She [the friend] turned her head, kept silent" (LJ, 102).

Unable to describe her "impression" of the Virgin, the narrator's foreign friend cannot comfortably translate between public religious experience and the world of linguistic signs. In Kuncewicz's text this discomfort is replayed as the result of a dualistic approach to the Marian tradition—accepting some of its tenets and rejecting others—which in turn inspires the narrator to explain the Virgin in her own words. Just like the early Christians, inspired by the sparse information about Mary to fill in the blanks with noncanonical writings,[16] Kuncewicz embroiders the given outline with her own designs. Similarly, instead of describing the painting of the Black Madonna, the narrator's friend translates her impressions through a landscape: "'Sunrise and sunset over the monastery [Jasna Góra] were marvelous, marvelous! . . . That grand tower against the golden-pink background. . . .' Her eyes filled with tears of wonder. 'Different gold in the morning, different in the evening, the pink different too. And those fortifications, that seriousness, those incomprehensible words, everything was losing gravity'." This way, although invisible, the Virgin appears to the listener as a combination of colors and images evocative of traditional litanies to her: "Tower," "Morning Star," "House of Gold," "Gate of Heaven."

Mary's invisibility and intangibility at Jasna Góra serve to catalyze an image painting of the monastery which symbolizes her on earth. The woman saint becomes everything the beholder can see around her; she melts into nature around the buildings. Such a metonymic description of Mary echoes the paradoxes of the Marian tradition, which both brings Mary closer to people by emphasizing her humanity and distances her from them by blotting out her sexuality, elevating her role in the divine plan by cleansing her of the "taint" of complete femininity.[17] Thus the originally mortal woman again becomes a hybrid of human and divine qualities. Mary's passive and silent acceptance of her mission in the Gospels corresponds to the silence and sense of passivity that Kuncewicz's narrator experiences after her question about the Virgin's well-being in "Ave Maria" and while asking her friend about the Black Madonna. Once disembodied, the woman saint cannot answer her worshipper's invocation: the believer-writer is left to interpret this silence in her own way.[18]

The necessity of such individual interpretation arises because, like Mary's, the believer's carnality, and especially the female believer's carnality in the Catholic church, has been excluded from what the church deems the proper experience of faith and worship. Removal of the woman's body as sinful in the Christian tradition came hand in hand with silencing of the female believer, who could express her religious life only through services to men: as a wife and mother, or as a pious and docile "hand" who helps decorate and maintain the sacred interiors. Inability to express their alienation as flesh-and-blood women, as creatures who bear the stigma of Eve's sin and cannot integrate their carnality into their faith, echoes clearly in the narrator's friend's inability to describe the Black Madonna. Since Mary should exist to the beholder primarily as a symbol of divine motherhood, and since the beholder has no means of asserting her own bodily presence within the Catholic tradition, we are given only a linguistic approximation of the "impression," not the Madonna-sister, the woman-goddess herself.

The general desexualization of members of the church regardless of gender follows logically from the notion of original sin. Adam and Eve were expelled from Paradise when they acquired "knowledge" about their bodies—hence the connection between women and sexuality as evil, and interpretation of Eve's disobedience as proof of women's vulnerability to temptation.[19] In such a context, the images of God's Mother's chastity and disembodiment serve as tools for control and punishment (Warner, 68–69). Forever tragically split into sinful bodies which they should resist and souls which should transcend earthly temptations, women are paradoxically supposed to aspire to be just like the Virgin, despite the impossibility of her miraculous achievements for any ordinary woman (Warner, 34–49). In revising these images, Kuncewicz's text shows that it is precisely the Virgin's body, restored in writing, that provides the connection necessary for a believer who wants to pray with both soul and body, who desires an embodiment of her belief.

As Margaret Homans stresses, there is a clear connection between body and language written into the figure of the Virgin, because "she not only represents an exaggerated version of the Aristotelian view of women's passive role in reproduction, but . . . also specifically articulates this view in terms of language, in the myth of the Virgin impregnated by the Word." To Homans, Mary's superficial power of divine motherhood, so glorified by the church, means just the opposite, as the point of the Marian myth is to show how little the Virgin had to do with her own body and the conception.[20] This clear connection between carnality and expression—a woman could bear the Word once she was desexualized—makes the narrator of *Listy* aware of how her own aching body underlies her prayers and religious meditations. More broadly, she sees her art of writing as a form of labor—the flood of birth waters and a child she creates within herself can be read as metaphors for language and the production of texts. She recalls laboring to give birth to her son in strongly biblical terms: "I was looking at my distended belly with disdain. The fetus grows, discomforts, makes me nauseous, but I didn't feel sick, only strange. . . . Where did the waters come from? Why did they break? Where did the flood come from? Why did it give in to Noah? Something gathered itself up and something subsided back to normal. The boy was born fit as a fiddle" (LJ, 112). It is easy to see in this fragment a parallel between the vision of giving birth/writing and Mary's wonder at her divine pregnancy and bringing forth of the Word. Mary's offspring comes out of the water—some etymologies give her name as meaning "mara," sea or ocean[21]—just as the narrator's son is born metaphorically from a flood of words that Kuncewicz records. Once again, the two women are brought closer together as creators of life and texts, as creators of stories.

Kuncewicz's private prayer to Mary in *Listy* emphasizes the mingling of spiritual and carnal aspects in her writing. Her works often explore the "soul" and "body" of texts, both the "divine" aspect of writing as spiritual creation and the "carnal" nature of texts as artifacts crafted in words and written with the author's hand. This dualism appears clearly in the quotation from *Listy* that opens this section and is as much about a religious experience as about a linguistic one. The Virgin of the Scriptures can be reinscribed into a woman's body by the believer once the verbal construction of the Angel's question has been examined. "Are you well, Mary?" is Kuncewicz's translation of the Latin inquiry into Polish, which she then examines on the syntactic and semantic levels. Through this examination, the narrator reveals Mary's carnal dimension—she can be well or unwell because she has a body that can feel either way. Moreover, the reader also witnesses the writer's passage from constructing the metaphorical meaning of her text to analyzing the mechanics of its making. The final phrase, "Be it unto me according to Thy word," acknowledges the verbal power available to the writer who can deconstruct it to mean "Do as you please with my body."

However, the same quotation anticipates the writer's awareness that her power over language is very precarious. In the fragment following her rewriting of Mary, Kuncewicz ponders the mysterious nature of words which "do unto us."

> [The sound], in which the act of will can be contained: "Let it be." I, a specialist in light-minded words, I, the so-called "femme de lettres" imprisoned in letters, am terrified of the Creator's words and of the Virgin Mother's words. At the end of an earthly day the Lord's Prayer and "Ave Maria" seem to me prayers surpassing human capacities. But despite that, I insist: "Our Father who *art, art,* certainly *art* in heaven! . . ." A moment to catch my breath and I ask: "Are you well, Mary?" And, as soon as I have greeted the supernatural beings, I implore them about my human problem. (LJ, 50)

As a writer, Kuncewicz is sure of her verbal powers but painfully conscious as well that she is also a reader responding to a larger text—the tradition and culture that surround her and provide contexts for her readings and writings. Therefore, her "carnal prayer" can be read as an exercise in rebellion of a woman believer caught in traditional Christian discourse—a specific Polish Roman Catholic version thereof—and of a writer who wants to wield power over language and the textual worlds she creates. Kuncewicz's narrator knows she is capable of rewriting her own belief, but she knows, too, that she cannot change the larger cultural and social scenario inscribing her as a woman, writer, Catholic, lover, wife, and mother. She can rewrite Mary in her own text, but she cannot literally change the "words of the Virgin Mother," which have petrified into a uniform, traditional reading through history.

Nevertheless, the narrator's very attempt to reread "Ava Maria" and the Lord's Prayer, her passionate emphasis on "Be it unto me," "Let it be," and her conspicuous repetition of "[Our Father] who *art, art,* certainly *art* [in heaven]" transform the meaning and suggest an alternative reading without changing the original words of the prayers. The context she gives to her prayers and the intense physicality of her worship let the reader understand the narrator's frustration and desire for rebellion. The text rewrites and rereads Catholicism from a woman's perspective, though it dares not change the words of the traditional narrative that superficially inscribes the writer as just another member of the church. Just as her struggle to embody her faith is visible in her rewriting of Mary as a "lady" with a body, her precarious situation as a writer with both infinite and very limited power over the Word is visible in her texts. Kuncewicz's works constantly question the "soul" and "body" of literary creation and spring from this inquiry to talk about the intertwining of spiritual and carnal within the concept of woman's faith constructed in her writings. In this way, Kuncewicz actually debunks the comparison of the writer's art with Adam's task of naming. Instead of passively submitting to God's will, she chooses to speak for herself and thus aligns herself with Mary's predecessor, daring Eve, who claimed knowledge for herself without God's permission.

From Virgin to Crone

The "true" I, after all, never gets reflected in the mirror; it is the "heart of darkness" of every human being. I am just not curious about this "heart of darkness" of mine. Perhaps I am afraid of it, maybe I can't see it. I also can't derive practical observations from my reflection in public opinion, I have no desire to alter my image in any direction. Because a mirror doesn't say who I am; it says what I look like.[22]

Kuncewicz analyzes the dichotomy between "soul" and "body" that informs her texts and faith in the early, youthful stories "Przymierze z Dzieckiem" ("Covenant with a Child," 1926) and "Twarz Mężczyzny" ("A Man's Face," 1928) and continues in her novels, *Cudzoziemka* and *Gaj Oliwny* (*The Olive Grove*, 1962) and in her notebook-autobiographies, *Fantomy, Natura, Przeźrocza* and *Listy do Jerzego*. This preoccupation with the dual nature of her art can be explained in terms of Julia Kristeva's theories of subjectivity in progress ("From One Identity to an Other") and the Christian construction of the feminine and the maternal ("Stabat Mater"). Kuncewicz's struggle to reconcile her art and religion involves a lifetime of writing which records all the important phases in the biological development of a woman. In writing an account of her life and faith, she also records her own story as a virgin, lover, wife, mother, and crone or wise woman—she creates a whole feminine narrative.[23]

Although it spans a woman's life from adolescence to old age, Kuncewicz's quest for religious expression is not simply subordinated to the chronological progression from youth to age. The beginner, who explored modernist techniques and pronounced feminine psychology and sexuality the stuff of women's prose in the 1920s, and the old woman of the late 1980s, who reassessed her life and achievements from the perspective of a cosmopolitan intellectual, are writing the same story. Comparisons and parallels between these two incarnations of one woman show different approaches to the same problem: Kuncewicz writes consistently, with the same expanding mind, but *within* a changing woman's body which becomes a document registering the past in the flesh.

Kuncewicz's ultimate text written upon the feminine body is imprinted with the experiences of flights of the unconscious—what she describes as her intangible "phantom" identity—and activities which produce material results, such as writing, housekeeping, gardening. This text is created by the soaring phantom—the soul—*and* the writer's body, the flesh trapped by biological determinism. The old woman's body in *Listy* is fleshed out in words that record the aches and pains of old age; it is the ultimate text through which she communicates and feels her creative and religious identity. In this respect, Kuncewicz's art and faith develop in a cyclical progression from the Virgin to the Crone, with the woman's body a point of reference in its ability to create, articulate, and nurture life, love, belief, ecstasy, and death. On the pages of Kuncewicz's books, sexual women—symbolized in the Bible by the unchaste temptress Mary Magdalene and sinful Eve—far from bringing about the fall of humanity, make it possible to reinterpret femininity within Catholic discourse. The punishment for Eve's, and all women's, curiosity—childbirth in pain—becomes a blessing that inspires artistic expression. For example, curiosity inspires reading and generating texts in Kuncewicz's short story "Dom" and the conversion of a little English girl in the novel *The Olive Grove*, where the Virgin appears as a fellow sufferer of women of all ages.

Such readings of Kuncewicz do not in the least aim to reinterpret theological doctrine. Rather, they explore how her writings react to cultural and social constructions of faith and belief in the Polish Roman Catholic church, and how these constructions in turn relate to twentieth-century women's writing in the West. In Kuncewicz's texts, the Kristevan other, the "unnameable" woman immersed in the realm of the semiotic, becomes her own text, asserts her independent power as author and believer. Just as Kristeva's theory maps the battle between the semiotic and symbolic spheres of language, between the maternal and feminine and the paternal and masculine,[24] Kuncewicz's texts construct a woman's identity from within the female body that creates woman's artistic and religious aesthetics in response and in opposition to the tradition writing her gender roles. By taking on the role of writer of the sacred, Kuncewicz embraces the Catholic faith as her own creation and as a function of the woman's body.

Such rewriting of Catholicism is clear in *Listy*, where Kuncewicz's cyclical narrative embraces the old woman's introspective personal journal and nostalgic readings of her nation's recent history. The narrator's memoirs are closely connected with the experiences of pain and pleasure written on the old woman's aching frame. When she prays, she engages her whole body in the act. At ninety, she conveys her supplication to God in the Lord's Prayer through powerful physical sensations:

> I hold on to this difficult prayer like a drowning person to the last straw of salvation. An old woman, approaching ninety, with a face anointed with cosmetics, with the bitterness of the last daily medication in her mouth, with pain in her bones, I clasp my hands and say loudly through my set teeth: "Our Father who art in heaven." I cross myself and shout: "Hallowed be Thy name! Thy kingdom come!" This doesn't sound like a prayer, this sounds like a prodigious child's reproach for having been rejected. . . . A difficult prayer. "Thy will be done, on earth as it is in heaven." Heaven and earth—a staggering distance. I agree to vast distances because I chose the Spirit. Yet I have not renounced the body. So I beg for daily bread and for forgiveness of my own and others' sins. (LJ, 49–50)

The images of violence and pain involved in the prayer to the Father—clasped hands, set teeth, shouting, aching bones, bitter taste—echo young women's simultaneous desire for and rejection of God in Kuncewicz's early stories and novels.[25]

As if to come back full circle to her first fascination with the body, *Listy* reminds its readers of Kuncewicz's young heroines' struggles to reconcile their sexual desires with spiritual needs and the social conventions of early twentieth-century Poland. Kuncewicz came to portray these dilemmas as the aspiring author of such stories about women's sexual awakenings as "Przymierze z Dzieckiem" and "Twarz Mężczyzny." Inability to pray to the distant Father is already familiar to young Terenia, a heroine of the latter text, who attends a church funeral:

> Terenia couldn't pray. God seemed so lost in attending to children's Christmas re-quests, to beggars' laments, to saints' silent madness that it wasn't proper to disturb Him. . . . The organ—at first babbling—finally gave in to the hands of the person play-ing: a cloud of sadness spread over the chapel, smoking, bleeding, just like at sunset. Different mortal affairs kept coming to her mind.[26]

Like the narrator of *Listy*, who cannot keep the aches of her body from disrupting her prayer, Terenia feels oppressed by the "mortal affairs" that invade her privacy and concentration within the church. Once inside, she feels separated from nature, reduced to an insignificant supplicant who should not disturb God. The man-made womb of the church is permeated with death—of the Savior and of the girl's young friend—and thus stands in sharp contrast to her thoughts about life. The adjective "mortal" is used ironically in this context, as it is "mortal" thoughts of love and sensuality that keep interrupting Terenia's prayers in the shrine symbolizing eternal life and triumph over death. She came to pray for a departed boyfriend, in a ritual celebrating passing into a "better life," and yet she "gives in to the hands of the person playing" the music (the writer?); she cannot free her thoughts from the images of fertile nature:

> The pond, where Stasiek used to gather forget-me-nots for Jadzia; that evening, when Anatol left, having lifted up his head of stiff hair, and *when the space for Truth remained empty amid the sky*; passion on beautiful lips that don't bear a name: love too heavy, too full-blooded, too suddenly fragrant for the people of a gray climate; mother's mumbling over a plate of fruit, father in his office—alone; and also her own room, filled with the air of the past. (TM, 105, my emphasis)

In contrast to the old woman in *Listy*, who embraces her body as a link between heaven and earth, the spiritual and the material, and the past and the present, the young woman in "Twarz Mężczyzny" cannot pray because she cannot free herself from the burden of the past. Terenia fears the future she will face as a female—deflowering and sex, childbirth, motherhood, deaths—stages suggested by the bleeding cloud sensed in the church. However, the physicality of their religious ex-periences unites these two women and records their lives on the changing female body. In Kuncewicz's cyclical writing of the woman's story, pain and suffering are inseparable from participation in the man-made religious ritual, as if the old woman's aches came as punishment for the young girl's "mortal" thoughts and de-sires, "too heavy, too full-blooded, too suddenly fragrant for the people of a gray climate."

Restricted by the enclosure of the church and the conventional prayer, the woman's body in both texts is still a temple of its own, enclosed in flesh and consecrated to the creation and worship of words as well as to the making and celebration of life.[27] For Terenia, this space puts forth her impulse to follow "mortal affairs"—to pursue life rather than acquiesce in the funeral mood of a ritual proclaiming death of the body. The outside world seems an extension of the young woman's being and is associated with life and sexual vitality; it contrasts sharply with the dark interior of the church, which is full of inertia and a never-ending "memento mori." In *Listy*, the narrator's painful inability to concentrate on the Lord's Prayer attests to the woman's continued desire to connect the carnal and the sacred, against the practices of the church that inscribe her body as sinful and defiled since it is a site of sex and reproduction. Between youth and old age, the two women symbolize two important incarnations of the sacred feminine—the Virgin and the Crone—a life-giving womb and a witness to this life's dying. In this respect, they share the potential both of a mother, creator of life, and of a writer, creator of words. Terenia and the narrator of *Listy* meet within Kuncewicz's ongoing text, recorded on and through the woman's body and celebrating its extremes: life and death.[28]

These two concepts of femininity in Kuncewicz's *Listy* meet metaphorically in the narrator's memories of her youth, spent "busy with singing, writing, and being in a state of wonder about anything, because that anything *was*, and I had always doubted that I was myself." Despite all that she has learned, she still realizes that, even in old age, every prayer is a struggle to connect the impossible extremes defining her and underlying her writing (LJ, 113, my emphasis). To Terenia in "Twarz Mężczyzny," her presence in the world swells beyond the space assigned to her within the church; she feels that important things "again floated somewhere up above, eclipsing the sun." The incongruity of her imagery and the nature of the ritual she attends indicate her alienation and otherness as a woman caught between the two worlds—spiritual and sensual. Just like the old woman of *Listy*, who shouts her prayer and struggles with it physically, so that perhaps God can hear her this time, Terenia prays in unlikely images soaked in blood and peopled with men who can kiss, break one's heart, and excite one's desire. Both women thus rely on their carnality to transmit their religious experiences. The old one clings to the traditional prayer; she rewrites it by reciting it with and through the pain in her bones. The young one rejects the priest, who "resembling a moth, rustled his garments; bent and opened his black-striped back before God," but prays with images and words of her own to express her true feelings for the departed friend (TM, 104–105). By rewriting the prayer and ritual to accommodate their femininity, both women assert themselves in their faith. They participate in traditional forms of worship while preserving and reaffirming their identities, rewriting Christian ritual for themselves.

Mother's Art

My art of writing results from an infinite sympathy for the suffering of my mother, and from an illumination about the fact that somebody can hurt so much because her art did not reach fulfillment. This type of human tragedy engaged me very much, it enchanted me for my whole life.[29]

Kuncewicz shows the need to redefine women's place in the Catholic tradition in her first novel, *Cudzoziemka,* which evokes late-nineteenth-century Warsaw under Russian occupation.[30] The heroine of this early text is an antithesis of the narrator-protagonist in *Listy,* as she fails to reconcile her need for religion with her sensuality and artistic desires. For Róża, failure to communicate with the deity—the spiritual transcendence she craves as an unfulfilled believer and artist—sentences her to a life of self-inflicted misery and torture. Róża associates her lack of genius as a violinist with her bad fortune in love, after her first passion for a man was thwarted and unconsummated because of his sexual infidelity. She blames God the Father for the tragic loss of her lover to another woman, "a shameless she-cat, a Moscow hussy who caused Michal's perdition with her insidious ways."[31]

> It was God who was guilty. It was He who had shown Himself to be an unworthy Father of His people. He has allowed evil to triumph over good. Perhaps He was not powerful enough to prevent evil? Thenceforward Rose treated God according to her mood—sometimes as an enemy, sometimes as a being weighed down by His own power. . . . In the storm Rose clearly heard the voice of God; at night she felt His dark presence among the stars. . . . When the weather was beautiful, when Nature seemed resplendent, she praised Him, desiring that He would not banish her from His paradise. But in the personal complexity of human affairs God seemed powerless to her. (S, 124)

However, no matter how she rebels against the injustice of the scenario God has written for her, Róża never doubts His existence and His right to govern her life. Brought up in the unquestioning patriarchal traditions of Poland and Russia, she looks at the indifferent Catholic God as just another unreliable man, as fallible in human affairs as her unfaithful lover. Unlike the heroines of Kuncewicz's earlier stories, who often dare to follow their nature against traditional dogma, Róża is afraid of her desires; she does not see until the day she dies that accepting them might offer liberation.

Róża's confusion arises primarily from her repressed sexuality, a condition to be expected in women of her time, caught in the vicious circle of nationalism, ethnic animosity, and Catholic tradition. In this respect, *Cudzoziemka* paints not only one woman's complex psychological portrait, but also a larger picture that inevitably accompanies it—the host of symbolic figures that Polish women were supposed to imitate in the turbulent times before independence was regained in 1918: these included the Virgin, the Mother, the Muse, and the National Heroine.[32] As Bianka Pietrow-Ennker stresses, women—"as Mary's successors on earth—were seen as entrusted with the task of caring for the smallest unit of the nation, the family, and seeing that it had Christian values instilled into it," but also had to "consecrate [their] maternal functions to the cause of national responsibility, to ensuring that [their] children were brought up across sex lines as patriots, as the coming saviors of the Polish nation."[33] In times of oppression, when the ideals of romantic love and noble national causes formed the stuff of poetry and music, women were expected to imitate the "holy mother of Poland" instead of searching for fulfillment as artists or as sexual beings."³⁴ Caught in these demands, Róża, with her mixed ethnic heritage, outlandish beauty, and hypersensitive nature, turns against femininity and thus against herself. Her first lover's infidelity makes her associate carnal love with destruction and shame. She sees sex as repulsive and the female body—the object of male desires—as a betrayer of idealistic dreams and a tool to avenge her tragedy. To spite her first love, she marries a man she will never love and takes pleasure in tormenting him with her beauty and denying him her love and passion. She submits occasionally to her husband's "needs" out of obligation to the institution of Christian marriage, and, without realizing how self-destructive she is, creates her own hell on earth.

Renouncing fulfillment in love and sex, Róża cherishes a dream of playing perfect music. Trying to use her artistic desires to sate the repressed carnal ones, Kuncewicz's heroine seeks to affirm the superiority of the sublime soul which, she has been taught, should transcend her weak body. Her painful failure in this endeavor one moonlit night provides further proof of her inadequacy as a woman and an artist. The night when she attempts to play Brahms's Violin Concerto in D major becomes a metaphor for her confusion:

> The music seemed to be the expression of ecstasy, brought about without any effort of hers. It was as if she were independent of physical laws. Freed from these laws, Rose seemed without the least difficulty to penetrate every sphere of feeling, spiritual elevation and sensual love. Her violin became imponderable, her bow seemed to change its shape and follow a zig-zag course like lightning. The division between the house and the world disappeared, the moonlit night melted into one dream and reality, sky and walls, mystery and knowledge; in the place of chaos there came the sounding, silky full moon. . . . Then a painful noise deafened her and troubled her. . . . Rose let her hands fall. She sat down, and her legs trembled. She dropped the bow. . . . A soundless chaos finally absorbed the harmony. Rose wept: "It is all my fault, my fault. I have spoiled it. I, miserable creature, by my incapacity have destroyed the beauty of this night."
> (S, 128–30)

Although she feels she is praying with her music and experiencing the highest spiritual power as it issues from her being, Róża cannot help translating the concerto into an expression of her repressed sensual nature. Kuncewicz's images are strongly erotic, and the pain Róża feels after failing to finish the piece projects her unfulfillment with excruciating physicality. She fails to play the difficult passage, just as she failed long ago to keep Michael's love. What follows this anticlimactic scene only affirms to Róża the fact that, even in art and prayer, she is trapped in her body. Her despised husband, excited by her music, drags her into the bedroom and rapes her. Róża's daughter is conceived that night, as further proof that being a woman is misery. In Róża's frustrated imagination, God must hate women because he has allowed such a brutal event just seconds after she almost touched the divine through her music.

Kuncewicz comments on her character's futile attempts to express her passionate nature in *Listy*, where she identifies Róża as a reflection of her own mother. Reminiscing about her mother's last rites, the narrator interprets Róża's death at the end of the novel as a simultaneous religious triumph and realization that she has at last found her faith through her body: "And what administering of the last application of holy ointments was this, what kinds of absolutions of sins? Where was God? There was only Johannes Brahms and his powerless human concerto condemned to divinity by my mother" (LJ, 18). It is through her body near death, through the painful falling and rising of her breast, aware that the last notes of her life are playing in her dying pulse, that Róża feels finally connected and at peace. She realizes her ability to rewrite her life—to be the designer of her own existence—as long as she has faith in herself. In a sense, this is also the discovery of a true religious faith. On her deathbed, Róża feels she can find pain, love, and compassion, even God, in herself. Connecting her body and soul in the last scene lets her re-create herself as a body and embrace her repressed femininity: "And now I am a real human being . . . Now I can . . . play it" (S, 221). Róża now sees her body, throbbing with music and desire, as good and holy, and she receives the last rites with understanding of her newly discovered and newly affirmed physicality. Though it is too late to live by her new beliefs, Kuncewicz's heroine dies knowing that both her misreadings and her rewriting of faith come from within herself.

Róża's problems with accepting her femininity can also be explained in light of Kristeva's theory that women exist within the symbolic sphere of patriarchal language, that is, within the masculine discourse of Catholic belief, as the *other* signifying defilement and abjection.[35] However, as *Cudzoziemka* shows, she also has the power to break free from the constraints of masculine theories of expression which denounce her body as a source of sinful lust. Kuncewicz's characters and autobiographical voices dare to explore what Kristeva would call a new discourse which records a new subject, "in infinite analysis . . . what a woman . . . can finally admit, aware as she is of the inanity of Being."[36] Such a concept of infinite reproduction and reproducing female discourse develops in Kuncewicz's other writings, which present women's bodies as texts rewriting the Christian tradition.

In light of Kristeva's theories on the feminine realm of the body and semiotic expression, Kuncewicz's insistence on the inherent carnality of even the most "spiritual" female experiences is even clearer. In her autobiographical *Natura*, she claims:

> Religion and art aren't, of course, the only sources of unconscious impulses. During childhood—an illusion of flight, during youth—Eros and sex offer unconsciousness, too. . . . But how to reconcile unconsciousness with the order and aesthetics of art? Sex disregards aesthetics. Eros demands it. Amor profano doesn't abhor ugliness and isn't afraid of ridicule. Amor sacro strives for asceticism. Now this isn't just a conflict, this is hair-splitting of a conflict. The Witness says: In the state of grace the conflicts cease; remember what you can from the revealed truth—and come back; we don't live in truth, we live in conflict. It follows that, in my case, activity results from the states of grace and passes within conflict. (N, 114)

In this passage, religion-spirituality and sexuality-carnality conflict on the aesthetic battlefield encapsulated within the woman's body, which registers "states of grace" and lives amid "activities." It is in the body, center of the passage's emphasis on spiritual and physical maturation, that Amor sacro and Amor profano meet. Thanks to the body, this meeting can be imagined and recorded. By thus translating religion and art through the body, Kuncewicz constructs faith as a carnal sensation and affirms the inherent sensuality of women's religious and literary experience. In her autobiography, many years after publication of the novel, she explains Róża's difficult quest in *Cudzoziemka* as a search for herself as a woman and believer. Kuncewicz shows the reader that individual faith can transcend and reinterpret church doctrine, and that it inspires writing that celebrates subjectivity in progress and connects the impossible extremes of religious and literary experiences within a woman's profane and sacred flesh.[37]

A Purely Private Matter: Writing the Phantom-Woman

> On the wall and on the chair cushion lie two squares of light which is seeping through the window, and on these lemon-colored squares of light the shadows of leaves struggle, float, drift away, and shiver. They shimmer, chase one another, run away, want to tear themselves away, cannot. Like my thoughts from you, Jerzy. The wall and the chair have become a screen onto which the birch from behind the window transfers the desperate effort of its leaves. I know nothing about the suicides of trees. They simply die, and not all of them "die standing upright." Do they complain that the leaves run away from them? I don't know. An abandoned human complains before the Creator. The Creator answers, I rarely understand the speech of the Creator. (LJ, 42)

The efforts of Kuncewicz's female characters to understand faith, to reinterpret disembodied tradition, imply coming to terms as much with their bodies as with the unbending words of patriarchal doctrine. Their collective re-embodiments of Catholicism culminate in the prayers of the narrator in *Listy*, who tries to read the language of the shivering shadows and to decipher the mysterious "speech of the Creator." In Kuncewicz's last text, the religious and artistic efforts of the believer and writer intertwine in an act of self-conscious textual creation. Since she has been able to "understand the speech of the Creator," the narrator now writes her own interpretation of the Word. In this way, she suggests a reversal of roles between God as Creator of the Word, and a believer who composes the world through her writings and reinterprets the tradition through her living and feeling body. In Kuncewicz's narrator's supplications, then, it is God who is not able to communicate with the narrator of *Listy*, who cannot provide her with consolation as she mourns departed physical love: "Now I was whispering terms of endearment with a fierceness I begrudged when I was young. . . . Why did I withhold for so long this erotic talk, this only heart's truth?" (LJ, 10).

In preferring Mary as a deity who can understand her, Kuncewicz's narrator not only relegates the male God to a secondary position in her text but also seems to combine sexual and chaste feminine images from the Bible in her private version of the Mother of God as all women: Eve and Mary, the Virgin and the Mother, the Crone and the Writer. The at once nightmarish and dreamy images of a wild female creature, Ałła Dżijan, who dances with and teases the narrator, and who is simultaneously a girl, a woman, a flower, and a vaginal sea anemone, are juxtaposed with icons of the Virgin. Yet both women belong to the world of the narrator's belief. It is as if she has combined the extremes—the Virgin and Mary Magdalene—to create a "gentle deity," a sexual woman who "doesn't know Satan" and who displaces the Father whose speech is "incomprehensible" to mortals.

As an artist of the word, Kuncewicz's narrator writes her own faith and God out of the impressionistic shadows of shivering images projected onto the screen of her imagination. Once again, we can see the mature women using Terenia's youthful discoveries in "Twarz Mężczyzny." The "space for Truth in the sky" may be empty, but it offers a field for one's own words. To Kuncewicz, who cannot rewrite the tradition that subjugates her gender, the Virgin's subservient words have a double meaning and become a supplicaton of God, who can no longer reach the woman believer. Mary's "Be it unto me according to Thy word" becomes a request of the deity who needs to be expressed anew, recaptured in words and images to attain meaning. Since the woman writer now has the power of the Word, since the Word is written into and through her body, Kuncewicz's God has to be reborn through the woman, has to literally come out of the body/text she keeps producing. In essence, *Listy* rewrites the original myth of a god's birth from a mortal woman's body; it proposes a reading of faith as every believer's individual textual creation.

Maria Kuncewicz constructs this intimate domain of fleeting moments of beauty and intense, emotional experiences of reality. As she describes it in her autobiographical text *Fantomy*:

> I consider my life to be mostly all that happens in the state of unconsciousness—spinning head, loss of breath, blindness, flight, forgetfulness . . . speed, lovemaking trance, vulnerability. I write to bring myself down to earth, to stop in the motion I force on myself: to regain consciousness from un-being. . . . [I]n the slow rhythm of writing self-knowledge emerges, I clutch onto an alien element . . . and begin to exist as a separate being. That is the reason for and aim of my writing—a purely private matter.[38]

The writer-believer from *Listy* can construct herself only on the pages of her books, where the two aspects of her writing—spiritual and carnal—intertwine and cross-fertilize each other. The shadow images of flight, speed, sexual trance, and breathless clutching take shape in the more tangible realm of the word—the "purely private matter" is expressed through the combination of "phantoms" and "pages." The undefinable narrator of the passage is caught in the net of syntactic and semantic structures and becomes a body pulled down to earth. The writer-believer must reconcile herself to constant molding through the "alien element" of language—the rigid system of signs—that makes it possible to discuss the "purely private matters" behind her art and craft. Kuncewicz's unceasing search for better and more astute ways to express her religiosity makes the characters in her novels into fanatical pursuers of their own "states of unconsciousness," and the narrators of her autobiographies into wanderers who progress from one epiphanic moment to another.[39]

This emphasis on gender in my discussion of Kuncewicz's writing and written subject is necessary for understanding her character's femininity as socially constructed. In another approach to *Cudzoziemka*, we can see Róża's fanatical hatred of life resulting from the fact that she can never be her phantom self from the past—the woman she wanted to become, the romantic heroine she could have been, had her flash of passion for Michal grown into a flame. Many years after *Cudzoziemka*, the narrator of *Przeźrocza* walks the streets of modern Rome trying to understand modern history as it takes place around her in theatrically lit Catholic rituals and blindingly brutal political events connected to Aldo Moro's kidnapping and murder by the Red Brigades. In both the novel about unrequited love and the *fin de siècle* autobiography, character and narrator discover that they can write their own stories even as gender and historical narratives write their lives. At the end of *Cudzoziemka*, Róża discovers her ability to "edit" her life, her power to become a different person, responsible for shaping her own concept of faith. The narrator of *Przeźrocza* challenges the dehumanizing bleakness of historical truth with a happy ending that attests to her unlimited abilities to re-create reality and provide hope. In all her texts, Kuncewicz endows her characters and narrators with profound faith in their abilities as authors and readers of their own existence.[40]

The examples of *Cudzoziemka* and *Przeźrocza* elicit further Kuncewicz's exploration of the nature of literary creativity—the inexplicable miracle of writing and generating meaning through words—and its final product, the artifact of the text. Her pursuit of the intangible innermost source of literary creativity is the exploration of the "states of unconsciousness" that must be recorded in her fictitious characters and fleeting images of herself on the necessarily autobiographical pages of all her works. On another level, her self-reflective critical analysis appraises the writer's more tangible realm of language—metaphorics and storytelling skills, her ability to construct people and worlds. Ultimately, her texts record an inquiry into this duality, into the "soul" and "body" of her writing. As she sums it up in *Natura*:

> History forces one to transform the subject into the object—in the end, I have come to observe myself through the eyes of the Witness, thus I have come to evaluate myself as a part of society. My Witness is a moralist in all its incarnations. . . . My nature is most fully compatible with: religion and art. In moments of happiness, I kneel down in adoration of something which "is not." In times of unhappiness, I place myself in the care of beings who "are not." . . . I don't always attend Mass, but—in case of the Day of Judgment—I always make the sign of the cross to cover myself before going to sleep. These unsconscious impulses demand expression.[41]

In her devotion to the dual nature of her occupation, Kuncewicz is thus an intensely religious writer. "Religious" because she writes with conviction and adheres to her specific concept of art/religion. She creates her phantom inner sphere as one would create one's own faith, having outgrown the rules and conventions of the church—in Kuncewicz's case, the traditional Catholic scenario. Yet she cannot help admiring the structure of traditional belief, the ritual, the outer shape of the doctrine, both religious and artistic, which she is trying to transcend. These two impulses—to break away and soar as a phantom, and to crouch close to the familiar and fascinating earth—inform her quest for a text that expresses both religion and art, the miracle of creativity and the resulting artifact, adequately and convincingly. Out of the convergence of these two spheres in Kuncewicz's writing arises the Witness, moralist and reader, able to understand her desire for an ultimate text written upon and from the woman's body.[42]

The intertwining of religion and art in Kuncewicz's writing happens through the woman believer's body, which is both a source of language and a means of identification with the deity. The cyclical power of rebirth such a text offers is symbolized in the combined figures of Ałła Dżijan and the Virgin Mary. The first is a demon, sister, daughter, mother, angel, and death crone who dances with the narrator of *Listy* in her dreams and waking moments: "The anemone tore itself away from her rock over the ocean and bloomed with lips in my street. It was a little girl . . . she was not a beautiful anemone-girl" (LJ, 5). The second is the "sister"-deity, mother and fellow woman imprisoned in the images constructed for her by patriarchal culture and language. At the end of *Listy*, Ałła Dżijan seems to be a rewriting of the Virgin—she is all women, as she emerges from the ocean like life on earth; she is the womb, the mother and the child, the writer's alter ego and untamed spirit: "a goblin created out of my fear of reality . . . a particle of physical pre-being . . . a dancer out of this world, my own caricature." In the last sections of *Listy*, Ałła accompanies the narrator-writer in death; they will "move" together into the other world, where the departed husband is perhaps keeping an apartment for his wife and for all her incarnations (LJ, 114). In its last glimpse of the world she has been so faithfully rewriting, Kuncewicz's ultimate text-body brings the writer and believer together with her faithful readers, who may see their own bodies rewritten and reborn in this author's intricately religious literary vision.

Notes

1. I am delighted that scholars such as Halina Filipowicz and Jadwiga Maurer are promoting feminist readings of Polish literature in the United States, but we have few such studies coming directly from Poland and available to the American reader. Paradoxically, since recent political changes in East and Central Europe have erased women's "privileges" in the workplace and reproductive freedom under communism, the Polish women's movement has been reactivated for the first time since the nineteenth century to fight institutionalized sexism. A member of the Polish Parliament, Barbara Labuda, claims that the main obstacle to democratic recognition of women's rights in Poland is the conservative position of the Catholic church. Nevertheless, most studies in English of Poland and the church's role during and after communism are oblivious to how women have been affected by the "Polish paradoxes." See, for example, Ronald C. Monticone, *The Catholic Church in Communist Poland, 1945–1985: Forty Years of Church-State Relations* (New York: Columbia University Press, 1986); Trevor Beeson, *Discretion and Valour, Religious Conditions in Russia and Eastern Europe* (Philadelphia: Fortress Press, 1982); Stanislaw Gomolka and Antony Polonsky, eds. *Polish Paradoxes* (London and New York: Routledge, 1990); Janine R. Wedel, ed., *The Unplanned Society: Poland during and after Communism* (New York: Columbia University Press, 1992) (with the exception of Teresa Holowka's "What Goes On in Catechism Class," pp. 193–204, containing one woman's approach to teaching religion and morals to contemporary Polish youth). See also John Moody and Roger Boyes, *The Priest and the Policeman:*

The Courageous Life and Cruel Murder of Father Jerzy Popieluszko (New York: Summit Books, 1987), an interesting look at religion and politics in Poland as exclusively male territories, and Thomas S. Gladsky, *Princes, Peasants and Other Polish Selves: Ethnicity in American Literature* (Amherst: University of Massachusetts Press, 1992), for a review of image-making Polish-American ethnic texts.

My generalizations about Polish history and culture exclude "nontraditional" Polish women—lesbians, Jews, Protestants, atheists. I choose the "traditional" perspective, limited to the Catholic and heterosexual majority, because of my focus on Kuncewicz's work and the limits of this short study.

2. The historical and cultural traditions of the Marian cult in Poland are the subject for a separate study. This brief overview presents a native's personal impressions rather than a scholarly perspective, in order to prepare the reader for my discussion of "personal impressions" in Kuncewicz's texts. There are many parallels between the Polish virtual deification of Mary and her worships in Ephesus, Spain, and Latin American (e.g., Our Lady of Guadalupe, declared the patron of Mexico in 1754 and of the Americas in 1910). For detailed studies, see Marina Warner, *Alone of All Her Sex: The Myth and the Cult of the Virgin Mary* (New York: Knopf, 1976); Carl Olsen, ed., *The Book of the Goddess: Past and Present* (New York: Crossroads, 1983); Anee Baring and Jules Cashford, *The Myth of the Goddess: Evolution of an Image* (London: Viking, 1991); David Kinsley, *The Goddess's Mirror: Visions of the Divine from East and West* (New York: SUNY Press, 1989).

3. Kazimierz Bukowski cites examples of Polish fascination with Mary, already widespread in the Marian songs and mysteries of the Middle Ages. See *Biblia a Literatura Polska* (*The Bible and Polish Literature*) (Poznan: Pallotinum, 1988).

4. Incidentally, this tradition always entailed a gender confusion, since Christ must be male, whereas Poland is anthropomorphized as female.

5. Częstochowa is not a unique shrine in Poland: Although less well known, the silhouette of the famous Marian church in Kraków often represents that city.

6. Maria Kuncewiczowa, *Listy do Jerzego* (*Letters to George*) (Warszawa: Instytut Wydawniczy PAX, 1988), p. 75. Subsequent references in parentheses preceded by LJ are to this edition. All translations from Polish are mine, unless otherwise indicated. For the sake of space I omit the original text.

7. Double publication dates correspond to editions published in Poland and in the "West," respectively.

8. Czesław Miłosz, *The History of Polish Literature* (London: The Macmillan Company, 1969), pp. 430–31. Note to Miłosz's comments on women writers in Poland: "Literary critics were puzzled by the invasion of women novelists who secured for themselves positions as the most widely read authors of fiction. Whether the often advanced explanation is valid or not (women supposedly had more time to write, while their husbands were busy being the breadwinners), the list of female writers is considerable."

9. See among Western criticism Anzia Yezierska, review of Kuncewicz's *The Forester, New York Times Review of Books*, September 12, 1954, p. 31; Mary Anne Schofield, "Underground Lives: Women's Personal Narratives, 1939–45," in David Bevan, ed., *Literature and Exile* (Amsterdam and Atlanta: Editions Rodopi B. V., 1990), pp. 123–29; Halina Janaszek-Ivaničková. "La contemporanéité et les archétypes ou le mythe de Tristan et Iseut dans l'oeuvre de Maria Kuncewiczowa," *Neohelicon* 3–4 (1975): 189–201.

Polish criticism includes, among many others Helena Zaworska, ed., *Rozmowy z Marią Kuncewiczowa* (*Conversations with Maria Kuncewicz*) (Warszaw: "Czytelnik," 1983); Barbara Kazimierczyk, *Dyliżans Księżycowy* (*The Moon-Coach*) (Warszawa: PAX, 1977); Włodzimierz Wójcik, ed., *W stronę Kuncewiczowej: Studia i Szkice* (*Toward Kuncewicz: Studies and Sketches*) (Katowice: Uniwersytet Śląski, 1988); Alicja Szalagan, "*Cudzoziemka* Marii Kuncewiczowej" ("Maria Kuncewicz's *The Stranger*"), *Pamiętnik Literacki* 72, no. 3 (1986): 241–76; Wojciech Natanson, "Niezliczone style pisarki" ("The Writer's Innumerable Styles"), *Życie Literackie*, September 17, 1989, p. 10.

10. Kuncewicz fought to obtain "world citizenship" for writers and artists in exile and wrote an appeal for it to the United Nations in 1948. Despite the support of prominent Western intellectuals, the UN disregarded the appeal. In 1971 Kuncewicz wrote about her efforts in *Natura*: "'Silly meaningless papers'—said the now deceased Duhamel. . . . I sift through the yellowed papers, and don't regret that I have amassed the pile of garbage" (110). See also Zdzisław Umiński, "'Mogliby być sobą gdyby nie byli mną'" ("They Could Have Been Themselves If They Hadn't Been Me"), *Kierunki*, March 10, 1974, p. 925, for an early glimpse of Kuncewicz as a political writer.

11. I obtained this information from Professor Hugh McLean of the Department of Slavic Languages and Literatures at the University of California in Berkeley, who kindly shared with me a copy of Kuncewicz's letter thanking him for writing a recommendation for her. Some of the most important awards she received are the Literary Award of the City of Warsaw (1937), the Golden Laurel of the Polish Academy of Literature (1938), the Włodzimierz Pietrzak Award (1966), the First Class National Award (1974), and the Medal of the Kościuszko Foundation for outstanding contributions to Polish and American cultures (1971).

12. Aside from studies such as Anna Węgrzyniakowa's "Kobieta-Fantom, czyli prawda Kuncewiczowej o kobiecie" ("Woman-Phantom, or Kuncewicz's Truth about Woman"), in Wójcik, *W strone Kuncewiczowej*, and Maria Janion's "Świat jako pamięć" ("World as Memory"), *Literatura*, August 21, 1975, pp. 1–6, discussing Kuncewicz's female characters and the author's biography. See also *Women in Polish Society*. ed. Rudolf Jaworski and Bianka Pietrow-Ennker (Boulder: East European Monographs, 1992), for a sociohistorical study of Polish women in the nineteenth century, a tradition very important for Kuncewicz's fiction.

13. Quoted after Zdzisława Mokranowska, "Zbudować fikcję prawdziwszą od życia" ("To Construct a Fiction More Real than Life"), in Wojcik, *W stronę Kuncewiczowej*, pp. 77–78.

14. Warner, *Alone of All Her Sex*, esp. pp. 14–24, 32–49, 193–205, 255–69, 333–39.

15. See also Baring and Cashford, *The Myth of the Goddess*, pp. 547–49.

16. It is impossible to list all the works that study Mary's transformation from flesh-and-blood woman to sublimated Virgin Mother, due to the church's need to erase any carnality from God's Mother's body. Paradoxically, beliefs in her special humanity and divinity resulted in pseudoepigraphical texts as early as the second century, although the dogmas of the Immaculate Conception and the Assumption of Mary were proclaimed surprisingly late by the Catholic church—1854 and 1950 respectively. For historical information see E. Ann Mater, "The Virgin Mary: A Goddess?" in Olson, *The Book of the Goddess*, pp. 80–96.

17. It is both appalling and fascinating to read the history of formative male perceptions of women, from the Aristotelian view of their passive role in reproduction, through John Chrysostom's consistent misogyny, Augustine's condemnation of women as the source of all evil, and Thomas Aquinas's conviction that women are defective creatures, to the Catholic church's contemporary approaches to contraception and marriage, which still refuse to recognize women as intelligent and independent sexual beings. See especially Uta Ranke-Heinemann, *Eunuchs for the Kingdom of Heaven: Women, Sexuality, and the Catholic Church* (New York: Doubleday, 1990).

18. I draw here on well-known feminist theories of *écriture féminine* discussed by Hélène Cixous, Judith K. Gardiner, Sandra Gilbert, Susan Gubar, Julia Kristeva, Nancy K. Miller, and others.

19. For a study of Eve as "beautiful evil," see John A. Phillips, *Eve: The History of an Idea* (San Francisco: Harper and Row, 1984). Phillips reads Adam's naming of Eve as a kind of silencing and rape "which formalizes a reversal of the normal course of events . . . she is born from him, not he from her" (32).

20. Margaret Homans, *Bearing the Word: Language and Female Experience in Nineteeth-Century Women's Writing* (Chicago: University of Chicago Press, 1986), pp. 156–57.

21. For etymologies of Mary's name, see Warner, *Alone of All Her Sex*, p. 14; Baring and Cashford, *The Myth of the Goddess*, p. 557. It is of course also important to note the Hebrew etymology, deriving "Mary" from a word meaning "bitter," related to such names as "Mariam" and "Miriam."

22. Maria Kuncewiczowa, *Przeźrocza* (*Slides*) (Warsaw: Instytut Wydawniczy PAX, 1985), 86.

23. The term "crone" is used with reference to Ursula Le Guin's essay "The Space Crone," in *Dancing at the Edge of the World* (New York: Harper and Row, 1989), pp. 3–6. See also Barbara Walker, *The Crone: Woman of Age, Wisdom, and Power* (San Francisco: Harper and Row, 1985).

24. In *The Powers of Horror*, Kristeva argues for the feminine realm of language, the semiotic, as constituting the "pure and proper" body, primary to paternalistic language of myth and symbol. This body, mapped within such a feminine, or maternal, "prelinguistic" realm, is separate and defined in opposition to the body drawn according to "paternal laws, within which, with the phallic phase and acquisition of language, the destiny of *man* will take shape." Kristeva emphasizes the separation between the semiotic body—mapped by the maternal and the feminine—and the symbolic body—mapped by the paternal and the masculine—as characteristic of the separations between the sexes imposed by cultures and religions. As masculine constructs, law and order perpetuate this separation through the repression of maternal authority and through erasure of the "corporeal mapping that abuts against them." Therefore, the body inscribed into religion and culture is the body defined according to male language which, insisting on erasing the maternal image, constructs it "through frustrations and prohibitions . . . into a territory having areas, orifices, points and lines, surfaces and hollows, where the archaic power of mastery and neglect, of the differentiation of proper-clean and improper-dirty, possible and impossible, is impressed and exerted" (71–72, my emphasis). Julia Kristeva, *The Powers of Horror: An Essay on Abjection*, trans. Leon S. Roudiez (New York: Columbia University Press, 1982).

25. This can be related to Elaine Scarry's theories of pain as inscribed into the power of God in Judeo-Christian scriptures and the nature of belief as a structure into which the faithful must fit. Elaine Scarry, *The Body in Pain: The Making and Unmaking of the World* (Oxford: Oxford University Press, 1985).

26. Maria Kuncewicz, "Twarz Mężczyzny," in *Nowele i bruliony prozatorskie*, p. 105. Subsequent references in parentheses preceded by TM are to this edition.

27. For a similar approach to women's language and physical experience, see Sibelan Forrester, "Body in Marina Tsvetaeva's Poetry," *Slavic Review*, Summer 1992, pp. 232–46. I am intrigued by Forrester's claim that Tsvetaeva's poetic depictions of Moscow's "female" church architecture "re-realize the female body," that being a poet for this East European woman means also "devoting all one's capacities to the production of one's own words rather than to reproduction of children," which distinguishes her from the Virgin Mary and makes her reach to alternative deities in the Orthodox tradition.

28. The concept of the Crone's cyclical connection with the Virgin and the Mother stages is based on Barbara Walker's theory of assimilation of these images of the ancient Goddess by Christianity, described in *The Crone*. See esp. pp. 12–31 for a historical overview of the emergence of the Marian cult, which combined worshippers' need for a female deity with church dogmas about Mary as a mortal woman.

29. Zaworska, *Rozmowy z Marią Kuncewiczowa*, p. 42.

30. Maria Kuncewicz, *The Stranger*, no trans. (New York: L. B. Fischer, 1945). Subsequent references in parentheses preceded by S are to this edition.

31. My translation of the original. Maria Kuncewiczowa, *Cudzoziemka* (Warszawa: Czytelnik, 1984), p. 27.

32. See also Małgorzata Czermińska, "Maria Kuncewiczowa, Istnieć 'Gdzie indziej'" ("Maria Kuncewicz: To Exist 'Elsewhere'"), *Literataura*, July 11, 1974, p. 4, for an analysis of Kuncewicz's writings as a recording of "collective Polish biography."

33. Jaworski and Pietrow-Ennker, *Women in Polish Society*, pp. 1–11.

34. See Jaworski and Pietrow-Ennker, *Women in Polish Society*, for a historical overview of Polish women's contributions to the national causes and their rebellion against patriarchal imposition of these roles.

35. As Kristeva writes in "From One Identity to an Other": "It is probably necessary to be a woman (ultimate guarantee of sociality beyond the wreckage of the paternal symbolic function, as well as the inexhaustible generator of its renewal, of its expansion) not to renounce theoreti-

cal reason but to compel it to increase its power by giving it an object beyond its limits." In her discussion of "poetic language," Kristeva proposes the feminine realm of the semiotic as maker of an alternative discourse to explore "what is heterogeneous to meaning . . . instinctual economies, always and at the same time open to bio-physiological sociohistorical constraints." Julia Kristeva, "From One Identity to an Other," in *Desire in Language: A Semiotic Approach to Literature and Art*, trans. Leon S. Roudiez (New York: Columbia University Press, 1980), p. 146.

36. In "Stabat Mater," interwining Kristeva's exploration of the images of motherhood in Christianity with a celebration of her own childbirth, we follow the remaking of law, which is given "flesh, language, and *jouissance*," and which "demands the contribution of women." Interestingly, her affirmation of the maternal, where "the speaking being finds a refuge when his/her symbolic shell cracks and a crest emerges where speech causes biology to show through," connects with the concepts worked out by Kuncewicz. It could be the author of *Listy do Jerzego* speaking of woman's phantom existence: "I am thinking of the time of illness, of sexual-intellectual-physical passion, of death." Like Kuncewicz, albeit in a very different literary expression, Kristeva elicits the states of unconsciousness through and within the female body. Julia Kristeva, "Stabat Mater," in *Ways of Reading: An Anthology for Writers* (New York: St. Martin's Press, 1990), pp. 360–81.

37. For a summary of theoretical approaches to this theme, see also Ann Rosalind Jones, "Writing the Body: Toward an Understanding of Écriture féminine," in *Feminist Criticism: Essays on Women, Literature and Theory*, ed. Elaine Showalter (New York: Pantheon Books, 1985), pp. 361–77.

38. Maria Kuncewiczowa, *Fantomy* (Lublin: Wydawnictwo Lubelskie, 1989), p. 186.

39. Anna Wegrzyniakowa praises Kuncewicz's ability to inscribe herself into her texts. She claims that reading this writer chronologically gives us a filmlike narrative recording the making of her vision. However, she also stresses that the portrait the reader receives is predominantly that of a woman "caught within life (that is: in tradition, physiology, history, everydayness . . . etc.)." Anna Wegrzyniakowa, "Kobieta-Fantom, czyli prawda Kuncewiczowej o kobiecie," in Wójcik, *W stronę Kuncewiczowej*, pp. 32–33.

40. In this insistence on the continuity between the experience of the writer and the reader of her own work, as well as between the writer and the characters inhabiting her texts, Kuncewicz's work contributes to a discussion of female readers and writers. See also Jonathan Culler, "Reading as a Woman," in *On Deconstruction: Theory and Criticism after Structuralism* (Ithaca: Cornell University Press, 1982), pp. 43–64.

41. Maria Kuncewiczowa, *Natura* (Lublin: Wydawnictwo Lubelskie, 1989), p. 114.

42. The development and implications of the Witness in Kuncewicz's art should be the object of a separate study. One may note, however, how this presence is both semi-authorial and semi-external; that is, it combines the author who is also her own reader and critic, as well as the alien reader and critic who come to evaluate Kuncewicz's work and become simultaneous participants and witnesses of her art. The Witness can also be related to Kaja Silverman's model of the "projected viewer," or third subject, who is the "spoken subject." In this sense, the Witness would be the subject who "agrees" to be signified by the author's (in Silverman, the filmmaker's) signifiers, as perceived by the external reader and critic who expect a certain text and meaning, and of whose presence and desires the author is aware (and perhaps a little afraid). See Kaja Silverman, "Suture," in *The Subject of Semiotics* (New York: Oxford University Press, 1983), pp. 198–99.

Select Bibliography of Maria Kuncewicz's Works

Kuncewicz(owa), Maria. *The Conspiracy of the Absent.* Translated by Maurice Michael and Harry Stevens, New York: Roy Publishers, n.d.

———. *Cudzoziemka.* Warszawa: Książka i Wiedza, 1984.

———. *Don Kichote i niańki (Don Quixote and the Nannies.)* Lubin: Wydawnictwo Lubelskie, 1989.

————. *Dwa Księżyce* (*Two Moons*). Lublin: Wydawnictwo Lubelskie, 1989.

————. *Fantasia alla polacca*. Warszawa: Czytelnik, 1979.

————. *Fantomy*. Lublin: Wydawnictwo Lubelskie, 1989.

————. *The Forester*. Translated by H. C. Stevens. London: Hutchinson, 1954.

————. *The Keys: A Journey through Europe at War*. New York, London: Hutchinson International Authors, n.d.

————. *Klucze* (*The Keys*). Lublin: Wydawnictwo Lubelskie, 1990.

————. *Leśnik* (*The Forester*). Warszawa: PAX, 1983.

————. *Listy do Jerzego*. Warszawa: PAX, 1988.

————. ed. *The Modern Polish Mind: An Anthology*. Boston and Toronto: Little, Brown, 1962.

————. ed. *The Modern Polish Prose*. Birkenhead: English-Polish Publications Committee, 1945.

————. "Moja wieża Babel" ("My Tower of Babel"). *Kierunki*, April 21, 1974, p. 6.

————. *Natura*. Lublin: Wydawnictwo Lubelskie, 1989.

————. N. t. *Twórczość*, December, 1968, pp. 113–15.

————. *Nowele i bruliony prozatorskie* (*Short Stories and Prose Notebooks*). Edited by Helena Zaworska. Warszawa: Czytelnik, 1985.

————. *The Olive Grove*. Translated by the author. New York: Walker, 1963.

————. *Polish Millstones*. Translated by Stephen Garry. London: P. S. King and Staples, 1942.

————. *Przeźrocza* (*Slides*). Warszawa: PAX, 1985.

————. "Refugees as World Citizens." *The London Times*, March 10, 1949, p. 6a.

————. *Rozmowy z Marią Kuncewiczową* (*Conversations with Maria Kuncewicz*). Edited by Helena Zaworska. Warszawa: Czytelnik, 1983.

————. "Smoczy jęzor pamięci" ("The Dragon's Tongue of Memory"). *Literatura*, November 21, 1974, p. 5.

————. *The Stranger*. New York: L. B. Fischer, 1945.

————. *Tristan*. New York: George Braziller, 1974.

————. *Tristan 1946*. Warszawa: Czytelnik, 1970.

————. *W domu i w Polsce* (*At Home and in Poland*). Warszawa: Czytelnik, 1958.

————. *Zmowa nieobecnych* (*Conspiracy of the Absent*). Warszawa: PAX, 1957.

TEN

Mother, Daughter, Self, and Other
The Lyrics of Inna Lisnianskaia and Mariia Petrovykh

STEPHANIE SANDLER

ONE OF THE most interesting innovations in recent feminist theory has been a shift away from the concern with difference toward a fascination with similarity. This is not a naive or nostalgic move, where the difficult questions of racial, class, sexual, and ethnic differences that divide women are cast aside in favor of a more soothing idea of all women as essentially alike. Rather, these theorists have kept the lessons of political difference well in mind as they explore how gender identification works in thought, speech, action, and cultural representation. The most provocative and also most sensitive work joins literary criticism, philosophical speculation, and psychoanalytic insight: I have in mind work done by Teresa de Lauretis, Ruth Leys, Luce Irigaray, and Judith Butler, among others.[1] Butler's formulation is a useful point of departure for this essay about Russian lyric poetry. She has argued that gender is culturally instantiated as a kind of coping—women learn to "be" women by looking or acting like a woman.[2] The fundamental cognitive move here is a search for kinds of similarity, and her quest takes her through many forms of imitation, mimicry, masquerade, reproduction, and repetition.

In lyric poetry, traditions of an individual speaker seeking self-definition through distinctiveness, a Romantic tradition that is still with us in Russian as well as in American cultures, can benefit from such a theoretical intervention. We can put aside, for the moment, a concern with the specificity of women's voices. Instead of generalizing how women's poetry is different from men's, we can explore how intimations of identity are released in tandem with cultural expectations about gender and proper behavior. These theorists also offer us a rich idea of subjectivity, one that is not embattled over the idea of whether or not there is any such thing as the subject (a stumbling point in much deconstructive theory that is artfully skirted here, even though the methods are rigorously deconstructive). We can accept the premise that women have agency, even when and where women have been oppressed. The question becomes *how*, not *whether*, poems articulate the subject. There is one other benefit for a discussion of Russian women's lyrics: the paradigm is, at its core, enormously dynamic, positing an interacting subject whose self-definitions and engagements with the world are self-questioning, self-conscious, and ever changing.

I offer here two kinds of lyric poems in which a woman's acts of self-definition energetically engage with an imagined other. The first part of this essay looks at mother-daughter lyrics, a genre that has the obvious appeal of letting the poet speak to someone whom she at once deeply resembles and is separate from. The

mother-daughter plot lets us situate these lyrics in the social context in which
much of women's sense of self is developed, and one in which cultural norms of
the feminine are powerfully reproduced.[3] The second part of the essay looks at a
different bond, that of one poet speaking to an earlier poet. Again, fundamental
similarities link speaker and addressee. The language of the poem I shall consider
does not render this connection a metaphorical version of the mother-daughter
bond.[4] What interests me is the interacting self-definitions of the poem, the way
one woman sees herself and her work in terms of another woman's example. I
hope that the resulting discussion in both parts of this essay will demonstrate that
a poet's act of self-definition and her deepest wishes for connection to another
person can be presented in poetry unsentimentally, even grimly.

The poems are by two women, Inna Lisnianskaia and Mariia Petrovykh, and I
expect this essay to contribute to our (remarkably scant) knowledge of them both.
Inna Lisnianskaia, born in 1928 in Baku and still writing poems in Moscow sixty-
five years later, is the author of nine volumes of verse,[5] hundreds of short lyric
poems that range in theme from religion and philosophy to ethical judgment and
personal revelation. These themes link her to the better-known poet Natal'ia Gorbanevskaia, though in her articulations of a self complexly connected to others she
strongly differs from Gorbanevskaia.[6] Among younger women poets, Elena
Shvarts's emotionally intense lyrics and Ol'ga Sedakova's philosophically specula-
tive poems may bear some comparison to Lisnianskaia's work; they, too, are more
generously translated in the West and more likely to be the subject of scholarly
study.[7] Lisnianskaia's quality of being little known, which in her verse is thematized
as a fascination with secrecy and with the unknowable, makes her especially attractive for our study here. The self imagined in her poems emerges uneasily and
partially; though a rigorous clarity of ideas characterizes Lisnianskaia's verse, her
secret writing of the self can be puzzling and resistant.

Mariia Petrovykh (1908–1979) was a poet, editor, and translator of little
renown outside a circle of Moscow and Armenian friends, many of whom were
also poets and writers. Her obscurity seems to have been at least partially of her
own making. Petrovykh's adult professional identity as editor and translator suitably allegorized the deferential, secondary position she came to prefer. Though she
occasionally saw her poems through to publication, beginning in 1926, a volume
of her verse appeared only at the initiative of her friends and family (in 1968).
Her poetry has recently been republished, along with memoir accounts of her.[8]
Petrovykh did not write a great deal, but she left some exquisite love lyrics and a
number of admirably precise poems of natural description. Her poems typically
include some revelation of spiritual truth, and in this they are comparable to work
by Anna Akhmatova, to whom Petrovykh knew she would be compared and come
out the poorer. As she writes in one poem, she lacked both Akhmatova's meekness
and Tsvetaeva's rage. Her lyrics, perhaps less complex in their self-presentations
than Lisnianskaia's, offer many shades of deference and denial, and from these
shaded regions a poet of considerable independence and courage can be heard
to speak.

Petrovykh had one daughter, Arisha Golovacheva (of Petrovykh's husband, little is said in published memoirs, though surviving friends of Petrovykh have said that he perished in Stalin's camps).[9] We will begin with her two lyrics to her daughter.

Mother/Daughter Lyrics

As a symbol of her willingness to help others, her gentle kindness to friends and family, Petrovykh's friends have noted that her favorite word was "my dear" (*milyi*).[10] One hears Petrovykh at her most tender in the following poem to her daughter. What will interest us is the loving declaration of tenderness in the context of the reduced expression of self.

Когда на небо синее Глаза поднять невмочь, Тебе в ответ, уныние, Возникнет слово: дочь.	When lifting one's eyes To the blue sky is impossible, One word will arise to answer you, Despair. It is: daughter.
О, чудо светлолицее, И нежен и высок,— С какой сравнится птицею Твой легкий голосок!	O bright-faced wonder, Both tender and lofty, What kind of bird is there to Compare with your light little voice!
Клянусь—необозримое Блаженство впереди, Когда ты спишь, любимая, Прильнув к моей груди.	I swear, the bliss ahead Is boundless, When you, my love, sleep Nestled in my breast.
Тебя держать, бесценная, Так сладостно рукам. Не комната—вселенная, Иду—по облакам.	Holding you, my treasure, Is a joy to the arms. This isn't a room, it's the universe, I walk across the clouds.
И сердце непомерное Колышется во мне, И мир, со всею скверною, Остался где-то, вне.	And a heart beyond all measure Flutters inside of me, And the world, with all its ugliness, Has been left somewhere outside, beyond.
Мной ничего не сказано, Я не сумела жить, Но ты вдвойне обязана, И ты должна свершить.	No word of mine has been spoken, I have not known how to live, But you are doubly bound to succeed, You must certainly complete my deeds.
Быть может, мне заранее, От самых первых дней— Дано одно призвание— Стать матерью твоей.	Perhaps, early on, From the very first days, I was given a single calling— To become your mother.
В тиши блаженства нашего Кляну себя: не сглазь! Мне счастье сгинуть заживо И знать, что ты сбылась.[11] (1937–1938)	In the quiet of our bliss I make this oath: let no evil come! I would gladly disappear entirely To know that you, my dream, have come true.

In this poem, danger lurks just beyond the world of mother/daughter intimacy (hardly surprising, given that the poem was written during the worst years of mass terror associated with Stalin's rule), but there is an enormous sense of consolation in just knowing that the daughter exists. The word "daughter" is capable of vanquishing the mother's despair; it is not a word she speaks to her daughter, it is a word that arises, as if from within her, to resist the sadness induced by the world. Holding this daughter in her arms, the mother can take on all threats—thus, in the fourth quatrain, she paces not their room but the heavens.

Having and holding her daughter empowers Petrovykh emotionally. But that is chiefly because her way of representing herself is so diminished. We see this more powerfully in the original Russian, though I have tried to keep Petrovykh's oblique self-references in the English translation. Her syntax of self-representation as a mother is passive, or at best reactive. Though she resists outside threats, and though her resistance suggests strength, this speaker's self-characterizations are consistently diminished. Even motherhood is described as something foretold for her.

She is someone who can barely bring herself to look at the sky, who has said nothing and was incapable of living (*Mnoi nichego ne skazano, / Ia ne sumela zhit'*—notice *mnoi* and *ia* in metrically unstressed positions). And she sees the world outside as foul. The glory of this daughter is in helping her keep that world at arm's length. The happiness, the "bliss" of a moment when her infant daughter sleeps at her breast, feels fragile, momentary, subject to vivid disappearance. Danger lurks in the final quatrain, where a command meant to ward off the evil eye (*ne sglaz'!*) marks the mother's oath of protection; her ultimate self-sacrifice is expressed in these lines as well, a readiness to give her life for her daughter's.

Fear also haunts a second poem to her daughter, written two years later. It, too, describes an arc of safety, tracing the same inclined maternal figure familiar from Russian icons.

Когда я склонюсь над твоею кроваткой,	When I bend over your little bed,
Сердце так больно, так сладко растет,	My heart so painfully, so sweetly swells up,
Стою не дыша и смотрю украдкой	I stand not even breathing, stealing a glance
На руки твои, на их легкий взлет.	At your hands, at their airy flight.
Я с горькой тоской спозналась глубоко,	I have come to know sadness bitterly, deeply,
В бессоннице я сгорела дотла,	In my sleeplessness I have been burned to the ground,
Но ты, ты нежна и голубоока,	But you, you are tender and blue-eyed,
Подснежник мой, ты свежа и светла.	My little snowdrop, you are freshness and light.
Мир твой не тронут горем и злобой,	Your world is not touched by grief or anger,
Страху и зависти доступа нет.	Terror and envy cannot get in.
Водзух тебя обнимает особый,	A separate air embraces you entirely,
Как будто всегда над тобою рассвет.	As if eternally dawning over you.
Когда я склонюсь над кроваткой твоею,	When I bend over your little bed,
Сердце растет в непосильной любви,	My heart swells in helpless love,
Смотрю на тебя и смотреть не смею,	I look at you, not daring to look,
И помню одно только слово: живи.[12]	And remember only one word: live.

1940

Again, the mother's adult and troubled world, marked by insomnia, anger, and fear, is separate from the innocence and freshness of her sleeping daughter.

This kind of delineation, however, is subverted, especially in the second poem, by the mother's identification with her sleeping daughter, by her desire to embrace within herself the innocence of her child. The mother who represents herself as if she, too, were a safely sleeping child also emerges as a much more powerful speaking subject than anything we might expect. In the first Petrovykh poem, near the end, the speaker refers to her own infancy (her *samykh pervykh dnei*). Her gaze is almost frightened, like a child's, as if she knows that she cannot bear to see too much at once. Like an infant, she knows the sweetness of an embrace with her hands and arms in the first poem (*Tebia derzhat', bestsennaia, / Tak sladostno rukam*). In the second poem, growth, a quality normally attributed to the chid, is taken up by the mother, whose heart figuratively grows with emotion (the phrase is repeated, in fact, in the first and final stanzas; I have translated *rastet* as "swells").

The mother is most like a young child, though, in her replication of the infant's way of learning to talk. She speaks as if she were an infant confronting the world for the first time, discovering her sensory perceptions one by one, naming the complexity of her relationship to her daughter with a toddler's simple, one-word ways. In the second poem, she seems in the last line to be telling us that she knows only one word to speak to her daughter, the imperative "live" (*zhivi*). In the first poem, it is in the first stanza that a one-word sentiment arises, and that word is "daughter" (*doch'*). These two words work metonymically to express what a mother/daughter lyric tries to do. "Live," spoken by the mother who has brought her to life, is the mother's word par excellence,[13] but these are moments when the mother, like a child, teaches herself to speak. Thus they give us a peculiarly compressed representation of the poetic calling. That gesture of reduction, of bringing many things down to one thing, occurs as well when the idea of a calling or vocation is mentioned: in the first poem, Petrovykh says, "I was given a single calling—To become your mother" (*Dano odno prizvanie— / Stat' mater'iu tvoei*). Petrovykh, who would not decide for herself to send her poems into a world she perceives here as evil and envious, surprises no one when she says her "calling" is that of a mother and that this is an exclusive vocation. Onto her daughter she projects a greater capacity for achievement (*No ty vdvoine obiazana, / I ty dolzhna svershit'*).

Petrovykh has, then, imprinted a constrained, limited self onto these poems, one opened out by an emotionally rich relationship with her sleeping daughter, perhaps. Petrovykh in various ways undoes the opposition between herself and the daughter to whom she speaks: she suggests a continuity between her own subjectivity and that of her daughter that was also aptly expressed in a line of poetry that Marina Tsvetaeva wrote to her daughter in 1918: "I don't know where you end and I begin" (*Ne znaiu, gde ty i gde ia*).[14] Perhaps Petrovykh asks that we see whole realms of possibility in the tiny, compressed space of her self-description (she is the one who knows not how to live—*ia ne sumela zhit'*—but whose emotional life is so complex that it burns through her sleep into insomnia—*V bessonitse ia sgorela dotla*).

How much can we glean about Petrovykh from her ways of representing her daughter? There is certainly a physical resemblance (in a photograph from 1946 their heads even incline at an identical angle, their expressions similarly kind and submissive), and "Arisha," the only name we usually get for her daughter, seems to have been her mother's closest companion.[15] We might provisionally read the similarities of mother and daughter as a ground for the exchangeability of subjecthood. Petrovykh, because she is imagining a world for both herself and her daughter, can create a zone of safety and intimacy. The readiness to sacrifice herself, almost a cliché of the maternal, produces something far less banal: Petrovykh creates a self who can provide comfort *to herself*; she is also able to be enfolded in the cocoon of safety she is spinning for her daughter.

There are other cases of mothers speaking to daughters whom they perceive as like them: Tsvetaeva tells her daughter Ariadna in an early poem that she will, like her mother, become a poet ("To Alia" ["Ale"], 1914). It is important that the similarity Tsvetaeva draws is that her daughter will come to write (especially since Tsvetaeva went so far as to include her seven-year-old daughter's verse in one of her published volumes: *Psyche* [*Psikheia*], 1923).[16]

In the poem, "To My Daughter" ("Docheri," 1983), Inna Lisnianskaia speaks to a daughter who is also a writer. Her daughter is Elena Makarova, the author of two volumes of stories at the time of the poem was written, and several since.[17] Makarova emigrated to Israel in 1990, though that is not relevant to this poem. What is relevant is Lisnianskaia's obvious sense of having failed her daughter and her fear that Makarova does not love her. Unlike Petrovykh, Lisnianskaia does not speak to a tiny, vulnerable child. Hers is a poem that neither idealizes the mother-daughter connection nor flinches at the thought that a grown-up daughter will have ideas of her own about the mother.

Дочери	To My Daughter
Казалось бы—и нечего сказать.	It would seem that there is nothing to say
Пред очевидностью такого факта,	Before the utter clarity of this fact:
Что я, твоя нелепейшая мать,	I, your most absurd mother,
Скончалась то ли так, то ль от инфаркта.	Have passed away, who knows how, maybe from a heart attack.
—Не надо плакать! —Вот что я скажу:	"Don't cry!"—that's what I will say.
Не я в гробу нарядная лежу	It is not I who lies in the grave, all dressed up
В платочке с розочками рококо,	In a little scarf of rose-colored Rococo.
А лишь пустая глина, но когда-то	No, it's empty clay, though there was a time
Ее сосочек, до крови намятый,	When her nipple, pressed and wrinkled to the point of bleeding,
Вливал в тебя скупое молоко.	Poured its meager milk into you.
Все мерки жизни и координаты	All the measures of life and all the points of location
Смерть изменяет быстро и легко:	Are changed quickly and easily by death:
Теперь ты от меня настолько близко,	Now you are as close to me
Насколько от тебя я далеко.	As I am far from you.

Теперь с пути мне сбиться нету риска,	Now there is no risk of losing my way.
Теперь в той самой я непустоте,	Now I am in that very non-abyss
Какую жизнь считала пустотою.	That, for life, was an abyss.
Не та здесь масса, скорости не те,	Here the weights are not the same, the speeds
	are not the same,
И даже сон не тот, что, в простоте,	And even a dream is not that which
Жизнь относила к вечному покою.	Life, in its simplicity, linked to eternal rest.
Теперь отпала надобность в очках,	Now the need for glasses has fallen away,
Отсюда вижу все твои веснушки—	And from here I see all your freckles,
Темней на скулах, золотей в зрачках,	Darker on the cheek bones, golden in the
	pupils of your eyes,
И вся ты—свет от пят до макушки.	And all of you, showered in light from top
	to bottom.
Не надо плакать! Холмик на опушке	Don't cry! The mound on the cemetery
Кладбищенской не есть последний дом,	Hill is not the last abode
Где забываются последним сном,—	Where one lapses into a final dreamed sleep.
То наших встреч таинственных площадка,	It is the site of our secret meetings
И нежным незабудкам—благодать.	And a blessing to the tender forget-me-nots.
Загадка—жизнь, но смерть всегда разгадка.	Life is a riddle, but death is always the riddle's
	answer.
О как мне эти слезы видеть сладко!	O how sweet it is for me to see these tears!
Поплачь еще, хоть я плохая мать	Cry some more, even if I am a terrible
	mother
По всем параметрам миропорядка.	By all the standards of the world's rules.
Нет, слуха твоего не оскорблю	No, I will not offend your ears
Тем оправданьем, что с пути я сбилась,—	With the excuse that I lost my way.
Все это ложь. Я так тебя люблю,	All of that is falsehood. I love you
Как дочерям заласканным не снилось.[18]	In a way that daughters lavished with
	affection never even dreamed.

1983

Like Petrovykh, Lisnianskaia takes a reticent stand toward language itself (seen in the refusal to offer justifications in the final strophe, and in the flat statement "there is nothing to say" [*nechego skazat'*] in the first line). But there is an extravagance of emotion hidden in this reduced self, just as the exhortation to her daughter *not* to cry gives way to the admission that the sight of those tears is a joy ("O how sweet it is for me to see these tears! Cry some more" [*O kak mne eti slezy videt' sladko! / Poplach' eshche*]).

Where this poem also differs from Petrovykh, however, is in its distance from all idealizations of maternal love and care: the promises that are possible to a sleeping infant are turned around to admissions of failure. This is an absurd, even bad mother (*tvoia nelepeishaia mat'*; *ia plokhaia mat'*), whose scant milk suggests a failure to nourish and to nurture (*vlival v tebia skupoe moloko*). That image, of a breast that provides insufficient milk, takes on directly the emblematic symbol of the maternal, the child happily sucking at the breast. Lisnianskaia replaces that image with a toughly physical representation of the nipple, bloodied and wrinkled by the infant's greedy sucking. It is an emblem of effort that cannot succeed, for either mother or child. The poem begins with a similar statement of inefficacy: the mother has nothing to say that can console her child, though the poem will offer up various things she might well say (an injunction not to cry, heard twice, then an encouragement to cry still more).

How are we to contextualize this failure, to judge its truth value, to know its meanings to the poet and to the poem? At the simplest level, we can consult Lisnianskaia's other poems and her published statements about her life, which include loving exclamations of pride in her daughter.[19] It is known, however, that after Lisnianskaia separated from Makarova's father, their daughter lived with him.[20] This guilt over having "abandoned" her daughter may be an impulse behind "To My Daughter." It finds confirmation in the daughter's writings. In Makarova's story "After Six Days Comes Sunday" ("Cherez kazhdye shest' dnei—voskresen'e," 1968) we discover a remarkable parallel to the family's living situation at a somewhat later point.[21] The heroine, Lenochka, sees her father more than her mother (named Inna). Inna is in a sanitorium, Lenochka in a center for children with spinal deformities. Both stays occurred—Lisnianskaia suffered a nervous breakdown, Makarova had something seriously wrong with her spine (in the story it is scoliosis); Makarova's use of her own and her mother's first names further suggests that the fiction has a basis in their lives. In her fiction, illness and physical confinement become the grounds for a narrative about love lost between daughter and mother.

A different scene of failure can be gleaned from Lisnianskaia's biography, this having to do with her troubled experience in reaching her readers. She was denied access to publication in the former Soviet Union after her participation in the almanac *Metropol'*.[22] Unlike Petrovykh, Lisnianskaia did not write only for the desk drawer; there were publications before and after the *Metropol'* scandal.[23] In 1983, when the poem was written, Lisnianskaia could refer to herself as a failure in this sense of having no access to her reading public—indeed, her daughter was then more widely published within the former Soviet Union. Lisnianskaia described herself in those years as having been a pariah.[24]

Such biographical explanation can take us only so far, of course. Certainly it would be difficult to assess judiciously whether Lisnianskaia was a "good" mother, whatever that is, and Lisnianskaia's frustrations in reaching her Russian readership were hardly unique. The real problem with the biographical reading I have suggested is that it tempts us to imagine Lisnianskaia's "failures" as the stuff of personal inadequacy. The poem itself contextualizes these flaws quite differently. They are the judgments of an external, horribly precise world (thus the language of measurement in the third and seventh stanzas).

Like Petrovykh's view of a world that threatens her sleeping daughter, Lisnianskaia rejects what is publicly and indisputably seen, including her death (a fact marked in line 2 by its *ochevidnost'*). She subverts this trope of the visible, the obvious, when she reiterates visual images to tell a different story, one that reveals an intensely hidden, private connection to her daughter. Thus the mother, having lost her need for glasses, sees her daughter's presence, from the tiny details of freckles to the whole body, with a new clarity. Thus, too, she sees the sight of her crying daughter, sees that eyes that seem as if they exist to take sights in (and judge them) in fact exist to shed tears of sadness and love.[25]

There is a further denial in the poem. It is one of many—there are fifteen moments in this thirty-seven-line poem when an action, a name, or a description is held up to be wrong. But it is the crucial negation, when in the second stanza the speaker says she is not the one who is lying in this grave (*Ne ia v grobu nariadnaia lezhu*, 1. 6). This rejected claim commands our attention because Lisnianskaia is separating her identity, her "self," from the scenario of death that this poem represents. She urges her daughter to believe and to take comfort in the fact that her essence is not contained in that scene of a dressed-up corpse. The dressing up is exaggerated, like so much else in the poem, accentuated by repetitions of sound (*v platochke s rozochkami rokoko*) that connote visual excess as well.

How else to read this costume except as the excessive masquerade of femininity, with its details of Rococo splendor and design of little roses? The head scarf emblematic of Russian women is rejected by Lisnianskaia here; she prefers to see herself as empty clay, a vessel with nothing left to give (and, as the failure in suckling suggests, a vessel that was never actually completely full). The rejection of the costume of femininity exemplifies precisely the mimicking feminine subject that Judith Butler has identified as a requirement of patriarchal gender norms.[26] Extending Joan Rivière's 1929 essay "Womanliness as Masquerade," Butler argues that gender is something that is performed, rather than authentically felt or demonstrated.

While Lisnianskaia insists that it is not she who lies there so attractively in the grave, still her poem imagines death as a liberation from the constraints of lived existence, a liberation that leads to new vision. The third and fourth stanzas describe these new freedoms with a thoroughly abstract vocabulary, and we return to concrete and enormously physical language in the fifth stanza. (That juxtaposition is not atypical for Lisnianskaia's way of contextualizing philosophical passages in her poetry with details of narrative and descriptive precision). All three stanzas describe a time and place where the physical dimensions and boundaries of the world as we know it are changed. The changes extend to inhabitants of this new world, for keener vision comes to one who drops her eyeglasses. What she sees is her daughter's body, a sight which adds to the resurgent concreteness in the poem. The prosaic detail of freckled skin also brings down the high philosophical tone, down all the way to the hilly earth, to a freshly dug grave, where those little roses on the woman's scarf are at last replaced with equally delicate but genuine flowers, another prosaic detail, the aptly named forget-me-nots. The dictions of fashion, physics, physical bodies, and geographic sites let Lisnianskaia speak perhaps deceptively easily through different registers, though nothing could be more obvious than the revelation that, rather than having nothing to say, this is a poet with only one thing she wants to say, and she saves it for the last, lingering line: "I love you / In a way that daughters lavished with affection never even dreamed" (*Ia tak tebia liubliu, / Kak docheriam zalaskannym ne snilos'*). In its cosmic claim, this line rewrites the world-measuring language of the third stanza; in its no-holds-barred self-certainty, it overcomes entirely the anxieties about risks or errors, and it entirely undoes the admission of being a "terrible mother" (*nelepeishaia mat'*). This final line could almost be read as the entire point of the poem, at least in terms of what it wants to say directly to the daughter. I say "almost" because I have already hinted at a way to reject this reading, yet in terms of its extravagance of emotion, this line has no near competitors in any other sentence of "To My Daughter."

What pushes us to see this poem as articulating more than a mother's implausible but deep love for her daughter is its urgent move through stylistic registers that include the abstractly philosophical. The poem addresses itself to the larger cultural idea of being a mother, as well as to the poet's own experience as a mother. We have seen a hint of how it does this in the repudiated Rococo scarf, where the poet finds herself unsuited for this particular cultural costume. The poem's overarching narrative makes a similar point in its appalling scene for this mother/daughter love (*nashikh vstrech tainstvennykh ploshchadka*) as the mother's grave. Because of its specificity in describing the site of the grave and the way the mother looks in her coffin, this imagining is more than an evocation of that moment when the mother "becomes a memory" (to cite another poem that Marina Tsvetaeva wrote to her daughter Ariadna).[27] The mother, who gives life, is invoked not in that capacity, but as a figure of death.[28]

To judge the significance of this move, I revert to recent feminist work on the symbolic value of the mother in a culture's imagination of itself as civilized. Luce Irigaray has written provocatively, even controversially, on the place of the mother in modern culture.[29] Irigaray, without relinquishing her authority to use the ideas of psychoanalysis, challenges Freud's views about motherhood. She has countered Freud's male-centered idea about the Oedipal origins of culture in *Totem and Taboo* with the claim that it was the death of the mother on which ancient culture was built (her example is the death of Clytemnestra in Aeschylus's *Oresteia*).[30] If Freud would have it that civilization emerges when obstacles are placed before the son who would murder his father, then Irigaray's feminist critique foregrounds myths in which it is the mother, not the father, who is put at risk, which pushes her to make the angry point that there are no equivalent taboos to stop the child who would kill off his mother. Irigaray demonstrates that patriarchal culture was founded over the mother's dead body, and in her view a feminist rereading of that culture can originate in a refusal "to kill the mother who was immolated at the origins of our culture for a second time."[31]

I want to suggest that this refusal to kill is at the center of Lisnianskaia's poem, and in that sense her poem is a revolutionary rethinking of the horrible myths of the maternal with which she and her daughter have lived their entire lives. Lisnianskaia gives us the mother's death *which is not really a death*. As the poem begins, the one thing she makes up her mind to say is "It is not I who lies in the grave all dressed up" (*Ne ia v grobu nariadnaia lezhu*), and she reiterates in the sixth strophe that the seeming grave is no place of final rest. Lisnianskaia refuses to take up that place of the mother lying in the grave. Throughout the poem, she uses negations to make her words sound like rejections. Not even death is what it seems ("Here the weights are not the same, the speeds are not the same" [*Ne ta zdes' massa, sko-rosti ne te*]). What has been called a death, what looks like separation and distance, becomes an affirmation of the mother/daughter bond. Lisnianskaia displaces the myth of the dead mother for a fearless acceptance of imperfection. She gives us not Clytemnestra, killed for her crimes, but the mother's lapses as part of her very human character. What Lisnianskaia repudiates as *lozh'* in the penultimate line only seems to be her excuses for failing her daughter; in fact, she rejects the lies that would have her a failure in the first place.

Luce Irigaray's work can also help explain how Lisnianskaia effects this displacement. There are two points here, both based on Lisnianskaia's imagery: the first has to do with the body. If we translate the title of Irigaray's essay literally, she would have us body to body with the mother.[32] Here is one innovation of Lisnianskaia's poem—that she realistically, prosaically evokes both the maternal body, represented as a suckled breast, and the daughter's body, seen by the mother as if for the first time. This body, dappled with light and skin markings, is itself a figure for the mother's imperfections. The move to render imperfections as physical appearance and the work of nature takes what might be construed as moral failings and turns them into a part of the natural order. Even these lapses are to be looked on with love: these lines, as much as the explicit declaration of love in the final sentence, demonstrate the mother's adoring gaze, but they also suggest a desire that the daughter look on her with the same kind of love. To be body to body with the mother, then, is to be one with her flaws. Lisnianskaia is opening up new possibilities for the mother as a subject in lyric poetry in this move: rather than the self-sacrificing or selfless speaker who projects all onto her child, Lisnianskaia gives us a canny, self-critical, but also self-accepting woman who as a result can offer her daughter a love beyond dreams.

The second figure that makes Lisnianskaia's transformation of the mother/daughter lyric possible is that of dreaming. Again, I cite Irigaray, who writes (in another essay): "Dreams are also riddles in that—during 'sleep,' and in order to 'keep' asleep—they recast the roles that history has laid down for 'subject' and 'object.'"[33] A rhetoric of dreaming lets Lisnianskaia do the work of recasting, not history, as Irigaray would have it, but the presentation of the self. Recall the references to dreaming in the poem: Lisnianskaia tells us in her fourth stanza that death contains a surprising dream (*I dazhe son ne tot, v prostote, / Zhizn' otnosila k vechnomu pokoiu*); and she returns to the figure of dreaming in her extravagant final line (*Ia tak tebia liubliu, / Kak docheriam zalaskannym ne snilos'*). These two lines seem similar. Both are negations, a syntactic structure used throughout the poem, and perhaps a way here to say that the dream in question is not quite what one would imagine, that it is a different sort of dream altogether. In the first instance, Lisnianskaia muses over the content of what we could call "life's dream," even though it is life's dream about death. This is not the mother's personal, idiosyncratic dream, it is that of an entire culture. I have looked at the idea of a shared cultural fantasy in this poem as one about the death of the mother, and said that it is a fantasy that Lisnianskaia refuses to inhabit. In that sense, her turn away from "life's dream" is part of what empowers her as a subject in this poem; it is a source of her strength as a speaker.

In the second reference to dreaming, the barely hinted notion of what a loved daughter might dream, we might sense a different notion of the subject. For in thinking about the daughter's dream, Lisnianskaia invites us to contemplate the imagination of her intended listener. She gives us, too, a flickering vision of Petrovykh's mother/daughter lyrics, in that a sleeping daughter is evoked. Another mother's imaginative version of her daughter's dreaming appears in "To My Daughter" ("Docheri," 1946) by Iuliia Drunina, where the poet conjures up exotic dreamed visions for her sleeping infant.[34] But the difference for Lisnianskaia when she speaks to a daughter who is a grown woman is enormous: this is very much a woman with her own dreams.

When Lisnianskaia places a fantasy of her daughter's love in the daughter's dream, she is joining their imaginations. Lisnianskaia gives us the lyric speech of the mother as a rejoinder to implicit messages from her culture (and perhaps from her daughter) that say "I wish you were dead" or that imply that, lacking subjectivity, one is dead. Having taken that dream into her own imagination, having turned it over and considered it not as a nightmare but as a complexly embedded cultural fantasy, Lisnianskaia emerges with a dream of her own. In her new dream, the "facts" of having nothing to say to your daughter, or of your own death, are transformed into closeness, connection, and words of love. I take the depth of wished-for connection to her daughter to emerge directly from the utter clarity with which Lisnianskaia describes their disjunction. Whereas Petrovykh, in two poems, subtly resists the fine lines that differentiate her from her daughter, and thereby writes her own subjectivity into her poem, Lisnianskaia premises her poem on a complete disaffection between mother and daughter, only to bring them together body to body, and dream to dream. Petrovykh achieves an assertion of self by means of identification with her daughter, but Lisnianskaia requires no image of herself as an infant coming to speech to create connections to her daughter. It is in Lisnianskaia's mother/daughter lyric that the myths of motherhood are most confrontationally taken on, and thus it is in Lisnianskaia that we find lines that can make something so simple as a mother's declaration of love for her daughter sound revolutionary.

Poet to Poet

I have been writing about these poets separately, but Mariia Petrovykh and Inna Lisnianskaia actually knew each other quite well and appear to have been very dear friends. We know this from Lisnianskaia's comments, which include grateful and gracious testimony to how much she benefited from Petrovykh's kindnesses. She called their friendship one of the most important in her life and stressed Petrovykh's support for her work: "Probably many of my poems would not have been

written were it not for her. No poet except for her so believed in my vocation and
so supported me in my times of deepest doubt."[35]

Lisnianskaia has dedicated three poems to Mariia Petrovykh to date.[36] We will
look at the one that most complexly figures a relationship between the two poets;
it also describes most fully their shared poetic vocation.

Марии Петровых	To Mariia Petrovykh
Вот книга твоя предо мною лежит—	Here your book lies before me—
И вижу твое лицо.	And I see your face.
Вот время твое предо мною бежит	Here your days rush past me
И свертывается в кольцо	And coil into the ring
Березы, под коей без снадобий спишь,	Of a birch tree, beneath which you sleep undrugged,
В колечко от табака,—	And into a little ring of tobacco smoke,—
Так, значит проснулась, и, значит, дымишь	And so, you've awakened, and you're smoking
За чаем наверняка.	Over a cup of tea, perhaps.
Давно ли я в двери звонила, а тут	Was it so long ago that I rang at the door, but here
Стучусь я в створку ствола:	I knock at the tree trunk's gates:
—Впусти меня, милая, на пять минут,	—Let me in, dear one, for five minutes,
Я книгу твою принесла!—	I've brought your book!—
И вижу: зажегся в березе глазок,	And I see: the little eye in the birch tree has lit up,
И слышу: скрипит кора:	And I hear: the tree bark creaks alive:
—Мне надо бы выправить несколько строк,	—I need to correct a few lines,
Да нет под рукой пера.—	But I don't have a pen at hand.—
—Впусти! Я тебе принесла и перо.—	—Let me in! I brought you a pen, too.—
—Чужое? Что делать с чужим?—	—Someone else's? What use is someone else's?—
. . . . Замкнулось березовое серебро	. . . . The birch tree of silver closed
И стало подобьем твоим.[37]	And became your likeness.
1983	

What will interest us in reading this poem is its narrative of exchange, so it is
worth some effort to identify precisely the scene, the book, and the speakers. One
obvious way to read the poem is that Lisnianskaia brings the first of Petrovykh's
two volumes of poetry, *Dal'nee derevo* (*Distant Tree*, 1968), to Petrovykh's grave.
The title of the volume, its tree, resonates with the birch tree that recurs in the
poem; Petrovykh's ironic response to this gift encodes wittily much that is known
about her—the self-deprecation, the exactitude, and a sense of privacy that was extreme, but maintained with kindness.

We know how much Lisnianskaia valued that kindness, and thus the emotions
behind this poem must certainly include loyalty, gratitude, a sense of shared craft
(and thus shared fate). In her first poems to Petrovykh (from 1976), they are joined
as the poem's "we"; this is a rare move for Lisnianskaia, whose lyrics more usually
evoke a solitary speaker. (Even in the poem "To My Daughter" discussed above,

Lisnianskaia finds only one occasion to join her fate to her daughter's, in the reference to "our place of secret meetings," the site of the mother's grave.) The sense of a speaking subject is probably the most significant difference between Lisnianskaia's and Petrovykh's verse—Lisnianskaia's focus is intensely inward, she relentlessly questions who the woman in her verse is, whereas Petrovykh's untroubled gaze appears to focus on the world of nature and of people. Petrovykh wrote what Anna Akhmatova called the most beautiful love lyric in twentieth-century Russian poetry, a genre that we would be hard-pressed to find in Lisnianskaia's verse (indeed, in a 1983 poem she asks wryly, where are the verses of love?).[38] Lisnianskaia's poems rarely have dedications or epigraphs, as if even formally she is reticent about showing herself in relationship to others. The poem to Petrovykh, then, is valuable in its dramatization of a relationship between two speakers. In this it moves beyond the poem "To My Daughter," for here Lisnianskaia gives us two sets of spoken words, and the speaking subject who emerges more vividly is the woman whom she addresses. Three motifs create the shift toward Petrovykh's world: the face, the ring, and the gift. Let us consider each in turn.

The poem opens with the emergence of a face from a book: "Here your book lies before me— / And I see your face" (*Vot kniga tvoia predo mnoiu lezhit—* / *I vizhu tvoe litso*). This can mean several things—that Petrovykh's self, as Lisnianskaia knows it, is contained in her poems; that the sight of this book is powerfully evocative of the memory of Petrovykh, now dead for four years; that the book and the face are interchangeable, the book able to stand in for the face of the absent other. The face is surely a metaphor for the self. Perhaps even more than in the West, the face is the locus of identity and self in Orthodox tradition, as the very idea of the icon would suggest. (The etymological connection between face, *litso*, and self or personality, *lichnost'*, also brings the concepts into close alignment.) Several Russian poets have read the face as the book of the self, and memorably; one thinks of the prose introduction to *Requiem*, admirably explicated by Susan Amert, with its focus on the faces of women in prison lines, and of the face etched with cuneiform lines in the first epilogue of *Requiem*.[39] But Lisnianskaia does not here move similarly to suggest the legibility of a face, or even the intelligibility of its suffering. The poem switches precipitously to Petrovykh's epoch, to the image of her just awakened, smoking, drinking tea. A simulacrum of Petrovykh, presumably of her face, returns in the last two lines, but it appears as a closed, and thus inaccessible, circle.

The poem gives us a number of circles and ring-shaped objects. There is the circular trunk of the birch tree of lines 3–4, beneath which Petrovykh sleeps in her grave; there is the ring of tobacco smoke in line 5, beneath which she sits at her tea. Circles unseen but strongly suggested include the hint of a teacup in line 8, a rolled cigarette in the line before it, the doorbell rung in line 9, the cylindrical tree trunk in line 10, the eye (suggested by a knot in the bark, presumably) that responds to Lisnianskaia's inquiry, the cylinder of a pen and rings around the birch tree, and the silver birch tree itself.

These repetitions are too many and too varied to go unnoticed, particularly when one considers how Lisnianskaia has used the geometric figure of the circle and the idea of circularity elsewhere in her writing. One poem to bring into this discussion is her 1974 cycle *The Circle* (*Krug*), for both its title and its form. This is a fifteen-poem "crown of sonnets," as the form is called in English (*venok sonetov* in Russian—thus both names evoke circularity), where the first lines of fourteen sonnets become in sequence the final poem. The "crown of sonnets" form involves a repeated circling back, a repeated recontextualizing of poetic lines. The form stands out because Lisnianskaia's work is almost entirely composed of short lyrics (say 12 to 32 lines, usually around 20), though she wrote one other "crown of sonnets" called *V gospitale litsevogo raneniia* (*In the Hospital for Face Wounds*, 1984).[40] The title evokes rich associations for our theme, with its suggestion of injury to face and identity.

By comparison with an intricate "crown of sonnets" form, there is little to distinguish the poem to Petrovykh (it is 20 lines of alternating 4- and 3-foot amphibraches, with alternating rhymes, all of them masculine). What we can say about the form is that it feels profoundly closed, partly because of the masculine rhymes, that it is like a circle in its shutting out of so much; it thus evokes Lisnianskaia's other poems where a circle is tightly closed. Two examples of that clenched circle come to mind, one from *The Circle*, when Lisnianskaia writes:

Стучат часы за голою стеной,	The clock strikes behind the blank wall,
Как стрелка, жизнь моя бежит, вращаясь	Like its pointing hand, my life runs on, turning
По замкнутому кругу предо мной.[41]	In a closed circle before me.

And there is another poem that begins "How complete is the circle in its closure!" (Как совершенен замкнутостью круг!).[42] The circle, then, works rhetorically like the image of the face (which is also, visually, round): it envelops something inaccessible. The circle encloses what the poet wants but cannot reach.

She tries to reach it by means of a gift. The story Lisnianskaia tells in this poem is that of a woman on a quest, one who brings a gift of a book to someone beyond her glance and grasp. Lisnianskaia recalls herself ringing the bell at Petrovykh's door, as if ever seeking after her; now she brings the book, even the pen with which to make corrections, only to be turned away, to be turned back to herself and her contemplation of the tree. The gift, too, performs a strange circularity of plot and identity, signaled in the poem largely by the line that seems to be about the pen, "Someone else's? What use is someone else's?" (*Chuzhoe? Chto delat' s chuzhim?*). This line raises the question that something "other" has invaded the tight circle that encloses this poem, or perhaps that one task of the poem is to define itself in terms of that "other" entity.

Whose book, we might ask, is the poet bringing as a gift? Here we must challenge our first presumption, that Lisnianskaia was bringing to Petrovykh a copy of Petrovykh's own book. On some level this question would be suggested by Petrovykh's biography, since it was her friends and not she who pushed her work toward publication, both before and after her death. Her books were inherently "not her own," then, but that is only the first solution to the riddle of possession. The second is suggested by the poem's last line, by which I mean its date: 1983. Petrovykh's first book, *Distant Tree (Dal'nee derevo)*, had been published since 1968; indeed, Petrovykh was alive to see it (she died in 1979). That makes *Distant Tree* an unlikely gift at this late date, for all the resonant associations with its title. The posthumous and much fuller collection of Petrovykh's work, *The Horizon Line (Cherta gorizonta)*, on which I have been drawing did not appear until three years after this poem was written, in 1986, so that cannot be the book at hand. What did appear in 1983 was a smaller posthumous collection entitled *Destiny (Prednaznachen'e: Stikhi raznykh let)*, and surely that is one impetus for Lisnianskaia's poem, even though its imagery pointed us in another direction.[43]

That suggestion of a misstep is no accident, because 1983 also saw the publication of another book that this poem has in mind as well. It was Lisnianskaia's own collection *Rains and Mirrors (Dozhdi i zerkala)*,[44] and it was a momentous thing for her, as she reaffirmed in a 1990 interview in Moscow.[45] As noted above, Lisnianskaia's work had not appeared in the Soviet Union since 1978, and even then it had been a volume with which she was enormously dissatisfied, as she said in the same interview.

I suggest, then, in a second reading of the poem, that it is her own book that Lisnianskaia brings to the grave, knowing how pleased her friend would be to see the volume. The demand to correct its lines now refers to Petrovykh's constantly having been an editor of others' work, though it could also be Lisnianskaia's own response to a volume published abroad that she may see as flawed.[46] Lisnianskaia becomes the poem's addressee, its "you" (*ty*) as in so many of her poems, where the circle of speech creates a voice for the poet to tell herself what she seeks to know. One thing that follows from imagining Lisnianskaia as the poem's "you" is that she puts herself in her own grave. Grotesque, perhaps, but it is probably the single most common location of her poems; we have seen it in "To My Daughter."

If the book can have been the work of either Petrovykh or Lisnianskaia, or both, then what of the poem's speaking subject? Given the comments on mimicry and resemblance with which this essay began, who, we might ask, is the one who sees a face in the book, who brings the book, offers the pen, and sees the tree trunk close in the end? She is more like Petrovykh, as texts have created her, than like Lisnianskaia. The poem's remarkably placid, even helpful tone could not be further from Lisnianskaia's usually dark, introspective speaker. Lisnianskaia would in fact be more likely to say wickedly, "Someone else's? What use is someone else's?" I base this characterization of Lisnianskaia on her self-descriptions as a troublemaker (in several poems, including *The Circle*, where she calls herself a difficult daughter, one who stirs things up, and has her mother tell her that she was proud and overly sensitive from the time she was in diapers).[47] In that last line, where the silver birch tree becomes a likeness of Petrovykh, Lisnianskaia for the moment, for this poem, has also become her likeness.

Lisnianskaia addresses Petrovykh as *milaia* in the poem, or, if you accept my transportation of the two, Lisnianskaia speaks this word (which we know to have been Petrovykh's favorite) in Petrovykh's voice. More than ventriloquism is at stake, however; the poem asks us to consider how we exchange words with those who are like our own second selves. The verbal imitation of an addressee is not unusual in lyric poetry: it is especially typical in poems that elegize the dead, as Lawrence Lipking has noted in his study of English and French poetry, and as we know well in the Russian tradition in poems from Baratynskii to Tsvetaeva to Brodskii.[48] Lisnianskaia has done something more interesting, I believe, by setting up an actual exchange of personae. She doesn't just address Petrovykh in words or tones that come from Petrovykh's poetic lexicon, she creates a dramatic scene in which it is finally indeterminate who speaks and who listens, who is alive and who is dead. There is an exchangeability of roles here, not unlike the scenario Petrovykh used in her second poem to her daughter, with the crucial difference being the atmosphere produced in the exchange: rather than the imagination of comfort and safety in a dangerous world, Lisnianskaia gives us a frustrating quest to offer up a gift where no amount of love can guarantee the completion of her task. Though the images and actions of this poem suggest the world of the fairy tale, with a birch tree coming to life and a questing heroine knocking at its bark, the ending is far from happy.

How to account for the sadder side of this mimetic scenario of identity? One answer is in Lisnianskaia's endlessly moving circle, where certainty of identity cannot be determined. The poem opens with the central insight that readers see faces in books, that they find in the poet's words the illusion of an identity. In suggesting a circularity of argument between book and self, this poem creates a circuit between speaker and addressee, between first- and second-person speech,[49] and thus between the identities of two women poets. It calls into question the idea of a discrete identity for the subject and refuses to let that question find an easy answer by displacing the subject, as in a sense Petrovykh does in displacing her identity onto that of her daughter.

Most of what we know about twentieth-century Russian women's poetry seems more an affirmation of identity, understandably so in the case of Akhmatova's insistent articulations of self in the face of Stalin's terror, the political and religious poetry of Irina Ratushinskaia and Natal'ia Gorbanevskaia, the fragile self-assertions of Bella Akhmadulina, and the polemical self-explorations of Marina Tsvetaeva.[50] Lisnianskaia's and Petrovykh's verse offers a different look at the woman behind poetry. They suggest that boundaries of the self change, that identities merge and are mutually constructed, that the individual identity of the one who speaks can never be stable or finally known. Elsewhere, Lisnianskaia demonstrates, for example in a poem about an invisible woman, that the illusion of women's presence is everywhere but ungraspable. She writes of faces (in Russian, *litsa*), but more often of masks (*lichiny*), as if embedding into her poems the sense of identity as masquerade, the sense of a self as something you put on or create anew with each poem.[51] I am once again drawing on Judith Butler's recent work in these formulations—her book is called *Gender Trouble*,[52] and it is a title particularly consonant with the self-articulations of this poet for whom making trouble is so much a part of her project. When Lisnianskaia dramatizes how "woman" recedes into the distance each time she is sought, she is making what we could call identity trouble. Petrovykh, so gentle and loving in her ways of dealing with the world, would not do anything so mischievous, but her poetic legacy gives us ample material to explore alternative strategies for reading the subject in Russian women's lyric poetry.

Notes

Comments from Pamela Chester and Sibelan Forrester were especially helpful in the final revisions of this essay, and I acknowledge them with gratitude.

1. See Teresa de Lauretis, *Technologies of Gender: Essays on Theory, Film, and Fiction* (Bloomington: Indiana University Press, 1987); de Lauretis, "Film and the Visible," in *How Do I Look? Queer Film and Video,* ed. Bad Object-Choices (Seattle, Wash.: Bay Press, 1991), pp. 223–63; Ruth Leys, "The Real Miss Beauchamp: Gender and the Subject of Imitation," in *Feminists Theorize the Political,* ed. Judith Butler and Joan W. Scott (New York: Routledge, 1992), pp. 167–214; Leys, "Mead's Voices: Imitation as Foundation, or The Struggle against Mimesis," *Critical Inquiry* 19, no. 2 (Winter 1993): 277–307; Judith Butler, "Imitation and Gender Insubordination," in *Inside/Out: Lesbian Theories, Gay Theories,* ed. Diana Fuss (New York: Routledge, 1991), pp. 13–31. Other work by Butler and Irigaray will be cited below.

2. Judith Butler, *Gender Trouble: Feminism and the Subversion of Identity* (New York: Routledge, 1990).

3. Russia's fascination with the figure of the mother, as recently popularized by Joanna Hubbs, may also be indirectly refined in the first part of the essay, for my material lends itself poorly to forms of idealization or myth. See Joanna Hubbs, *Mother Russia: The Feminine Myth in Russian Culture* (Bloomington: Indiana University Press, 1988). For an essay that takes on Hubb's approach far more directly than I will here, see Barbara Heldt, "Motherhood in a Cold Climate: The Poetry and Career of Maria Shkapskaya," in *Sexuality and the Body in Russian Culture,* ed. Jane Costlow, Stephanie Sandler, and Judith Vowles (Stanford, Calif.: Stanford University Press, 1993), pp. 237–54.

4. Some feminist literary scholars have, of course, explored women's literary traditions as a species of kinship arrangements. See, for example, Sandra Gilbert and Susan Gubar, *The Madwoman in the Attic: The Woman Writer and the Nineteenth-Century Literary Imagination* (New Haven: Yale University Press, 1979); Sandra Gilbert, "Life's Empty Pack: Notes toward a Literary Daughteronomy," *Critical Inquiry* 11, no. 1 (1985): 355–83; and, for a very different view, Betsy Erkkila, *The Wicked Sisters: Woman Poets, Literary History and Discord* (New York: Oxford Universtiy Press, 1992).

5. Lisnianskaia, *Eto bylo so mnoiu* (1957); *Vernost'* (1958); *Ne prosto—liubov'* (1963); *Iz pervykh ust* (1966); *Vinogradnyi svet* (1978); *Dozhdi i zerkala* (1983); *Na opushke sna* (1985); *Vozdushnyi plast* (1990); and *Stikhotvoreniia* (1991). The 1983 and 1985 volumes appeared in the West; they overlap, and much of their content is also in the 1990 and 1991 volumes. Since 1987, many of these poems, and some new ones, have appeared in journal publications in Russia, some of which I cite below. Lisnianskaia has also written a critical study of Akhmatova's *Poem without a Hero*: Lisnianskaia, *Muzyka "Poemy bez geroia" Anny Akhmatovoi* (Moscow, 1991).

6. Gorbanevskaia (b. 1936) has published prolifically, including translations and journalistic accounts. Among her poetry collections that I especially admire are *Angel dereviannyi* (Ann Arbor: Ardis, 1982), which includes poems from earlier collections, and *Chuzhie kamni* (New York: Russica, 1983). For translations into English, see *Contemporary Russian Poetry,* ed. Gerald S. Smith (Bloomington: Indiana University Press, 1993), pp. 100–111; *Selected Poems by Natalya Gorbanevskaya,* ed. Daniel Weissbort (Oxford: Carcanet Press, 1972); and, on her arrest and trial, Gorbanevskaya, *Red Square at Noon,* trans. Alexander Lieven (New York: Holt, Rinehart and Winston [1972], and London: Deutsch, 1972).

7. For translations of Sedakova and Shvarts, see Sedakova, *The Silk of Time*, ed. Valentina Polukhina (Keele, Staffordshire: Ryburn Publications, 1994); Shvarts, *"Paradise"*, trans. Michael Molnar, with additional translations by Catriona Kelly (Newcastle-upon-Tyne: Bloodaxe Books, 1993); *Contemporary Russian Poetry*, pp. 246–79; *Third Wave: The New Russian Poetry*, ed. Kent Johnson and Stephen M. Ashby (Ann Arbor: University of Michigan Press, 1992), pp. 129–36, 211–22; *The Poetry of Perestroika*, ed. Peter Mortimer and S. J. Litherland (Newcastle-upon-Tyne, England: Iron Press, 1991), pp. 91–93, 99–101; *Child of Europe: A New Anthology of East European Poetry*, ed. Michael March (London: Penguin Books, 1990), pp. 197–204 (Shvarts only). None of these collections includes Lisnianskaia. Interviews with Shvarts and Sedakova appear in *Brodsky through the Eyes of His Contemporaries*, ed. Valentina Polukhina (London: St. Martin's Press, 1992), pp. 215–60.

　　　For criticism, see Barbara Heldt, "The Poetry of Elena Shvarts," *World Literature Today* 63, no. 3 (Summer 1989): 381–83; Tat'iana Goricheva, "'Tkan' serdtsa rassteliu Spasiteliu pod nogi . . . ,'" *Grani* 120 (1981): 198–214; Mikhail Epshtein, *Paradoksy novizny* (Moscow: Sovetskii pisatel', 1989), pp. 159–69 (on Sedakova); Darra Goldstein, "The Heartfelt Poetry of Elena Shvarts," in *Fruits of Her Plume*, ed. Helena Goscilo (Armonk, N.Y.: M. E. Sharpe, 1993), pp. 239–50; and Catriona Kelly, *A History of Russian Women's Writing (1820–1992)* (Oxford: Oxford University Press, 1994), which includes excellent essays on both poets.

　　8. I will generally be referring to Mariia Petrovykh, *Cherta gorizonta: Stikhi i perevody. Vospominaniia o Marii Petrovykh* (Erevan: Sovetakan grokh, 1986). Other recent republications are mentioned below.

　　9. Some of my information about Lisnianskaia and Petrovykh has come to me through conversations with Sarah Babyonysheva and Viktoria Schweitzer, and I take this occasion to thank them for their help.

　　10. Petrovykh, *Cherta gorizonta*, p. 330.

　　11. Ibid., pp. 30–31. The translation into English, as throughout this essay, is my own; it is meant as a literal gloss, with few of the poetic attributes of the original, and some of the syntax has been changed to make the English sensible.

　　12. Ibid., p. 32.

　　13. *Zhivi*, as an imperative, can also be read as the mother's injunction to herself to keep on living so that she can protect her daughter. The word reminds us, too, that except in a reading where the mother speaks to herself, her poems are addressed to a being incapable of answering her; these are not even lullabies meant to soothe a child loudly expressing itself. Quite a lot of lullabies were, though, written at this time, and the lullaby may well be the most canonical form of a mother's poetic speech to her child. See in particular Ol'ga Berggol'ts, "Pesnia docheri" (1936), "Kolybel'naia drugu" (1940), and "Kolybel'naia" (1939), where it is her husband she is lulling to sleep; in Berggol'ts, *Izbrannye proizvedeniia* (Leningrad: Sovetskii pisatel', 1983), pp. 143–44, 166–67, 187–88.

　　14. Tsvetaeva, *Stikhotvoreniia i poemy*, 5 vols. (New York: Russica, 1980–90), vol. 2, p. 29.

　　15. See Petrovykh, *Cherta gorizonta*, for the photograph (following p. 320) and for a description of Arisha as "just as suppressedly delicate as Mariia Sergeevna, but not quiet—she is ardent, quick, at times even fitful in her movements" by Natella Gorskaia (p. 308).

　　16. The frequency with which I have recourse to Tsvetaeva for examples of mother's poems to daughter is worth noting: this is not just because her poems are useful emblems, but also because there are not, strictly speaking, all that many poets who have written in the genre.

　　17. Makarova's publications include *Katushka: Povesti* (Moscow: Sovetskii pisatel', 1978), *Perepolnennye dni: Rasskazy i povesti* (Moscow: Sovetskii pisatel', 1982), *"Osvobodite slona"* (Moscow: Znanie, 1985), *Leto na kryshe* (1987), and *Otkrytyi final* (Moscow: Sovetskii pisatel', 1989). In *Balancing Acts*, ed. Helena Goscilo (Bloomington: Indiana Unitersity Press, 1988), pp. 328–29, one of her stories, "Herbs for Odessa," is translated into English; the collection provides biographical and bibliographical information as well.

　　18. Lisnianskaia, *Stikhotvoreniia: Na opushke sna* (Ann Arbor, Mich.: Ardis, 1984), pp. 93–94.

　　19. Inna Lisnianskaia and Elena Stepanian, "O Zhizni i o Knige," *Literaturnoe obozrenie* 4 (1990): 30–34; see p. 30. For two other poems by Lisnianskaia to her daughter, see "Ne na strune

sed'moi" (1971), in Lisnianskaia, *Stikhotvoreniia*, p. 154; and "Bereza i aloe," in Lisnianskaia, "Iz tetradi 1993," *Novyi mir* 12 (1993): 108, the latter with clear references to Makarova's having taken up residence in Israel.

20. As told to me by Viktoria Schweitzer, and hinted by Helena Goscilo in *Balancing Acts*, p. 329.

21. The parellel was suggested to me by Sarah Babyonysheva. For "Cherez kazhdye shest' dnei—voskresen'e," see Makarova, *Katushka*, pp. 5–72. Makarova is a remarkably good writer, and this story merits attention in its own right. Its real interest is the tale of young Lenochka's friendship with a slightly older and dominant girl, Sveta, and its extraordinary descriptions of children with all kinds of braces, crutches, enclosures, and the like, so that painful "cures" become a figure for the onset of adolescence. This is more than a variant on what one could call the orphanage tale, and not just because parents come and go in crucial ways. Largely in the absence of parents, the girls' relationships with each other structure their expanding sense of self, and the resulting story is an unusual examination of female friendship and antagonism that shares the lack of sentimentality I will be attributing to Lisnianskaia's poetry.

22. Elena Stepanian, "Dar samootrechen'ia," *Literaturnoe obozrenie* 10 (1988): 46–48, describes Lisnianskaia's exclusion from official literary life quite eloquently, and quotes several passages from her poetry that take up this theme.

23. For publications since 1987, see, for example, *Ogonek* 42 (1987); *Znamia* 9 (1987): 127–30; *Oktiabr'* 11 (1988): 130–32; *Iunost'* 3 (1988); *Druzhba narodov* 1 (1988): 242–47; *Literaturnoe obozrenie* 10 (1988): 48–50; *Literaturnaia gazeta*, August 2, 1989; and *Literaturnoe obozrenie* 4 (1990): 34–46.

24. Lisnianskaia and Stepanian, "O Zhizni i o Knige," p. 33.

25. Sarah Babyonysheva has also told me that during Lisnianskaia's breakdown, one of her symptoms was temporary blindness. That experience might well be one reason for the way seeing is used in this poem, especially the keen sense of seeing something as if after not being able to see it.

26. Butler, *Gender Trouble*, pp. 43–57 and 128–41.

27. Tsvetaeva, *Stikhotvoreniia i poemy*, vol. 2, p. 31.

28. For an extraordinary and painful posing of this possibility in a poem that mourns the lost daughter, see Marina Tsvetaeva's 1920 poem on the death of her daughter, Irina (ibid., p. 275).

29. See Luce Irigaray, "Le corps-à-corps avec la mère," in *Sexes et parentés* (Paris: Editions de Minuit, 1987), pp. 19–34; translated into English as "Body to Body: In Relation to the Mother," in Irigaray, *Sexes and Genealogies*, trans. Gillian C. Gill (New York: Columbia University Press, 1993), pp. 7–22; and Irigaray, *Speculum of the Other Woman*, trans. Gillian C. Gill (Ithaca, N.Y.: Cornell University Press, 1985), published in French in 1974. For a very good analysis of how Irigarary has become controversial, and why the turn away from her ideas represents a misreading of them, see Naomi Schor, "This Essentialism Which Is Not One: Coming to Grips with Irigaray," *differences* 1 (Summer 1989): 38–58. This issue of *differences* is devoted to the topic of essentialism and feminism: other essays there by Diana Fuss and Teresa de Lauretis also raise questions related to what I argue here about motherhood.

30. Relying on Irigaray, Marianne Hirsch and Margaret Homans have studied modern women writers who wrote against this matricidal norm. See Hirsch, *The Mother/Daughter Plot: Narrative, Psychoanalysis, Feminism* (Bloomington: Indiana University Press, 1989); and Margaret Homans, *Bearing the Word: Language and Female Experience in Nineteenth-Century Women's Writing* (Chicago: University of Chicago Press, 1986).

31. Irigaray, "Le corps-à-corps avec la mère," p. 30.

32. The figurative meaning of her title, as her translator has noted, is importantly different: "corps-à-corps" means something more like "hand-to-hand combat."

33. Irigaray, *Speculum of the Other Woman*, p. 138. Lisnianskaia also includes the language of riddles, in her line about life and death in the penultimate strophe, which leads me to think that this quotation from Irigaray might suggest a richer reading of this poem than I can offer here. Other passages in *Speculum* show how, for Irigaray, the cognitive structure of riddles can participate in a radical rethinking of patriarchal culture.

34. The poem is included in *Antologiia russkikh sovetskikh poetov*, 2 vols. (Moscow, 1957), vol. 2, p. 492.

35. Lisnianskaia and Stepanian, "O Zhizni i o Knige," pp. 33–34.

36. I have written about one of the other poems from Lisnianskaia to Petrovykh in "The Canon and the Backward Glance: Akhmatova, Nikolaeva, Lisnianskaia, Petrovykh," in Goscilo, *Fruits of Her Plume,* pp. 113–33.

37. Lisnianskaia, *Stikhotvoreniia: Na opushke sna*, p. 32.

38. The poem is "Pronzeny polovetskimi strelami russkie sny," in ibid., p. 15. The curious love lyrics that Lisnianskaia has published would themselves make a fine object of study, including "Penelopa-zanuda" (dated 1983; ibid., p. 84) and "Voz'mi menia, Gospodi, vmesto nego" (dated 1978, *Dozhdi i zerkala*, p. 181).

39. Susan Amert, "Akhmatova's *Song of the Motherland*: Rereading the Opening Texts of *Rekviem*," *Slavic Review* 49, no. 3 (Fall 1990): 374–89, esp. pp. 377–78. A version of this essay also appears in her book *In a Shattered Mirror*, cited below.

40. This cycle was published in *Druzhba narodov* 1 (1988): 242–47, and it is the concluding poem of Lisnianskaia, *Stikhotvoreniia* (Moscow: Sovetskii pisatel', 1991), pp. 223–33.

41. Lisnianskaia, *Dozhdi i zerkala*, p. 86.

42. Ibid., p. 80, dated 1971, but compare the version published in *Oktiabr'* 9 (1990): 69, where the poem is dated 1972; in Lisnianskaia, *Stikhotvoreniia* (1991), the poem is dated 1971 (p. 69).

43. One more volume of Petrovykh's poetry has now appeared in Russia, a testimony to increased interest in her work, perhaps. See Petrovykh, *Izbrannoe* (Moscow: Khudozhestvennaia literatura, 1991).

44. Thus she brings a volume entitled *Rains and Mirrors*, and the action of mirroring (like the figure of the circle) is what is at stake in the poem. Lisnianskaia uses mirrors very often in her poems, less to invoke the shattered mirrors of Akhmatova's late verse, that is, the mirror that gives back a distorted image, than to call up a mirror that reflects nothing at all. One particularly frightening image from a 1980 Lisnianskaia poem comes to mind: the poet stares unseeing into a mirror and is given not the image of her face but a dreamed tale of exile and execution. See Lisnianskaia, *Dozhdi i zerkala*, p. 204.

45. Lisnianskaia and Stepanian, "O Zhizni i o Knige," p. 33.

46. The urge to make corrections may also be Lisnianskaia's own response to the volume, which was published in Paris and may contain errors that she would have caught had the publication process been nearer at hand (this is not just speculation on my part, I might add, in that several poems from this volume, and from her 1984 Ardis collection, have appeared in the Soviet press in the last few years with changed dates of writing). We also know that Lisnianskaia felt dissatisfied with the 1978 volume *Vinogradnyi svet*. She chastised herself for letting it appear in so distorted a form in a recent interview: "It's shameful even to say it, but I did it for money. My daughter was in the hospital, I had just been released from the hospital." See Lisnianskaia and Stepanian, "O Zhizni i o Knige," p. 31.

47. Lisnianskaia, *Dozhdi i zerkala*, pp. 86, 84, 85, respectively.

48. See Lawrence Lipking, *The Life of the Poet: Beginning and Ending Poetic Careers* (Chicago: University of Chicago Press, 1981). I am referring to Baratynskii's poem on Pushkin's death, "Kogda tvoi golos, o poet," to Tsvetaeva's poems to Blok, Mandel'shtam, and others, and to Brodskii's elegies on Donne, Auden, and others.

49. On first- and second-person speech, see Lisnianskaia's remarkable long poem "Postskriptumy (Poslanie B. Ia. B.)" ("Postscripts: Epistle to B. Ia. B."). It concludes the volume *Dozhdi i zerkala*, pp. 241–52, where it is dated 1982. It also appeared in *Druzhba narodov* 1 (1990): 41–47. The prose preface to this poem recounts Lisnianskaia's search for the second-person speech, and in some sense for a "you," in the process of which she loses first-person speech; the poem cycle, like other of her works, shifts back and forth between first- and second-person self-address, thus enacting the claims about grammar and identity that begin the poem.

50. These characterizations of Ratushinskaia, Gorbanevskaia, and Akhmadulina will seem routine, I expect, but the condensed description of Akhmatova's later lyrics depends on Susan

Amert's remarkable book *In a Shattered Mirror: Akhmatova's Later Lyrics* (Stanford, Calif.: Stanford University Press, 1992); Catherine Ciepiela's dissertation, "Lyric's Fatal Lure: Politics and the Poet in Tsvetaeva's 'Krysolov'" (Yale University, 1992), has shown me the importance of polemic in Tsvetaeva's poetry.

51.   See in particular "I know this woman as I know myself" ("Etu zhenshchinu ia znaiu, kak sebia," 1973), *Dozhdi i zerkala*, p. 19. The poem ends with a repetition of the first line, thus is a kind of circle, that suggests how elusive is the knowledge that is supposed to "be" identity: "I know this woman by her face, / But she for a long time now has not known herself" (*Ia–to znaiu etu zhenshchinu v litso, / No ona sebia davno uzhe ne znaet*). The poem evokes a woman with black bangs, one of Petrovykh's trademarks, and thus might also be a poem to her, though it is also likely that Lisnianskaia writes to herself as both women, thus knowing and unknowing at once.

52.   Some other recent feminist work on autobiography has also posed the question of how tales of the self might depend on something more like a postmodern, unstable subject. Among others: Sidonie Smith, *Subjectivity, Identity, and the Body: Women's Autobiographical Practices in the Twentieth Century* (Bloomington: Indiana University Press, 1993); Smith, *A Poetics of Women's Autobiography: Marginality and the Fictions of Self-Representation* (Bloomington: Indiana University Press, 1989); Leah D. Hewitt, *Autobiographical Tightropes: Simone de Beauvoir, Nathalie Sarraute, Marguerite Duras, Monique Wittig, Maryse Condé* (Lincoln: University of Nebraska Press, 1990); and *Life/Lines: Theorizing Women's Autobiography*, ed. Bella Brodzki and Celeste Schenck (Ithaca, N.Y.: Cornell University Press, 1989), where the essay by Celeste Schenck on lyric poetry is especially pertinent.

ELEVEN

Women-Centered Narratives in Contemporary Serbian and Croatian Literatures

JASMINA LUKIĆ

Willia Shakespeare

"Listen, Tina, your mother will tell you: If Shakespeare were a woman, she would never have let so many people die; not even old Hamlet, no! But, as primitive masculine 'logic' dictates: a rival must not live."

"But weren't they competing a little over a throne?"

"The throne was peripheral, as I see it. In the first place, there's love, tenderness, caring, and even passion—if we are to be frank. *Willia* would never choose so-called great people—to amuse a crowd—kings, and queens, and princes. . . . She would write about more modest, but not less emotional characters. Because their problem is in itself *already big enough.*"[1]

THE DIALOGUE QUOTED here from Hana Dalipi's novel *Weekend at Mother's* obviously refers to Virginia Woolf's essay "A Room of One's Own," in which Woolf speculates about the possible destiny of some unknown but wonderfully gifted sister of William Shakespeare. But the person who speaks about Shakespeare—herself significantly named Vilja, a near-translation of "Willia"—is not presented in the novel as someone who could be aware of the intertextual connection. Although not educated as a feminist—and probably not knowing much about such matters—she declares here the need for a critical reinterpretation of traditional values, which might be called feminist—with some reservations, of course, for Dalipi's heroine Vilja has no clear concept of the implications her plea for Willia, a female Shakespeare, might have. When she asserts that Willia Shakespeare—her reproduction of Woolf's imaginary sister of Shakespeare—would write about modest people whose problems are also *big enough*, she is obviously thinking of herself and the other women she knows.

It is through her own experience that Dalipi's Vilja attained this level of self-awareness, which might easily have led her to a real feminism. But although she saw the difference between male and female circumstances, she never went much further than this recognition. She never thoroughly questioned or rejected the established model of femininity. Her position is characteristic for many women who feel the oppression of accepted gender roles but do not see any way out. They usually escape into their dreams, or into reading romances. The same thing is recognizable in Vilja's attitude. In her reading of Shakespeare, she significantly gives primary importance to emotions, to love, tenderness, and passion, in a way that echoes the typical schemes of romantic novels. She projects the same scheme, mixed with some elements of common female destinies, onto her image of the king and queen. She considers the king, Hamlet's father, just a self-indulgent, uncaring husband, and the queen a neglected wife who longed for love and tenderness, thus creating a situation in which the queen becomes the real victim of the play. For Dalipi's heroine this interpretation has a precise meaning: to be able to identify with the role as an actress, she needs to justify the queen. In fact, her reading of the play is related not so much to Shakespeare as to her own need to defend women in general. It might be taken as the first step toward her true liberation.

The Emergence of the Female Voice

Weekend at Mother's is just one of the series of prose works written by women and published throughout the 1970s and 1980s in both Croatian and Serbian literatures.[2] For both these literatures the last decade was important and marked by great success, despite the social crisis that foreshadowed the coming tragedies in the former state of Yugoslavia. Literary life was intense, with many influential names and movements on the literary scene; among them, a group of women writers introducing female issues into contemporary Croatian and Serbian prose writing emerged as particularly important. Of course, it should not be forgotten that some distinguished women authors were well known and appreciated before that period, though their literary careers were not part of any more comprehensive affirmation of women's creativity, but rather exceptions in a masculine world. It was only in the late seventies and the eighties that a conscious female voice entered Serbian and Croatian literatures, with the clear intention of changing the way in which women were commonly presented.

This change in the literary presentation of women was definitely related to a parallel process of introducing and spreading feminist ideas through fairly strong feminist circles in both Zagreb and Belgrade. Some prominent authors, such as Slavenka Drakulić and Rada Iveković, were closely linked to a feminist group formed in Zagreb. Others were not formally associated with the feminist movement, but their ideas were obviously a part of their cultural milieu, as was the case with Biljana Jovanović in Belgrade or Dubravka Ugrešić in Zagreb. And although some of these women writers, such as Milica Mićić Dimovska, may even deny any direct connection with feminism, the books they wrote display an undeniable change in their understanding of the female position, one which can be explained only within an interpretive frame of feminist criticism.

At the beginning, throughout the seventies and in the early eighties, the new kind of women's prose writing did not receive adequate critical recognition. It was possible for a piece of narrative displaying the new quality of female self-awareness to be underestimated and critically misinterpreted, not so much because of the fact that it was written by a woman, but because of its subject. In the course of time, and with the increasing production of such works, critical attitudes gradually changed. There was a growing willingness to admit the literary quality and importance of these books, but they were still for the most part analyzed with little or no interest in problems of gender. The result was a critical recognition of women writers who wrote about women, while the real changes they brought into both Serbian and Croatian literatures were largely overlooked.

Disclosure of Gender Roles, or Female Subversion in the Male Kingdom

The case of Milica Mićić Dimovska is probably the best example of such misunderstanding in critical evaluation of the new kind of women's writing. She was among the first to analyze thoroughly an established model of femininity within a dominant, basically patriarchal model of culture, and she did this by subverting the dominant narrative model in Serbian literature of that time.

Throughout the seventies and the early eighties, the Serbian literary scene was dominated by a group of (male) prose writers who introduced a new narrative model, labeled by some critics as "the new realism." They were mostly interested in recognizable everyday reality, often emphasizing its dark side, and in socially disapproved phenomena. They insisted upon naturalistic details and developed a particular form of quasi-documentary narration. As the term "new realism" was at first used in a somewhat pejorative sense, authors whose names were associated with the term resented it as misleading and felt that its use unjustly ignored the creative differences between them.[3] But no better one was invented to describe their particular narrative style, and so the term will be used here, without intending to refer to any preconceived ideas.

Generally speaking, within "new realist" prose production much attention was given to a model of patriarchal society with clearly defined gender roles.[4] This is not a result of the authors' willingness to deal specifically with masculinity and femininity, but rather a consequence of their choice of topics, taken mostly from a rural or suburban social milieu, where patriarchal norms persist, determining the positions of both sexes.[5] The "new realists" were deeply interested in social relations, and they rightly recognized the importance of gender roles in any given surroundings. They mainly wrote about women who were abused and victimized by their families or by society. But although they created some very convincing female characters in their works,[6] the "new realists" were not interested in women per se. Female destinies were always taken as highly significant illustrations for other points they wanted to make, and, however sympathetic toward women, the "new realist" position remained always clearly masculine. Being so distinctly marked by gender differences, this "new realism" was quite susceptible to female subversion. This was the path of Milica Mićić Dimovska, who followed the characteristic narrative pattern very closely but from a female point of view.

Dimovska's first book, *Stories about a Woman*,[7] appeared quite early, in 1972, and although it did not receive much public attention, it was well received in professional circles, where Dimovska was recognized as a talented writer. The same was true of her two subsequent novels, *Acquaintances* (1980) and *Phantoms*

(1987);[8] there was not much talk about them, but it was agreed that Dimovska's work was interesting, even important. Finally, her most recent book, *Defrosting: Cosmetic Stories* (1991),[9] won a prestigious prize, which in a way legitimized her professional position. Still, many critics were obviously baffled by Dimovska; they had to recognize the value of her writings, yet they felt they were missing something about her books. That "something" was the subversive potential of Dimovska's narratives within an overly masculine dominant model.

Most of the "new realists" were particularly interested in socially marginalized people, the poor and humiliated, whose situation allowed them to express their critical attitude toward actual social reality. Dimovska took such an orientation to its ultimate limits; putting women into the center of her writings, she recognized them as the biggest and most important marginalized group in society. However, she also indicated that women and their specific problems could not be presented only within some more general social framework, as they were by most of the "new realists," but must be recognized in their own particularity. Social criticism as an important aspect of the "new realist" aesthetic concept, in the writings of Milica Mićić Dimovska, thus became a critique of gender roles.

Primarily interested in what may be called the common female destiny, Dimovska recognized the existence of several irreconcilable concepts of femininity within the same cultural frame. On the one hand, it is expected that a woman will find happiness and fulfillment in performing her highly routine everyday duties, often without any emotional response from those she is related to. This is the sort of life which subjugates her completely to her chores, taking away any form of individuality. On the other hand, she is expected to be happy, attractive, desirable, and inspiring. Her everyday life, so hard and so dull, leaves her with strong feelings of loneliness, uselessness, and abandonment. At the same time, she faces a false image, imposed through the media as an ideal to follow, of a woman who easily performs all her tasks, rich and happy, successful in all she does. "You could be the same, if you only tried hard enough," seems to be the message she constantly receives from the outside world, which only arouses a strong feeling of inadequacy in her.

In Dimovska's writings women are practically trapped in that feeling of inadequacy, facing the gap between their aspirations, the way they see themselves, and the reality of their lives. They may even feel guilty because of their inability to fulfill the role which is assigned to them, however hard or senseless it might be. They tend to resign themselves to their position rather than to oppose whatever makes them feel miserable. But they are not just disappointed losers; in the almost cruel clarity with which they recognize their own position, a quiet resistance against accepting it may be perceived.

Dimovska usually focuses on moments in the lives of her characters when they clearly see and understand the circumstances determining their positions. Usually, these situations are not of particular importance for the outer world, but for her characters they appear to be moments of truth. Hence there is not much action in her writing; even if events are highly dramatic, linked with death, insanity, or illness, they are only outlined, and the author's real interest is in emotions and personal reactions. Dimovska rarely narrates in the first person but prefers the position of an omniscient narrator, combining it with her characters' internal monologues; this enables her to draw an outer picture of events, and to analyze introspectively all the reactions that a character might have in a given situation. She is also aware that to speak of gender does not mean to speak only about women, and that it is almost impossible to present a relevant model of femininity while omitting the masculine side. She makes an effort to introduce some important aspects of the masculine role, and she does so with the same sharpness that characterizes her presentation of the female side. But this is not the primary issue in her narratives; when it comes to men, what interests her is the interplay of two sides, male and female, and their mutual feelings of discontent in life.

Dimovska has not conceptualized her writings as specifically feminist. "I write about women simply because I know them better," she usually says. But her writing has contributed significantly to a change of perspective on women's issues.

The Quasi-Autobiographical Model of Narrative

Generally speaking, the change which the new generation of female authors brought into both Serbian and Croatian literatures was essentially related to the presentation of women. It was noticeable in all literary genres, in poetry and drama as well as in prose, but it was most evident in the novel as the dominant form. For this new kind of novel we have adopted the term "woman-centered," not only because these works are focused on women characters and determine a particular female position; what marks them out among other prose works also concerned with women is the fundamental attitude in their treatment of the issue, their quality of female self-awareness. In Mary Eagleton's words, we can say that this new production of "woman-centered" prose works deals with women as "active, productive, historical beings," and not "as a sign, a construct created in culture."[10] Most of these narratives have a basically similar structure, a form of quasi-autobiography; they are usually narrated in the first person, by a character in many respects very close to the author herself.[11] The model of quasi-autobiography dominates both Croatian and Serbian production of the new kind of "woman-centered" narratives, but some differences can be noted in the author-narrator relationship. In Serbian literature a clear distance was kept, emphasizing the fictional character of the narratives. In Croatian literature, the points of identification between author and narrator were more obvious, and the authors' personal experiences more openly used.

Hana Dalipi in *Weekend at Mother's* carefully preserves the distance between the author and the narrator. The novel takes the form of a long conversation between a mother and daughter. The mother is an actress in her fifties, not a famous and glorious one, but an actress playing small roles and living an ordinary female life. Her daughter is a painter, who lives on her own and comes to her mother's place to stay for a weekend. They talk all day about their common past, and through their conversations the daughter tries to re-create some of the most important events of her childhood. Although their voices are introduced as parallel, we recognize the daughter as the principal narrator. She is also closer to the author herself: their ages are similar, they live in the same city and have a similar family background, and the childhood that the narrator re-creates with her mother could easily, in many respects, be a reproduction of the writer's own childhood. The author's photograph on the cover even shows Dalipi herself as a small girl in her mother's and father's arms. Still, it would be a mistake to identify Hana Dalipi herself with the narrator, for she never does this openly, in any unambiguous way. She obviously wants her characters, including the narrator, to remain fictional.

In Serbian literature, the basic model of quasi-autobiographical narrative was provided in two novels by Biljana Jovanović, who was the first to introduce a new kind of female character. Her novel *Avala Is Falling*[12] was published in 1978, and at that time it was a rather shocking event; the reading public was not at all used to young women writers speaking openly about the sexual needs and frustrations of their characters, nor to self-aware literary heroines unashamed of their own bodies. The second novel, *Dogs and Others* (1980),[13] provoked some unpleasant disputes about the possible identity of the author herself with the main character of the novel. This was important insofar as it exposed a typical chauvinistic narrow-mindedness in understanding women's roles, also proving the need to preserve a distance between author and narrator in narratives which take on socially provocative issues.

Both novels by Jovanović were seen as provocations because she presents a different concept of woman, which many saw as disturbing and dangerous. She speaks of young, rebellious, self-aware persons who consciously refuse to accept the established and desirable model of femininity. The heroine of *Avala Is Falling* is a flute player—and it is significant that an artistic profession is frequently ascribed to the protagonists of new woman-centered narratives. There are two basic reasons for that. On the one hand, it offers the possibility, within a quasi-autobiographical model, of associating the protagonist with the author on the basis of their occupation. On the other hand, it is generally acknowledged that people concerned with art are freer to differ from others; hence it makes it easier to emphasize a character's unwillingness to accept conventions related to gender.

It is through their bodies that the heroines of both Biljana Jovanović's novels reject an established model of femininity. They are highly aware of their own sexuality, and they feel their bodies to be an unknown area which has to be explored and understood. In sexual life, they refuse to play a conventional role; both promiscuous, which is denounced in a patriarchal society, they also use their bodies as a means of getting even with the world. Jelena Belovuk in *Avala Is Falling* dresses and behaves in a provocative manner, but at the same time she refuses to accept her aunt's recipe for seductiveness: she does not want to wear a girdle, buy small high-heeled shoes, or pretend with the help of her clothes that she has big breasts—all of which would serve to build a recognizable image of female attractiveness. This rejection is not just a matter of choice between different concepts of female beauty, a traditional one, represented by Jelena's aunt, and a liberated one, which Jelena herself has chosen; clothes and outlook, as well as provocative behavior, are signs of her personal, desperate revolt against her situation and a role she does not want to accept.

Dogs and Others introduces a really taboo theme in Serbian literature, that of lesbian love. Lydia, the narrator of the novel, who speaks about her own life, has a short but intense lesbian affair, which she passes through with mixed emotions of love and hatred. But it proves to be a very deep, very true emotion, hard to bear once the affair is over. Lydia describes it as a "search for uterine warmth," thus alluding to her need for love and her complex and unhappy relationship with her mother. But her mother and her lover belong to a female world in which she herself does not fit. The difference between them is significantly marked in their looks: Lydia's mother is beautiful, and she is not; her lover has delicate white skin, while Lydia's is dark and rough. Lydia feels that she cannot compete with either of them, and this makes her almost always feel out of place.

For Biljana Jovanović in both her novels, the mother-daughter relationship appears to be of particular importance, as is often the case in new woman-centered narratives. In Jovanović's novels it is seen as one of the major factors in creating a female personality, but also as a possible source of great frustration. As a selfish person unable to love her children, Lydia's mother in *Dogs and Others* induces a feeling of abandonment and a desperate need for love in her daughter, as well as in her son. Lydia wishes to reject all that her mother represents, but she is unable to do so effectively, until her brother kills himself in a mental hospital and she has to face the fact that all her mother wants is to protect herself. In *Avala Is Falling* the heroine's mother is insane, and that insanity hounds Jelena Belovuk until she is no longer able to distinguish between herself and her mother. Biljana Jovanović uses both these cases of insanity—that of Jelena and that of Lydia's brother—to criticize institutional psychiatric practice, particularly psychoanalysis.

The basic model of quasi-autobiography is also recognizable in the works of several other female authors, such as *The Golden Booklet* by Vesna Janković, or *Traces of Braking* by Judita Šalgo.[14]

The Other Side of the Romance

In Croatian literature, before the appearance of the new kind of woman-centered narratives, the female issue was raised in a very specific kind of literary pastiche. In 1981 Dubravka Ugrešić published a short novel, *Steffie Speck in the Jaws of Life*,[15] a "female" story, a humorous replica of stereotypical formula romances. The novel was warmly received because of its witty style. Ugrešić offered her audience the possibility of laughing heartily at her heroine, the humble Zagreb typist Steffie Speck, and readers gladly seized the opportunity.

However, the book is much more than an amusing literary game. On the one hand, it seems to be a sort of inventory of clichés related to a dominant model of femininity. Taken together, these clichés outline the frame in which women are expected to remain; at the same time, they reveal some of the most influential preconceived ideas associated with femininity, widely accepted not only by men, but by women themselves. On the other hand, *Steffie Speck in the Jaws of Life* was one of the first novels in Croatian literature to use some of the most characteristic postmodern narrative strategies. Ugrešić's later books also proved to be closely related to the poetics of postmodernism; in that sense, her work undoubtedly represents one of the most important projects of contemporary Croatian literature.

The subtitle of *Steffie Speck in the Jaws of Life* is *A Patchwork Story*, referring to the way the novel is structured, for it copies the form of the sewing patterns which can be found in many popular women's magazines. The pointers which usually assist the user of a sewing pattern in cutting out some article of clothing serve in Ugrešić's novel to lead the reader through the text, pointing out where she/he has "to *cut* the text along the line"; "to *pleat:* on both sides of the author's seam make big narrative stitches"; "to make a metatextual noose and insert it as you wish." Also, the whole procedure of making a book is presented as something analogous to the process of making a piece of clothing, or a patchwork quilt.

By equating writing with sewing, and her text with a garment, Ugrešić points to the intended stereotypical artificiality of the female world she has created. This world is made according to the model of femininity supported by women's magazines of a certain type, which create the image of a seemingly well-integrated woman, successful in all fields, as mother, housewife, and often (though not necessarily) professional, who keeps her family together and remains attractive and desirable despite her everyday work and repeated pregnancies. Through a whole series of references, *Steffie Speck in the Jaws of Life* reproduces the horizon of expectations created for women in this kind of publication. At the beginning of each chapter the reader finds advice on cooking, or keeping house, or taking care of one's health. Also, in the first chapter the author explains that Steffie Speck, the heroine of the novel, was chosen as the type of person who writes to her favorite magazine asking for advice on how to lead her life. Steffie Speck is young, she lives with her aunt, works as a typist, and feels lonely; her problem is to find someone she likes and to fall in love. She goes for advice to her aunt, then to her friends; she makes some futile attempts at dating men; she tries to read and educate herself (significantly, she reads Flaubert's *Madame Bovary*); she becomes desperate; and finally she finds love in an evening school English class for adults. Each episode is shaped according to some recognizable model of behavior, linked with some typical problem that women face, such as dieting, feeling depressed, or dating a married man. It is all very funny, but also tellingly familiar.

The author comments on her heroine, on her choices of narrative strategies in the novel, and on different possibilities for resolving Steffie's dilemma. At one point, the author gives a version of an ending according to the pattern of popular romances (Steffie goes to Palma de Mallorca, there she meets a very rich but unhappy film director, etc., etc.), imitating the characteristic style of the genre. Of course, such a version must be put aside, to remain just one piece in the narrative's patchwork. But this episode is significant as an intertextual connection with a literary genre closely related to the female reading public. Many women prefer to read romances, and consider them the real "female" literary form; they search in them for their dreams, for all that was promised to them when they were taught to play their female roles so well. As Janice Radway shows,[16] many romance readers search for escape in their favorite novels. They are well aware that the characters and events described in romances do not resemble what they see in their everyday lives, but they simply want to escape from their own reality into a world they like better. Hence they want their romances to follow the well-known pattern, the one they enjoy the most. In other words, they choose the repertoire of clichés they prefer.[17]

This is the point where cliché proves to belong as much to the context as to the text itself; the choice of preferred genre depends on the reader's ideas about life, which also very easily follow the pattern of some recognizable cliché. Dubravka Ugrešić is well aware of that. Hence the story of Steffie Speck is only provisionally closed. Steffie meets Mr. Frndić, but what next? Pretending to be confused, the author—as one of the characters in the novel—goes to her mother's to discuss the problem, and there she meets a group of middle-aged women, all willing to help her to end the story. Their reflections on Steffie's possible destiny reveal that they simply cannot imagine anything other than stereotypes. And they are happy with them. In the final episode of the novel, the author's mother, along with her friends, is leafing through "a colorful collection of the world's most fascinating men." Warmed by a bit of liquor, they choose, among some of the most famous heartthrobs, whom they would like to make love to; thus each of them creates her own private novel plot, a romance.

After *Steffie Speck*, Ugrešić published a collection of short stories entitled *Life Is a Fairy Tale*,[18] in which most of the stories are based on some well-known classical text, such as Nikolai Gogol's "The Nose," or Leo Tolstoy's "Kreutzer Sonata," or Lewis Carroll's *Alice in Wonderland*, all of them retold in Ugrešić's specific, witty manner. But from the point of view of gender roles, the most interesting story is "Lend Me Your Character," related to the well-known question from Sandra Gilbert and Susan Gubar, "Is the pen a metaphorical penis?" In "Lend Me Your Character," as with *Steffie Speck in the Jaws of Life*, Ugrešić proves that gender roles themselves may be seen as a sort of genre, with a given repertoire of recognizable clichés. The story is about a love affair between two writers, who become close over a story which the heroine published in some magazine. The hero likes it and wants to borrow a female character from it for an erotic fantasy he himself is writing. The two writers quarrel over the literary character, but they discover that they like each other and decide to move in together. Their family life quickly turns into mutual literary description of each other's behavior.

Discussing the narrative styles of the stories they write, and the situations into which each of them has put the same character, the two writers in fact re-create dominant models of masculinity and femininity. They also demonstrate how these models interfere with their own concepts of literature. The heroine, as a writer, detests pornography and wants "a decent boyfriend" for her character. The hero thinks that the character in her story is sexually neglected and needs a more efficient partner. The heroine wants to compile a "Dictionary of Female Literary Characters"; she writes about "Beauty and the Beast," an essay called "Pinocchio: A Typical Example of the Masculine Erotic Imagination"; she discusses the question, "Why Did Anna Karenina and Emma Bovary Kill Themselves?" etc.—covering separate, particular, seemingly insignificant problems. Her partner at first writes erotic stories, then turns to more general problems, such as "the relations between the individual and society" or "the attitude of an individual to himself." Whenever he feels unsuccessful in his writing, he wishes to prove himself as a lover (thus answering Gilbert and Gubar's question), while the heroine, in love, turns into an "emotional pudding" and instead of writing devotes herself to housework as if that were the real object of her creative potential. They both, as man and woman, follow the traditional scheme precisely. But Ugrešić lets her heroine realize that gender roles are assigned to them in the same way that they both, as writers, determine the roles of their literary characters.

Dubravka Ugrešić often writes about writing and writers, as in her novel *Fording the Stream of Consciousness.*[19] The central event of the novel is an international writers' conference, held in Zagreb, where different people from different cultures meet and mingle for several days. All sorts of things happen at such an occasion, from anecdotal and amusing ones to events of crucial importance. In characteristic postmodern manner, Ugrešić combines elements of various genres and narrative styles in *Fording the Stream of Consciousness*, making the novel a compendium of possible approaches to literature.

Fording the Stream of Consciousness also explicitly raises the issue of gender, and again it is related to writing. Ugrešić has found an intriguing way to introduce two radically opposite viewpoints on women's role in literature. This is done through an episode modeled on Marta Tikkanen's book *Men Cannot Be Raped*, but in Ugrešić's version the initial crime which demanded revenge was not a physical assault but an intellectual humiliation, a creative castration which aims to deprive women of equal access to the symbolic order. Namely, one of the distinguished guests at the conference is a local critic who detests women's writing. He claims that women belong in the kitchen only, for they cannot invent anything but gossip. Three women, Cecilia Sørensen, who came to the conference as a guest from Denmark, and two local writers, Dunja and Tanja, decided to punish him for this; they lure him into Cecilia's room, tie him up on her bed, and then humiliate him, covering his body with glue and feathers. In the end, the unhappy critic is even raped by Cecilia.

Cecilia Sørensen is a representative of so-called *écriture féminine*, and her letters home from Zagreb display the distinctive features of that narrative procedure. Dunja and Tanja are also self-aware women. All three of them share the same attitude of active, liberated persons willing to maintain control over their lives. But the conference takes place under the hovering shadow of a woman who longed for something similar, never really able to realize what it was that she was searching for. The woman's name is Emma Bovary. Recalling her destiny through a reception where only dishes from Flaubert's novel were served, Ugrešić has introduced the other side of this tragic female story, much more common, and with an unavoidable tragic end. It is the story of a woman who has to be sacrificed because she dares to disturb the established social order.

Autobiography Rediscovered

In the 1980s, the Croatian literary scene was somewhat different from the Serbian one, and this also affected the way in which female authors were received. On the one hand, Croatian literature of the time was generally more oriented toward poetry and literary theory, with a less prolific prose production, and hence there was greater readiness for positive reception of new tendencies in prose writing. On the other hand, the reading public was better prepared for the new female voices. This was partly a result of the fact that the feminist circle in Zagreb was stronger and more influential than the one in Belgrade. Founded in 1978, it gathered many prominent women from public life, who helped to promote women's issues in the mass media. Slavenka Drakulić, as one of the best-known members of that feminist circle, published as her first book a collection of her newspaper articles entitled *The Mortal Sins of Feminism*,[20] with the intention of unmasking different forms of discrimination in a society where the equality of the sexes was legally proclaimed, but where sexism was preserved in practice in many ways. Some other members of the circle, such as Lydia Sklevicki, a sociologist, and Rada Iveković, a philosopher, wrote much and often about different aspects of feminism. Hence, when the new kind of woman-centered narratives appeared, both the general public and literary professionals were already acquainted with a more global process of female revolt.

In such an atmosphere it became much easier for women authors to speak openly about their own personal experiences; they felt that they did not need the disguise of a fictional narrator, but wanted to speak in their own voices. The first to do so was Irena Vrkljan, in her prose works *Silk, Scissors* (1984) and *Marina, or About Biography* (1986),[21] in which she wrote about her own life and the ways she had to face the dominant concept of femininity. Both books were written in Berlin, where Vrkljan has lived intermittently since 1966, and the distance from which she wrote about her previous life in Zagreb and people she knew there probably helped her to be so frank and open with her memories and emotions.

Vrkljan was already known as a poet when *Silk, Scissors* appeared, and the book was immediately very well received both by the public and by critics. It takes the form of autobiographical reminiscences from the author's earliest childhood until the moment when, as an adult, she left Zagreb and, symbolically, the frame of the life she wanted to change. The book's title refers to an episode from Vrkljan's early childhood, when she went with her mother to buy some silk. The material was decorated with small sea horses, and the girl watched unhappily as the salesman's scissors cut one in half; half a sea horse remained in the store, the other half ended up in the hem of the girl's skirt. The episode is significant, for Vrkljan's own life finally becomes like that sea horse, cut in half and divided between Zagreb and Berlin.

Silk, Scissors can hardly be called a novel; rather, it is a piece of poetic prose, abounding in symbolic images. The book is fragmented, and the past is brought back discontinuously, following the course of emotions, not of time or events. Still, it is possible to reconstruct all the crucial moments in the author's life. In *Silk, Scissors* Vrkljan successfully combines a highly sophisticated, poeticized style of writing with verity in the evocation of actual events, which makes her narrative both intriguing and attractive. *Marina, or About Biography* is written in the same manner.

But, however personal, *Silk, Scissors* was written not only because Irena Vrkljan wanted to rethink her own past from a distance of personal and creative maturity. What she really intended was to understand the basic determinants of her previous life, and particularly her *female* position, which preconditioned her to feel and react in a certain way, as a *woman*. In other words, to turn back meant for Vrkljan the possibility of recognizing the pattern of the gender role she was taught to accept. From Vrkljan's point of view, the family appears to be the prime factor in imposing that role on women; more precisely, it is the middle-class family, where the positions of parents are clearly defined and children are expected only to follow their example.

Looking back at her own family, Vrkljan sees both her mother and her father as deeply unhappy people, unable to realize that it was their own way of life which made them so miserable. When she was little, she used to take her father's side, blaming her mother for all his disappointments and discontent. Once she became a grown woman herself, she realized how cruel life had been to her mother, leaving her without any real possibilities for fighting her problems. Vrkljan describes her mother as a "child-wife," and she may be seen as an extreme example of identification with the model of a woman's role which practically destroys one's individuality. Most of the other women Vrkljan knew, including herself, were also in some way affected by the same basic concept of femininity, for weakness and dependence as distinctive traits of female character are still cherished by society as a whole, and particularly by the family, which proves to be the most efficient mechanism for the protection of traditional gender roles.

In *Silk, Scissors*, Irena Vrkljan wanted to make this visible by using real examples, and she realized that it was not only her own personal frustrations that were deeply rooted in her family life; the same was true of most of the other women she was close to, her sisters and her friends. They were all confined within their families—those they were raised in or those they made themselves. There they were taught how to play their female roles, which often implied a certain self-denial and submission. What Vrkljan particularly wanted to explore was the price that women have to pay for renunciation of their true selves. This she did in *Marina, or About Biography*, where the destinies of three women are juxtaposed, seen as three different possible responses to the oppression of gender roles: rejection, adaptation, and withdrawal.

This book is structured around the most important events from the biography of the famous Russian poet Marina Tsvetaeva, but Vrkljan also speaks about her own life and the life of Dora Novak, an actress from Zagreb. Tsvetaeva refused to compromise in life. Dora Novak was the one who chose to withdraw; after a promising professional start in Zagreb and a good marriage, she shut herself in her room and ceased to communicate with the outside world. Vrkljan sees herself as the one who took a middle road, mimicking a good girl throughout her childhood and youth in order to avoid trouble. An emblematic detail is used to illustrate this: as a child, when she had to draw, she always made the same picture—a brown tree with green leaves, no experiments, no risks, but no freedom. By contrast, Tsvetaeva as a small girl used to talk with a devil she saw in her sister's room; no one else saw it besides Marina, and she liked it despite everything she was taught.

Vrkljan is obviously fascinated by Tsvetaeva, in the first place as a poet, but also as a woman. In Tsvetaeva's tragic destiny, Vrkljan sees an example of rebellion against any form of falseness in life. Tsvetaeva always remained faithful to herself, as a poet and as a woman, and Vrkljan makes significant use of an anecdote from Tsvetaeva's life to depict this faithfulness. It is the story of a bead found in the Crimea, in 1911, when Marina was eighteen and her future husband only seventeen years old. They met on a beach where the pebbles included various kinds of semi-precious stones, and Marina told herself that she would marry that young man and never leave him if only he found her favorite stone, a sort of carnelian bead. Sergei Efron found one in the sand and offered it to Marina on the first day of their acquaintance. "Was it nothing but a romantic act? Blue sea, a beautiful, pale, tubercular young man, her favorite stone? No, for Marina it would be much more than that, it would be a golden ring, an iron ring already closed around her future. [. . .] The story of the bead is beautiful, because it can be told. But the real secret lies behind it, in Marina's attitude to words, to a given word as well as to a written one. Unable to betray a word, she was unable to betray a man. The word is life. It is the beginning."[22]

The consequences of Tsvetaeva's choice to remain faithful to her word did not refer only to her poetry. It also significantly affected her female life, because the choice she made in the Crimea eventually led her to a very difficult position. She had to pay for her decision to remain with Efron by exile from Russia and extreme poverty, which made her daily life a difficult task. She had to bring up her children in extremely hard conditions, which made her female work much more demanding and exhausting. Still, she continued writing her poetry throughout this time, and her persistence in writing was almost incredible. It is as if she really existed only in her poems and letters, which revealed the great richness of her soul. While she wrote, she never allowed the miseries of her life to harm that richness. And when she gave up writing in 1939, she actually gave up living. The rest was only a matter of time.

Speaking about Tsvetaeva's writing in between cooking and sewing and washing, Irena Vrkljan also refers to all the other women who have had to steal the time for their creative work from their everyday duties. "Doors of youth, doors of female life. Behind them there are always untidy rooms, children's shouting, rumpled beds. And never enough time to pull ourselves together. And art is a shining star in the white, clean rooms of men, locked up in books with titles in gold, in heavy monographs, in chambers furnished only with writing desks. [. . .] When Marina passed through a room (and she would still do the same, if she were alive), in a deep pocket of her apron she always had some paper, a pencil, and a notebook. And I can hear her words: 'I have entirely withdrawn into my notebook.'"[23] There, Marina Tsvetaeva was free. But she had to pay a high price for that freedom.

Facing the Female Body

Speaking of woman-centered writing, Rosalind Coward has stated that "confession of sexual experience is one of the most characteristic features of contemporary feminist writings." She also recognizes it as an important feature of quasi-autobiographical narratives, where the voice of the central protagonist "frequently offers itself as 'representative' of women in general, firstly claiming sexual experience as a vital terrain of all women's experience, sometimes also making generalities as to the oppressive nature of that experience."[24]

Although sexuality as such is not so overtly present in Serbian and Croatian literatures, in some of the writers mentioned here it is of primary importance. The case of Biljana Jovanović is the most illustrative in Serbian literature. In Croatia, the topic of female sexuality has been significantly raised by Slavenka Drakulić, whose treatment of the issue is strongly marked by her feminist engagement. What she wishes to illuminate in her narratives is what it means, and how it feels, to be a woman. Feelings related to one's own body are seen in her works as one of the most important aspects of more general female self-awareness.

The first novel by Slavenka Drakulić, *Holograms of Fear*,[25] is autobiographical. It is based upon a very particular and also extremely difficult experience, the kidney transplant Drakulić herself had undergone several years before. After many years as a kidney patient, she faced illness in a very stark form, but she never accepted it as the reality of her life. *Holograms of Fear* is a book about the battle with illness, through which its very nature is exposed. Illness always draws attention to the corporeal dimension; to be ill means to be fully aware of one's own body, of its particular needs. At this level, *Holograms of Fear* does not appear as a woman-centered novel, for the experience of sickness seems to overshadow the question of gender. But that is only the first impression.

The world Drakulić creates in *Holograms of Fear* is clearly a female one. This is so not only because male characters are few, and have only secondary importance, while all the main relationships are established between women, and all the conflicts to be solved are between them. It is the author/narrator who very clearly displays an awareness that she belongs to a specific female world, different from the male one, and that this identification unavoidably marks her. Her illness only strengthens this feeling, for there are no men around her at the crucial moments of her healing; support is always offered by women.

The particularity of the female world is indicated in the novel in many ways, but the most striking is the episode in which Drakulić speaks of her friend's suicide, stating that the female ritual of dying is different from the male one. If her friend had been a man, Drakulić says, he probably would have shot himself, leaving bloodstains all around; but the young woman who decided to end her life did it quite differently. She cleaned up her apartment, washed the dishes, put her laundry to soak in the bathtub although she knew there would be no more chance for her to wash it, and left a note, "Caution, gas," for the first person to enter her place. She cared about all these things and felt obliged to leave everything in order behind her—as if all that were more important than her own death.

Apart from sickness and health, the most important issue in the novel is the mother-daughter relationship. The narrator appears in both roles, as a mother and as a daughter. She even sees her mother, herself, and her daughter as a triple mirror; the link between them is strong and everlasting. But the meaning of this relationship is not equal in both directions. As a mother, the author/narrator feels close to her daughter and self-confident. She recognizes in her own motherhood one of the most important experiences of her life, but it does not help her to get closer to her own mother. The basic relationship between them is just a deep silence. Instead of real communication, her mother offered her only food and meals that she prepared for the family, while the daughter did not want to accept that. "Stubbornly, I wanted *words*," she says.

The lack of communication between mother and daughter is also very important in Slavenka Drakulić's second novel, *Marble Skin*,[26] where she raises directly the question of female sexuality. The story is relatively simple. A teenage girl, whose mother marries for the second time, gets involved in a sexual relationship with her stepfather. In fact, she is abused by him, but she tolerates his nightly visits, wishing through his body to get closer to her mother, who cares so much for him. Here again, the male character is only of secondary importance. The issue is the sexual maturation of a girl, a process which is strongly determined by her relationship to her mother. The girl is taught by her mother that the body must be controlled, that the stains of menstrual blood are to be hidden and thoroughly cleaned, that being a woman is a sort of burden. At the same time, her mother's body is sending the girl quite different messages—that something very important is hidden on the other side of the wall, in her mother's bedroom. All this confuses the girl, who wants at first to destroy that physical, sexual aspect of her mother; at one point, she tries to shred her mother's sexy nightgown with a small pair of manicure scissors. The scissors are a well-chosen detail here: later in the novel, the mother will use them to cut out all the male faces from the photographs she keeps; this small tool, which is intended to help women to be more beautiful and attractive, is used here for quite a different purpose, to excise men from the female world. With their bent blades, practically useless for any real cutting, these scissors reveal all the futile despair the two heroines have shared in their attempts to change reality.

The effort to change the mother is useless; hence the girl goes the other way, getting close to her mother's lover. Through this relationship, she wants to share the same feeling of contentment with her body, to realize and recognize what it is that makes her mother so distant from her and so attracted to the other person. It is the first step of liberation from the restraints she accepted as a child; she has decided to become aware of her own body.

The mother's behavior, on the other hand, involves a dimension of castration. She does not want her daughter to grow up, to recognize her sexual maturation. Marking the blood which proves that maturation as something evil which she is strongly determined to repudiate, she is in fact marking her daughter's body as something similarly impure and undesirable. When her daughter finally confesses to her that she has been raped, the mother does not want to believe it, and this is not so much out of a wish to protect her man as out of unwillingness to accept consciously that her daughter is also a grown woman. When her daughter leaves home, the mother keeps on the wall only pictures of her as a small girl; the adult does not exist for her.

In *Marble Skin*, Slavenka Drakulić moves from a clearly autobiographical to a quasi-autobiographical model of narrative. The author and narrator are not to be identified here, although they are close in many respects. (Drakulić narrates here in the first person, and her heroine is an artist, more precisely a sculptor; the choice of profession is no accident, for it also underlines the book's general focus on tactile and bodily sensations.) But, as was the case with Biljana Jovanović, this is all just a part of the game.

Something similar happened with Irena Vrkljan, who moved from autobiography in *Silk, Scissors* to a quasi-autobiographical form in *Marina, or About Biography*, where her personal experiences are of lesser importance. Some other female authors in Croatia have also tried to combine the two models. Neda Miranda Blažević, in *American Prelude*,[27] merges her travels in America with the fictional biography of a female emigrant of Czech origin, whose destiny might easily have been the author's own destiny, if only she had decided to emigrate. Similarly, in her treatise-like novel *Slowness-Pungency*,[28] Rada Iveković rethinks her own youth and relations within her family, but her experiences are only the pretext for more general reflections on different topics, some of them related to women in particular.

Generally, it seems that female authors in Croatia at first recognized in autobiography a form in which they could freely express their need to speak in their own voices. However, once the barrier was broken, pure autobiography as a literary form became too limited to communicate all the aspects of newly born female self-awareness. When personal experiences were to be understood and explained within a larger framework, it proved to be easier if author and narrator were somehow separated. Hence, the quasi-autobiographical structure dominated the new kind of women-centered narratives in both Croatian and Serbian literatures.

————

THE UNFORTUNATE DISMEMBERMENT of the former Yugoslavia and the breakout of the war in 1991 necessarily changed the literary scene in the region, and it also strongly affected women's writing. Nearly as soon as they were recognized as important and highly interesting from a literary point of view, female issues were pushed aside within the new social reality.[29]

Women, of course, have continued to write, but inevitably their creative force has been influenced by the general situation. In a way, the war forced itself as a topic for many writers, journalists, and intellectuals, who felt obliged to react to a given situation. Different women naturally reacted to the war in different ways, depending on their personal beliefs and political opinions, but many of them reacted strongly against the war and tried to preserve a critical approach in highly uncritical surroundings, struggling against the oversimplification, one-sided ideologies, and totalization forced within new or newly redefined countries.[30]

Probably the best example of this is the case of Dubravka Ugrešić, who began to write literary essays on current topics. Her first collection of such essays, *Have a Nice Day*,[31] was written during the first year of the war in the former Yugoslavia, but from a particular point of view.

Have a Nice Day is in fact a sort of dictionary, a "fictionary," as Ugrešić explains in the introductory essay, "My American Fictionary." It was written as a series of articles for a paper in Amsterdam from October 1991 until August 1992. At that time, Ugrešić was in the U.S. At home, in Zagreb, there was a war, and everything was undergoing dramatic changes; in Middletown, at her temporary residence, a whole new world was waiting to be recognized and accepted, as if nothing untoward were happening on the other side of the globe. It was impossible to face one of these worlds without comparing it to the other. Sharpening her eyes through her distinctive position, Ugrešić offers here a series of witty and funny, but bitter and unmistakably precise observations on different topics, from the simple "Mail box" or "Cappucino" to others which reveal the hidden structures of everyday life in the United States, such as "Jogging," "Harassment," or "Contact," and to those which deal with basic concepts and sources of the drama in her homeland, "Refugee," "ID," or "Missing." In all these essays Ugrešić constantly juxtaposes two parallel, in many respects entirely distinct but in other respects very similar worlds, America and Europe, West and East, Us and Them.

Speaking of the two prevalent cultural models which are linked with the concepts of East and West, Ugrešić depicts them as two sisters, one beautiful and successful, the other less affluent. "And suddenly I see that same Eastern Europe. It's sitting at my table, we look at each other as in a mirror. I see a neglected complexion, cheap make-up, an expression of condescension and defiance on its face. It wipes its lips with its hand, talks too loudly, gesticulates, raises its eyebrows. I see in its eyes a glint of simultaneous despair and cunning, I see a panic-stricken need to stop being a second-class citizen and become someone. My sister, my sad Eastern Europe."[32]

On the other hand stand Western Europe and self-confident, self-sufficient America, uncritically convinced of their own values. The American dream, states Ugrešić in this book, has become a stereotype which today produces the American way of life, where success and good luck have become a sort of social obligation, even a dictate imposed on people—just as in a particular restaurant in Los Angeles, where the most important stereotypes of Americana can be found. "It was a museum of Americana and everything was there: real and fake quotes from American films and television series, from American history (which we know, of course, from American films and television series), from American everyday life, American painting (pictures which reflected that everyday life hyperrealistically). Everything was there: quote by quote, quote on quote; everything was mixed up with everything else in a kind of vast American salad" (72–73). In this restaurant, there were also members of the staff whose duty it was to assess the "level of happiness" among the visitors. "Do you think that kitsch is a typical product of communist systems?" one of Ugrešić's students asks while she is lecturing about Kundera's novel *The Unbearable Lightness of Being,* thus revealing, for Ugrešić, a deep misapprehension of the phenomena which also characterize American everyday life (177).

Similar processes, though much more dramatic, could now be observed in Ugrešić's homeland. "Once long ago some bloody reality produced the Balkan Myth, today it is the Balkan Myth that is producing our bloody reality," writes Ugrešić in the entry "Yugo-Americana" (110), which argues that the two myths, the American one and the Balkan one, however different they may seem, present two parts of the same picture.

Dubravka Ugrešić went to the U.S. at the beginning of the war in former Yugoslavia. Leaving the country, she faced the fact that "horror can't be eliminated by moving away from it. The price of going away is two-fold fear: fear for one's family, friends, city, and for one's 'emotional property'" (10–11). *Have a Nice Day* is a book marked with this horror, carried around like a sort of "emotional baggage." But to face the tragedy and comply with it does not mean to lose the possibility of perceiving the other side of human reality, even a reality which is marked by enormous suffering and unhappiness. Ugrešić has always been highly sensitive to banality, stereotypes, kitsch in all its different forms. She does the same things in *Have a Nice Day* that she did in her previous books—with just one crucial difference. In the 1970s and 1980s, when general circumstances were different, all of it seemed so funny. After Vukovar and Sarajevo, there is not much room left for simple laughter.

Another book is worth mentioning here. It is a project realized by four writers from different parts of the former Yugoslavia. The outbreak of war inevitably meant the destruction of a common cultural milieu within the previous country, which for most people living in the region in practical terms meant a complete break in communication with everyone living on the other side of the new frontiers. But four women who liked and felt close to one another refused to accept this new reality. In the midst of war and division, from early June 1991, when the whole thing started, until November 1992, Biljana Jovanović (who lived in Belgrade and Ljubljana), Rada Iveković (Zagreb and Paris), Maruša Krese (a poet who lived in Ljubljana and Berlin), and Radmila Lazić (a poet living in Belgrade) wrote letters to one another, sharing their fears, desperation, unhappiness, and mutual friendship, the only devices they had to overcome the horror we were all forced into. Later, their letters were gathered and published in a book which equally engages reason and the emotions.[33]

Finally we must say that this is just the beginning: Reactions to the war and changes in the region are still to come. Many books comprising these experiences are probably being written now, or will be in the near future. Women's stories from the early nineties are still to be told, both in Croatian and in Serbian literatures.

Notes

1. Hana Dalipi, *Vikend u materini* (Belgrade: BIGZ, 1986), p. 57. Here and elsewhere all translations are my own except where otherwise indicated.

2. This was a period when Serbian and Croatian literatures were closely related. They both participated in the same cultural milieu, which they shared and created with the other national literatures within the common state of Yugoslavia. Particularly close were the literatures written in the same language, known as Serbo-Croatian. Spoken by several nations (Serbs, Croats, Montenegrins, and Bosnian Moslems), Serbo-Croatian tended to differentiate into several variants. Among them, the Croatian variant, with its own linguistic norms, was more obviously distinct than the others. But the basic unity of the Serbo-Croatian language as a whole was not seriously questioned.

I do not intend to open here the issue of language, which was already highly volatile in the former Yugoslavia, but rather to emphasize a simple fact of great importance for both the literatures we are dealing with. In their common country, Serbian and Croatian writers shared very much the same reading public, and all important events in one national culture also affected the other.

When the war broke out, things changed. For political rather than linguistic reasons, Croatian and Serbian are now being recognized and named as separate languages, although they still share a common grammatical structure and most of the same vocabulary. But, no matter how things develop in the future, mutual influences and close relations remain important characteristics of the literary life of previous decades, which deeply affected both Croatian and Serbian literatures.

3. The term "new realism" was linked with the names of Dragoslav Mihailović, Milisav Savić, Miroslav Jošić Višnijć, and Vidosav Stevanović as its most prominent representatives. They are all powerful creative personalities, whose works differ from one another in many respects. Still, earlier in their careers there were significant similarities between them in their understanding of literature, as well as in the dominant narrative strategies they used in their writings.

4. This is particularly obvious in the works of Radoslav Bratić, whose stories are situated in the small Hercegovinian village of Biš, practically separated from the rest of the world. In this highly patriarchal milieu, women "know their place"—in the story "Clear Are the Waters of the River Trebišnica," from the collection *Fear of the Bell*, he speaks of a proposal which resembles bargaining over a horse more than offering to marry a girl. Women there are always in black, mourning for some departed member of the family; they often speak in a particular way, in a specific metaphorical, mythical language, where evil is voluntarily evoked in order thus to be defeated. Radoslav Bratić, *Strah od zvona* (Belgrade: SKZ, 1991).

5. Milisav Savić, in "Young Men from Raška" and "School of Raška," often speaks of the cruelty a small city such as Raška shows toward any woman who disobeys the established rules for her social position and gender. A girl's innocence is a target to be attacked and defeated, women's honor is a treasure to be preserved, and prostitutes are simply inferior beings, to be despised by the whole community. Milisav Savić, *Mladići iz Raške* (Belgrade: Vidici, 1969) and *Raška škola* (Belgrade: Slovo ljubve, 1978).

6. The best example is the excellent novel by Dragoslav Mihailović *Petrija's Wreath,* where the destiny of a peasant woman named Petrija is recounted in the first person, in a female voice. The novel is about the senselessness of human suffering, and Mihailović chooses a female character as his protagonist in order to emphasize the point. D. Mihailović, *Petrijin venac* (Belgrade: SKZ, 1975).

Mihailović has also created several highly persuasive female characters in the short stories from his collection *Good Night Fred*, especially the story "Lilika," about a small girl molested by her mother and her stepfather. D. Mihailović, *Frede, laku noć* (Novi Sad: Matica srpska, 1967).

Another name to mention here is Miroslav Jošić Višnjić. His story "The Fifth Soldier," from the collection *Beautiful Jelena*, shows a young woman who is becoming a prostitute as she slowly learns how to live with her new profession. M. J. Višnjić, *Lepa Jelena* (Belgrade: Vidici, 1969).

7. Milica Mićić Dimovska, *Priče o ženi* (Novi Sad: Matica srpska, 1972).

8. Milica Mićić Dimovska, *Poznanici* (Novi Sad: Matica srpska, 1980); *Utvare* (Novi Sad: Matica srpska, 1987).

9. Milica Mićić Dimovska, *Odmrzavanje, Kozmetičke priče* (Novi Sad: Matica srpska, 1991). The book was awarded the Ivo Andrić prize for the best short-story collection. Of course, it is not my intention to identify literary value with official awards; it is mentioned here only because Dimovska's case is illustrative of the process of recognition of female authors. During the literary promotion of *Defrosting* I was even advised by a well-meaning colleague not to interpret Dimovska's stories from a feminist point of view, for that could only harm her professional reputation.

10. Cf. Mary Eagleton, ed., *Feminist Literary Theory* (Oxford: Basil Blackwell, 1990), p. 45.

11. Rosalind Carter has recognized the quasi-autobiographical structure as strikingly common for "woman-centered" novels of the new kind. Cf. R. Coward, "'This Novel Changes Lives': Are Women's Novels Feminist Novels?" in Eagleton, *Feminist Literary Theory*, pp. 155–56.

12. Biljana Jovanović, *Pada Avala* (Belgrade: Prosveta, 1978).

13. Biljana Jovanović, *Psi i ostali* (Belgrade: Prosveta, 1980).

14. Vesna Janković, *Zlatna knjižica* (Belgrade: Prosveta, 1985); Judita Šalgo, *Trag kočenja* (Novi Sad: Književna zajednica Novog Sada, 1987).

15. Dubravka Ugrešić, *Stefica Cvek u raljama života* (Zagreb: Grafički zavod Hrvatske, 1981), English edition: "Steffie Speck in the Jaws of Life," trans, Celia Hawkesworth, in *In the Jaws of Life* (London: Virago Press, 1992).

16. Janice A. Radway, "Women Read the Romance: The Interaction of Text and Context," in Eagleton, *Feminist Literary Theory*, pp. 128–31.

17. In this way Radway explains the difference between "good" and "bad" romances according to the opinions of Dorothy Evans's customers, who reject aggressiveness, promiscuity, or pornography in their romances, preferring a gradual development of love between the characters, lots of empathy and tenderness, and a one-woman-to-one-man scheme.

18. Dubravka Ugrešić, *Život je bajka* (Zagreb: Grafički zavod Hrvatske, 1983).

19. Dubravka Ugrešić, *Forsiranje romana-reke* (Zagreb: August Cesarec, 1988); English edition: *Fording the Stream of Consciousness*, trans. Michael Henry Heim (London: Virago Press, 1991).

20. Slavenka Drakulić, *Smrtni grijesi feminizma* (Zagreb: Znanje, 1987).

21. Irene Vrkljan, *Svila, škare* (Zagreb: Grafički zavod Hrvatske, 1984); *Marina, ili O biografiji* (Zagreb: Grafički zavod Hrvatske, 1986), English edition: *Marina, or About Biography*, trans. Celia Hawkesworth (Zagreb: The Bridge and Dirieux, 1991).

22. Vrkljan, *Marina, ili O biografiji*, p. 20.

23. Ibid., p. 35.

24. Eagleton, *Feminist Literary Theory*, pp. 156–57.

25. Slavenka Drakulić, *Holorami straha* (Zagreb: Grafički zavod Hrvatske, 1987); English edition, *Holograms of Fear*, trans. Ellen Elias-Bursać (New York: Norton, 1992).

26. Slavenka Drakulić, *Mramorna koža* (Zagreb: Grafički zavod Hrvatske, 1989); English edition: *Marble Skin* (New York: Norton, 1994).

27. Neda Miranda Blažević, *Američka predigra* (Zagreb: Grafički zavod Hrvatske, 1989); the title might also be translated as *American Foreplay*.

28. Rada Iveković, *Sporost-oporost* (Zagreb: Grafički zavod Hrvatske, 1988).

29. An extreme social situation such as a war, necessarily imposed by different primary

interests on the whole of a society, favors patriotic feelings and national topics in all domains of public communication. With the general crisis and deep changes in the new societies in the Balkans, challenged by both war and transition, the position of writers and of literature in general has also changed in many respects. There is an obvious process of general marginalization of literature itself and of writers as socially influential individuals within their communities—unless they want to play the role of national bards, which many have performed only too well in the last few years.

30. Many women have gathered around peace initiatives; many joined together in active groups which help other women, victims of war, and refugees in general. In a way, the situation created by war in parts of the former Yugoslavia has urged women to think critically about their own positions, and stoked feminist activity, contrary to the general patriarchalization of the newly created societies in the region.

31. Dubravka Ugrešić, *Američki fikcionar* (Zagreb: Durieux, 1993); English edition: *Have a Nice Day: From the Balkan War to the American Dream*, trans. Celia Hawkesworth (London: Jonathan Cape, 1994).

32. Ugrešić, "Refugee," in *Have a Nice Day*, pp. 22–23.

33. The first edition of this book was issued in Germany under the title *Briefe von Frauen über Krieg und Nationalismus* (Edition Suhrkamp, 1994). A few months later it also appeared in the original languages, Serbo-Croatian and Slovenian, under the title *Vjetar ide na jug i obrće se na sjever/Veter gre, proti poldnevu in se obrača proti polnoči* (Belgrade: Radio B92, 1994).

Contributors

Diana L. Burgin is Professor of Russian, Chair of the Department of Modern Languages at the University of Massachusetts at Boston, and a fellow of the Russian Research Center, Harvard University. She is the author of numerous books, articles, and translations, including *Richard Burgin: A Life in Verse* and *Sophia Parnok: The Life and Work of Russia's Sappho*. She is currently working on a book-length study of Marina Tsvetaeva and female same-sex love.

Pamela Chester is an independent scholar affiliated with the Russian Research Center at Harvard University. Previously she taught at Wellesley College. Her publications deal with Lev Tolstoy and Marina Tsvetaeva as well as women's fiction and autobiography. She is currently at work on a book about the cycle of "creation myths" in Tsvetaeva's autobiographical prose.

Jane Costlow is Associate Professor of Russian at Bates College. She is the author of *Worlds within Worlds: The Novels of Ivan Turgenev* and coeditor, with Stephanie Sandler and Judith Vowles, of *Sexuality and the Body in Russian Culture*. The author of articles on various aspects of women's writing in nineteenth-century Russia, she is currently at work on a series of essays on the writing of nature in Russian prose.

Halina Filipowicz, Associate Professor of Polish Literature at the University of Wisconsin–Madison, is the author of *A Laboratory of Impure Forms: The Plays of Tadeusz Różewicz*. She is currently working on a book examining gender mythology and national mythology in Polish nineteenth- and twentieth-century drama. Her research for the essay in this volume was supported by a fellowship from the National Endowment for the Humanities.

Sibelan Forrester is Assistant Professor of Russian at Swarthmore College; she formerly taught at Oberlin College. She has published articles on Marina Tsvetaeva and other Russian poets and authors and specializes in twentieth-century Russian poetry. She is now finishing a book on body, language, and gender in Tsvetaeva.

Natasha Kolchevska is Associate Professor of Russian at the University of New Mexico. Her publications include articles on women's memoir and autobiographical writing, post-perestroika prose, and the development of Soviet film and theater in the 1920s and 1930s. She is currently writing a study of Russian women's autobiographical practice in the twentieth century; coediting a book of interviews with contemporary Russian women; editing and translating a collection of essays on photographic theory and practice in the 1920s and 1930s; and completing a study of Anastasiia Verbitskaia.

Jasmina Lukić is a Lecturer at the Women's Studies Center in Belgrade, Yugoslavia; she also lectures at the Women's Studies Center in Zagreb, Croatia. She has worked since 1976 as a professional literary critic, and her collection of essays on contemporary poetry, *The Other Face (Drugo Lice)*, was published in Belgrade.

Solomea Pavlychko is a Senior Research Associate in the Institute of Literature, Academy of Sciences of Ukraine in Kiev. She is the author of *Letters from Kiev* and of three monographs in the fields of American and English literature, published in Ukraine. She is currently writing a study of modernist discourse in Ukrainian literature.

Sarah Pratt is Associate Professor of Slavic Languages and Literatures at the University of Southern California. She is the author of *Russian Metaphysical Romanticism: The Poetry of Tiutchev and Boratynskii* and *The Semantics of Chaos in Tiutchev* and of a number of articles on the critic Lidiia Ginzburg. She is currently working on a book on the poet Nikolai Zabolotskii as a representative of both cultural disjunction and cultural continuity in the Soviet period.

Stephanie Sandler is Associate Professor of Russian and Women's Studies at Amherst College. She is the author of *Distant Pleasures: Alexander Pushkin and the Writing of Exile* and coeditor, with Jane Costlow and Judith Vowles, of *Sexuality and the Body in Russian Culture*. She is presently at work on a book about myths of Pushkin as Russia's national poet.

Magdalena Zaborowska is Assistant Professor of English at Furman University, specializing in American Literature, American Studies, and Women's Studies. She published *How We Found America: Reading Gender through East European Immigrant Narratives* and is currently writing a book about masculinity in transcultural narratives of the nineteenth and twentieth centuries and conducting research for a bilingual biographical and literary-critical study of Maria Kuncewicz.

Index